Law, Science, Rationality

AF786316

Law, Science, Rationality

Antonia Waltermann, David Roef, Jaap Hage and Marko Jelicic (Eds.)

eleven
international publishing

Published, sold and distributed by Eleven International Publishing
P.O. Box 85576
2508 CG The Hague
The Netherlands
Tel.: +31 70 33 070 33
Fax: +31 70 33 070 30
email: sales@elevenpub.nl
www.elevenpub.com

Sold and distributed in USA and Canada
Independent Publishers Group
814 N. Franklin Street
Chicago, IL 60610, USA
Order Placement: +1 800 888 4741
Fax: +1 312 337 5985
orders@ipgbook.com
www.ipgbook.com

Eleven International Publishing is an imprint of Boom uitgevers Den Haag.

ISBN 978-94-6236-989-4
ISBN 978-94-6094-448-2 (e-book)

© 2020 The authors | Eleven International Publishing

This publication is protected by international copyright law.
All rights reserved. No part of this publication may be reproduced, stored in a retrieval system, or transmitted in any form or by any means, electronic, mechanical, photocopying, recording or otherwise, without the prior permission of the publisher.

Table of Contents

Preface

In The Morality of Law, Lon Fuller tells the story of King Rex who tries – and spectacularly fails in numerous ways – to make law for his subjects: his rules are not made public, they are contradictory or incomprehensible, there is no consistency between the rules and their application, and so on, with Rex's subjects complaining that they cannot follow rules like this. The story ends with Rex dying, deeply disillusioned, and his successor, Rex II, deciding to place the powers of government in the hands of psychologists and public relations experts, in order to make his subjects happy without the need for rules. But what, one might ask, do psychologists have to do with law?

There are different views on what law actually is – is it a social phenomenon, something that can be analysed by means of 'practical sociology', is it an answer to the question what we should do, or some alternative? If we take law to be something that has the purpose of guiding (human) behaviour, as Fuller's tale suggests, if we regard law as a means to an end, we need to know how and in what way law can best fulfil its purpose. How do we find out?

First, we need to know in what direction to guide (human) behaviour, of course – what purpose or end do we want to achieve? This question is philosophical, ethical, and/or political in nature and not the focus of the present volume, although Rex II seems to consider that the purpose is making people happy. Second, and irrespective of the purpose or end, we need to know what legal measures will influence (human) behaviour in what way. This is where, in Fuller's tale, the psychologists come in. Arguably, in our day and age, not only psychology, but the much broader multidisciplinary field of the cognitive sciences (including but not limited to cognitive psychology) can tell us a great deal about (human) behaviour and decision-making. Rex II considers replacing all lawyers with psychologists and public relations experts – but is that the right choice, or too hasty? As a discipline, law has a different (normative) function, is independent of the cognitive sciences and defines its own concepts. Should these be informed, adapted or even replaced, in light of insights from the cognitive sciences?

All the questions we have raised thus far relate to something more fundamental, namely the relationship between law and the cognitive sciences and more specifically, the following two questions: what is that relationship and what should it be?

These questions form the starting point and rationale for this edited volume, which is divided into two parts. The first part addresses these questions from a more general, theoretical perspective, for example by asking in what way and to what extent insights from the cognitive sciences can and should impact legal concepts, rules and paradigms. The second part uses the field of criminal responsibility to illuminate and exemplify the relationship between law and the cognitive sciences, with several authors analysing specific elements of criminal responsibility in light of insights from the cognitive sciences.

The following sets out a brief reading guide of this volume, indicating the subject matter each chapter deals with, and offers some notes on the focal question of this volume, namely the relationship between the cognitive sciences and law.

In the first part, Jan Christoph Bublitz approaches the relationship between law and the cognitive sciences by asking what (if anything) is wrong with hungry judges, referring to the trope of Legal Realism that justice is what the judge had for breakfast and a recent study by Danziger *et al.* that seems to confirm this trope. Specifically, he looks into whether findings about the cognitive processes underlying a legal decision provide grounds to challenge, review or appeal those decisions. He finds that the study shows skewed patterns of judgments that remain unobservable from a traditional legal perspective that looks predominantly at individual cases, written documents and records. New perspectives like those offered by the Danziger *et al.* study are valuable to social institutions in pursuit of justice, because they offer new vantage points.

In his chapter, Jaap Hage takes insights from the cognitive sciences to critically assess the law of contracts. Using the anchoring bias as an example, he argues that there are good reasons to assume that the conclusion of a contract is often not a rational event, yet the law seems to presuppose that it is. There are two ways in which the law of contract can deal with the fact that it is not: use existing tools to deal with the irrationality, or redesign substantive parts of contract law. After analysing possible justifications for the phenomenon that contracts create legally enforceable obligations, he comes to the conclusion that relying on existing tools would be justified if subjective preferences are generally formed in a rational manner. This is the kind of question that the cognitive sciences can answer.

In her chapter, Antonia Waltermann considers the possibility to regard non-human entities as agents in the law. She argues that different non-human entities have been regarded as legal agents at different times. Analysing the conceptualisation of legal agency and legal acts underlying the different legal agents reveals that this is sometimes done for metaphysical reasons and sometimes for normative reasons. Cognitive science offers grounds to question the metaphysical reasons, which can have an impact on what (kinds of) entities are regarded as agents for what reasons. According to Waltermann, there are three broad topics that need to be investigated in future research: (i) the metaphysical presuppositions that underlie the law need to be explicated, which is a task for legal scholars; (ii) the accuracy of these metaphysical presuppositions needs to be investigated, which is a task for cognitive scientists broadly understood; and (iii) a normative theory according to which law regards a non-human entity as a legal agent is required, taking into account the insights from (i) and (ii), which is a task for legal scholars and legal decision-makers.

In the second part of this volume, Federica Coppola critically examines the punitive responses to violence in criminal law, drawing on insights from a robust body of behavioural and neuroscientific studies regarding the significance of emotion in moral and social behaviour. These insights indicate, inter alia, that harsh punitive measures promote violence instead of preventing it. How should such insights be incorporated into criminal law? Coppola argues that they can foster a more comprehensive understanding of violent crimes, especially when it comes to the culpability and punishment of violent perpetrators, but that this requires a normative reform of the general standard of culpability first. Such reform could promote the social rehabilitation of violent perpetrators.

In his chapter, Gerben Meynen begins by considering the relevance of free will, rationality, and Aristotle for legal insanity. He argues that rather than free will and rationality, the Aristotelean model for responsibility offers a straightforward way to explain the insanity defence and proposes to include in the insanity criteria the elements of knowledge (to be interpreted morally) and control. In particular with regard to the latter element, control, the behavioural sciences and moral philosophy play a role, as the term is commonly used there as well, bringing these disciplines and criminal law together.

In his chapter, Sjors Ligthart considers the relationship between new technologies such as neuroimaging and the protection of (human) rights, focusing in particular on coercive neuroimaging in criminal justice. He argues that coercive forensic neuroimaging is comparable to compulsory medical interventions to obtain evidence of a crime in the context of article 3 of the European Convention on Human Rights, that is, the prohibition of torture and inhuman or degrading treatment. Whether a specific case of coercive forensic neuroimaging violates the prohibition of ill-treatment depends on factors such as necessity, proportionality, subsidiarity, and the health risks involved. This chapter provides an analysis of the limits a legal system can set to the use and impact of insights or methods from the cognitive sciences within the law: the relationship between law and the cognitive sciences goes both ways.

In his chapter, Paul Catley uses insights from cognitive sciences to plead for a change in English criminal law: his chapter explores situations where brain lesions are associated with changes in personality that lead to criminal behaviour. English law operates a binary divide of responsible or not-responsible with no room for gradations of responsibility for the determination of guilt or innocence, with tests that would lead to judgments of not-responsible based on medico-scientific knowledge of the 1800s. He argues that introducing a partial diminished capacity defence would not only bring this aspect of English criminal law into the 21st century, but that it would also be desirable on normative grounds, such as reducing stigma.

In their chapter, Anna Goldberg and David Roef offer a comparative analysis of the role addiction plays when it comes to capacities and criminal responsibility, looking at the common law system of England and Wales, and the civil law systems of Germany and the Netherlands. In doing so, they show that the latter allow for a more realistic and flexible assessment of addiction in criminal law cases, and that neuroscientific insights on the impaired capacities of addicts can help us to inform the criminal policy regarding addiction. They come to the conclusion that a defence of diminished responsibility is the most suitable approach to addicted defendants. This links their chapter to the previous one in its recommendation, although the two chapters address different grounds for (a lack of) criminal responsibility.

In her chapter, Lisa Claydon uses insights from the cognitive sciences to critically assess the criminal culpability of those who are ordered or coerced into committing a criminal act. These insights indicate that coercion changes the sense of agency of individuals. Claydon focuses in particular on the situation of individuals who have suffered long term abuse and are, within this context, coerced into committing a criminal act, highlighting a tension in the law between fairly recognising the negative experience of those in such a situation and protecting society from the dangers such an individual may represent. Claydon suggests that cognitive neuroscience has a part to play in helping the law establish greater consistency in its reasoning regarding culpability.

Lastly, Marieke Hopman and Dorris de Vocht focus on the criminal responsibility of children in the Netherlands. They analyse how Dutch judges distinguish between child and adult defendants in light of the Criminal Law for Young Adults which allows judges a certain amount of discretion in deciding if a juvenile defendant should be tried as an adult or a young adult defendant as a juvenile. Critically assessing these findings from the perspective of sociology of childhood, they find that the judicial treatment of these cases is linked more to folk psychological intuitions than to scientific findings.

This volume suggests that there is a mutually beneficial relationship between law and the cognitive sciences. The cognitive sciences can offer insights that lead to a critical assessment and rethinking of legal concepts (such as agency or criminal responsibility) or entire fields of law (such as the law of contracts), inviting a viewpoint external to the law. At the same time, insights from the cognitive sciences can be used within the law, subject to the conditions of the law (which is an internal legal viewpoint). In turn, law can pinpoint specific issues for further research by cognitive scientists, such as the accuracy of presuppositions underlying the law, and set limits to the permissible use of insights, methods, and technologies emerging from the cognitive sciences. Each chapter of this volume highlights a different aspect of this relationship.

Antonia M. Waltermann
David Roef
Jaap Hage
Marko Jelicic
Maastricht 2019

1 What Is Wrong with Hungry Judges? A Case Study of Legal Implications of Cognitive Science

C. Bublitz

1 Introduction

Legal studies are at an interesting *empirical*, and more specifically, *psychological* turn. Cognitive science reveals more of the psychology behind moral and legal decision-making, with sometimes unexpected and sometimes commonsensical results. Some speak about a 'New Legal Realism'.[1] This chapter explores one of the normative questions posed by these developments: do findings about psychological processes underlying legal decisions afford to infer anything about their correctness? Should they provide grounds to challenge (review, appeal) decisions? These questions are addressed through a case study on judgments by the proverbial hungry judge. That "justice is what the judge ate for breakfast" was a trope of Legal Realism. And, evidently undercomplex, it was not infrequently turned against it: how ridiculous the Realists' ideas![2] However, a recent study by Shai Danziger and colleagues found precisely that: decisions of an Israeli parole board, staffed by professional judges with a mean expertise of more than twenty years of judging, varied significantly in relation to the time of the last meal break.[3] Chances of a positive outcome for applicants were less than half as high in the three last decisions after a meal break than in the first three decisions. Thus, provided that cases were distributed randomly and no other confounding factors were at work, the time of the meal seems to have causally affected judgments in these cases. This makes one wonder about the normative implications of such a finding: how do such influences relate to the correctness of decisions – do they falsify it, should they give grounds

1 C.R. Sunstein & T. Miles, 'The new legal realism', *University of Chicago Law Review*, Vol. 75, 2008, pp. 831-851.

2 D. Priel, 'Law and Digestion: A Brief History of an Unpalatable Idea', 2017 (preprint SSRN, http://dx.doi.org/10.2139/ssrn.2982716), traces the historical development of the hungry judge slogan.

3 S. Danziger, J. Levav & L. Avnaim-Pesso, 'Extraneous factors in judicial decisions', *Proceedings of the National Academy of Sciences*, Vol. 108, 2011, pp. 6889-6892.

for review, or could decisions, in the terminology of contemporary debates in philosophy, be 'debunked'?[4]

This chapter proceeds as follows: after a brief introduction of the study in the first section, the second section seeks to explain the decisions and analyzes whether they are correct in light of several criteria, from extralegal factors over bias to rules of precedents. This requires elaborating on sources of legal errors, the distinction between context of discovery and context of justification, and visible and invisible parts of a judgment. The third section addresses the main normative problem, inconsistent judging across cases. It runs contrary to legal principles such as equal treatment before the law. As the idea of equal treatment is exposed to come under some criticism, and as its scope and importance are not always clear, the chapter sketches a brief justification of equal treatment as an inherent feature of reciprocal relations in a social contract model. With respect to the concrete decisions of the study, however, the chapter argues – perhaps counterintuitively – that decisions affected by the time of the meal and related factors are regularly *neither* incorrect, *nor* violate rights of affected parties. Rather, they follow from features of the law such as indeterminacy, reasonable disagreement and a diverse judiciary. Under non-ideal circumstances, unequal treatment as exposed by the study might thus be justifiable. Nonetheless, legal systems are called upon to create conditions facilitating more consistent rulings.

2 The Hungry Judge Study

The study by Danziger and colleagues (henceforth: 'the study' and 'the researchers') surveyed over a thousand parole board decisions (n = 1112) which had only two possible outcomes: granting or denying applicants' requests (which concerned release, conditions of parole, or related matters). The main finding is that favorable and unfavorable decisions wavered during the course of the day, but they did not do so randomly, but in shifting patterns. As time went by, judges tended to decide more dismissively; and this trend was affected and partly reversed by meal breaks. The researchers summarize their findings:

> [T]he likelihood of a favorable ruling is greater at the very beginning of the work day or after a food break than later in the sequence of cases … [T]he likelihood of a ruling in favor of a prisoner spikes at the beginning of each session – the probability of a favorable ruling steadily declines from ≈0.65 to nearly zero and jumps back up to ≈0.65 after a break for a meal. … From the

4 H. Sauer, *Debunking Arguments in Ethics*, 1st edn, Cambridge University Press, Cambridge 2018; S. Nichols, 'Process Debunking and Ethics', *Ethics*, Vol. 124, 2014, pp. 727-749.

perspective of the prisoner, there is a clear advantage to appearing at the beginning of the session (*i.e.*, either at the beginning of the day or immediately following the break).[5]

The following graph may help to illustrate their findings:

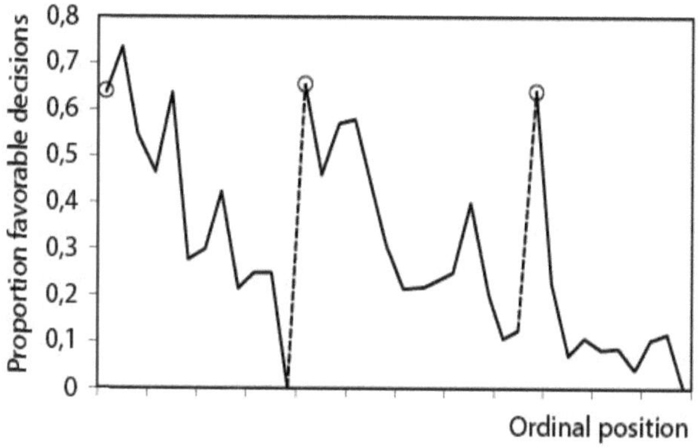

Fig. 1 Proportion of rulings in favor of the prisoners by ordinal position. Circled points indicate the first decision in each of the three decision sessions; tick marks on *x* axis denote every third case; dotted line denotes food break. Because unequal session lengths resulted in a low number of cases for some of the later ordinal positions, the graph is based on the first 95% of the data from each session.

The researchers offer the following explanation:[6] previous studies demonstrated that repeated judgments deplete mental resources.[7] Depleted resources seem to influence the content of decisions towards upholding the status quo, which supposedly means here: dismissing the application.[8] Therefore, the researchers note, "as judges advance through the sequence of cases ..., they will be more likely to accept the default, status quo outcome: deny a prisoner's request."[9] Meal breaks restore mental resources, and this reverts chances of positive decisions (almost) back to the initial level. Whether this change is mediated by increased glucose levels, increased mood or another factor cannot be discerned from the study. Since it only collected behavioral data, statements about the underlying psycholog-

5 Danziger, Levav & Avnaim-Pesso 2011, pp. 6889-6892, at p. 6890.

6 Figure 1, adapted from Danziger, Levav & Avnaim-Pesso 2011, pp. 6889-6892, at p. 6890. Reprinted with kind permission from the National Academy of Sciences.

7 A classic statement of the idea of ego-depletion is R.F. Baumeister, 'Ego Depletion and Self-Control Failure: An Energy Model of the Self's Executive Function', *Self and Identity*, Vol. 1, 2002, pp. 129-136.

8 I only wish to note that it is not clear why *denying* requests is supposed to be the default outcome in terms of the law. Domestic law usually has default rules for different types of parole decisions, and often they are guided by the idea *in dubio pro libertate*. The default outcome would then be *granting* requests.

9 Danziger, Levav & Avnaim-Pesso 2011, pp. 6889-6892, p. 6889.

ical processes are educated speculations.[10] The researchers also speculate that "judges may simplify their decisions", without further elaborating what simplification means here more precisely. One may thus wonder: does granting applications and deviating from the status quo require more mental resources, or does it cause more paperwork, or is the status quo easier to justify?

The study has been met with skepticism and criticism, not only from members of the (directly affected) Israeli judiciary. One reason is that doubts have been cast on the overarching psychological theory – ego-depletion theory – as key studies failed to replicate.[11] Suspicion is also raised by the large effect size in the study (Cohen's *d* of 1.96). Chances of positive outcomes dropped by over 50%; an effect allegedly much larger than in similar studies.[12] Some critics suspect that the findings result from non-random scheduling of cases, so that effects are not due to time of the meal, but rather to the complexity of cases, duration of hearings, or availability of legal assistance, and therewith, legally relevant factors.[13] Danziger and colleagues have replied to some of these criticisms.[14] I wish to remain uncommitted about the validity of the study, and only wish to note that prima facie, its general thrust, namely the suggestion that judicial decision-making might be affected by the time of the last meal, and thereby factors as glucose, hunger, mood, or mental fatigue,

10 Instead of exhibiting an implicit status quo orientation, it might as well be the cases that judgments become harsher, or more risk-averse, the hungrier or more impatient judges become.

11 M.S. Hagger *et al.*, 'A Multilab Preregistered Replication of the Ego-Depletion Effect', *Perspectives on Psychological Science*, Vol. 11, 2016, pp. 546-573.

12 A. Glöckner, 'The Irrational Hungry Judge Effect Revisited: Simulations Reveal That the Magnitude of the Effect Is Overestimated', *Judgment and Decision Making*, Vol. 11, 2016, pp. 601-610; Ø. Daljord, O. Urminsky & J.M. Ureta, 'The Status Quo Theory of Depletion Does not Explain the Israeli Parole Decisions', 2017 (preprint, http://home.uchicago.edu/ourminsky/Status_Quo_Theory_Revisited.pdf), suggest that the status quo depletion theory is the wrong explanation, but do not call the general finding of the study into question.

13 K. Weinshall-Margel & J. Shapard, 'Overlooked factors in the analysis of parole decisions', *Proceedings of the National Academy of Sciences*, Vol. 108, 2011, E833-E833; *see also* Glöckner 2016.

14 S. Danziger, J. Levav & L. Avnaim-Pesso, 'Reply to Weinshall-Margel and Shapard: Extraneous factors in judicial decisions persist', *Proceedings of the National Academy of Sciences*, Vol. 108, 2011, E834-E834;

seems plausible. It ties in with other studies demonstrating physiological, psychological, or situational influences on moral decision-making of lay persons[15] and legal experts.[16]

As my interest lies in the normative consequences of findings of this kind, I shall assume *arguendo* that those of the study are, by and large, correct. I shall further assume that two related variables are among its causes: blood glucose levels, as the relevant physiological factor most directly affected by a meal and supposedly related to "ego-depletion", as well as mental fatigue, the lowering of mental resources, as the relevant psychological factor in the eyes of the researchers.[17] The legal argument, however, does not hinge on peculiarities of these factors. They rather exemplify *biological* and *psychological factors* which may influence judicial decisions. In the near future, cognitive science will likely show the influence of more of such factors on moral and legal reasoning. The study may thus serve as a test case for the normative relevance of these factors.

What are the normative consequences of the findings of the study: are these decisions incorrect, or some of them, and why? Does the study provide grounds for review, and should it? These are at one level simply questions of positive law which different jurisdiction may answer differently. One may, for instance, consider parole board judgments as a matter of administrative law, or as an annex to sentencing and thus criminal law. Parole

15 D.C. Molden *et al.*, 'Motivational Versus Metabolic Effects of Carbohydrates on Self-Control', *Psychological Science*, Vol. 23, 2012, pp. 1137-1144; C.M. Barnes *et al.*, 'Lack of sleep and unethical conduct', *Organizational Behavior and Human Decision Processes*, Vol. 115, 2011, pp. 169-180; M. Kouchaki & I.H. Smith, 'The Morning Morality Effect: The Influence of Time of Day on Unethical Behavior', *Psychological Science*, Vol. 25, 2014, pp. 95-102; K.C. Yam, X.-P. Chen & S.J. Reynolds, 'Ego depletion and its paradoxical effects on ethical decision-making', *Organizational Behavior and Human Decision Processes*, Vol. 124, 2014, pp. 204-214; *cf.* J.Z. Siegel & M.J. Crockett, 'How serotonin shapes moral judgment and behavior', *Annals of the New York Academy of Sciences*, Vol. 1299, 2013, p. 42; F. Gino *et al.*, 'Unable to resist temptation: How self-control depletion promotes unethical behavior', *Organizational Behavior and Human Decision Processes*, Vol. 115, 2011, pp. 191-203.

16 Sleep deprivation increases severity of punishment, K. Cho, C.M. Barnes & C.L. Guanara, 'Sleepy Punishers Are Harsh Punishers: Daylight Saving Time and Legal Sentences', *Psychological Science*, Vol. 28, 2017, pp. 242-247. Losses in football games affects punishment severity in professional judges, probably via the induction of negative emotions, *see* O. Eren & N. Mocan, 'Emotional Judges and Unlucky Juveniles', *American Economic Journal: Applied Economics*, Vol. 10, 2018, pp. 171-205. The authors conclude that "it is noteworthy that the judicial decisions are in fact impacted by emotions that are unrelated to the merits of the case". In a different study by the Institute for Advanced Studies Toulouse (IAST), 'This Morning's Breakfast, Last Night's Game: Detecting Extraneous Influences on Judging', 2016 (working paper, http://iast.fr/pub/31020), shows in a *within-subject* study that asylum applications are more likely successful the day following a win of the local football team, and less likely when the weather is bad. Berdejo & Chen 2013 show that US federal appeal court judges decide more along political lines in the two quarters before elections.

17 M.T. Gailliot & R.F. Baumeister, 'The Physiology of Willpower: Linking Blood Glucose to Self-Control', in *Personality and Social Psychology Review*, Vol. 11, 2007, pp. 303-327; J.L. Orquin & R. Kurzban, 'A meta-analysis of blood glucose effects on human decision making', *Psychological Bulletin*, Vol. 142, 2016, p. 546.

decisions might be understood as an act of mercy with little judicial oversight, or they might be fully reviewable. Such matters depend on broader and sometimes historically contingent considerations of particular legal orders about which there is no right or wrong. While it is interesting to ponder how the jurisdictions one is familiar with would handle an appeal grounded in such findings, details of particular jurisdictions are not of present concern. Presumably, such findings by themselves do not provide grounds for review in most jurisdictions. The following explores whether they *should* do so, irrespective of more specific doctrines and considerations specific to each jurisdiction. Moreover, the present interest is not constrained to parole board decisions, but encompasses administrative or judicial acts potentially affected by such factors more broadly.

Danziger and colleagues summarize that their "findings suggest that judicial rulings can be swayed by extraneous variables that should have no bearing on legal decisions."[18] One intuitively shares their sentiment. Rulings have gone astray, they were influenced by something that ought not be there, something that affects or taints or contaminates decisions and renders them incorrect. Capricious rulings resulting from such extralegal factors appear as a paradigmatic instances of what it means to be 'at the whim of a judge'. Or, in the words of the former US Supreme Court Justice William Douglas: there will be no "justice under law if a negligence rule is applied in the morning but not in the afternoon."[19] In other words, if justice is indeed what judges ate for breakfast, there is no justice.

Or so it seems. The reasons for why the rulings of are wrong and further implications of these findings merit more attention than legal theorists have devoted to it. Exposing errors will prove more complicated and legal implications more nuanced than the foregoing suggests. In fact, I shall argue that framing the problem as one of 'extralegal factors' contaminating decisions is misleading. Extralegal factors are *not* the problem in these cases and deflect from the true – and more intricate – problem that lies elsewhere. To appreciate this, let us take a look at correct and incorrect legal decisions

3 Legal Errors

3.1 *Correct and Incorrect Decisions*

At the outset, it is important to note the following: each and every decision of the study might be incorrect for the ordinary reasons: rules were wrongly applied, facts wrongly

18 Danziger, Levav and Avnaim-Pesso 2011, pp. 6889-6892.
19 W.O. Douglas, 'Stare Decisis', *Columbia Law Review*, Vol. 49, 1949, pp. 735-758, at p. 736.

established, relevant criteria such as the likelihood of reoffending wrongly assessed. Identifying such errors would require engaging with each case, the factual circumstances and the legal reasoning, in short: ordinary legal case analysis. This is beyond the scope of this chapter, and also beyond its interest. The challenging question raised by the study is whether such findings add something *new*, a novel perspective on correct legal reasoning and judicial decisions. The following thus focuses on the impact of the supposedly wrong-making factors such as time of the meal, glucose levels or mental fatigue.

A further clarification: I assume there is a correct answer to every legal question, although not necessarily a single one, there could be several, *i.e.*, a set or range of equally reasonable but mutually exclusive answers. Let us call this the *set of ideal outcomes.*[20] Our interest lies in the correctness of particular legal decisions.[21] Generally speaking, a decision is correct if and only if it conforms to the law. This means, *substantively*, that the outcome is a member of the set of ideal correct outcomes, and *procedurally*, that requisite *modi operandi* were followed. For finding the substantively correct outcomes, the law stipulates an ideal method: applicable norms have to be identified (and sometimes interpreted) by the means legal methodology provides (whatever they precisely are, and potentially all the way down to principles and Constitutions). Norms then have to be applied to the facts, as established by procedural rules of evidence. The result of these operations, if performed perfectly, is the set of ideal outcomes. It forms the substantive standard of correctness for particular judgments.

Courts and administrations seek to reach correct judgments by approximating these steps, though in a non-ideal fashion and under non-ideal epistemic conditions. While often on target, they sometimes fail. Showing that an actual judgment is wrong on the merits requires showing that is not within the set of ideal outcomes. However, identifying this set is frequently impossible under non-ideal circumstances, or requires severe and sustained efforts. Therefore, actual judgments are often challenged on the basis of errors that likely lead to incorrect outcomes. Accordingly, motions to review judgments may highlight errors which probably skewed the outcome (without showing its effects all the way down). Our present

20 What judges should do when the set has more than one member (*i.e.*, when there are several correct answers) and when they "run out of reasons" to adjudicate between alternatives is an issue we have to sidestep here. It may suffice to note that in most proceedings before courts or administrations, the law stipulates burdens of persuasion or other presumptions which determine outcomes in situations of *non-liquet* (in which no party can make a convincing case for their claim, be it in questions of law or fact). Thus, the Dworkinian 'single-right-answer' thesis can largely be bracketed for present purposes, R. Dworkin, *Taking Rights Seriously*, Harvard University Press, Cambridge Massachusetts 1977.

21 'Decision' and 'judgment' are used interchangeably.

question might thus be put in this way: should influences such as time of meal breaks, glucose, fatigue, qualify as errors of the kind that gives grounds for review?

A couple of further differentiations need to be drawn. Some errors such as the false application of a norm are *explicit* in the sense that they can be identified in the reasoning laid down in relevant records, documents such as written legal opinions or judgments. These errors may not be obvious, but they can, in principle, be identified by engaging with the relevant material and records. Other errors, by contrast, are *invisible* or *imperceptible* from this perspective, they remain unspoken and cannot be extracted from records because they are not contained in them. Written judgments, for instance, are not comprehensive statements of all relevant facts and applicable norms, but only of the most salient ones. Many legal and factual premises remain unstated. Some decisions come without an explanation, other with only brief remarks (parole decisions as in the study are typically of this kind). Yet, there might be errors in the unreported parts of a judgment, too (*e.g.* false application of a norm). Furthermore, not only the reporting but also the decision-making process is regularly *incomplete*. For instance, assessing whether an applicant still poses a threat, how likely his future conviction is, or whether he satisfies other conditions of parole requires protracted fact finding and reasoning that judges do not (and cannot) make all the way through and have to cut at some point. Moreover, reasoning and decision-making always remain partly in the dark even to decision-makers (judges) themselves. Factors of which they remain unaware are *implicit*. For instance, judges do not explicitly apply all norms, concepts, or background considerations to reach a conclusion, but draw on assumptions and implicit knowledge, use shortcuts and heuristics. Because of this, their reasoning is susceptible to influences such as implicit biases. These biases are regularly not identifiable in written judgments, but there are nonetheless good reasons to assume that they may have shaped outcomes. They are operative in the hidden, deeper layers of the decision-making process, such as the psychology of judges, and may lead them astray. Accordingly, judicial reasoning is partially – and inherently – incomplete and implicit and a range of potentially biased factors contributing to a judgment remain imperceptible. In this way, relevant wrong-making factors may exert influence while remaining imperceptible in the explicit parts of the decision. Implicit biases are a good example. Arguably, their influence should give grounds for review, they might even constitute a wrong in itself, despite their invisibility in judgments (they are, after all, widely implicit even to decision-makers).[22]

22 For an introduction to implicit biases, *see* the introduction of M. Brownstein & J. Saul, *Implicit Bias and Philosophy, Volume 1*, Oxford University Press, Oxford 2016. For empirical research on implicit biases of judges, see J.A.J. Wistrich & J.J. Rachlinski, 'Implicit Bias in Judicial Decision Making: How it affects judgment and what judges can do about it', *in* S. Redfield (Ed.), *Enhancing Justice (2017)*, American Bar Association, 2017, pp. 87-130.

Decisions suffering from *explicit* failures do not pose particularly interesting novel challenges for legal theory. Every legal system has rules and doctrines to address them. The intriguing aspect of the study is that it demonstrates *imperceptible* factors – the time of the last meal, glucose levels, mental fatigue – which seem to sway judgments without appearing in the records. Such factors may, of course, *indicate* explicit errors in judgments and motivate further scrutiny, which may lead to reviews on traditional grounds. But beyond that, even when particular judgments *are not explicitly* flawed, these factors might still be normatively relevant. This is the theoretically interesting aspect explored in the following. I shall thus assume *arguendo* that an expert review of the cases would fail to find explicit flaws in reasoning or fact finding. Prima facie, decisions fall within the set of ideal outcomes. And still, something seems wrong.

3.2 *Context of Discovery and Context of Justification*

It is important to keep apart the actual reasoning and decision-making process, *i.e.*, the psychological operations in the mind of a judge or a collegiate of judges, and the normative justification of a decision. The former is sometimes called 'context of discovery', and at least in theory, it can be fully explained by the natural and social sciences. It stands in contrast to the normative level, the 'context of justification', which is not concerned with factual reasoning processes but with the content and structure of reasons, deductions, inferences, conclusions, and better arguments. Ultimately, this is the level of interest for law and ethics, the substantive correctness of a judgment is decided here.

The written judgment and the accompanying reasons are not, and should not be mistaken for, representations of the actual decision-making process, the context of discovery. They may speak about the 'reasoning of the court', but not in a psychological sense. Drafted *ex post*, judgments are rhetorically stylized to let conclusions appear inevitable and unassailable. They concern the context of justification.[23] Cognitive and social science, by contrast, concern psychological, sociological and other facts about the context of discovery. The study, for instance, is not analyzing rightness or wrongness of decisions, but external facts about institutionalized decision-making and judicial psychology. Because such facts address discovery, they are usually held to be of minor relevance for matters of justification. How judges came to a conclusion is regularly irrelevant, what matters is whether the conclusion is right (*i.e.*, falls within the set of ideal outcomes). It is not a condition of the substantive

23 This does of course not rule out that there might be cases in which writing the judgment motivates a reconsideration, as previously unthought problems or arguments may arise. Also, *post hoc* writing of judgment neither entails, nor excludes *post hoc* reasoning in the Legal Realist sense, namely that other factors determine the outcome which then steers rationalizations.

correctness of a decision that is has been reached on a particular way. A decision is not wrong because, for instance, judges relied on intuitions, hunches or heuristics.[24] Explanation and justification of a judgment are simply different subject matters.

The key question is then how cognitive and social science might be of relevance for issues of justification at all. I wish to suggest here that descriptive facts about the context of discovery may be relevant for purposes of legal justification in an *epistemic* way. Facts about discovery may *indicate* that an outcome is incorrect, on the merits, because the process is unreliable to produce correct outcomes. Imagine a judge decides cases by throwing dice. This fact about discovery would suffice to distrust the outcome – without engaging with arguments on the merits. Cognitive science may bring to light unreliable decision-making processes (whether they are unreliable needs surely thorough normative argument). Here is an example: if cognitive science can show that actual reasoning of judges is implicitly biased (context of discovery), we have reason to assume that judgments are wrong, even though no explicit errors are found (context of justification). Biases may nonetheless have had distorting influence in the imperceptible parts. As rule of thumb: if a factor that renders a decision-making process prone to error is identified in the context of discovery, and if it is not rectified subsequently, caution is warranted with respect to the correctness of the decision. This is the *epistemic* relevance of the context of discovery. Note that it also implies that if there was a complete and transparent *explicit* justification, a written opinion enumerating every relevant point of law and fact, every background consideration, every weighing of values and probabilities, then facts about discovery may *not* add anything relevant. Every error could then be identified in the judgment, and if none is to be found there, it is immune to further challenges based on facts about its genesis. However, complete and transparent justifications never exists in law.

3.3 *Extralegal Factors?*

Against this backdrop, let us explore what may have gone wrong in the cases of the study. Although the decisions are, *ex hypothesi*, not explicitly erroneous, they nonetheless appear incorrect because of the causal influence of irrelevant or 'extraneous factors'. But let us take a closer look: in which sense are the last time of the meal, glucose levels, or mental fatigue 'extraneous' or 'extralegal factors'? No legal norm refers to them. In that sense, they are rather *alegal factors*. However, 'extralegal' suggests more: something akin to what natural sciences call a confounding factor, the presence of something that ought not be

24 For the relation between heuristics and law, *see* the contributions in G. Gigerenzer & C. Engel (Eds.), *Heuristics and the law*, MIT Press in cooperation with Dahlem University Press, Cambridge Massachusetts 2006.

there, something that distorts and contaminates outcomes. Perhaps the argument can be put this way:

1. Legal decision D is affected by factor F (empirical premise).
2. F is an extralegal factor.
3. Correct decision are not affected by extralegal factors.

Conclusion: D is not correct.

This would be a strong understanding of 'extralegal factor' as wrong-making factor (3). A weaker version would be the epistemic variant just described:

3*. Causal influence of extralegal factors *indicates* that D may be false (but it could be correct).

In light of the study, it may appear tempting to suggest that glucose is an extralegal factor. However, this would come with a commitment to the proposition that *legal decisions should not be causally influenced by glucose.* This is unpersuasive. Legal decision-making is embodied, with minds and brains of judges running on glucose. Until AI overtakes the judiciary, every full *causal* explanation of a legal judgment involves glucose. Its presence is not the problem.[25] Nor does it provide reasons to think the decision is incorrect.

However, glucose levels and mental fatigue may matter more indirectly in how they affect mental capacities for judging. They might fall below a point at which a judge is no longer fit to judge. 'Depletion' of mental resources *sensu strictu* may denote such an incapacity. But there are no indications that mental capacities of judges in the study fell below this threshold. More likely, they simply experienced the familiar everyday swings of mental energy, clarity and fatigue, patience and annoyance, calmness and irritations. They do not qualify as instance of 3 or 3*.

It might be helpful to disambiguate 'extralegal factors'. In the law, it commonly refers to extralegal *reasons*, *i.e.* invalid inputs into the decision-making process, considerations which courts should not take into account. The phase of the Moon-Cycle, or more worrisome, race of an applicant, are clearly irrelevant and in this sense, legally invalid reasons. If they affect a decision, it is probably incorrect. So there is grounds for epistemic concern (3*). But none of this applies to the cases of the study, which is silent about reasons.

25 Nor, I should add, are specific glucose levels. Attempts to define *right levels of glucose for legal decision-making* are probably futile for medical reasons. Glucose levels vary considerably between persons and are regularly modified via medication (*e.g.*, diabetes).

'Extralegal factors' there does not refer to reasons, but to glucose or mental fatigue. They lie on different levels. Glucose is one of the causes of the cognitive machinery on which legal reasoning runs and mental fatigue is an indication of its functioning. Both refer to *causes*, not reasons, and they are not evident instance of 3 or 3*.

To put it differently: the researchers open their paper with the rhetorical question "are judicial rulings based solely on laws and facts?" Their aim is to show that this is not the case. But this way of framing it tends to conflate categories. If they take their study to provide a dismissive answer to their question in a strict sense, then *no* judicial ruling is based 'solely on laws and facts.' There are always further causal factors, the physical realizers, the embodiment of the decision-making process – but they are not 'extralegal'. Moreover, judges of the study supposedly *did* base their rulings on laws and facts, and not on morality, aesthetics, personal proclivities, the weather, or the time of the lunch. At least nothing suggests that they entertained such considerations ("let us deny this application quickly so we can have lunch"). Therefore, neither extralegal reasons, nor extralegal causes are helpful categories in capturing the problem.

3.4 *Procedures & Biases*

The foregoing drew on a substantive idea of correctness. Let us briefly turn to the procedural side. Procedural rules stipulate *modi operandi* for fact-finding and, to some extent, deliberation. Breaches may provide grounds for review, they may *indicate*, again epistemically, that judgments might be incorrect on the merits. Moreover, some breaches violate principles of procedural justice and therefore constitute wrongs in themselves, and may give rise to remedies for that reason alone. But the problem of the study does not seem to lie in irregular proceedings. Quite conceivably, all procedural rules were observed.

However, one might be inclined to think that judges were *biased*. This would violate a central principle of procedural justice (its relevance is underscored by the fact that the 'rule against bias' is considered one of two principles of natural justice in common law).[26] Whether judges were indeed biased depends on what constitutes bias in a legal sense. Not every bias in psychology is one in law. The legal idea of bias is rooted in the demand of judicial and administrative impartiality. It prohibits (dis-)favoring a party for undue rea-

26 M. Groves, 'Rule against Bias', *Hong Kong Law Journal*, Vol. 39, 2009, p. 485; H. Stout, 'Bias', *Judicial Review*, Vol. 16, 2011, pp. 458-482.

sons.[27] The classic conflict of interest between the role of the judge as a neutral arbiter and personal interests ("no one be a judge in her own case") does not apply here. But judges might exhibit treat one party unfairly for other reasons.[28] However, the study does not provide indications that judges *knowingly* disfavored later applicants. They might have done so *implicitly*. But how precisely would implicit bias work in these cases? Usually, it is triggered by properties of the party, *e.g.* gender or ethnicity. Yet again, there are not indications that this has been the case. The same is true for motivated cognition; nothing indicates that judges desired a particular outcome.[29] Therefore, behavior of judges does not fit traditional conceptions of bias as lacking impartiality.

Perhaps a related idea, 'predetermination' in common law, is a better candidate. It denotes the "minimal requirement of impartiality in legal disputes, an attitude of openness to and lack of pre-judgment upon the claims of the disputants."[30] It is interesting to ponder what this means more precisely. Common law draws a distinction between a judge's predispositions and predetermination.[31] As Keith Lindblom, former Judge at the English High Court, summarizes:[32]

> The jurisprudence on ... predetermination, in the planning decision-making context, is mature and uncontroversial. It recognizes the clear and crucial distinction between predisposition and predetermination. Predisposition is normal and acceptable. Predetermination, when it occurs, is unacceptable. What distinguishes one from the other is that in the case of the former, at the time when the decision in question is made, the decision-maker's mind is open; in the case of the latter, that mind is closed.

However, even though the jurisprudence might be uncontroversial, clear distinctions are probably hard to draw in concrete cases. When is the mind open, when is it closed? This seems to be a gradual affair, related to the sensitivity of judges to relevant reasons.[33] But is there any way to render these notions more concrete? Mind seems closed if every

27 The demand of impartiality is expressed in Art. 6 of the ECHR; Art. 41 and 47 of the EUCFR. On the convergence between legal cultures in this regard, *see* M. Allars, 'Disqualification for Bias and International Tribunals: Room for a Common Test', *Missouri Law Review*, Vol. 78, 2013, pp. 379-411.

28 Stout 2011.

29 A.M. Sood, 'Motivated Cognition in Legal Judgments – An Analytic Review', *Annual Review of Law and Social Science*, Vol. 9, 2013, pp. 307-325.

30 W. Lucy, 'The Possibility of Impartiality', *Oxford Journal of Legal Studies*, Vol. 25, 2005, pp. 3-31, at p. 15.

31 J. Maurici, 'The Modern Approach to Bias', *Judicial Review*, Vol. 12, 2007, pp. 251-260.

32 *R (Harris) v Haringey London Borough Council* [2009] EWHC 2329, at para. 62.

33 P. Havers & A. Henderson, 'Recent Developments (and Problems) in the Law on Bias', *Judicial Review*, Vol. 16, 2011, pp. 80-93.

application at a particular time or place in the order were denied, irrespective of the submissions of the party. But the study does not show such strong effects. Probability of a favorable ruling dropped significantly before the first and the second break, but it still ranged around 30% and 20% respectively. So judges apparently did listen and granted persuasive applications. Only at one point in the afternoon, chances approximate zero for a short interval. But this might be a statistical artefact as it rises again shortly after.[34] The picture is slightly different with respect to the ordinal number of the case. If judges made more than nine decisions before a food break, chances of positive outcomes for later decisions dropped below 10%. Perhaps, this is indicates closed-mindedness. But it affected only a handful of cases. Apart from them, the effect size is not big enough to speak of minds being closed in a pronounced sense. Rather, one may say judges were more open-minded towards applicants' cases at some points in times, and more towards the opposing (prosecutorial) side at others. Such fluctuations do not seem to qualify as predetermination.

Objective or Apparent Bias

Furthermore, there is an objective or apparent side to bias. Because of the importance of impartiality, a real possibility or the appearance of bias suffices to disqualify a judge or member of the jury. In Lord Hewart's proverbial saying, justice should not only be done, but also be seen to be done. And as often reiterated by the ECtHR, it is of great importance that "courts inspire confidence in the public and the parties."[35] Suppose a new applicant comes before the parole board, constituted in the way as it was during the study. His case is the last before lunch break. Made aware of the study by his attorney, it may *appear* to him that his case is not judged impartially, that the cards are stacked against him. This impression is understandable. But does it suffice to disqualify judges, or provide grounds for subsequent review? Under the European Convention, it is not the perspective of the applicant but of a 'fair-minded' observer which is decisive.[36] How would proceedings appear to such an observer? Mainly, I think, this depends on the still outstanding explanation of the judgments. Without it, the appearance of bias seems hard to deny. Worth noting is the fact that the problematic aspects have likely not occurred to anyone involved in the proceedings. Neither parole board judges, nor applicants or their attorneys supposedly entertained the idea that ordering of cases had an impact on outcomes. Thus, the appearance of bias, probably due to imperceptible factors, is revealed through the study. This is an interesting indirect effect cognitive science (and social science) may have on the law. Once the study is out, the law cannot deny its findings.

---

34 See Figure S.2. in the supporting information of Danziger, Levav & Avnaim-Pesso 2011, pp. 6889-6892.

35 ECtHR (GC), 15 December 2005 (*Kyprianou v. Cyprus*), app. no 73797/01.

36 *See* W. Schabas, *The European Convention on Human Rights: A commentary*, Oxford University Press, Oxford 2016.

3.5 *What Then Is the Problem?*

Let us take stock: hitherto, we could neither find faults in procedure, nor *ex hypothesi* in explicit reasoning of decisions. Nonetheless, something seems wrong. The main piece of evidence is the pattern of outcomes. If cases are randomly distributed and their number is large enough, a more equal distribution pattern is expected. At least under one condition: *that cases are measured by the same standard.* This is where the problem seems to lie. More precisely, it arises from the conjunction of two phenomena: meal-related influences affect imperceptible parts of judgments, and their operations are brought to light through a comparative juxtaposition of many decisions. The view on the particular case, the usual focus of the law and of judicial review, does not reveal them.

How may this happen? Imperceptibility is related to legal indeterminacy. Judging requires applying loosely defined concepts or broad standards to a concrete case, tailored to its circumstances through interpretation. Interpretation is intertwined with assessments of facts of the case. Going back-and-forth between facts and norms is common in rendering the latter more precise to fit the former. For instance, take a central consideration in the type of decisions of the study. Granting parole requires that the applicant no longer poses a threat. To assess this, normative thresholds for threats have to be defined, and be related to the factual likelihood of reoffending (in any case only educated guess). This may have to be done with respect to different types of misconduct and severities of potential harms. They will be weighed in light of general considerations about the values of public security and individual freedoms, not always free from influence by the prevailing political climate. Accordingly, determining whether an offender still poses a threat easily turns into a complex calculation involving forecasts, probabilities, and values. A single right outcome is often hard to find, several reasonable outcomes remain. Within this spectrum, judges have leeway. It is here that legal reasoning becomes susceptible to biases and influences, including psychological and physiological ones. Mental fatigue may make judges more risk-averse and low glucose levels less trustworthy. But notably, they do not render decisions incorrect. Both old and new assessments of thresholds and standards may fall within the range of the reasonable. Divergences nonetheless suffice to shift judgments from one category to the other, from approval to rejection. Thus, judges may subtly – and implicitly – change concepts and standards by which they evaluate the facts of the case, but do so within the bounds of the law, without trespassing conceptual or normative boundaries. This may explain the patterns of decisions without presupposing bad faith, bias, or (non-comparatively) wrong outcomes.

4 Normative Implications

4.1 *Treating Like Cases Alike*

If this explanation is, by and large, correct, what follows for particular decisions? Applying different standards, overtly or subtly, runs contrary to the maxim to treat like cases alike or the idea of equal treatment before the law. If outcomes depend on the time of the day or ordering of hearings, two relevantly similar cases might be decided differently. As a formal principle, treating like cases alike is a central idea of justice, deeply rooted in the western tradition and tied to idea of the rule of law. Its corollary on the personal level is the right to equal treatment before the law. Legal orders may construe its material scope, interferences, and remedies differently. Whereas some, as Art. 14 of the European Convention, conceive it as an accessory to substantive rights, it is a stand-alone right in others (*e.g.* Art. 26 Covenant Civil and Political Rights).[37] In substance, it may prohibit unequal treatment *tout court*, or only if based on specific enumerated grounds (such as race, gender, sexual orientation). Interferences may also be justified differently. Again, rather than reviewing particular theories, let us consider analytically how the law should deal with such situations.

4.2 *Precedent and Stare Decisis*

First and foremost, a judgement in contravention of equal treatment is *relatively* or *comparatively* incorrect, not in itself (non-comparatively). Accordingly, in the absence of a diverging ruling in another case, applicants have no grounds to complain. There are no *independent* reasons for the incorrectness of the decision (provided, as assumed here all along, that decisions fall within the range of correct outcomes). *Secondly*, legal orders in which binding precedent plays a central role (a feature of common law) may hold that subsequent decisions have to be decided pursuant to the first because the (temporally) former sets the standard: *stare decisis*. The first decision (more precisely, its *ratio decidendi*) binds later courts. Then, strictly speaking, a diverging second decision on the same point does *not* fall within the range of permissible outcomes, as this range has been narrowed down by the previous decision. One may surely ask why the first decision should be binding. This touches upon foundational questions of precedent and *stare decisis*. Apart from familiar problems of establishing *rationes* and likeness, critical voices cast doubts on

37 For the ECHR, *see* Schabas 2016; for the CCPR, *see* Human Rights Committee, 'General Comment No. 18 - Non-discrimination', 1989. A comprehensive comparative work is J.H. Gerards, *Judicial review in equal treatment cases*, M. Nijhoff Publishers, Leiden 2005.

the plausibility of temporal priority as a normative criterion. If the law is truly indeterminate in the first decision, why should the concretization by the first bind following courts? If there are no prevailing reasons for a particular decision in the first case, there are none in the second.[38] Binding precedent means that an arbitrary decision is perpetuated, without better reasons in its favor. In the eyes of critics, this is a 'foolish consistency' conferring undue powers to the past.[39] Subsequent decisions, handed down in view of previous ones, may seem epistemically advantageous and further develop the law. This view prompts thorny questions about the lawmaking powers of the judiciary, the value of legal consistency and stability. As they may lead us astray here, we may perhaps sidestep them with the following: courts should not be barred in principle from deviating from former decisions – and thereby, treating like cases *unlike* – if persuasive reasons suggest so (this position seems to correspond to the actual realities in many precedent-based jurisdictions). However, with respect to the present inquiry, it would not be persuasive to conceive diverging second decisions as advancements of the law, given the repeated and *unreasoned* tossing and turning throughout the day. Not following precedent in these cases does not seem to further any valuable goal. Therefore, these cases interfere with (a modest understanding of) the rule of precedent, or the idea of equal treatment. This needs justification.

4.3 *Criticism of Equal Treatment*

This leads us, *thirdly*, to a line of critic against the value of equal treatment which has resonated in civil law thinking. As an example, here is a remark by Hans Kelsen:

> What of the special principle of so-called equality before the law? All it means is that the machinery of the law should make no distinctions which are not already made by the law to be applied. If the law grants political rights to men only, not women, ... then the principle of equality before the law is fully upheld if in concrete cases the judicial authorities decide that a woman ... has no political rights. This principle has scarcely anything to do with equality any longer. It merely states that the law should be applied as it is meant to be applied. It is the principle of legality ...which is by nature inherent in every legal order regardless of whether this order is just or unjust.[40]

38 A. Marmor, 'Should like cases be treated alike?', *Legal Theory*, Vol. 11, 2005, pp. 27-38.

39 C.J. Peters, 'Foolish Consistency: On Equality, Integrity, and Justice in Stare Decisis', *Yale Law Journal*, Vol. 105, 1996, pp. 2031-2115.

40 H. Kelsen, 'What is justice?', *in* H. Kelsen, *Essays in Legal and Moral Philosophy*, Springer, Dordrecht 1973, p. 15.

Distinguishing equality *before* the law from equality *in* the law, Kelsen notes that the former only consists in the principles of legality, the correct application of existing law. It does not confer an additional right over and above the non-comparative rights which the person possesses. This *equality skepticism* is echoed in influential more recent contributions arguing that equal treatment or comparative justice is "empty" or "tautological".[41] If two decisions about the same facts diverge, so the argument goes, the law has been misapplied in at least one. However, this modern equality skepticism overlooks what has been emphasized in the foregoing, the realms of indeterminacy and imperceptibility. Wherever several outcomes are prima facie right, unlike treatment (within this range) does not run afoul of *other* requirements of the law. Whether like cases should nonetheless be treated alike is then a non-redundant and distinct question, which skeptical arguments regularly fail to adequately address.[42] Furthermore, skeptics often note their troubles with locating deeper sources of the value of equal treatment, over and above the correct application of other substantive criteria. But they may not need to look in too faraway places, the idea of equality might be enshrined in the very foundations of state authority.

4.4 *Social Contract & Equal Treatment*

Here, *fourthly*, is the sketch of an argument for the inherent value of equal treatment. It lies in the basic arrangement that confers legitimacy to state authority in the first place: the social contract. Equality is part of the pre-contractual condition, in the sense that no one has any claims or prevailing rights over others. It is then incorporated into the contract and adopted as a general principle, provided the contract is indeed one between free and equal partners. Any plausible construal of an arrangement of equals will include equality before the law. And as a principle of contract law, one party is bound to perform its contractual duties if and only if the others do so likewise (*do ut des* in the civil law tradition). This leads to reciprocal relations between all parties. This implies that every citizen is bound to give up her freedoms only to the extent that others do likewise. Otherwise, the reciprocal relationship is violated. Accordingly, if A has to give up her liberty, say in the interest of public safety – and provided that decision is not erroneous for other reasons –, B is expected to do the same under equal circumstances. The first case thus sets a standard against which others are to be measured. If a lesser burden is imposed on B, *ceteris paribus*,

41 P. Westen, 'The Empty Idea of Equality', *Harvard Law Review*, Vol. 95, 1982, pp. 537-596; Peters 1996.

42 One reason for this neglect is that the possibility of several correct outcomes seems a peculiar feature of (applied) law and might have escaped the attention of some philosophers. For other arguments to the same result: A.R. Miguel, 'Equality before the Law and Precedent', *Ratio Juris*, Vol. 10, 1997, pp. 372-391; F.K. Thomsen, 'Concept, Principle, and norm – equality before the law reconsidered', *Legal Theory*, Vol. 24, 2018, pp. 103-134.

A can complain that her contribution to the common good was heavier. This deviation needs justification, which may often be impossible under *ceteris paribus* conditions. As a consequence, A was overcharged, triggering some kind of remedy.

With this, we have justified a basic system of equal treatment and precedent: State authority grounded in an arrangement of equals standing in reciprocal relations cannot treat some parties favorably or unfavorably. It is bound to adhere to general contractual principles and to commit itself – as all actual states do to some degree – to the idea of equal treatment. Equality before the law is thus an *architectonical feature* of plausible social contract models. Accordingly, by default, everyone has to be treated equally, and later decisions should follow former ones. Nonetheless, precedent can be overturned but this requires sound justification, additional reasons.

Moreover, *fifthly*, most authors agree on the *instrumental* value of equal treatment: clarity and predictability of the law. Although some may see this as a 'status quo bias', normative stability is an important background condition for social coordination and cooperation.[43] Therefore, good reasons speak in favor of conceiving equal treatment as an independent right. This supports the default rule that legal systems should treat like cases alike.

4.5 Limits to Equal Treatment: Disagreement and Diversity

Nonetheless, *sixthly*, equal treatment is not an absolute or indefeasible right. It comes with costs, and it might be overridden by countervailing reasons. One set of such reasons might summarily be referred to as diversity, pluralism, decentralization, and feminist standpoint epistemology. Although I wish to remain uncommitted to the merits of the latter, it underscores the undeniable truth that perspectives and life experiences differ. Insofar as legal indeterminacy is generated by incommensurable values and diverging assessments of facts, equal treatment would, somewhat ironically, buttress majoritarian views. To put it bluntly: if the perspectives of privileged white men who made up the overwhelming part of the judiciaries for the last centuries are complemented by more diverse and diverging perspectives, more variance in judgments, even on similar facts, are to be expected. There is room for reasonable disagreement. This point relates back to the discussion of bias. Judges differ in their life experiences and outlooks, and *dédoublement*, the separation

43 N. Bostrom & T. Ord, 'The Reversal Test: Eliminating Status Quo Bias in Applied Ethics', *Ethics*, Vol. 116, 2006, pp. 656-679.

between role and person, only goes so far.[44] In the words of Stephen Schwebel, former President of the International Court of Justice:

> We are all prisoners of our own experience. Such measure of objectivity as may be humanly possible may come more easily to some than others, depending in part on that experience, in which the legal and political culture that conditioned it is important.[45]

Disparities in adjudication between judges are well known and wide spread.[46] As long as outcomes of particular decisions stay within the bounds of the permissible, they follow from a *prima facie* welcome development. Diversity comes with costs to decisional consistency. With this, we can assess the still hovering charge of subjective bias. If diverse personal experiences and backgrounds of judges explain differences in judgments, the impression of bias and unfair treatment *disappears*.

Nonetheless, *seventhly*, wide variations between outcomes are still somewhat unsatisfactory. Lawmakers are of course free to narrow down indeterminacy and streamline decision-making. They may introduce more finely knit rules, vest judges with less discretion, or step in whenever the judiciary treats too many like cases unlike. But these interventions face technical and practical limits. The law is to some extent necessarily general and abstract to fit the multifaceted and hard to anticipate situations which it seeks to regulate. Inflexibility, over-rigidity, and failure to afford 'right' decision in individual cases are typical downsides of tighter regulatory regimes.[47] Some tensions between equality, indeterminacy, discretion, and diversity thus remain. But this does not seem to pose pressing problems of legitimacy, neither for the entire legal order, nor for individual cases, provided their outcomes stay within the correct range. To assuage remaining worries, H.L.A. Hart once suggested to 'identify … the optimum conditions for the exercise of discretion, because

44 G.I. Hernández, 'Impartiality and Bias at the International Court of Justice', *Cambridge Journal of International and Comparative Law*, Vol. 1, 2012, pp. 183-207.

45 S.M. Schwebel, 'National Judges and Judges Ad Hoc of the International Court of Justice', *International and Comparative Law Quarterly*, Vol. 48, 1999, pp. 889-900, at p. 895.

46 An interesting model to measure disparities and extrapolate error-rates provides J.B. Fischman, 'Measuring Inconsistency, Indeterminacy, and Error in Adjudication', *American Law and Economics Review*, Vol. 16, 2014, pp. 40-85.

47 *See* D.A. Strauss, 'Must Like Cases Be Treated Alike?', University of Chicago Public Law Research Paper No. 24, 2002, https://ssrn.com/abstract=312180. Noteworthy, many actual legal systems do not invest much in ensuring consistency between individual cases, only in coherence in law on a higher level of generality, mainly through high courts. Given that administrations and courts in mass society routinely deal with many potentially alike case, databases affording comparisons could easily be established. The lack of will to do so may indicate that consistency is not perceived as a pressing goal, at least on this level of implementation. This may change once Big Data enters judicial practice.

where we cannot be sure of being right, we can at least do what we can to obtain the best conditions for decisions."[48] However, Hart explicitly understood this to not encompass "psychological conditions of the sound exercise" of discretion, but only conditions of the normative-legal sphere.[49] In this point, studies as the one by Danziger and colleagues suggest that Hart might have been wrong. Every decision has bio-psychological conditions which may influence outcomes, especially where the indeterminacy of the law affords leeway. Excluding them from the interest of legal theory is a shortcoming.

Hitherto, a permissive view with respect to variations and divergences has been formulated. It needs two specifications. *Eighthly*, more restrictive limits have to be drawn to unequal treatment with respect to discrimination on grounds of unchosen personal characteristics (*e.g.*, race, gender, ethnicity) or of expressions of fundamental rights (*e.g.*, religion, opinion). Such criteria should never, or only in the rarest of circumstances, be allowed to make a difference. Accordingly, unequal treatment on these grounds is regularly discriminatory and requires "very weighty" justificatory reasons (ECtHR).[50] For our purposes, we can leave open the vexing question whether discrimination has to be intentional (or whether implicit bias suffices).[51] It bears noting that the additional strength of these prohibitions derives not from equal treatment alone, but from general considerations about societal problems (racism, sexism, xenophobia) in combination with the importance of the protected basic liberties, as well as the equal moral status of everyone.[52] In light of these considerations, discrimination of this sort arguably constitutes an independent wrong in itself. Therefore, even though a decision falls within the range of ideal outcomes, it is wrong if it discriminates on these specific grounds.

The foregoing suggests drawing a distinction between unequal treatment based on characteristics of affected persons and of judges. The latter is regularly justifiable whereas the former is not. However, this needs, *ninthly*, restrictions with respect to personal preferences of judges. Consider one of the classic claims of Legal Realism, namely that judicial decisions are strongly influenced by the political views of judges ('attitudinal model').[53] Assuming

48 H.L.A. Hart, 'Discretion', *Harvard Law Review*, Vol. 127, 2013, pp. 652-665.

49 Id., p. 653.

50 J. Gerards, 'The Discrimination Grounds of Article 14 of the European Convention on Human Rights', *Human Rights Law Review*, Vol. 13, 2013, pp. 99-124.

51 Whereas even apparent bias suffices to *disqualify* a judge, the question is here whether it also violates equal treatment, which usually has stronger ramifications.

52 For an argument against equality skepticism along these lines, *see* P.S. Shin, 'The substantive principle of equal treatment', *Legal Theory*, Vol. 15, 2009, p. 149.

53 J.A. Segal & H.J. Spaeth, *The Supreme Court and the attitudinal model revisited*, Cambridge University Press, Cambridge 2002; E. Braman, *Law, politics, & perception: how policy preferences influence legal reasoning*, University of Virginia Press, Charlottesville 2009.

that this is – to some extent – descriptively true, does the view laid out here not confer on judges an evaluative *carte de blanche* to implement their attitude, hidden behind a veil of vagueness and indeterminacy? Such a consequence is clearly wrong, it contravenes a role-expectation of judges: political neutrality. However, where judges are tasked with exercising discretion, they are supposed to make, among others, policy considerations and value decisions. The crucial difference is that these decisions should not be based on personal preferences or prejudices, but on the values and principles inscribed in the legal order. And of course, the value of diversity cannot override the rule of law. Even though *de facto*, personal preferences and policy considerations may intermingle to a degree at which they become inseparable, they differ in theory, and judges are called upon to keep them apart. Thus, if judges pursue their own policy preferences – even within the bounds of the permissible –, they fail to discharge their duty. But whether this violates applicants' rights is a different matter. If one assumes, as argued here, at least a weak priority of precedent, deviating exercises of discretion because of judges' personal preferences violate comparative justice.

5 Assessing the Study

Against the backdrop of these considerations, we can finally assess unequal treatment in the study. It is, we have assumed, neither intentional, nor based on personal characteristics of applicants, or on judges pushing personal preferences. Rather, the causes of unequal treatment are best described as order effects which stem from shortcomings of the legal order to provide a decision-making process that rules consistently and uniformly. They are due to what one may call 'technical limitations', biological constraints and psychological weaknesses of humans, glucose levels and mental fatigue, which shift assessments and standards within the indeterminate legal realm. As long as rulings fall within this range, they are (non-comparatively) correct. But as they contravene equal treatment and precedent (however strong their bind may be), they are in need of justification.

As argued, diversity on the bench and plural perspectives among judges may justify unequal treatment because a diverse judiciary will deliver diverging judgments. Regularly, parties do not have a right to a judge with particular characteristics (*e.g.* same gender, race, or religion).[54] They are thus exposed to the shifting standards of a diverse judiciary, but this does not give grounds for grave concerns. Rather, this is an inevitable feature of the law and relates to what Jeremy Waldron describes as "luck in one's judge". This idea is partic-

54 It should be noted that the idea of having a right to a particular jury is not as far-fetched as it may seem, especially with a view on minorities regularly judged by a jury of peers with a different background.

ularly familiar to common law countries where jury selection and juror exclusion generate an entire field of controversies. More broadly, luck in one's judge or jury is a variation of the phenomenon of legal luck. As Waldron points out, "legal systems face this element of luck with some disdain: luck may be present; we may wish it were not; we are certainly not going to take any positive action to promote it."[55] Nonetheless, luck seems inevitable, as the alternative, a strict positivistic rule-bound system, fails – in terms of justice – because of its inflexibility. Therefore, variances between outcomes resulting from inter-judge disparities are justifiable insofar as they inevitably follow from a diverse judiciary.

Then, transferred to the question before us, fluctuating decisions *within* a judge might be tolerable as well. If, as we assume, the fact that the judge in one case applies standards different to those she applied previously does not, by itself, violate non-comparative rights. The remaining question is whether unequal treatments are justified. From the perspective of rights of applicants, it seems irrelevant whether shifting standards are due to inter- or intrajudge disparities as long as they are roughly similar in size. Intra-judge differences seem inevitable to the extent that they stem from ordinary biological and psychological functioning of humans. There is a minor difference though. Discrepancies between judges derive from diversity, a value of its own. Intra-judge differences, derive from fluctuations not valuable by themselves. They are thus not worth preserving and should be prevented by the law. Nonetheless, insofar as they are factually inevitable features of human judgments, they are justifiable. Then, the cases in the Danziger study fell short of violating applicants' rights.

This conclusion may come as a surprise. It may provoke the objection that the judiciary is not even called upon to adjudicate consistently. But I wish to suggest the contrary: if intra-judge disparities were *not* inevitable, the weak bounds of precedent should prevail. Non-ideal justifications demand reasonable attempts to approximate the ideal. So to the extent that inconsistencies can be overcome, they should. This remains true even though disparities fall short of violating applicants' *subjective* rights. Consistency and equal treatment are nonetheless objective values which legal orders embrace and should aspire to attain. In addition, as judges are surely better judges the more aware of influences they are, they should be educated about them, enabling them to factor them into their reasoning. If possible, 'debiasing' (in a psychological sense) strategies should be developed. Perhaps, inconsistencies might be alleviated through several short breaks, glucose replenishments or other intervention such as coffee. Judges can also learn to be more sensitive about indications of mental fatigue or "ego depletion". And there might be structural solutions: judges might be asked to be more explicit about thresholds and standards. Thus, even

55 J. Waldron, 'Lucky in Your Judge', *Theoretical Inquiries in Law*, Vol. 9, 2007, pp. 186-216, at p. 187.

though decisions may not have violated applicants' rights, the study does put pressure on legal orders and should motivate further research into the psychological conditions of legal reasoning.

6 Conclusion

The foregoing discussion proceeded under some counterfactual assumptions. In reality, a set of a thousand decisions surely contains some that are explicitly erroneous in substance or procedure. In others, judges might have been partial and biased. Nonetheless, the study raises interesting theoretical questions, over and above such ordinary problems of any judiciary. Even when judges act in good faith and judgments are not explicitly incorrect, they can be influenced by biological and psychological factors that enter the law through loopholes of indeterminacy and imperceptibility. Contrary to first appearance, the normative problem with such influences does not lie in them being extralegal factors, but rather in the absence of consistency in judgment across time and cases. This runs counter to the ideas of equal treatment and precedent. However, it might be justified.

In non-ideal conditions, the judiciary can only attempt to provide consistently judging courts. Shortcomings of the human psychology should be addressed, but normative demands must be shaped by what is descriptively possible: *ought implies can*. Other studies have revealed, and future ones will continue to do so, physiological, psychological and situational factors which may affect judgments, from hormone levels to medications, from mental disorders to personal problems, from sleep deprivation to current political and social events.[56] Judges are, as Jerome Frank and the Legal Realists reminded us some decades ago, humans – and their reasoning susceptible to such factors.[57] This is not an invitation for complacency, but a realistic assessment of what is possible. Therefore, insofar as judiciaries attempt to create condition of consistent judging, the setbacks to equal treatment fall short of violating rights (again, provided that outcomes are within the bounds of the permissible).

The Danziger study is intriguing because it shows skewed *patterns* in judgments that remain unobservable from the traditional legal perspective on the individual case and written documents and records. These perspectives fail to reveal these influencing factors, even though they merit attention and call for explanations. Only a comparative look at a

56 See infra.

57 J. Frank, 'Are Judges Human? Part One: The Effect on Legal Thinking of the Assumption That Judges Behave like Human Beings', *University of Pennsylvania Law Review and American Law Register*, Vol. 80, 1931, p. 17.

greater number of cases renders them visible. This is the power of statistics, and the study shows that the law is well advised to muster it more often, at least for purposes of quality control. A social institution in the pursuit of justice must be interested in gaining vantage points from which it can detect patterns unobservable from the 'internal point of view'.

If further studies replicate the findings or reveal more of such factors, legal systems might need to devote more attention to the psychology of legal reasoning. This may also put pressure on the secrecy of court's deliberation. Usually, it is shielded from access by parties or the public to ensure judicial independence. But the contexts of discovery and justification touch each other here. Imperceptible failures remain *de facto* unreviewable without access to discovery. In individual judges, the psychological processes of judging are by their nature hardly accessible. Group deliberations, however, may provide clues for detecting biases and influences. Secrecy is thus a double-edged sword: obtaining evidence for errors would run counter to independence.[58]

Comparative studies such as the present one are then one of the few ways to acquire knowledge about distorting factors. Since they provide only aggregate information about sets of cases, they may not afford inferences about particular cases. Nonetheless, they shed light on the darker sides of the workings of the law, a perspective that should be openly embraced rather than dismissed by legal orders.

58 For instance, in the UK, it is an offence to seek to obtain any information about the jury deliberations, pursuant to Section 8 (1) of the Contempt of Court Act 1981.

REFERENCES

Allars, M., 'Disqualification for Bias and International Tribunals: Room for a Common Test', *Missouri Law Review*, Vol. 78, 2013, pp. 379-411.

Barnes, C.M., Schaubroeck, J., Huth, M. & Ghumman, S., 'Lack of sleep and unethical conduct', *Organizational Behavior and Human Decision Processes*, Vol. 115, 2011, pp. 169-180.

Baumeister, R.F., 'Ego Depletion and Self-Control Failure: An Energy Model of the Self's Executive Function', *Self and Identity*, Vol. 1, 2002, pp. 129-136.

Bostrom, N. & Ord, T., 'The Reversal Test: Eliminating Status Quo Bias in Applied Ethics', *Ethics*, Vol. 116, 2006, pp. 656-679.

Braman, E., *Law, politics, & perception: how policy preferences influence legal reasoning*, University of Virginia Press, Charlottesville 2009.

Brownstein, M., & Saul, J., *Implicit Bias and Philosophy, Volume 1*, Oxford University Press, Oxford 2016.

Chen, D.L., 'This Morning's Breakfast, Last Night's Game: Detecting Extraneous Influences on Judging', 2016 (working paper, http://iast.fr/pub/31020).

Cho, K., Barnes, C.M. & Guanara, C.L., 'Sleepy Punishers Are Harsh Punishers: Daylight Saving Time and Legal Sentences', *Psychological Science*, Vol. 28, 2017, pp. 242-247.

Daljord, Ø., Urminsky, O. & Ureta, J.-M., 'The Status Quo Theory of Depletion Does not Explain the Israeli Parole Decisions', 2017 (preprint, University of Chicago, http://home.uchicago.edu/ourminsky/Status_Quo_Theory_Revisited.pdf).

Danziger, S., Levav, J. & Avnaim-Pesso, L., 'Extraneous factors in judicial decisions', *Proceedings of the National Academy of Sciences*, Vol. 108, 2011, pp. 6889-6892.

Danziger, S., Levav, J. & Avnaim-Pesso, L., 'Reply to Weinshall-Margel and Shapard: Extraneous factors in judicial decisions persist', *Proceedings of the National Academy of Sciences*, Vol. 108, 2011, E834-E834.

Douglas, W.O., 'Stare Decisis', *Columbia Law Review*, Vol. 49, 1949, pp. 735-758.

Dworkin, R, *Taking Rights Seriously*. with a new appendix, Cambridge Massachusetts, Harvard University Press, 1977.

Eren, O. & Mocan, N., 'Emotional Judges and Unlucky Juveniles', *American Economic Journal: Applied Economics*, Vol. 10, 2018, pp. 171-205.

Fischman, J.B., 'Measuring Inconsistency, Indeterminacy, and Error in Adjudication', *American Law and Economics Review*, Vol. 16, 2014, pp. 40-85.

Frank, J., 'Are Judges Human? Part One: The Effect on Legal Thinking of the Assumption That Judges Behave like Human Beings', *University of Pennsylvania Law Review and American Law Register*, Vol. 80, 1931, p. 17.

Gailliot, M.T. & Baumeister, R.F., 'The Physiology of Willpower: Linking Blood Glucose to Self-Control', *Personality and Social Psychology Review*, Vol. 11, 2007, pp. 303-327.

Gerards, J., 'The Discrimination Grounds of Article 14 of the European Convention on Human Rights', *Human Rights Law Review*, Vol. 13, 2013, pp. 99-124.

Gerards, J.H., *Judicial review in equal treatment cases*, M. Nijhoff Publishers, Leiden 2005.

Gigerenzer, G. & Engel, C. (Eds.), *Heuristics and the law*, MIT Press in cooperation with Dahlem University Press, Cambridge Massachusetts 2006.

Gino, F., Schweitzer, M.E., Mead, N.L. & Ariely, D., 'Unable to resist temptation: How self-control depletion promotes unethical behavior', *Organizational Behavior and Human Decision Processes*, Vol. 115, 2011, pp. 191-203.

Glöckner, A., 'The irrational hungry judge effect revisited: Simulations reveal that the magnitude of the effect is overestimated', *Judgment and Decision Making*, Vol. 11, 2016, pp. 601-610.

Groves, M., 'Rule against Bias', *Hong Kong Law Journal*, Vol. 39, 2009, p. 485.

Hagger, M.S. *et al.*, 'A Multilab Preregistered Replication of the Ego-Depletion Effect', *Perspectives on Psychological Science*, 11, 2016, pp. 546-573.

Hart, H.L.A., 'Discretion', *Harvard Law Review*, Vol. 127, 2013, pp. 652-665.

Havers, P. & Henderson, A., 'Recent Developments (and Problems) in the Law on Bias', *Judicial Review*, Vol. 16, 2011, pp. 80-93.

Hernández, G.I., 'Impartiality and Bias at the International Court of Justice', *Cambridge Journal of International and Comparative Law*, Vol. 1, 2012, pp. 183-207.

Human Rights Committee, 'General Comment No. 18 – Non-discrimination'. 1989.

Kelsen, H., 'What is justice?', *in* H. Kelsen, *Essays in Legal and Moral Philosophy*, Springer, Dordrecht 1973.

Kouchaki, M. & Smith, I.H., 'The Morning Morality Effect: The Influence of Time of Day on Unethical Behavior', *Psychological Science*, Vol. 25, 2014, pp. 95-102.

Lucy, W., 'The Possibility of Impartiality', *Oxford Journal of Legal Studies*, Vol. 25, 2005, pp. 3-31.

Marmor, A., 'Should like cases be treated alike?', *Legal Theory*, Vol. 11, 2005, pp. 27-38.

Maurici, J., 'The Modern Approach to Bias', *Judicial Review*, Vol. 12, 2007, pp. 251-260.

Miguel, A.R., 'Equality before the Law and Precedent', *Ratio Juris*, Vol. 10, 1997, pp. 372-391.

Molden, D.C. *et al.*, 'Motivational Versus Metabolic Effects of Carbohydrates on Self-Control', *Psychological Science*, Vol. 23, 2012, pp. 1137-1144.

Nichols, S., 'Process Debunking and Ethics', *Ethics*, Vol. 124, 2014, pp. 727-749.

Orquin, J.L. & Kurzban, R., 'A meta-analysis of blood glucose effects on human decision-making', *Psychological Bulletin*, Vol. 142, 2016, p. 546.

Peters, C.J., 'Foolish Consistency: On Equality, Integrity, and Justice in Stare Decisis', *The Yale Law Journal*, Vol. 105, 1996, pp. 2031-2115.

Priel, D., 'Law and Digestion: A Brief History of an Unpalatable Idea' (preprint SSRN, www.ssrn.com/abstract=2982716).

Sauer, H., *Debunking Arguments in Ethics*, 1st edn, Cambridge University Press, Cambridge 2018.

Schabas, W., *The European Convention on Human Rights: A commentary*, Oxford University Press, Oxford 2016.

Schwebel, S.M., 'National Judges and Judges Ad Hoc of the International Court of Justice', *International and Comparative Law Quarterly*, Vol. 48, 1999, pp. 889-900.

Segal, J.A. & Spaeth, H.J., *The Supreme Court and the attitudinal model revisited*, Cambridge University Press, Cambridge 2002.

Shin, P.S., 'The substantive principle of equal treatment', *Legal Theory*, Vol. 15, 2009, p. 149.

Siegel, J.Z. & Crockett, M.J., 'How serotonin shapes moral judgment and behavior', *Annals of the New York Academy of Sciences*, Vol. 1299, 2013, p. 42.

Sood, A.M., 'Motivated Cognition in Legal Judgments – An Analytic Review', *Annual Review of Law and Social Science*, Vol. 9, 2013, pp. 307-325.

Stout, H., 'Bias', *Judicial Review*, Vol. 16, 2011, pp. 458-482.

Strauss, D.A., 'Must Like Cases Be Treated Alike?', University of Chicago Public Law Research Paper No. 24, 2002, https://ssrn.com/abstract=312180.

Sunstein, C.R. & Miles, T., 'The new legal realism', *University of Chicago Law Review*, Vol. 75, 2008, pp. 831-851.

Thomsen, F.K., 'Concept, Principle, and norm – equality before the law reconsidered', *Legal Theory* Vol. 24, 2018, pp. 103-134.

Waldron, J., 'Lucky in Your Judge', *Theoretical Inquiries in Law*, Vol. 9, 2007, pp. 186-216.

Weinshall-Margel, K. & Shapard, J., 'Overlooked factors in the analysis of parole decisions', *Proceedings of the National Academy of Sciences*, Vol. 108, 2011, E833–E833.

Westen, P., 'The Empty Idea of Equality', *Harvard Law Review*, Vol. 95, 1982, 537-596.

Wistrich, J.A.J. & Rachlinski, J.J., 'Implicit Bias in Judicial Decision Making: How it affects judgment and what judges can do about it', *in* S. Refield (Ed.), *Enhancing Justice (2017)*, American Bar Association, 2017, pp. 87-130.

Yam, K.C., Chen, X.-P. & Reynolds, S.J., 'Ego depletion and its paradoxical effects on ethical decision-making', *Organizational Behavior and Human Decision Processes*, Vol. 124, 2014, pp. 204-214.

2 Autonomy, Reason and Bias in Contract Law

J. Hage

1 Introduction

This article is part of a larger project that aims to take stock of recent developments in the cognitive sciences and their possible implications for law. The focus of the present contribution is on the implications for contract law if it proves to be the case that human decision-making in general, and in contracting in particular, is less rational than is often assumed. A possible consequence of this finding might be that contract law should be completely rewritten, or perhaps even abolished.

The autonomy of legal subjects is the cornerstone of private law in general, and contract law in particular. Private law deals with the mutual relations between private legal subjects. Originally[1] the role of state organs was confined to the enforcement of the legal positions and relations that legal subjects created themselves. For example, legal subjects determine who owns what, and the role of the state is confined to protecting those property rights. The much-heralded freedom of contract provides another illustration. The law of contract makes it possible for cooperating legal subjects to modify their legal positions by undertaking contractual obligations. The freedom of contract involves both the power of legal subjects to create the obligations that they want to undertake, and the permission to do so.[2] By using this freedom, legal subjects express their autonomy,[3] and this empowerment of legal subjects' autonomy goes hand in hand with the assumption that this autonomy is exercised rationally.[4] As we will see in Section 2.4, support for this link between autonomy

1 After the heyday of the night-watch state and free-market liberalism, the interference of the government in what were originally considered to be private relations has increased. As a result, topics that used to belong to private law only, have partly become the object of public law too. Labor relations provide an illustration of this shift from private to public.

2 J.C. Hage, 'Rechtstheoretische analyse van de partijautonomie in het contractenrecht. Twee dimensies van contactsvrijheid', *in* I. Samoy (Ed.), *Evolutie van de basisbeginselen van het contractenrecht*, Intersentia, Antwerpen 2010, pp. 241-261.

3 K. Larenz & M. Wolf, *Allgemeiner Teil des bürgerlichen Rechts*, 9th edn, Beck, München 2004, p. 393.

4 The close relationship between autonomy and rationality is a cornerstone of Kant's philosophy of practical reason. It is well worth exploring whether this element of Kant's philosophy has influenced the development of contract doctrine in continental Europe, but this possible connection will not be elaborated here.

and rationality in actual contract law can be found in the situations where the law limits the freedom of contract.

Psychological and neurological research of the last decennia has shown that human decision-making is often less rational than was traditionally assumed. Investigations (inspired) by Festinger, Ryle and Gazzaniga have made it clear that humans sometimes confabulate the motives that made them act.[5] In a number of papers, Kahnemann and Tversky have shown that human judgments are often based on heuristics that are less than fully rational, and that they suffer from biases.[6] Moreover, recent research into the brain has begun to reveal the neural mechanisms that implement decision making; specifically, it has revealed that the parts of the brain closely related to our emotions, actually play an important role in the decision-making process.[7]

The assumption that adult and mentally healthy persons have always had the capacity to act rationally lies at the heart of contract theory. However, in light of these recent psychological and neurological findings, I will try to show in this article that a thorough reconsideration of contract theory and of the foundations of contract law is necessary. To this purpose, I will discuss the 'anchoring bias'. This bias is one of the biases that were identified by Kahnemann and Tversky. I will argue that the existence of this bias and of other biases should at least lead to an adaptation of the doctrine of contract formation. Perhaps it is even better to completely replace contract law by rules that immediately aim to promote the interests of legal subjects, rather than empowering legal subjects to promote their interests on the basis of their subjective preferences.

In Section 2 I will argue that the central role of the will or intention of contract partners is best considered as a stand-in for the interests of contract parties, and also that the present law is primarily focused on interests rather than on autonomy, but that this focus has been inconsistent.

Section 3 discusses the anchoring bias, and shows that many more contracts than only those based on misrepresentation, duress, mistake, or fraud, are the result of irrationality.

---

5 D.M. Wegner, *The Illusion of Conscious Will*, The MIT Press, Cambridge Massachusetts 2002, pp. 171-186.
6 D. Kahneman, *Thinking, fast and slow*, Penguin, London 2011.
7 A. Damasio, *Descartes' Error. Emotion, reason and the human brain*, Putnam, New York 1994; F. Cushman, L. Young & J.D. Greene, 'Multi-System Moral Psychology', *in* J.M. Doris (Ed.), *The Moral Psychology Handbook*, Oxford University Press, Oxford 2010, pp. 47-71; R.M. Sapolsky, *Behave. The Biology of Humans at Our Best and Worst*, Bodley Head, London 2017.

Section 4 deals with the consequences the law should attach to the fact – if it is one – that the behavior of legal subjects is often irrational. In a conservative approach, irrationality raises the question whether and under which conditions contracts that were irrationally concluded should be avoidable. In a more radical approach, the question becomes whether the social practice of contracting should even be supported by law. This article is summarized and concluded in Section 5.

2 The Justification of Contractual Obligations

Traditionally, contract law assigns an important role to the will or intention of the contracting parties, when it comes to determining whether a contract was concluded. The point of the present section is to argue that the will or intention of the contract partners is a heuristic stand-in for the interests of the partners. In the end, the interests count, not the will or intention. This is already the case in contract law as it presently is, although it is not always clearly visible. We can discover the role of will, intention, and interests, if we ask what justifies the existence of contractual obligations. Why should the partners in a contract have obligations, merely because they promised each other to do something?

Let me introduce an example that will facilitate the discussion that follows. Anne offers her house for sale to Bob for € 430,000. Bob makes a counter-offer of € 400,000, which is accepted by Anne. In this example, the questions that need to be answered are why Anne has the obligation to transfer the house to Bob and why Bob has the obligation to pay Anne € 400,000. The answers to these questions belong to one of three kinds. The first kind emphasizes the mutual reliance that is created by making contractual promises. For example, Anne promised Bob to transfer her house and Bob's reliance on this promise justifies that Anne has the obligation to perform. The second kind of answer refers to the autonomy of the contract partners. Anne's autonomy gives her the power to undertake contractual obligations by expressing her will to do so. Anne's acceptance of Bob's counter-offer is an exercise of this autonomy, by means of which she undertook the obligation to transfer the house. This justifies the existence of the obligation to transfer. The third kind of answer does not focus on concrete contracts, but on the social practice of contracting, which has been laid down in contract law. Concrete contractual obligations can then be justified by invoking the practice: there is a rule which attaches the obligation to transfer to the contract.

In the Sections 2.1 and 2.2 it will be argued that the first two of these reasons do not cut ice. The third reason, invocation of the social practice of contracting, is the right one, but presupposes a justification of this very practice. This justification is the topic of the Sections

2.3-2.5, and in studying it, we will discover that interests play a more important role than will or intention.

2.1 *Reliance on Specific Promises*

One classic answer to the question of why contract partners derive obligations from their contract is that a contractor induces her partner, by means of the contract, to do something which he would otherwise not have done. The contract creates reliance, and this reliance is awarded with an obligation on the partner who induced it.[8] At first sight, this reliance theory of contractual obligation has its attractions, but on closer inspection the theory fails. It will turn out that reliance can only be justified if contracts lead to obligations. However, if that is the case, the reliance cannot be the reason why contracts create obligations.

Suppose that Anne told Bob that her house is somber when it is cloudy and that on a cloudy day she would happily transfer her house to anyone offering at least € 100,000. On a cloudy day, Bob offers Anne € 100,000 and relies on it that Anne will transfer the house. Based on this reliance, Bob sells his own house to C for € 110,000, which is considerably less than the market value. Is Anne under an obligation towards Bob to transfer her house to him, against payment of € 100,000?

Reliance only leads to obligations if it is justified. This raises the question of under which circumstances reliance counts as justified and leads to obligations. Perhaps it might be argued that in the above example, Bob was justified in relying on Anne's remark. Perhaps Anne is the kind of woman whose remarks are a reliable predictor of what she will do. However, reliance on a trustworthy predictor of future behavior is not the relevant kind of reliance for the creation of obligations. Bob should not rely on a mere prediction of Anne's future behavior. This becomes immediately clear if the prediction is not based on the behavior of Anne herself, but on that of some other person. Suppose that Geraldine, Anne's sister, knows Anne well, and can make trustworthy predictions of Anne's future behavior. Bob's reliance that Anne will transfer the house would, legally speaking,[9] not be justified if Geraldine predicted the transfer.

8 P.S. Atiyah, 'Fuller and the Theory of Contract', *in* P.S. Atiyah, *Essays on Contract*, Clarendon Press, Oxford 1986, pp. 73-92; *see also* J.M. Smits, *Het vertrouwensbeginsel en de contractuele gebondenheid*, Gouda Quint, Arnhem 1995.

9 The alternative for legally justified reliance is epistemically justified reliance. The very point of the present example is that if a person is epistemically speaking justified in relying on something, this does not automatically mean that this person is also legally speaking justified in relying. Legally justified reliance presupposes contract law, while epistemically justified reliance does not.

Reliance based on trustworthiness would not even be justified if Anne herself would have made this prediction of her future behavior. Bob should rely on it with justification, not merely that Anne will transfer her house, but that Anne placed herself under an obligation to transfer the house. That is only possible, however, if Anne could place herself under this obligation independent of Bob's reliance. However, if Anne could do this, it means that the obligation does not depend on the reliance, and is not justified by it. It is rather the other way around: the reliance is justified by the obligation which came into existence independently of the reliance. Because contracts lead to obligations, a contract partner is justified in relying on the assumption that other contract party will perform.

2.2 *Autonomy, Will and Intention*

The second kind of answer to the question of why contracts lead to obligations, is that because contractual obligations are undertaken voluntarily and they are willed by the contract partners, they are in that sense expressions of their autonomy.

The problem with this answer is that it is either vague, or unconvincing. To see how it can be vague, one only needs to consider the circumscription of autonomy as given in the *Stanford Encyclopedia of Philosophy*:

> [...] to be autonomous is to be one's own person, to be directed by considerations, desires, conditions, and characteristics that are not simply imposed externally upon one, but are part of what can somehow be considered one's authentic self.[10]

The reference to what can *somehow* be considered one's *authentic* self illustrates that this notion of autonomy is in need of elucidation. In the absence of such elucidation, this kind of autonomy cannot play a serious role in the justification of contractual obligations.

Similarly problematic is the view that contractual obligations are justified because they were willed. The very notion of the will is vague. The will is not a conscious event. For instance, it would not make sense to say "A minute ago, I willed to sell my house."[11] A better view is that the will is a disposition to act in a particular way. It makes sense to say "I always willed (wanted) to make a trip to Venice." That would mean that the person with this will, will make the trip as soon as a suitable opportunity presents itself. However, if

10 J. Christman, 'Autonomy in Moral and Political Philosophy', *in* E.N. Zalta (Ed.), *The Stanford Encyclopedia of Philosophy*, Winter 2017 edn, https://plato.stanford.edu/archives/win2017/entries/autonomy-moral/.

11 G. Ryle, *The Concept of Mind*, Hutchinson, London 1949, pp. 61-67.

the will is such a disposition, it is not clear why having a will justifies a contractual obligation. The person who expresses a will to take a trip to Venice does not need a contract for his motivation to make the trip. Moreover, he has no interest in concluding such a contract: why add an obligation to an already existing motivation? The other contract party may have an interest in the existence of an enforceable obligation and therefore in a contract. However, it does not seem to make sense that this obligation would exist for the mere reason that the first contractor was motivated to make the trip. We can conclude that the will that some action will be performed is not a good reason to justify the existence of an obligation.

Perhaps the view that contractual obligations exist because they were undertaken voluntarily[12] is more promising than the idea that these obligations exist because the obligated behavior was willed. The idea that contractual obligations are undertaken voluntarily may seem to be helpful, at least if the notion of voluntary action is used in the traditional sense of an action not being caused by conditions which should not have caused it.[13] However, it is unclear why the fact that an obligation was *undertaken* voluntarily shows that the obligation itself is justified. If an agent undertakes an obligation, then this agent has an obligation, no matter whether the obligation was undertaken voluntarily. 'Undertaking' is in this respect a success-verb: one can only undertake a task or an obligation if one has this task or obligation after having undertaken it. If voluntariness is a condition, it is a condition for the capability to undertake, not for the existence of what was undertaken.

If this sounds too abstract, perhaps the following example can illustrate my point. If a mountaineer climbs a mountain, she will reach the top by definition of what 'climbing a mountain' means. It does not matter for this purpose whether she did this voluntarily. Whether she climbed voluntarily or not, does not matter for the issue of whether she reached the top. However, on some definitions of climbing, involuntary climbing is impossible. A person who 'climbed' involuntarily was actually dragged to the top of the mountain. The voluntary nature of the event determines whether we call it climbing or being dragged, but not whether the mountain top was reached. Similarly, the voluntariness of undertaking an obligation does not determine whether an obligation came into existence. However, it may be relevant for whether the event could be called 'undertaking' an obligation, rather than having an obligation imposed.

12 Joseph Raz, 'Voluntary obligations and normative powers', *Aristotelian Society*, Supplementary Vol. 46, 1972, pp. 79-101.

13 The alternative is that an action is voluntary if it is based on a free will. When it comes to vagueness, this notion of a free will can compete with the notion of autonomy: we hardly have a clue what it might be.

The same reason which makes that the voluntariness of undertaking obligations does not justify the existence of these obligations also applies to the intentionality of undertaking obligations. An agent can contract with the intention to undertake in that way a particular obligation. The precise contents of the obligations are strongly influenced by the intentions of the contract partners. However, the fact that intentions influence the *contents* of the obligations, does not prove that these intentions also justify the *existence* of the resulting obligations. Contracting with the intention to create particular obligations only makes sense if the contracting parties already know that their behavior will lead to the intended obligations. This knowledge presupposes the existence of a social practice according to which contracting leads to obligations. If this practice exists, it justifies the existence of contractual obligations. Then, there is no need for additional intentions however.

Perhaps the mountain climbing example can make this clearer again: intentionally climbing a mountain is only possible for a person who knows that her behavior will lead her to the mountain top. An intentional mountain climber can only know this, if his climbing will bring him actually to the top. This means that reaching the top cannot depend on the intention to do so.

I conclude that specific contractual obligations are not justified by the autonomy, will, or intention of the contracting parties. Together with the finding that these obligations are not justified by reliance either, the conclusion must be that the traditional theories of the justification of contractual obligations fail if they are interpreted as theories about the justification of specific obligations. However, this does not mean that they also fail as theories of why the social practice of contracting is justified.

2.3 Preferences and Interests

The social practice of contracting consists of a set of rules that specify which kinds of actions count as contracting, which obligations or other legal consequences result from valid contracts, and which legal steps can be undertaken in case a contractual obligation is not performed. For my present purposes, the details of these rules – which vary from one jurisdiction to another – are not relevant. Even if there exists a social practice of contracting which justifies contract-based obligations, the question may be raised whether such obligations are 'really' justified. The answer depends on whether the social practice itself is justified. If the practice is bad, it cannot justify obligations, but if the practice is a good thing, it can justify obligations. It turns out that if contractual obligations are justified by invoking the social practice of contracting, the success of this justification depends on the justification of the practice itself. This leads us to the question whether the existence of a social practice of contracting is justified. In answering this question, both reliance and autonomy play a role.

It is efficient in the economic sense of 'efficiency', if there is a social practice which makes it possible for agents to undertake obligations in exchange for obligations undertaken by other agents. To see why, it is useful to introduce the notion of a Pareto-improvement, named after the Italian economist Vilfredo Pareto. A Pareto-improvement in the division of goods (in a broad sense) over a population is a change in the distribution which makes at least some members of the population better off, while it makes nobody worse off. A voluntary exchange will normally[14] lead to a Pareto improvement for both[15] parties involved. For example, if Anne values her house on € 380,000, while Bob values the house on € 420,000, a sale of the house from Anne to Bob for an amount in between € 380,000 and € 420,000 will lead to a Pareto-improvement. If goods are distributed over a population in such a way that no Pareto-improvement is possible anymore – any exchange will make somebody worse off – the distribution is said to be Pareto-efficient.[16]

Normally, in a voluntary sale both parties will improve their situations if the exchange takes place immediately, and nobody runs the risk that the other party will not perform. However, it is often better if the performance of one or both of the parties takes place later. For instance, Bob only needs the house three months from now, but if he can rely on it that the house will be transferred then, he can already sell his own house to Carol, and use the money to pay Anne. At the same time, Anne can count on receiving the money after three months, and already book the cruise around the world that she always wanted to make. Such delayed exchanges can only function in a reliable way, if there exist mechanisms to enforce them. Reputation is one such mechanism, contract law is another. By making enforcement of contracts and therefore also reliance possible, the practice of contracting facilitates delayed exchanges and will therefore contribute to a Pareto-efficient division of goods and services over society. At least, so it seems.

2.4 *If Preferences and Interests Do not Match*

Pareto-improvements have to do with making members of the population better or worse off. What precisely makes a participant better or worse off is not specified in this charac-

14 Later, I will argue that the clause 'normally' is crucially important here.
15 I ignore multi-party contracts, but including them would not change the argument considerably.
16 More details on Pareto-improvements and Pareto-efficiency can be found on https://en.wikipedia.org/wiki/Pareto_efficiency and on www.econlib.org/library/Enc/bios/Pareto.html (last visited on 31 December 2017).

terization. There are both subjective and objective tests for what makes an agent better off.[17] The typical subjective test is preference satisfaction:[18] the situation of an agent is improved if more of his actual preferences are satisfied to a higher degree.[19] A more objective variant of this test takes only informed preferences into account.[20] The typical objective test is based on the interests of an agent, regardless of whether the agent prefers these interests to be satisfied. This test leaves the question open what precisely count as an agent's interests. A traditional answer to this question is that an agent has only one ultimate interest: maximization of happiness.[21] A related answer is the maximization of well-being.[22] There are also pluralist theories according to which there are several interests which must somehow be combined.[23]

Contracts are based on subjective preference satisfaction. They are voluntary transactions, and it seems unlikely that an agent will voluntarily engage in a transaction which violates his actual preferences. Legal subjects do not contract to realize the preferences which they would have under ideal circumstances. Either they do not know what these ideal preferences would be, and can therefore not act upon them, or they know their ideal preferences, but then these have become their actual preferences, since ideal preferences are the preferences which persons would actually have under ideal circumstances. Further, legal subjects do not contract to realize what is good for them, unless they have the subjective preference to do so.

There are several possible reasons why the subjective preferences of a person do not reflect his real interests. First, a subjective preference may be short-lived, and perhaps last only a few minutes. A far-fetched example would be an agent who is under hypnosis and has a preference which disappears as soon as the hypnosis ends. Second, the agent may suffer from a general lack of capacity to form adequate subjective preferences. Obvious examples

17 From here on, I will ignore the possibility that an agent is worse off as the result of some transaction, but the argument on when an agent is better off applies *mutatis mutandis* also to being worse off.

18 S. Ove Hansson & T. Grüne-Yanoff, 'Preferences', *in* E.N. Zelta (Ed.), *The Stanford Encyclopedia of Philosophy*, Winter 2017 edn, https://plato.stanford.edu/archives/win2017/entries/preferences/.

19 I will ignore the trade-off between the satisfaction of more preferences and a higher degree of satisfaction of less preferences. For a discussion of this trade-off, *see* J.C. Hage, 'Comparing Alternatives', *in* J.C. Hage, *Studies in Legal Logic*, Springer, Dordrecht 2005, pp. 101-134.

20 *See* Ove Hansson & Grüne-Yanoff 2017 on 'filtered' preferences.

21 J. Bentham, *An Introduction to the Principles of Morals and Legislation*, J.H. Burns and H.L.A. Hart (Eds.), Methuen, London 1970, Chapter I, Section 2.

22 *See* the discussion of welfarism in R. Crisp, 'Well-Being', *in* E.N. Zalta (Ed.), *The Stanford Encyclopedia of Philosophy*, Fall 2017 edn, https://plato.stanford.edu/archives/fall2017/entries/well-being/ and J. Griffin, *Well-being. Its Meaning, Measurement and Moral Importance*, Clarendon Press, Oxford 1986.

23 E. Mason, 'Value Pluralism', *in* E.N. Zalta (Ed.), *The Stanford Encyclopedia of Philosophy*, Summer 2015 edn, https://plato.stanford.edu/archives/sum2015/entries/value-pluralism/.

are young children, some aged people, and persons suffering from a mental handicap or illness. Third, a subjective preference may be badly informed and would have been different if well-informed. An example would be if Bob wants to buy Anne's house, because he believes that there will be a good railway connection from the house to his working place. However, the railway company intends to end this railway connection. If Bob had known this, he would not have wanted to buy the house.

All three examples have in common that an agent has preferences which do not (necessarily) reflect his interests. Often, the law takes this discrepancy into account. A juridical act performed under hypnosis will sometimes be avoidable, and the same holds for juridical acts performed by very young persons, or by persons who are for other reasons not capable to 'form their will'. This last formulation is telling, since almost all persons are capable to form a will.[24] The problem in the mentioned cases is not that people cannot form a will, but that their will may not reflect their interests. From the fact that the law attaches consequences to situations in which the subjective preferences of contract partners do not reflect their real interests, we may conclude that what counts in law is not only people's subjective preferences, but also their interests.

Perhaps, we should even go one step further. It is possible to interpret the importance which the law attributes to the subjective preferences of persons as an indication that these preferences are seen as evidence for their interests. In this interpretation of law, only interests count, and the subjective preferences that people have are relevant as indicators of what their interests are. Indeed, it is easier to establish subjective preferences than to establish interests, and substituting subjective preferences for real interests may in many cases be a responsible epistemic strategy.[25] However, as soon as it becomes clear that the subjective preferences may deviate from a person's real interests, the law provides tools to correct the legal consequences of juridical acts based on unrepresentative preferences. An example from Dutch law would be the following. If a 13-year child old child uses their savings to buy reasonably-priced study books, the contract will be normally valid. However, if they use the money to buy a motor cycle on impulse, the contract can be vitiated.[26]

---

24 A *caveat* is in place here, because the expression 'form one's will' suggests that will-formation is under control of the agent. Even if this is sometimes the case, very often it is not. One's will is typically something that just happens to a person.

25 As Jan Smits pointed out to me, in a meta-ethical non-cognitivist view, there may not be real interests over and above subjective preferences. In that case the satisfaction of subjective preferences coincides with the satisfaction of real interests. Such a non-cognitivist view is in my opinion not very attractive, as it does not even distinguish between subjective and informed preferences.

26 Art. 1:234 S. 3 Burgerlijk Wetboek.

The tool that is most often used for this purpose is the possibility to avoid juridical acts that do not serve the interests of the agents who performed these acts. The details differ between jurisdictions. In Dutch law, avoidability is – under conditions – available to minors, persons under wardship, persons suffering from a mental disorder, or persons acting under a 'defect of consent', such as mistake, fraud, threat and undue influence.[27] [28]

If a contract does not serve the interests of one of the contract parties,[29] it will often be in his interest to avoid the contract. If the other contract partner relied on his performance, this other party's interests will typically be violated. For example, Bob receives word that the railway company will end the train connection between his working place and Anne's house. The acquisition of Anne's house no longer serves Bob's interests, and he may want to avoid the sales contract for the house. However, Anne has booked the cruise around the world that she always wanted to make and if the sale is discontinued, she may have a financial problem. More in general, if it becomes easy to avoid contracts if it turns out that they do not serve the interests of one of the contract parties, it becomes more difficult to rely on contracts. Contracting becomes less attractive, fewer contracts will be concluded, and fewer Pareto-improvements will be realized. Allowing avoidance to protect private interests damages the public interest, and this damage needs to be balanced against the interest of one of the contract partners in avoiding the contract.[30]

2.5 *Conclusion on the Justification of Contractual Obligations*

We have considered three possible justifications for the existence of contractual obligations. The first two justifications invoke reliance and autonomy and we have seen that they both presuppose the existence of the very obligations that they aim to justify. Reliance that a contract will be performed is only justified if it may be assumed that a contractual obligation

27 J.M. Smits, *Contract Law. A comparative introduction*, Edward Elgar, Cheltenham 2014, pp. 91-100 and 159-175.

28 Notably, the conditions for avoidance typically do not directly mention the interests of the person who is empowered to avoid. Instead the conditions tend to refer to the mental condition of the agent which made it difficult for him to safeguard his interests himself.

29 If a contract disadvantages both parties, they can terminate the contract consensually.

30 Actually it is slightly more complicated, because it is also a public interest that private interests are safeguarded. To determine what serves the public interest best, it is necessary to balance the decreased number of Pareto-improvements against the better protection of private interests. It depends on many circumstances what the best outcome of this balancing operation will be. There exists a lot of theory dealing with this issue under the headings of duties to inquire and to inform. *See* A.T. Kronman, 'Mistake, Disclosure, Information, and the Law of Contracts', *Journal of Legal Studies*, Vol. 7, No. 1, 1978, pp. 1-34 and R. Sefton-Green, *Mistake, Fraud and Duties to Inform in European Contract Law*, Cambridge University Press, Cambridge 2005.

exists. The autonomy to create obligations by means of contracts presupposes the possibility to create obligations by contracting.

The third justification invokes the social practice of contracting. A particular contractual obligation is justified because the contract is an event that according to this practice leads to obligations. The social practice of contracting can only justify particular obligations if this practice actually exists and if it is justified itself. Both reliance and autonomy play their role here again, but this time in an indirect way. The protection of reliance is a reason for recognizing contractual obligations because this recognition and the enforcement that goes with it, facilitates the use of this practice, which itself leads to Pareto-improvements. Autonomy consists in part in empowerment, and the social practice of contracting empowers legal subjects to arrange their own affairs by creating obligations.

However, the role of autonomy in this connection is in need of further justification. It turns out that the law does not unconditionally recognize the autonomy of legal subjects to undertake contractual obligations. The power to undertake these obligations is limited when there is reason to assume that it will not be used in the interest of the subject exercising this power, as when he is a minor, or mentally ill. This suggests that the aim of the law in advancing individual autonomy does not have this autonomy as its final goal, but rather sees it as an instrument to promote individual interests. Moreover, the use of this instrument is limited by the interests of other legal subjects.

We can see this in the possibility to avoid some contracts. The reasons to avoid a contract always relate to the circumstances of concrete cases. The social practice of contracting, laid down in contract law, provides rules which provide that, in general contracts lead to the obligations that the parties intended to undertake by means of the contract. This practice is assumed to be justified because it leads to a more Pareto-efficient society, and reliance pays an important role in this connection. The justification of concrete obligations need not refer to other circumstances than that the parties followed the procedure for undertaking contractual obligations. If one of the parties nevertheless wants to argue that one or more of the obligations do not hold, it must refer to the special circumstances of the concrete case. In this connection, an important argument is that the intention of the party that wants to nullify the contract did not properly reflect his interests. This means that if contracts are seen as reflections of the tension between will and reliance, the role of reliance is most important for the justification of contracting as a social practice, while the will has its most important function in justifying exceptions to the general practice in concrete cases. This role of the will derives its importance from the fact that the intentions of contracting parties do not always reflect the interests of these parties. In the next section

I will use the anchoring bias as a tool to demonstrate that this discrepancy between intention and interest is more common than is typically assumed.

3 The Anchoring Bias

The anchoring bias involves a situation in which people must answer a question or take a decision that involves quantities. They tend to let their answer or decision be influenced by a quantity that was placed in their mind just before. This occurs even if this quantity is completely irrelevant for the question or decision. For example,[31] a wheel of fortune was rigged to make 10 or 65 the only possible outcomes. After a spin of the wheel – which gave 10 or 65 as result – students of the University of Oregon were asked whether the percentage of African states as members of the UN was larger or smaller than the result of the wheel. This planted either the number 10 or the number 65 in their minds. After that, the students also had to answer the question what is, in their opinion, the percentage of African members of the UN. Students who had 10 as outcome of the wheel estimated the percentage of African members states on the average to be 25. However, students who started from 65 estimated the percentage of African members states on the average to be 45. Somehow the student's estimations were 'drawn' towards the outcome of the wheel of fortune, even though the students were very much aware that this outcome was not relevant for their estimation. The result of the wheel functioned as an 'anchor' for the judgment about the percentage of African UN member states. This anchor biased the judgment of the students, and that explains the name 'anchoring bias'. Other examples of the anchoring bias are the fact that the price a potential buyer is willing to offer for a house is influenced by the asking price, or that a car driver who just left the highway and must now drive at a lower speed, may be tempted to drive too fast.

It turns out that there are two explanations for the existence of the anchoring bias, which complement each other. The one explanation is that there is often uncertainty about the correct answer to a question or decision. An anchor influences the answer, because the respondent takes the anchor as starting point for adaptations towards the 'correct' answer. If Anne asks € 430,000 for her house, Bob will think this amount too high, and adapt it downward to € 400,000. That might be a correct price (uncertainty) and since the reasoning started from a higher price, it stops at the highest amount in a range of possibly correct prices. If Bob would have started the negotiations with an offer of € 300,000, Anne would have adapted that amount upwards until the range of possibly correct prices has been

31 The present discussion, and all examples are based on Kahneman 2011, pp. 119-128, which contains references to more specific research.

reached. Let us assume that this range goes from € 350,000 to € 400,000. Then, if Anne starts adapting from € 300,000, she will arrive at € 350,000 as the first possible correct price. It is well possible that she will give this as a counter-offer, which may be accepted by Bob. In this way, the first price mentioned in the negotiations about the sale of a house influences the price for which the house will be sold. It turns out that this anchoring effect even influences the estimations of real estate agents who are aware of the existence of the anchoring bias.

The second explanation for the existence of the anchoring bias is that mentioning an amount before a question is asked somehow influences the answer to the question by association. Where the anchor exercises a conscious influence on the answer in the first explanation, it has an unconscious influence in the second explanation. The example of the percentage of African UN members illustrates this. The students who had to estimate this percentage will not have taken the outcome of the wheel of fortune as starting point for conscious adaptations. It is more likely that the result of the wheel unconsciously affected their judgements. Nevertheless, even where there is clearly no connection between the answer that must be given and a number planted in the mind of the respondent to a question, the planted number still 'primes' the answer.[32]

What is the relevance of this anchoring bias for contract law? If an anchor influences the decision that somebody makes, it depends on the anchor what the decision will be. There are then two possibilities. One is that no matter what the anchor, the decision will fall within a range of outcomes that are equally good for the decision maker. Then the anchor does not influence the quality of the decision for the decision maker. In case of contracts this means that the anchor does not influence the (dis)advantages which a contract has for a party. Then the anchoring bias is not relevant for contract law. Although this is theoretically possible, it will not often happen that an anchor that influences a contract has no influence on the attractiveness of this contract for a contract partner.

The other possibility seems more likely. Anchoring means that a contract will influence the interests of the contracting parties. The most frequent situation will be that the party whose decision has been influenced by the anchor will conclude a less advantageous contract than he would have done without the anchor. If Anne asks € 430,000 for her house, this will most likely influence the amount that Bob is willing to pay for the house. In our example the parties agreed on an amount of € 400,000. However, they might have agreed on a lesser amount, for instance € 380,000, if Bob's willingness to pay had not been influ-

32 This unconscious 'priming effect' also plays a role in different settings than those of anchoring. *See* Kahneman 2011, pp. 52-58.

enced by the asking price. Then, the anchoring effect costs Bob € 20,000. Bob's will (to pay € 400,000) did not reflect his interest, which would have been served better if Bob had bought the house for € 380,000.

4 Coping with Irrationality

The anchoring bias illustrates the more general phenomenon that human decision making is often far from rational. People take decisions which they know, or at least could easily have known, not to reflect their interests optimally.[33] The law has traditionally recognized a number of these situations, and has provided tools to limit the effects of irrationality. However, recent psychological, behavioral-economic, and neurological research has shown that the situations in which people act irrationally are more frequent than was traditionally assumed. How should law deal with the results of this research?

For the purpose of exposition, I will ignore the possible answer that law should do nothing with these results. Moreover, I will confine myself to considering only two extreme ways of taking the recent insights into account. One way is to expand the use of the existing tools. If people are more often irrational than was traditionally assumed, the law might consider more contracts as null and void, and allow contract partners more often to avoid contracts they irrationally concluded. Of course, these possibilities should still take the interests of the other contract partners and of trade in general into account. The precise outcome of this approach cannot be described here, but it is possible to characterize this approach. It is a continuation of present contract law, with minor adaptations to accommodate new scientific insights. Most likely, this is what will actually happen, because law is – for good reasons – a conservative institution.

The question should be raised, however, whether the recent scientific insights reveal that our image of mankind as a rational decision maker who sometimes lapses, is fundamentally wrong. Perhaps human beings are not very good at promoting their own interests. Perhaps the satisfaction of subjective preferences is not at all a good way to create a Pareto-efficient, or otherwise good, distribution of goods. There are no satisfactory answers to these questions yet, but the recent scientific developments justify that serious attempts are made to find such answers. Moreover, the willingness should in principle exist, if it turns out that subjective preferences are not reliable indicators of interests, to strongly limit the role of autonomy in contract law. It is even imaginable that the very phenomenon of contracts, where subjective preferences play a crucial role, should be replaced by transactions which

33 The assumption here is that rationality consists, at least to a large extent, in promoting one's own interests.

better reflect the interests of legal subjects. If that would happen, it would be a very radical change in law indeed. Radical, but also exciting, and worthy of additional study.

5 Conclusion

The cognitive sciences provide us in high frequency with insights in the functioning of the human mind. One of these insights – perhaps not even very new – is that human decision-making is often not rational. The law has tools to deal with lapses of rationality, but it works on the basis of an image of mankind according to which humans are, and typically act, rationally. This raises the question of whether law should be more adaptive to the stream of new insights produced by the cognitive sciences.

The present article aims to answer this general question for an important field of law: the law of contract. It shows in Section 3, on the basis of the anchoring bias, that there are good reasons to assume that the conclusion of a contract is often not a rational event. Yet, by making the satisfaction of subjective preferences a cornerstone of contracts, the law seems to presuppose the opposite. Is it therefore necessary to change the law considerably, or is it possible to limit the changes or even to ignore the new insights from the cognitive sciences?

These questions cannot be answered without insight into the essence of a field of law, in our case, of contract law. Section 2 aimed at providing this insight into the essence of contract law by discussing three possible justifications of the phenomenon that contracts lead to legally enforceable obligations. It turned out that two of these justifications, the ones that focused on particular obligations, are unsatisfactory. The justification of particular obligations on the basis of a general social practice of contracting fared better. However, the discussion of this kind of justification also made clear that the social practice of contracting implicitly assumes that subjective preferences are a stand in for objective interests. This assumption can only be made if subjective preferences generally are formed in a rational manner. However, this very assumption is the topic of the doubts created by the cognitive sciences.

The law can follow two strategies[34] in dealing with the insight that contracts, and – extrapolating a bit – juridical acts in general – are often not created rationally. One strategy is to use the tools which law already has for dealing with irrationality for newly discovered

34 Of course, more strategies are possible, but they will often be intermediates on a scale of which the two mentioned possibilities are the extremes.

kinds of cases such as the anchoring bias. Another, is to redesign substantial parts of the law to take into consideration that subjective preferences often do not reflect objective interests. Which strategy is the best depends on the frequency of situations in which subjective preferences do not reflect objective interests. Is it still rational to use subjective preferences as indicator for objective interests?

The last question cannot be answered here, but suggests a line of research that has become important in the light of the developing cognitive sciences. We need to find out which presuppositions the law makes about the functioning of the human minds. Then we can check whether these presuppositions still hold. If the presuppositions turn out to be outdated, the law must be modified on the basis of insight into the essence of its subfields and on the basis of our recent insights into the functioning of the mind.

References

Atiyah, P.S., 'Fuller and the Theory of Contract', *in* P.S. Atiyah, *Essays on Contract*, Clarendon Press, Oxford 1986, pp. 73-92.

Bentham, J., *An Introduction to the Principles of Morals and Legislation*, J.H. Burns and H.L.A. Hart (Eds.), first edn 1789, Methuen, London 1970.

Christman, J., 'Autonomy in Moral and Political Philosophy', *in* E.N. Zalta (Ed.), *The Stanford Encyclopedia of Philosophy*, Winter 2017 edn, https://plato.stanford.edu/archives/win2017/entries/autonomy-moral/.

Crisp, R., 'Well-Being', *in* E.N. Zalta (Ed.), *The Stanford Encyclopedia of Philosophy*, Fall 2017 edn, https://plato.stanford.edu/archives/fall2017/entries/well-being/.

Cushman, F., Young, L. & Greene, J.D., 'Multi-System Moral Psychology', *in* John M. Doris (Ed.), *The Moral Psychology Handbook*, Oxford University Press, Oxford 2010, pp. 47-71.

Damasio, A., *Descartes' Error. Emotion, reason and the human brain*, Putnam, New York 1994.

Griffin, J., *Well-being. Its Meaning, Measurement and Moral Importance*, Clarendon Press, Oxford 1986.

Hage, J.C., 'Comparing Alternatives', in *Studies in Legal Logic*, Springer, Dordrecht 2005, pp. 101-134.

J.C. Hage, 'Rechtstheoretische analyse van de partijautonomie in het contractenrecht. Twee dimensies van contactsvrijheid', *in* Ilse Samoy (Ed.), *Evolutie van de basisbeginselen van het contractenrecht*, Intersentia, Antwerpen 2010, pp. 241-261.

Kahneman, D., *Thinking, fast and slow*, Penguin, London 2012.

Kronman, A.T., 'Mistake, Disclosure, Information, and the Law of Contracts', *Journal of Legal Studies*, Vol. 7, No. 1, 1978, pp. 1-34.

Larenz, K. & Wolf, M., *Allgemeiner Teil des bürgerlichen Rechts*, 9th edn, Beck, München 2004.

Mason, E., 'Value Pluralism', *in* E.N. Zalta (Ed.), *The Stanford Encyclopedia of Philosophy*, Summer 2015 edn, https://plato.stanford.edu/archives/sum2015/entries/value-pluralism/.

Ove Hansson, S. & Grüne-Yanoff, T., 'Preferences', in E.N. Zalta (Ed.), The Stanford Encyclopedia of Philosophy, Winter 2017 edn, https://plato.stanford.edu/archives/win2017/entries/preferences/.

Raz, J., 'Voluntary obligations and normative powers', *Aristotelian Society*, Supplementary Vol. 46, pp. 79-101.

Ryle, G., *The Concept of Mind*, Hutchinson, London 1949.

Sapolsky, R.M., *Behave. The Biology of Humans at Our Best and Worst*, Bodley Head, London 2017.

Sefton-Green, R., *Mistake, Fraud and Duties to Inform in European Contract Law*, Cambridge University Press, Cambridge 2005.

Smits, J.M., *Het vertrouwensbeginsel en de contractuele gebondenheid*, Gouda Quint, Arnhem 1995.

Wegner, D.M., *The Illusion of Conscious Will*, The MIT Press, Cambridge Massachusetts 2002.

3 Why Non-Human Agency

A. Waltermann

1 Introduction

There are increasingly more entities created by human beings but not themselves human that shape our lives, our social and legal reality, such as tables, books, computers, corporations, states and artificial intelligence. Next to churches, states and corporations have been on this list for centuries, but stock-trading algorithms, autonomous weapons and self-driving cars are newer additions. From a legal perspective, churches, states and corporations as well as artificially intelligent entities have in common that they raise the question of whether and how such entities are and should be regulated. This entails questions such as whether and how they can act and when they are and should be liable for their actions. From a moral perspective, one can ask similar questions: can these entities act and are they – or should they be – morally responsible for their actions?

Questions of moral responsibility or legal liability are on the public, political and academic agenda, with the European Parliament calling for 'electronic personhood'[1] for autonomous and artificially intelligent robots and with self-driving cars beginning to drive on US roads, but also with an on-going debate regarding corporate criminal liability in Germany,[2] to give only three examples. In the context of moral responsibility or legal liability, it is often (but not necessarily) presupposed that the entity in question has acted, or more generally that there was conduct of some kind. This is not obvious, however. Are non-human entities able to act for the purpose of moral responsibility or of legal liability?

In this paper, I want to focus on the topic of acts of non-human entities and sketch out why I consider this a relevant field of research for academics from law, philosophy, the social and the cognitive sciences in addition to the questions of responsibility that are already being asked. As such, this paper is meant to identify relevant research questions and to out a research agenda. It is not yet meant to answer these questions, only to provide impetus for future research.

1 European Parliament, Report with recommendations to the commission on Civil Law Rules on Robotics, A8-005/2017

2 *Cf.* K. Volk, K. LuDerssen & Eberhard Kempf, *Unternehmensstrafrecht*, De Gruyter, Berlin 2012.

I seek to identify areas in which different fields can learn from one another, in particular areas in which law can learn from philosophy and the cognitive sciences broadly construed, and to identify questions that are relevant to ask in connection to non-human agency. In order to do so, I will first look at examples of different types of non-human entities that have historically or are currently regarded as agents in the eye of the law (in different legal systems), examining the reasons why these have been or are regarded as such (Section 2). This examination reveals a number of (metaphysical) assumptions commonly made regarding agency (both human and non-human), forming the 'metaphysical frame of reference' of agency (Section 3 and 4). This paper will posit (in Section 5) that agency in the law is constructed, but that its construction is often based on an unqualified and uncritical application of the metaphysical frame of reference and is as such insufficiently theorised. Insights from philosophy and the cognitive sciences broadly construed are relevant for an investigation of the metaphysical frame of reference and in future theorising on the matter. The paper concludes in Section 6 by summarising the main argument and pointing out questions for future research.

2 Non-Human Actors and the Law

In everyday life, we routinely make a distinction between agents and things. This holds intuitive appeal. Greene and Cohen summarise:

> Looking out at the world, it appears to contain two fundamentally different kinds of entity. On the one hand, there are ordinary objects that appear to obey the ordinary laws of physics: things like rocks and puddles of water and blocks of wood. These things do not get up and move around on their own. They are, in a word, inanimate. On the other hand, there are things that seem to operate by some kind of magic. Humans and other animals, so long as they are alive, can move about at will, in apparent defiance of the physical laws that govern ordinary matter. Because things like rocks and puddles, on the one hand, and mice and humans, on the other, behave in such radically different ways, it makes sense, from an evolutionary perspective, that creatures would evolve separate cognitive systems for processing information about each of these classes of objects. There is a good deal of evidence to suggest that this is precisely how our minds work.[3]

3 J. Greene & J. Cohen, 'For the Law, Neuroscience Changes Nothing and Everything', *Philosophical Transactions: Biological Sciences*, 2004, pp. 1775-1785, at p. 1782, references omitted.

Chopra and White similarly hold that "[i]ntuitively, an agent is something able to take actions. One way to distinguish agents from other entities is that agents do things, as opposed to have things happen to them."[4] This distinction between agents and other entities seems to correspond to the animate-inanimate distinction outlined by Greene and Cohen.

When it comes to agency in law, I want to distinguish between two notions of agency: on the one hand, there is the notion of agency that relates simply to doing things in the eyes of the law, as a baseline conception of agency; on the other hand, there is a more specific notion of agency used more frequently in the legal context: that of agency in the sense of an agent – principal relationship in the law of agency. These two uses of 'agency' are not always clearly distinguished.[5] By the baseline conception of agency, I mean that the entity is regarded as "a being with the capacity to act",[6] and by act I mean that there can be conduct by that entity.[7] Being an agent in an agent – principal relationship presupposes this more basic sense of agency: here, the agent acts on behalf of another, the principal.[8] In this paper, I am not interested primarily in the more specific notion of agency in the sense of an agent – principal relationship so much as in the more fundamental question why the law regards an entity to be capable of action at all.

Currently and over the centuries, different sets of entities have been regarded as legal agents. It is not the case that all human beings have been or are regarded as legal agents at all times, nor is it the case that only human beings have been or are regarded as legal agents. In the following, I will consider three non-human entities that are or have been regarded as legal agents: corporations and States as current examples and animals in the Middle Ages as a historical example.

2.1 Corporations

It is no exaggeration to point out that corporations are ubiquitous in modern society, or that they impact human lives and the environment more generally on a (near-)constant

4 S. Chopra & L. White, *A Legal Theory for Autonomous Artificial Agents*, University of Michigan Press, Ann Arbor 2011, p. 11.

5 By way of example, *see* id. Perhaps they did not see the need to make the distinction.

6 M. Schlosser, 'Agency', *in* E.N. Zalta (Ed.), *The Stanford Encyclopedia of Philosophy*, Fall 2015 edn.; https://plato.stanford.edu/archives/fall2015/entries/agency/.

7 Conduct includes omissions. I will ignore the complication of omissions for the rest of this paper.

8 For an amusing recapitulation of agency theory, *see* S.P. Shapiro, 'Agency Theory', *Annual Review of Sociology*, Vol. 31, 2005, pp. 263-284. *Cf. also* https://en.wikipedia.org/wiki/Law_of_agency, last accessed 1 March 2019.

basis at this point in time. The fields of corporate law (in particular corporate criminal law) and corporate moral responsibility have considered the question whether corporations can act and offer different conceptions of the corporation that lead to different answers.

Criminal law has traditionally been perceived of as "designed for natural persons, as only individuals can act, so it is argued, and only human beings are considered to be morally blameworthy"[9] but has since moved on to recognize corporate crime in many jurisdictions. As such, the way corporate criminal law conceptualizes corporations and corporate wrongdoing (which, notably, includes *doing* in some form) offers fertile grounds for investigating the reasons why law – at least this field of law – regards corporations as agents, or why it does not.

There are two main conceptions of the corporation here: the nominalist approach and the organisational approach.

The nominalist (or atomist) approach regards the legal entity as nothing more than a legal fiction. Under this view, the corporation is nothing more than a sum of its human parts, a collection of individuals instead of an entity separate from the individuals that make up the corporation. For corporate criminal law, this approach means that the criminal liability of the legal person is 'necessarily derived from the wrongdoing of a natural person'.[10] The *actus reus* (act or omission) and *mens rea* of a natural person are attributed to the legal person, which means that there can be no corporate act (or omission) without a natural person having acted (or omitted to act).

The organisational (or realist) approach views the corporation as a separate entity instead, capable of acting independently from its individual human parts. For criminal liability, this means that the corporation can act and be at fault separately from individual human action and fault; it is not required that an individual's *mens rea* and *actus reus* are first identified and then attributed to the corporation. This approach takes into account the insight that corporations and corporate attitude may influence the conduct of their members.

French considers that to reduce the corporation to "biological referents", that is, to human beings is fallacious and argues that the corporation is a non-eliminatable subject of

9 D. Roef, 'Corporate Criminal Liability', *in* J. Keiler & D. Roef (Eds.), *Comparative Concepts of Criminal Law*, 3rd edn, Intersentia, Antwerp 2019, p. 335.

10 Id., p. 336.

responsibility in a way that, for example, a mob is not.[11] This means that while a mob's actions are reducible to the actions of its individual human parts, the same is not true for a corporation, because the mob has – according to French – no intentionality beyond that of its individual human parts, while the corporation does:

> We can describe many events in terms of certain physical movements of human beings and we also can sometimes describe those events as done for reasons by those human beings, but further we can sometimes describe those events as corporate and still further as done for corporate reasons that are qualitatively different from whatever personal reasons, if any, component members may have for doing what they do. Corporate agency resides in the possibility of CID Structure [corporate internal decision structure] licensed redescription of events as corporate intentional.[12]

Because of a corporation's structure of decision-making, consisting of an organisational flow chart of corporate power structures and corporate policy, a corporation can be said to act in ways that are different and for reasons that are different than the acts and reasons of the human members. This argument rests on an understanding of actions as those events that can be described under an aspect that makes them intentional. For French, this means that a corporation acts intentionally when its act is "consistent with, an instantiation or an implementation of established corporate policy", because it is then proper to describe that act has having been done for corporate reasons, rather than for whatever reasons, if any, the directors or shareholders may have for doing the same thing.[13]

With this, French rejects as unhelpful (for his purposes) a theory that recognises corporations as pre-legal sociological persons:

> Underlying the theory is the view that law cannot create its subjects, it only determines which societal facts are in conformity with its requirements. At most, law endorses the pre-legal existence of persons for its own purposes.[14]

Neumann offers a compelling argument against this approach: because it is a question of decision whether and what legal consequences are attached to a particular social fact or situation, the existence of a pre-legal act by a pre-legal person says nothing about whether

11 P.A. French, 'The Corporation as a Moral Person', *American Philosophical Quarterly*, Vol. 16, No. 3, 1979, pp. 207-15, at p. 210.
12 Id., p. 212.
13 Id., p. 213.
14 Id., p. 209.

this is to be recognised as a legal act or the entity as a legal person.[15] For this, a normative argument is required. Kelsen recognised this when he held that

> To define the physical (natural) person as a human being is incorrect, because man and person are not only two different concepts but also the result of two entirely different kinds of consideration. Man is a concept of biology and physiology, in short, of the natural sciences. Person is a concept of jurisprudence, of the analysis of legal norms.[16]

This can be expanded on for present purposes: in the same way in which 'person' is a concept of jurisprudence, 'action' (or more generally, 'conduct') is also a legal concept, with the law determining what legal consequences attach to an event or situation and whether that event or situation is to be classified as an act (or more generally, as 'conduct'). According to this view, which Neumann calls normativism (*Normativismus*),[17] it is a question of decision whether something counts as a legal act and whether an entity counts as a legal agent. Therefore, the existence of a pre-legal act or agent says nothing about whether this is to be recognised. From a legal perspective, so Neumann, an action is not a natural, but an institutional fact which is constituted by legal or social recognition.[18]

2.2 States

The Draft articles on Responsibility of States for Internationally Wrongful Acts (hereafter: ARSIWA) and commentaries thereto adopted by the International Law Commission in 2001 provide a good starting point to consider the question when a State has acted. They 'seek to formulate, by way of codification and progressive development, the basic rues of international law concerning the responsibility of States for their internationally wrongful acts.'[19] One of the issues covered by these articles includes 'determining in what circumstances conduct is to be attributed to the State.'[20]

15 Volk, LuDerssen & Kempf 2012, p. 16.
16 H. Kelsen & A. Wedberg, *General theory of law and state*, Harvard University Press, Cambridge Massachusetts 1945, p. 94.
17 Volk, LuDerssen & Kempf 2012, p. 16.
18 Id., p. 17.
19 International Law Commission, Draft articles on Responsibility of states for Internationally Wrongful Acts, with commentaries, 2001, p. 31.
20 Id.

Article 1 of ARSIWA states that "[e]very internationally wrongful act of a State entails the international responsibility of that State." The commentary to this article holds that one or more actions or omissions or both may constitute an act in the sense of this article.

Article 2 of ARSIWA states that "[t]here is an internationally wrongful act of a State when conduct consisting of an act or omission: (a) is attributable to the State under international law; and (b) constitutes a breach of an international obligation of the State." The commentary to this article is of particular interest for present purposes. Under (5), it is held that

> [f]or particular conduct to be characterized as an internationally wrongful act, it must first be attributable to the State. The State is a real organized entity, a legal person with full authority to act under international law. But to recognize this is not to deny the elementary fact that the State cannot act of itself. An 'act of the State' must involve some action or omission by a human being or group: 'States can act only by and through their agents and representatives.'[21]

According to this, a State is real and can act, but not of itself. It can only act where a human being or group has acted (or omitted to act). This is reminiscent of the nominalist approach to the corporation; in international relations literature, it is called the functional theory and can be contrasted to the agential theory. Fleming summarises the two as follows:

> According to the *agential theory*, states can be held responsible because they are moral agents like human beings, with similar capacities for deliberation and intentional action. State responsibility is essentially individual responsibility scaled up. According to the *functional theory*, states can be held responsible because they are legal persons that act vicariously through individuals. States are principals rather than agents, and state responsibility is akin to the vicarious responsibility of an employer for the actions of her employee. The two theories of state responsibility depend on different understandings of how corporate entities can act.[22]

These two theories of state action and state responsibility closely resemble the realist and nominalist approaches to the corporation.

---

21 Id., p. 35, citing the German Settlers in Poland case, Advisory Opinion, 1923 PCIJ (Ser. B) No. 6, at 22.'

22 S. Fleming, 'Moral Agents and Legal Persons: The Ethics and the Law of State Responsibility', *International Theory*, Vol. 9, No. 3, 2017, pp. 466-489, at p. 467, references omitted.

2.3 Animals

In the Middle Ages and the Renaissance, animals were regarded as criminally liable by both secular and religious authorities and prosecuted accordingly, with wild animals generally falling under the jurisdiction of ecclesiastical courts and domestic animals under the jurisdiction of ordinary criminal courts.[23] More than two hundred cases of animal trials are recorded in Western Europe; most from the period of the 15th to 17th century, but with medieval record keeping notoriously spotty, the actual numbers are likely higher.[24] There are documented trials against 'an unspecified number of rats, which were prosecuted in the ecclesiastical court of Autun for having feloniously eaten and wantonly destroyed local barley,'[25] sows and other animals for infanticide,[26] bees, bulls, horses and snakes for homicide,[27] field-mice for fraud and foxes for theft.[28] Punishments for those found guilty ranged from a reprimanding knock on the head to excommunication or capital punishment.[29] A sow, for example, was tried in a court of law for infanticide in Falaise (France) in 1386 and sentenced to death. The sow 'was dressed in human clothes, mutilated in the head and hind legs, and executed in the public square by an official hangman' after '[h]aving been duly tried in a court of law'.[30] Despite the examples mentioned here, it is not the case that these trials were privileging the human plaintiffs or finding for them invariably.[31] These trials, it seems, were conducted in accordance with due process at the time:

> The animals were indeed fortunate, since they received due process of law every bit as good as that provided for humans. They were certainly not executed summarily, as would be the case today of an animal that ate a baby. In fact, the prosecutors were so careful to apply the law equally to animals, that they even placed them on the rack and tortured them for a confession. [...] [Animals] were only treated cruelly by the criminal law to the same extent that humans were.[32]

---

23 W. Ewald, 'Comparative Jurisprudence (I): What Was It Like to Try a Rat?', *University of Pennsylvania Law Review*, Vol. 143, No. 6, 1995, pp. 1889-2149, at p. 1903 *et seq.*

24 Id., p. 1903.

25 P. Beirnes, 'The Law Is an Ass: Reading E.P. Evans' the Medieval Prosecution and Capital Punishment of Animals', *Society and Animals*, Vol. 2, No. 1, 1994, pp. 27-46, at p. 30.

26 Id., p. 31.

27 Id.

28 Id.

29 Id.

30 Id.

31 Ewald 1995, p. 1902.

32 Beirnes 1994, p. 39, citing G. Newman, *The punishment response*, J.B. Lippincott, Philadelpia 1978, p. 93.

This was because "animals were apparently regarded as having the same sort of responsibility for their actions as humans", meaning that "justice and fairness demanded that animals should be treated in the same way as humans."[33] In sentencing, too, animals were treated similarly to human beings:

> Animals condemned to death were executed in various ways. Some were burnt at the stake; others merely singed and then strangled before the body was burned. Frequently the animal was buried alive. A dog in Austria was placed in prison for a year; at the end of the seventeenth century a he-goat in Russia was banished to Siberia. Pigs convicted of murder were frequently imprisoned before being executed; they were held in the same prison, and under substantially the same conditions, as human criminals.[34]

It seems that animal trials took place from at least the 12th to the 19th century in a variety of Western countries. There are indications, however, of animals being held criminally liable in non-Western countries and long before the Middle Ages: Beirnes cites evidence of animal trials in classical Athens and indicates that it is known that "the ancient Persians, for example, considered animals as responsible beings, and punished them for their misdeeds."[35]

It bears keeping in mind that these animal trials took place in a different context from trials today. Cohen (1986) points out that "one cannot settle in purely empirical terms the question of whether animal trials existed either outside the occident or in pre-medieval Europe" because any such determination depends to a large extent on what is seen as counting as an animal trial.[36]

With this caveat in place, there are some indications why animals were put on trial and prosecuted. Beirnes notes that there is "no solid evidence of a general belief that the volition and intent of animals was of the same order as those of humans"[37] though apparently, they were believed to be responsible for their own actions in the same way as human beings.[38] The *lex talionis* is one possible – and likely – factor contributing to the trials of animals in the Middle Ages. Similarly,

33 Id., p. 38.
34 Ewald 1995, p. 1905.
35 Beirnes 1994, p. 37.
36 Id., citing E. Cohen, 'Law, folklore and animal lore', *Past and Present*, No. 110, 1986, pp. 6-37.
37 Id., p. 29.
38 Id., p. 38.

> [i]n the Athenian Prytaneum, in the common hearth of the city, a special court was convened to try unknown murderers, inanimate objects such as stones and beams, and animals that had caused human death. In cases of wrongful death it was necessary formally to try these three categories of malefactor because, in reasoning similar to that underlying the *lex talionis*, an unavenged murder would disturb the moral equilibrium and the physical health of the community, the wrath of the Furies would be aroused, and the soul of the deceased would be unable to find rest.[39]

Beirnes further points out that "numerous purposes have been allotted animal trials, quite apart from the use of biblical precepts as justifications for them. Thus, it is said that animal trials were conducted in order to deter other animals from committing similar crimes",[40] but he this considers unlikely, as medieval folk apparently did not "parade their animals in front of the gibbet on which executed pigs were left by the hangman for public display"[41] – or that the animal trials were designed to deter those "responsible for an offending animal's dangerous actions."[42] Ewald rejects explanations that sever the link between an animal's guilt and the animal's punishment as unsatisfactory.[43] When it comes to deterrence as a reason for putting animals on trial and punishing them, he holds that it explains the punishment, but not the trial itself – after all, the animal could have been killed and its body displayed without a trial as well. Animal trials seem to suggest that animals (from cows and wolves to insects and mice) were seen as "creatures who, like humans, could be brought to trial for their deeds and cruelly punished; but from some points of view this must be seen as a sign of moral respect" and as "fellow creatures who enjoyed certain basic rights that can be vindicated at law."[44] Today, we do not think of animals in the same way anymore:

39 Id., p. 37.
40 Id., p. 38.
41 Id.
42 As a footnote, it is interesting to point out here that the determination of responsibility – certainly in the case of legal liability – is something a trial would have to establish in the first place. If it is the animal that is capable of being responsible for its own actions, legally speaking or in some other meaning of the word, this phrasing would point back to the animal as the one responsible for its own behaviour. Out of the context, it is apparent that Beirnes here means human beings – in particular the owners of the animal. This is apparent because Beirnes continues: "If so, animal trials served as vehicles to convey to animal owners a moral message to oversee their charges. In a case of 1567 where a pig was executed for having killed an infant in Senlis in France, therefore, the judge warned the inhabitants of the village "not to permit the like to go unguarded on pain of an arbitrary fine and of corporal chastisement in default of payment". *See* id. While context makes clear what the statement refers to, the ambiguity of it hinging on the word 'responsibility' is noteworthy.
43 Ewald 1995, p. 1906.
44 Id., p. 1915.

> [...] we draw a sharper distinction between the animals and ourselves, and are more inclined to view them as automata, as parts of the material world. And when we do accord them some degree of moral respect, there has been an important change in the standard we apply: the higher animals are not to be mistreated, not because they are the handiwork of God, but because they are like us.[45]

What lies at the heart of the animal trials and modern difficulties with grasping their rationale full is a difference in what may be termed the metaphysical frame of reference:[46] who we regard as legal agents today and what forms of punishment we are willing to inflict on them seems influenced, to a large extent, by modern moral sensibilities and intuitions. Questioning the rationale behind animal trials and seeking to understand why animals were regarded as legal actors and both tried and punished accordingly invites questioning the rationale of our current metaphysical frame of reference as well.

What is our current metaphysical frame of reference and how does it impact our (legal) view of non-human entities as actors?

3 THE METAPHYSICAL FRAME OF REFERENCE OF ACTION

The law can, in principle, define its own concepts and create its own frame of reference entirely without the need for metaphysics or to refer to an existing frame of reference. This is the point Neumann makes with regard to corporate criminal liability[47] and which Brozek makes regarding personhood in the law when he holds that it "has a technical character and is not connected with any concrete philosophical content."[48] With regard to personhood as well, however, Naffine points out that the law does not do this cleanly or neatly.[49] Instead, it oscillates between different approaches to or models of personhood[50] with different metaphysical "baggage".[51]

45 Id.

46 Id., pp. 1916-1921.

47 Volk, LüDerssen & Kempf 2012, p. 16 *et seq.*

48 B. Brozek, 'The Troublesome Person', *in* V. Kurki & T. Pietrzykowski (Eds.), *Legal Personhood: Animals, Artificial Intelligence and the Unborn*, Springer, New York 2017, p. 8.

49 N. Naffine, 'Who Are Law's Persons? From Cheshire Cats to Responsible Subjects', *The Modern Law Review*, Vol. 66, No. 3, 2003, pp. 346-367.

50 Id.

51 Brozek 2017, p. 6.

While the law may assign an entity the status of agent independently of concrete philosophical content or particular physical characteristics, this can (and often will) be influenced by philosophical thought and folk psychological understandings of the notion of agency on the one hand; it also can (and often will) influence philosophical and folk psychological understandings on the other hand. While the law is independent of philosophy, moral theory, folk psychology, etc. this does not take away the possibility (and indeed likelihood) of mutual influence.[52]

We have seen above that when it comes to the agency of corporations and States, the law shifts between different models as well. In corporate law, particularly corporate criminal law, the nominal approach seems to assume that only events caused by human beings can count as actions proper and that only human beings can have intentions. It accepts that those actions can then be attributed to a composite entity such as the corporation of the state and in this sense, corporations and states can and do act, but their acts are always derivations of and reducible to human acts. In contrast, the organisational approach does not take human beings as the prototypical agents on whose actions all other forms of action must be based. International law is consistent in treating States as incapable of non-derived actions. In international law, a State can only act where its acts are reducible to human acts or, conversely stated, where human action is attributable to the State. This could be taken as emphasising the distinction between the legal notion of action and other conceptions, but this strikes me as the wrong conclusion to draw. The phrasing of the International Law Commission of it being an "elementary fact" that an act of a State must be preceded by human action that is attributable (and actually attributed) to the State suggests not a deliberate choice for distinctness from other fields. Instead, it seems a reference to a metaphysical frame of reference that is presumed to be "fact" – and elementary fact at that.

Synthesising the findings from the sections on corporations, states and animals above, two approaches can be identified with regard to legal agency. Under both approaches, non-human entities can and do act. The difference lies in how they are able to perform an action, that is, in the conceptualisation of their action. Under one model, non-human entities act only when the act of a human being is attributed to them. The action of a human being counts as the action of a corporation or a state and as such *is* the action of that corporation or state or other non-human entity. Under this model, however, the actions of the non-human entity are necessarily always reducible to the action of a human being. Human beings take a central and special role as the only non-reducible actors. The implication here is that there is something about human beings that other types of entities such

52 Chopra & White 2011, pp. 2 and 154 respectively, although the point is made in different words on the respective pages.

as corporations, states, animals, rivers or artificially intelligent entities lack and as such, it speaks of a particular metaphysical frame of reference. This approach is reflected in international law as well as the nominalist model of the corporation.

Under the other model, human beings do not hold the same special place in the metaphysical frame of reference, although human beings are still treated as prototypical. Some events caused by human beings are actions and some events caused by non-human beings are actions with no necessary link between the two. Non-human beings can be agents in the same non-reducible sense as human beings, and human beings can be actors in a reducible sense (as when there is an agent-principal relationship). The latter holds true, by the by, for the first model as well. This second approach is growing more prevalent. This is what French argues for with regard to corporations and what is reflected in the realist theory of corporations as well as the agential theory of states that is prevalent in international relations. Under this approach, genuine non-reducible action of non-human entities is taken to be possible; a non-human entity can act, provided it fulfils certain conditions that are taken to be necessary for 'genuine' or 'real' action.

To summarise, there are two variants of the metaphysical frame of reference currently reflected in the law. Non-human entities can act under both; in the one case they are 'only' capable of derived action reducible to human action, in the other case they are capable of non-derived action because they are in some way sufficiently similar to human beings. This takes for granted that human beings are non-reducible agents because they have certain characteristics, and that non-human entities can – at times – have the same characteristics. Under this view, it is those characteristics that make the entity an agent.[53]

In this context, two types of arguments regarding agency in law can be identified: on the one hand, there are normative arguments; on the other hand, there are metaphysical arguments. By the former, I mean arguments that regard the law as distinct from folk psychology or the metaphysical frame of reference and embed determinations of agency in a normative argument, for example in one regarding the problems regarding a kind of entity as a legal agent would solve and the desirability thereof. The normativistic approach of Neumann and Kelsen (cited above) reflects this. By the latter, I mean arguments that determine the question of agency by reference to the metaphysical frame of reference, depending on whether the entity has particular metaphysical characteristics, such as intentionality. French's approach (cited above) reflects this.

53 The normativistic approach, meanwhile, does not presuppose this, or it holds only that the conditions for 'genuine' or 'real' *legal* action are whatever conditions the law requires.

The example of animals being treated as agents as well as increased insights from philosophy and the cognitive sciences generally give us reason to question our metaphysical frame of reference:[54] it strikes me as important to carefully consider the metaphysical frame of reference that determinations of legal agency are based on, for the following reason: law-makers (broadly understood) can in principle posit that legally speaking, an entity is an agent. If they do so by reference to the metaphysical frame of reference and it turns out that this frame of reference is flawed or incorrect in some way, this may remove the foundation for regarding that entity as an agent for the reasons that it has particular metaphysical characteristics. Let me give an example to clarify this point: I can choose to go to the train station daily at 3pm to pick up a friend who arrives at that time. If I learn my friend is not arriving at the train station at all today, I can still choose to go, but my reason for doing so is gone. Does it still make sense for me to go to the train station, then? Perhaps – but not for the reason that my friend is arriving, because she is not. I might go for different reasons, or I might have reason to go somewhere else (for example, if she tells me she will arrive at the airport instead). It seems to me that the principle is the same for law and what entities it treats as actors and for what reasons. Using international law by way of example:

> International law is currently positing that a State can only act when a human being has acted, and that action is attributable to the State for the reason that it takes it as a fact that only human beings can act ('properly', that is, in a non-derived manner).
>
> There are good reasons to believe that it is not a fact that only human beings can act ('properly', that is, in a non-derived manner).

What conclusion should be drawn from this?

The conclusion that international law should no longer posit that a State can only act when a human being has acted and that action is attributable to the State is too quick even when one ignores the logical invalidity of that derivation. What the above argument suggests, to me, is the following:

1. We should carefully investigate whether there are indeed good reasons to believe that it is not a fact that only human beings can act; that is, we should investigate and think about our metaphysical frame of reference. This is a task predominantly for the cognitive sciences broadly understood.
2. International law should not posit that a State can only act when a human being has acted, and that action is attributable to the State *for the reason* that only human beings

54 More on the role of philosophy and the cognitive sciences in Section 4.

can act, if it turns out that this reason appears misguided. This does not take away that it posits the same for different reasons. This requires normative arguments and is a task for legal scholars and practitioners, taking into account the insights from the cognitive sciences regarding (1).

4 Investigating the Metaphysical Frame of Reference

How can we investigate our metaphysical frame of reference and whether or not it is misguided that only human beings can act in a non-reducible manner and draw conclusions from this for legal agency? It seems to me that we need three things in order to do so successfully: firstly, we need to explicate the metaphysical frame of reference and investigate the metaphysical presuppositions that underlie the law, where such presuppositions are being made. Section 2 of this paper indicates that it is the case that such presuppositions are being made, but it does not constitute anything close to a full account of them, nor did I attempt to give such a full account in that section. Further investigation is required in this regard.

Secondly, we need insights from philosophy, neuroscience and the cognitive sciences more generally. Both philosophical argument and the cognitive sciences indicate that the division between subjects and objects, agents and things, persons and non-persons may not be 'out there' in an ontologically objective, mind-independent world. This entails that it is not the case that some entities can, as a matter of brute fact, act, while others cannot; that some entities are 'really real' actors and others are not. Intentionality, agency or personhood are not natural kinds, despite the fact that our minds may work in ways that suggest to us that they are via our intuitions.[55]

Some example can give us insight into what these fields can offer regarding the investigation of the metaphysical frame of reference. Farah and Heberlein suggest that

> [t]here is evidence from neuroscience and developmental psychology that these intuitions may come from innate brain mechanisms, separate from those used to learn about other concepts. Whereas the mental categories day and night, mountain and molehill are learned primarily by induction from experience with the world, we come into the world equipped with the tendency to categorize certain entities as persons and to treat them accordingly. Things with such

55 M.J. Farah & A.S. Heberlein, 'Personhood and Neuroscience: Naturalizing or Nihilating?', *The American Journal of Bioethics*, Vol. 7, No. 1, 2007, pp. 37-48; Greene & Cohen 2004.

> trigger features as humanlike faces and/or contingent movement and/or natural language will tend to elicit from us the 'intentional stance' (the assumption that the entity is acting according to its own beliefs and desires; Dennett 1978) and a certain moral regard.[56]

It seems that we attribute intentionality, agency or personhood (and many other things) to ourselves and to others. Dennett puts this in clear terms when summarising his take on the intentional stance and on intentional systems:

> An Intentional system is a system whose behaviour can be (at least sometimes) explained and predicted by relying on ascriptions to the system of *beliefs* and *desires* (and other Intentionally characterized features [...]). There may *in every case* be other ways of predicting and explaining the behaviour of an Intentional system – for instance, mechanistic or physical ways – but the Intentional stance may be the handiest or most effective or in any case *a* successful stance to adopt, which suffices for the object to be an Intentional system.[57]

Taking this intentional stance toward an entity does not require or entail that this entity has any "particular intrinsic features"[58] or that intentional interpretation of some entities are "objectively true".[59] It seems that our intuitions at times lead us to take the intentional stance also to stick figures or geometric shapes moving on a screen.[60] Moreover, a physical explanation for the behaviour of intentional systems may be possible in every case – including in the case of human beings.

Brozek and Janik indicate that what entities we take this intentional stance toward and regard as moral agents is culture-dependent:

> Moral agents must be recognised as such: to be a moral agent, an individual must be treated as a moral agent by other members of the community.[61]

56 M.J. Farah & Andrea S. Heberlein, 'Response to Open Peer Commentaries on "Personhood and Neuroscience: Naturalizing or Nihilating?": Getting Personal', *The American Journal of Bioethics*, Vol. 7, No. 1, W1-W4, at W2.

57 D.C. Dennett, 'Conditions of Personhood', *in* A. Oksenberg Rorty (Ed.), *The Identities of Persons*, University of California Press, Berkeley 1976, p. 179.

58 Id.

59 Id., p. 181.

60 F. Heider & M. Simmel, 'An Experimental Study of Apparent Behavior', *The American Journal of Psychology*, Vol. 57, No. 2, 1944, pp. 243-259.

61 B. Brożek & B. Janik, 'Can Artificial Intelligences Be Moral Agents?', *New Ideas in Psychology*, 2019, p. 3.

Moreover,

> to be recognised as a moral agent one has to fit within the concept of agency adopted in the given culture (and the folk psychology associated with it). Some cultures may consider animals or even inanimate objects (rivers, volcanoes, etc.) as capable of moral agency; others may exclude from the pool of moral agents some human beings (slaves, enemies, people belonging to other tribes).[62]

The folk psychology of a given culture and its concepts of agency, intentionality and personhood are all part of what I call the metaphysical frame of reference in this paper. Insights from the cognitive sciences broadly understood (including philosophy) can aid us in explicating and testing the metaphysical frame of reference that – at times – underlies the law and legal determinations of the agency of entities.

Thirdly, and in light of this and in light of the fact that law is *in principle* distinct from the metaphysical frame of reference and free to determine its own concepts, a normative theory is required. The normative theory is necessary in order to determine what the relationship between folk psychology and the life experiences of individuals (which are based on intuition and the metaphysical frame of reference), the law and insights from the cognitive sciences broadly construed should be. In other words, it is required to determine in how far law should take insights from the cognitive sciences into account or how closely it should reflect folk psychological notions of, for example, agency.

5 The Relevance of Investigating the Metaphysical Frame of Reference

If it turns out that the metaphysical frame of reference is misleading or incorrect,[63] and where the law refers only to the metaphysical frame of reference as reason for regarding an entity as agent, this takes away the foundation of that determination. Let me use international law as an example again:

> If it turns out that it is not an elementary fact that only human beings can act in a non-reducible manner, this takes away the foundation for international law holding that a State can act only when the acts of a human being are

62 Id., p. 4.

63 Whether 'misleading' or 'incorrect' is the more accurate term also needs to be investigated. This depends on whether it is a matter of truth in the sense of corresponding to objective (or social) reality, or whether it is something that is more or less useful, depending on its purpose.

> attributable and attributed to the State *because* it is an elementary fact that only human beings can act in a non-reducible manner. This does not mean that international law cannot hold that a State can act only when the acts of a human being are attributable and attributed to the State, but it takes away the reason why this is currently being held.

Moreover, the emergence of more and new kinds of non-human entities such as artificially intelligent entities gives a very practical reason to investigate the metaphysical frame of reference and the law's relationship to it: the question how to regulate these new entities will need to be settled and is already on the agenda of, for example, the European Parliament.[64] Questions such as whether these artificially intelligent entities should be regarded as legal agents, under what circumstances and for what reasons will need to be answered. I hope to have shown that we should not answer them on the basis of unreflective intuitions (probably) stemming from our metaphysical frame of reference.

6 CONCLUSION

In this paper, I have argued the following:

- Different non-human entities have been regarded as legal agents at different times. The conceptualisation of legal agents and legal acts underlying the choice as to which entities to regard as legal agents shows that this is – at times – done for metaphysical reasons: by reference to the metaphysical frame of reference. At other times, it is done for normative reasons.
- There are reasons to investigate the metaphysical frame of reference.
- If it turns out that the determination of legal agency is made on the basis of references to the metaphysical frame of reference and if it turns out that the metaphysical frame of reference is incorrect or misleading in this regard, the reason for that particular determination of legal agency *on that particular basis* disappears. This does not take away that the same determination can be made for other reasons.

This – and the fact that the number of non-human entities that may need to be regulated is on the rise – leads me to conclude that the topic of non-human agency is a worthwhile subject for legal scholars and cognitive scientists to investigate. I have identified three (very broad) main topics that need to be investigated in order to successfully investigate non-human agency in the law:

---

64 *See* introduction.

1. Firstly, the metaphysical presuppositions that underlie the law need to be identified and explicated, where the law makes such metaphysical presuppositions. This is a task for legal scholars primarily and concerns a critical investigation of the reasons for which the law regards different non-human entities as agents.
2. Secondly, the metaphysical frame of reference needs to be investigated. This entails investigating whether the metaphysical presuppositions made by the law are correct, although these investigations need not be geared toward law specifically. I consider this a task for cognitive scientists broadly understood (and firmly counting philosophers amongst their numbers).
3. Lastly, a normative theory is necessary in order to determine for which reasons law should regard a non-human entity as a legal agent and in which situations the law should identify an event or situation as a legal act. This theory will also need to determine what the impact of the (moral) intuitions of individuals (based on folk psychology/the metaphysical frame of reference) or of insights from the cognitive sciences (that is, point 2) should be for determinations of legal agency. I consider this a task for legal scholars and legal decision-makers, taking into account the information under 2.

Insights from 1 and 2 are input that is required for the normative theory (3). Taken together, these three questions provide the foundation for a project on non-human agency that will – ideally – enable legal decision-makers to make well-founded choices regarding the agency of non-human entities such as corporations, States, churches, rivers or artificially intelligent entities.

References

Beirnes, P., 'The Law is an Ass: Reading E.P. Evans' The Medieval Prosecution and Capital Punishment of Animals', *Society and Animals*, Vol. 2, No. 1, 1994, pp. 27-46.

Brozek, B., 'The Troublesome Person', *in* V. Kurki & T. Pietrzykowski (Eds.), *Legal Personhood: animals, Artificial Intelligence and the Unborn*, Springer, New York 2017.

Brożek, B. & Janik, B., 'Can Artificial Intelligences Be Moral Agents?', *New Ideas in Psychology*, 2019, p. 3.

Chopra, S. & White, L., *A Legal Theory for Autonomous Artificial Agents*, University of Michigan Press, Ann Arbor 2011.

Cohen, E., 'Law, folklore and animal lore', *Past and Present*, No. 110, 1986, pp. 6-37.

Dennett, D.C., 'Conditions of Personhood', *in* A. Oksenberg Rorty (Ed.), *The Identities of Persons*, University of California Press, Berkeley 1976.

Ewald, W., 'Comparative Jurisprudence (I): What Was It like to Try a Rat?', *University of Pennsylvania Law Review*, Vol. 143, No. 6, 1995, pp. 1889-2149.

Farah, M.J. & Heberlein, A.S., 'Personhood and Neuroscience: Naturalizing or Nihilating?', *The American Journal of Bioethics*, Vol. 7, No. 1, 2007, pp. 37-48.

Farah, M.J. & Heberlein, A.S. 'Response to Open Peer Commentaries on "Personhood and Neuroscience: Naturalizing or Nihilating?": Getting Personal', *The American Journal of Bioethics*, Vol. 7, No. 1, 2007, W1-W4.

Fleming, S., 'Moral agents and legal persons: the ethics and the law of state responsibility', *International Theory*, Vol. 9, No. 3, 2017, pp. 466-489.

French, P.A., 'The Corporation as a Moral Person', *American Philosophical Quarterly*, Vol. 16, No. 3, 1979, pp. 207-215.

Greene, J. & Cohen, J., 'For the Law, Neuroscience Changes Nothing and Everything', Philosophical Transactions: Biological Sciences, 2004, pp. 1775-1785.

Heider, F. & Simmel, M., 'An Experimental Study of Apparent Behavior', *The American Journal of Psychology*, Vol. 57, No. 2, 1944, pp. 243-259.

Kelsen, H. & Wedberg, A., *General theory of law and state*, Harvard university press, Cambridge Massachusetts 1945.

Naffine, N., 'Who Are Law's Persons? From Cheshire Cats to Responsible Subjects', *The Modern Law Review*, Vol. 66, No. 3, 2003, pp. 346-367.

Newman, G., *The punishment response*, J.B. Lippincott, Philadelpia 1978

Roef, D., 'Corporate Criminal Liability', *in* J. Keiler & D. Roef (Eds.), *Comparative Concepts of Criminal Law*, 3rd edn, Intersentia, Antwerp 2019.

Schlosser, M., 'Agency', *in* E.N. Zalta (Ed.), *The Stanford Encyclopedia of Philosophy*, Fall 2015 edn., https://plato.stanford.edu/archives/fall2015/entries/agency/.

Shapiro, S.P., 'Agency Theory', *Annual Review of Socioly*, Vol. 31, 2005, pp. 263-284.

Volk, K., LüDerssen, K. & Kempf, E., *Unternehmensstrafrecht*, De Gruyter, Berlin 2012.

4 Bringing (the Right) Feelings Back: Culpability, Punishment, and Violence in the Era of Social and Affective Neuroscience

F. Coppola

1 Introduction

Violence[1] is the core of criminal law and justice. Most of the times, discussions of crime are discussions of violence. Public fear of crime is, essentially, fear of violence.[2] Political discourses on public security and safety,[3] and even the media,[4] rely upon violence. These public forms of communication fuel a distorted imagery of individuals who engage in violent crimes by depicting them as unscrupulous bad people or dangerous monsters. They do so with the aim of legitimizing criminal justice policies based on exclusion and punitiveness. In some systems, such strategies may even create or increase gaps between different social classes or ethnic groups. Accordingly, attempts to reform criminal law and justice toward decriminalization or more lenient sentencing are often complicated or impeded by this specific narrative on crimes of violence.

1 This chapter embraces an understanding of violence that includes acts of interpersonal physical aggression, which may result in crimes of assault, robbery, or homicide. This chapter does not consider sex offences.

2 U. Gabriel & W. Greve, 'The Psychology of Fear of Crime: Conceptual and Methodological Perspectives', *British Journal of Criminology*, Vol. 43, No. 3, 2003, pp. 600-614.

3 K. Dowler, 'Media Consumption and Public Attitudes Toward Crime and Justice: The Relationship Between Fear of Crime, Punitive Attitudes and Perceived Political Effectiveness', *Journal of Criminal Justice and Popular Culture*, Vol. 10, No. 2, 2009, pp. 109-126; C. Bogert, 'How the Media Help Drive Harsh Criminal Justice Policies', *Los Angeles Times*, 31 May, 2019.

4 N. Kalmoe, 'Yes, Political Rhetoric Can Incite Violence', *Politico Magazine*, 30 October, 2018.

The normative dimension of violence[5] – that is, the culpability[6] and punishability of violent perpetrators – is tied to such intuitive imagery of violence that is endorsed in everyday criminal justice discourse. As for culpability, the normative construct of the violent perpetrator reflects the rationalist paradigm of a culpable agent that has found traction in Western criminal law. Based on this paradigm, the typical violent perpetrator is perceived as basically a rational individual whose choice to commit or threaten physical harm is the result of his or her instrumental reasoning (often dictated by evil motives).

This normative picture of the typical violent perpetrator may also encompass further attributes that typically apply to criminal violence. For instance, common sentencing criteria for violent crimes include the heinousness of the offence or the individual's dangerousness. These criteria are designed to promote and echo retributivist and incapacitative perspectives and attitudes toward violence and, above all, toward the people who commit violence. The fusion of normative and social/descriptive dimensions of violence is most visible in punitive responses to violence. From a normative standpoint, the punitive approach to violence relies on the same legal-psychological assumptions as culpability. Because criminal violence is often perceived as being worse than any other offense, the punishment for perpetrators of violent crimes must be more severe accordingly. By implicitly echoing public demands, the severity of the punitive responses to violence often translates into restrictive forms of punishment, which are characterized by social exclusion and isolation. In fact, exclusion and isolation are still presumed to be efficacious means of punishing, neutralizing and 'transforming' violent perpetrators. The assumption on which this punitive approach to violence is based is that social isolation and exclusion are just conditions for perpetrators of violent crimes to understand the wrongfulness of their misdeed; furthermore, these outcomes are presumed to encourage perpetrators to refrain from re-offending in the near future.[7]

5 The substantive criminal law of violence typically includes crimes that involve the threat of physical force as well as those that involve actual physical harm, such as homicide, robbery, assault, or rape. However, the range of behaviors that should fall within "violence" have been subject to disagreements among different fields of study. For a critical overview, *see* A. Ristroph, 'Criminal Law in the Shadow of Violence', *Alabama Law Review*, Vol. 62, No. 3, 2011, pp. 570-621. *See also* R. Ferguson, 'Violence, Crime, and Violent Crime', *International Journal of Conflict and Violence*, Vol. 3, No. 1, 2009, pp. 23-29.

6 For the purposes of this chapter, I espouse a mixed or hybrid understanding of culpability, one that embraces and combines a descriptive dimension including the particular mental states provided for in the definition of the criminal offenses, and a normative dimension including blameworthiness. For a similar account, *see* K. Kesser Ferzan, 'Holistic Culpability', *Cardozo Law Review*, Vol. 28, No. 6, 2007, pp. 2523-2543.

7 This assumption draws on expressivist accounts of punishment, according to which a major purpose of punishment is to express moral condemnation of criminal acts; as a consequence, the perpetrator must (be able to) understand the moral wrongness of his or her act. *See, e.g.*, W. Sinnott-Armstrong & K. Levy, 'Insanity Defenses', *in* J. Deigh & D. Dolinko (Eds), *The Oxford Handbook of Philosophy of Criminal Law*, New York, Oxford University Press, p. 313 (observing that "[w]e condemn rapists as bad people even if they suffer losses for what they do. Fines would be not enough for rape even if they worked to prevent it.

The narrow normative view of violence stands in contrast to a robust body of behavioral and neuroscientific studies about the critical role of emotions in moral and social behavior. Research from the fields of social and personality psychology, and social and affective neuroscience has emphasized that morally adaptive behaviors are strongly influenced by specific social emotions and emotion-related capacities coupled with protective social environmental factors. As for violence, the same body of empirical research has suggested a connection between violent and aggressive behavior, negative socio-environmental influences and dysfunctional emotional dynamics. These findings suggest that violence is a far more complex behavioral phenomenon than criminal law and popular understandings assume.

The specific contribution of brain research to understandings of violence has concerned clinical populations. There is no neurobiology of violence nor is violence a disease of localized brain dysfunction. Nonetheless, over the past few decades, neuroimaging studies have improved understandings of the relationship between specific brain dysfunctions and diagnostic factors that are linked to an increased risk of engaging in violent conduct. Notably, neuroscientific studies on certain clinical categories, including psychopathy and post-traumatic stress disorder, have suggested that several common psychological traits (e.g., callousness, low empathy, poor emotion regulation) shared by members of these clinical populations are associated with altered functioning in emotion-related brain regions that appear to be significantly involved in social functioning.

While uncovering the psychological and neurobiological cues of violence, empirical studies have also highlighted that punitive approaches to violence risk exacerbating the emotive risk factors of violence. Contrary to commonsense-based views, restrictive and exclusionary

---

We also wish to proclaim to society that rape is morally wrong and, ideally, to make rapists understand its wrongness. . ."). *See also* R. A. Duff, 'Restoration and Retribution', *in* A. VonHirsch, J. Roberts, A. Bottoms, K. Roach & M. Scheff (Eds), *Restorative Justice and Criminal Justice: Competing or Reconcilable Paradigms*, Oxford, Hart Publishing, 2003, p. 53 (proposing that punishment has to be seen as "a kind of secular penance: [as] a burden undertaken by the wrongdoer, which aims to induce and express her repentant and apologetic understanding of the wrong she has done. . ."). This theoretical background most likely backs the harsher and more exclusionary regimes that apply to violent perpetrators across different legal systems. *See, e.g.*, J. Whitman, *Harsh Justice: Criminal Punishment and the Widening Divide Between America and Europe*, Oxford University Press, New York 2003, p. 71 (observing that European legal cultures and prison practice, by contrast with the American, "have grown harsher *only with regard to a shrinking class of mostly violent offenders* [. . .] terrorists, certain sex offenders, drug dealers"). For an analysis of the purposes of punishment behind the supermax security regime for mafia leaders in Italy, *see* S. Romice, 'Brevi Note sull'Art. 41 Bis', *Giurisprudenza Penale Web*, No. 12, 2017, pp. 1-50. For analyses of public beliefs about the (harsher) punishment for violent perpetrators, *see, e.g.*, F. Cullen, B. Fisher, & B. Applegate, 'Public Opinion about Punishment and Corrections', *Crime and Justice*, Vol. 27, 2000, pp. 1-79; M. Vasiljevic & G. Tendayi, 'Dehumanization, Moral Disengagement, and Public Attitudes to Crime and Punishment', *in* P. G. Bain, J. Vaes & J. Leyens (Eds), *Humanness and Dehumanization*, New York, Psychology Press, 2014, pp. 129-146.

punitive measures in scarce environments not only risk promoting the same negative feelings (e.g., shame and humiliation) that have been found to stimulate violent behavior, but also discourage individual paths for positive behavioral change. Hence, some authors have suggested that criminal justice responses to violence should motivate prosocial feelings that inhibit violence against others, such as self-esteem, self-respect, empathy with the suffering of others, and feelings of guilt and remorse regarding impulses to harm others. Importantly, some have also argued that these emotions are best created in socially rich and stimulating environments, thereby suggesting the implementation of alternative programs designed to allow a wide range of inclusionary, socially rehabilitative strategies in community-like settings or therapeutic communities.

Behavioral and neuroscientific studies on emotions, social behavior and violence provide some challenging information for criminal law and justice. First, emotions are critical to moral and (pro)social behavior. Second, the social environment profoundly shapes the social brain and behavior. Third, excessively severe and exclusionary punitive measures promote rather than prevent violence.

The intention of this chapter is to address this information and provide several arguments on how empirical insights into social behavior and violence can foster more comprehensive understandings, evaluations and responses with respect to violent crimes. Notably, the chapter addresses the potential impact of this body of knowledge on the culpability and punishment of violent perpetrators. As for the former, the chapter argues that for the (neuro)science of emotions and social behavior to have repercussions on the culpability status of violent perpetrators, there first needs to be a normative reform of the general standard of culpability and, consequently, of culpability-related doctrines. That reform should include emotions and emotional faculties among its relevant legal-psychological set. However, as will be discussed, this scenario will remain purely theoretical in the near future. As regards the latter issue, this chapter argues that findings on the psychological and neurobiological cues of violent behavior are more likely to affect punitive responses to violence. Notably, (neuro)scientific research could contribute to changing the narrative behind criminal violence and re-directing or strengthening criminal justice responses to violence to promote inclusion, dialogue and social rehabilitation. Such initiatives would ideally take place in stimulating and minimally restrictive institutional settings that still ensure public safety.

The chapter proceeds as follows. It begins by briefly illustrating the legal rationalist view of the capacity for rational moral agency, upon which criminal law grounds the paradigms of culpability and punishment, including for violent perpetrators. It then moves to the controversial role that criminal law attributes to emotions in its theories and docrines, and it explores how such a view of emotions applies to criminal violence. It then measures the legal rationalist model of violence against behavioral and neuroscientific literature on the role of emotions and socio-environmental influences on moral and social behavior. It then analyzes empirical works about the individual and structural risk factors for violence, by considering both nonclinical and clinical populations. Based on this analysis, the chapter addresses challenges that this body of scientific knowledge poses to the current legal view of criminal violence and provides an argument regarding how, and to what extent, this body of scientific knowledge can affect both the culpability of violent perpetrators and punitive responses to violence. The chapter concludes with several remarks and suggestions for future research.

2 Culpable Agency and the Narrative of the Typical Violent Perpetrator

In Western legal traditions, there is general consensus that individuals may be held criminally responsible and punished because they are capable of rational moral agency.[8] In the eyes of criminal law, individuals are capable of rational moral agency when they are aware of, or can understand what they are doing and that what they are doing is wrong and yet choose to act unlawfully.[9] The legal notion of rational moral agency that grounds an attribution of criminal responsibility and the infliction of punishment essentially encompasses the fusion of two elements: cognition and volition.[10]

Current paradigms of culpability and punishment are deeply rooted in a cognition-based view of rational moral agency. Embracing the rationalist view of rational thought and behavior – law-abiding and antisocial alike – endorsed by classical and neo-classical thinkers,[11] criminal law identifies rational moral agency with cognitive faculties such as

8 *See, e.g.*, S. J. Morse, 'Reason, Result, and Criminal Responsibility', *University of Illinois Law Review*, 2004, pp. 363-444; D. Husak, 'Broad" Culpability and the Retributivist Dream', *Ohio State Journal of Criminal Law*, Vol. 9, 2012, pp. 449-485.

9 See H.L.A. Hart, *Punishment and Responsibility: Essays in the Philosophy of Law*, Oxford University Press, Oxford 1967; R. A. Duff, 'Choice, Character, and Criminal Liability', *Law & Philosophy*, Vol. 12, No. 4, 1993, pp. 345-383; D. O. Brink & D. K. Nelkin, 'Fairness and the Architecture of Responsibility', *in* D. Shoemaker (Ed.), *Oxford Studies in Agency and Responsibility* Vol. 1, New York, Oxford University Press, 2013, pp. 284-313.

10 Across different legal systems, culpability-based notions like *mens rea* and legal insanity are all based on the interdependency between cognition and volition. *See* J. Keiler & D. Roef (Eds.), *Comparative Concepts of Criminal Law* 2nd edn, Intersentia, Cambridge 2016.

11 *See, e.g.*, R. Faqir, 'The Philosophy of Punishment: A Study to the History of Classical and Positive Schools of Penology', 1 *Forensic Research & Criminology International Journal*, Vol. 1, No. 6, 2015, 1-8.

reasoning, thinking, planning, learning and *understanding.*[12] Cognition is allegedly the mental faculty that drives decision-making, intention-formation, and planning. It is also what guides individuals' practical moral reasoning about what they ought and ought not to do.[13] Based on this assumption, the cognitive dimension of the mind is the source of criminal choice and behavior. As such, the cognitive dimension of the mind is the essential precondition in culpability assessments.

This 'atomistic' and 'individualistic'[14] understanding of culpable agency is related to and legitimizes both the retributivist and consequentalist justifications for punishment.[15] Indeed, the narrative that cuts across these justifications for punishment aligns with the legal understanding of rational moral agency: the state inflicts harm upon the wrongdoer not only because the wrongdoer deserves it but also because, through punishment, the wrongdoer will understand the negative consequences of his or her misbehavior[16] and choose to behave lawfully in the future.[17]

The normative construct of the ideal culpable agent is emblematically represented by perpetrators of violent crimes. The prototypically culpable violent perpetrator is an intelligent individual who knowingly chooses to threaten or to inflict physical harm. While the pejorative view of criminal violence is imperceptible in the general canons of culpability – there are no general culpability doctrines that are especially or uniquely tailored to violence – , two contexts distinguish criminal violence from other crime types: sentencing and the execution of punishment. As for sentencing, the violent character of the perpetrator or of the crime he or she committed are usually valued as aggravating factors. The particular cruelty or heinousness of the crime or the modalities of perpetration, and the assessed dangerousness of the perpetrator, are typical aggravating factors of the perpetrator's blameworthiness that entail harsher sentences.[18] Harshness in punishing perpetrators who

12 C. Anyagwe, *Criminal Law: The General Part*, Langaa RPCIG, 2015, p. 249 (reporting that "[t]he cognitive functions are our intellectual functions, that is, our ability to assimilate information from the environment, remember it, organise and process it in a rational manner, drawing rational conclusions, and making appropriate decisions. Thus, they include our functions of perception, thinking, reasoning, understanding, judgement and recall.").

13 *Id.*, p. 249 ("[a] person's ability to distinguish between right and wrong; to know when certain conduct would be wrong according to the standards of law, society and/or morality; and to decide on an appropriate course of action, depends on that person's cognitive functions.").

14 J. Claessen, *Forgiveness in Criminal Law Through Incorporating Restorative Mediation*, Wolf Legal Publishers, Oisterwijk 2017, p. 55.

15 *See* R.A. Duff, *Trials and Punishments*, Cambridge University Press, Cambridge 1986.

16 R. Lippke, 'Retribution and Incarceration', Public Affairs Quarterly, Vol. 17, 2003, pp. 29-48.

17 C. L. Johnson, 'The Effects of Imprisonment', *in* F. Cullen & P. Wilcox (Eds.), *The Oxford Handbook of Criminological Theory and Criminal Justice*, New York, Oxford University Press, 2013, pp. 672-690.

18 *See, e.g.*, S. Bibas, *The Machinery of Criminal Justice*, Oxford University Press, New York 2012, p. 59 ("[s]entencing decisions are swift and impersonal. To the extent that they reflect the underlying merits at

have committed violent offenses may not only equate to longer sentences. Rather, it often equates to more severe restrictions during the execution of punishment, which are characterized by greater social exclusion and, sometimes, isolation.

The legal view of criminal violence mutually echoes the typical and often stereotypical depictions of violent perpetrators in mainstream criminological accounts. According to David Garland, whereas one side of the criminological debate 'normalizes' violent offenders and depicts them as 'rational opportunists,' more politicized and 'crime-control-focused' views of the 'collective unconscious' promote a strategy of 'essentialized difference.'[19] From this perspective, a violent perpetrator is depicted as an 'alien other', whose antisocial character reflects wantonness, amorality and dangerousness, with little social value and little resemblance to 'us.'[20] Thus, as Garland has argued, the only practical response to such people is incapacitation, to 'take them out of circulation'[21] for the protection of the public. Policymakers have attempted to achieve such an outcome through the implementation of incapacitative criminal policies, including mandatory minimum sentences and maximum-security regimes.

Overall, the fictional picture of the typical violent perpetrator that emerges from the combination of substantive criminal law and social discourse is humanized and dehumanized at the same time.[22] The violent perpetrator is a rational being who commits acts that do not reflect human nature. As such, the typical violent perpetrator deserves to – and must – be removed, both physically and figuratively, from the rest of society.

3 Emotions and the Criminal Law's Construct of Violence within Culpability and Punishment

The rationalist vein that emerges from the status of culpability and punishment is also manifest in the negligible, or at least one sided and negative role that criminal law attributes to emotions within its theories, doctrines and practices. The orthodox view is that in

all, they are tied to the individual defendant's badness and need for retribution, deterrence, and incapacitation. They tend to be static, backward-looking assessments of blame and dangerousness that fit neatly into mechanical compartments.").

19 D. Garland, *The Culture of Control: Crime and Social Order in Contemporary Society*, Oxford University Press, New York 2001, p. 135.

20 *Id.*

21 *Id.*, p. 136.

22 *See* S. Stolk, 'A Sophisticated Beast? On the Construction of an 'Ideal' Perpetrator in the Opening Statements of International Criminal Trials', *European Journal of International Law*, Vol. 29, No. 3, pp. 677-701 (discussing the frequent stereotyping of perpetrators of mass atrocities as "inhuman human" beings).

principle, unlike cognition, emotions may compromise volitional capacities and disturb rational thought and behavior.[23] Nevertheless, emotions are not positive essential components of (the capacity for) rational moral agency. Hence, as long as the individual exhibits intact cognitive faculties, emotional influences on decision-making and behavior are not essential in either assessing or excluding an individual's criminal responsibility. On the other hand, an individual's lack of certain emotional faculties is not indicative of a compromised capacity for rational moral agency. To the contrary, emotional absence indicates even stronger rational capacity.[24]

The theoretical dichotomy 'cognition *versus* emotion' endorsed by substantive criminal law theory is also manifest in its doctrines and practices. First, emotions or emotional capacities are not included among the essential descriptive elements of culpability doctrines, such as *mens rea* or legal insanity. On the other hand, certain emotions are central to certain 'lack-of-choice/self-control' excuse defenses, such as overwhelming fear in duress[25] or (in common law systems) uncontrollable – yet reasonable – rage in diminished capacity/heat of passion to reduce murder to manslaughter.[26] However, when a given crime is accompanied by – even pathological – emotional absence (e.g., callousness), during the perpetration of the crime, this condition usually warrants a recognition of criminal responsibility.[27]

The emotional dimension of the perpetrator, especially in cases involving criminal violence, may gain circumstantial weight – either aggravating or mitigating – in sentencing. For instance, negative emotional factors that may have a link with the violent crime – such as the perpetrator's past emotional traumas or a history of abuse – *may* be considered as mitigating factors for sentencing, at the decision-makers' discretion. Likewise, perpetrators' expressions of specific emotions, such as remorse or regret for the violent crime committed, *may* be considered in sentencing decisions.[28] On the other hand, when the perpetrator

23 N. Finkel & G. Parrot, *Emotions & Culpability: How the Law is At Odds with Psychology, Jurors, and Itself*, American Psychological Association, Washington D.C. 2006.

24 *See* F. Coppola, 'Motus Animi in Mente Insana: An Emotion-Oriented Paradigm of Legal Insanity Informed by the Neuroscience of Moral Judgments and Decision-Making', *The Journal of Criminal Law and Criminology*, Vol. 109, No. 1, 2019, pp. 1-68.

25 *See* Eimear Spain, *The Role of Emotions in Criminal Law Defenses: Duress, Necessity, and Lesser Evil*, Cambridge University Press, New York 2011.

26 American Law Institute, Model Penal Code, 1962, § 210.3(1)(b). *See also* R. G. Fontaine, 'Adequate (Non)Provocation and Heat of Passion as Excuse Not Justification', *University of Michigan Journal of Law Reform*, Vol. 43, No. 1, 2009, pp. 27-51.

27 *See* S. Morse, 'Psychopathy and Criminal Responsibility', *Neuroethics*, Vol. 8, 2008, pp. 205-212.

28 While this situation is generally less common in continental Europe (*see* Claessen 2017, p. 63), in the United States expressions of remorse are afforded greater circumstantial value – however discretional – in sentencing. However, a large body of literature has underscored the unequal consideration of these emotional elements by decision-makers based on the perpetrator's ethnicity and social status. *See, e.g.*, S. Bandes, 'Remorse and Criminal Justice', *Emotion Review*, Vol. 8, No. 1, 2016, pp. 14-19; S. Pillsbury, 'Emotions and Criminal

expresses emotional absence (e.g., lack of remorse, callousness) at trial, this circumstance may aggravate his or her sentence.[29]

From a more practical – yet related – standpoint, the emotional dimension of perpetrators, especially those who engage in violent crimes, is hardly addressed during the execution of punishment. As implied above, justice responses to violence are constructed around a fear-based rhetoric: *the state must punish violence.* By virtue of this rhetoric, exclusionary and disempowering mechanisms in the execution of punishment prevail over the emotional (and social) needs of those who have harmed others.[30] A punishment that excludes, leaves behind and isolates people, rather than including and healing them, is still often viewed as the natural response to violence, for it allegedly achieves retributivist, incapacitative and deterrence goals, and it also satisfies public demands. Paradoxically, such punishment is also assumed to lead to rehabilitative outcomes.

According to Ristroph, the rhetoric of violence in criminal justice policy does far less than it could to address and prevent violence. The popular depictions of violence that have seized the public imagination than including and healing them, is still appear to have produced legal outcomes 'that do not so much prevent violence as redistribute it.'[31] This is particularly true in countries like the United States where 'tough on crime' policies have left racial minorities and the poor especially exposed to violence. All in all, as Ristroph has observed, 'the greatest source of violence might be the criminal law itself.'[32]

4 Emotions, Socio-environmental Factors and (Pro)social behavior

In *Women and Human Development*,[33] philosopher Martha Nussbaum offers a rather objective list of universal 'functional capabilities' that she holds to be central to human

Punishment in Theory and Practice', 2016, http://emotionresearcher.com/emotion-and-criminal-punishment-in principle-and-in-practice/.

29 *See, e.g.*, B. H. Ward, 'Sentencing Without Remorse', *Loyola University Chicago Law Journal*, Vol. 38, No. 1, 2006, pp. 131-167.

30 *See, e.g.*, J. Woodall, R. Dixey, & J. South, 'Control and Choice in English Prisons: Developing Health-promoting Prisons, *Health Promotion International*, Vol. 29, No. 3, 2013, pp. 474-482; P.J. Askar & D.T. Kenny, 'Views from the Inside: Young Offenders' Subjective Experiences of Incarceration', *International Journal of Offender Therapy and Comparative Criminology*, Vol. 52, 2008, pp. 584-597; J.A. Schnittker, 'Enduring Stigma: The Long-term Effects of Incarceration on Health', *Journal of Health and Social Behavior*, Vol. 48, 2007, pp. 115-130.

31 Ristroph 2011, p. 616.

32 *Id.*, p. 621.

33 M. Nussbaum, *Women and Human Development*, Cambridge University Press, New York 2000.

life. Many of the capabilities she lists are intimately connected to human experience, such as

> [b]eing able to have attachments to things and people outside ourselves; [n]ot having one's emotional development blighted by overwhelming fear and anxiety, or by traumatic events of abuse or neglect [Emotions]; [b]eing able to form a conception of the good and to engage in critical reflection about the planning of one's life [Practical Reason]; [b]eing able to . . .recognize and show concern for other human beings, to engage in various forms of social interaction; to be able to imagine the situation of another and to have compassion for that situation . . . Having the social bases of self-respect and non-humiliation [Affiliation].[34]

According to Nussbaum, these components are separate, yet strictly interrelated. Moreover, these elements are of central and equal importance to being and behaving as uniquely and completely human.[35]

Nussbaum's list embraces a multidimensional conception of the central capabilities innate to the nature of humans as fundamentally social beings. Notably, Nussbaum's account finds large support within not only social and personality psychology, but also social and affective neuroscience. Findings in these fields have underscored the critically influential and informative role of emotions and emotion-related capacities (e.g., empathy or emotion regulation), coupled with socio-environmental factors, in the deliberative processes that lead to morally adaptive behavior in social contexts.

Both disciplines have attributed evaluative,[36] motivational,[37] adaptive[38] and regulatory[39] functions to emotions in decision-making processes and social behavior. Importantly, both disciplines have suggested that emotional states or faculties exert an influence on cognitive functions, including attention, cognitive performance and cognitive control.[40]

---

34 *Id.*, p. 79.
35 *Id.*, p. 81.
36 A. Moors et al., 'Appraisal Theories of Emotion: State of the Art and Future Development', *Emotion Review*, Vol. 5, pp. 119-124.
37 N.H. Fridja, 'Emotions and Actions', *in* A. Manstead, N. Fridja & A. Fisher (Eds), *Feelings and Emotions*, Cambridge, Cambridge University Press, 2004, pp. 158-173.
38 R.W. Levenson, 'The Interpersonal Functions of Emotions', *Cognition and Emotion*, Vol. 13, N. 5, 1999, pp. 481-504.
39 A. Damasio, *The Feeling of What Happens: Body and Emotions in The Making of Consciousness*, Harcourt Trade, San Diego 1999.
40 *See, e.g.*, H. Okon-Singer et al., 'The Neurobiology of Emotion–Cognition Interactions: *Fundamental Questions and Strategies for Future Research*', *Frontiers in Human Neuroscience*, Vol. 9, 2015, pp. 1-14.

Furthermore, the neuroscientific literature has indicated the large artificiality of the divide between emotion and cognition at the neural level.[41] Rather, neuroscientific studies have suggested the strict interrelation of prototypically cognition-related and prototypically emotion-related functions in decision-making processes, especially in moral contexts.[42] Overall, neuroscientific studies have critically indicated a *mutual* dependent relationship between emotion and cognition in guiding moral decision-making and, consequently, in influencing social behavior.

Personality and social psychology studies have explored the various roles that different emotions – both basic and social –[43] and emotion-related faculties[44] play in (pro)social behavior at both dispositional and situational levels. For instance, several studies have indicated the prosocial function of compassion[45] and regret[46] in motivating altruistic and morally adaptive behaviors. Other studies have focused on the varying impact of self-conscious negative emotions – notably, guilt and shame – on prosocial behavior.

Specifically, several accounts across the literature have contrasted the adaptive function of guilt with the maladaptive function of shame.[47] Shame has been defined as 'the intensely painful feeling or experience of believing that [*oneself is*] flawed and therefore unworthy

---

41 *See, e.g.*, R. Davidson, 'Cognitive Neuroscience Needs Affective Neuroscience (and Vice Versa)', *Brain and Cognition*, Vol. 42, 2000, pp. 89-92.

42 *See, e.g.*, J. Blair & K. Fowler, 'Moral Emotions and Moral Reasoning from the Perspective of Affective Cognitive Neuroscience: A Selective Review', *European Journal of Developmental Science*, Vol. 2, 2008, pp. 303-323; L. Pascual, P. Rodriguez & D. Gallardo-Pujol, 'How does Morality Work in the Brain?', *Frontiers in Integrative Neuroscience*, Vol. 1, 2013, pp. 1-8.

43 P. Ekman, 'Basic Emotions', *in* T. Dalgleish & M. J. Power (Eds.), *Handbook of Cognition and Emotion*, New York, John Wiley & Sons Ltd., 1999, pp. 45-60; J. Haidt, 'The Moral Emotions', *in* R. Davidson, K. Scherer, & H. Hill Goldsmith (Eds.), *Handbook of Affective Sciences*, New York, Oxford University Press, 2003, pp. 852-870.

44 N. Eisenberg, N. Eggum & L. Di Giunta, 'Empathy-related Responding: Associations with Prosocial Behavior, Aggression, and Intergroup Relations', *Social Issues Policy Review*, Vol. 4, No. 1, 2010, pp. 143-180; M. S. Lebowitz, & J. F. Dovidio. 'Implications of Emotion Regulation Strategies for Empathic Concern, Social Attitudes, and Helping Behavior', Emotion, Vol. 15, 2015, pp. 187–194.

45 G. Coricelli, R.J. Dolan, & A. Sirigu, 'Brain, Emotion, and Decision-Making: The Paradigmatic Example of Regret', *Trends in Cognitive Science*, Vol. 11, pp. 258-265.

46 K. Preckel & T. Singer, 'On the Interaction of Social Affect and Social Cognition: Empathy, Compassion, and Theory of Mind', *Current Opinion in Behavioral Science*, Vol. 19, 2018, pp. 1-6.

47 *See, e.g.*, R.F. Baumeister, A.M. Stillwell, & T.F. Heatherton, 'Guilt: An Interpresonal Approach', *Psychological Bulletin*, Vol. 115, No. 2, 1994, pp. 243-267; J.P. Tangney, J. Stewing & D.J. Mashek, 'Moral Emotions and Moral Behavior', *Annual Review of Psychology*, Vol. 58, 2007, pp. 345-372. *Cf.* N. Harris, 'Reassessing the Dimensionality of Moral Emotions, *British Journal of Psychology*, Vol. 94, No. 4, 2003, pp. 457-473; J. Sabini & M. Silver, 'In Defense of Shame: Shame in the Context of Guilt and Embarrassment', *Journal for the Theory of Social Behavior*, Vol. 27, No. 1, 2001, pp. 1-15.

of love and belonging.'[48] It usually occurs following negative public exposure – that is, when somebody is shamed by somebody else (external shame) – or in private events (internal shame). In the latter case, shame typically involves a sense of imagined self-exposure.[49]

In brief, shame occurs when individuals evaluate themselves as failures.[50] Hence, shame may involve intense feelings of humiliation, powerlessness, worthlessness, low self-esteem and low self-respect, all of which result from global evaluations of one's self-concept.[51] The experience of shame, at both the dispositional and situational levels, is likely to lead to negative reactions by the individual (e.g.., anger, rage, or hostility) as well as maladaptive action tendencies (e.g., aggression) cognitive disortions (e.g., avoidance, neutralization of negative behavior) and externalization of blame.[52]

On the other hand, guilt is a less painful internal experience than shame, for the focus of the negative evaluation is the act, not the self. The feeling of guilt occurs when individuals evaluate *their behavior* as negative.[53] Hence, when feelings of guilt precede a potentially harmful behavior, such as harming others, people simply avoid engaging in the behavior that might make them feel guilty and suffer the negative consequences of such potential misbehavior. When feelings of guilt follow harmful behaviors, people are more prone to feel remorse for the harm done, to take responsibility for it, to make amends, and to attempt to repair the damage.[54] Overall, guilt serves an adaptive function in most people by protecting them from the risk of engaging in antisocial behavior, and suffering the negative consequences.[55]

Several studies have accounted for the different effects of guilt and shame on social behavior based on their respective relationship with empathy – which is positive in guilt

48 B. Brown, *I Thought It Was Just Me (But It Isn't): Making the Journey from "What Will People Think?" to "I Am Enough"*, Gotham Books, New York 2007, p. 29.

49 R.H. Smith et al., 'The Role of Public Exposure in Moral and Nonmoral Shame and Guilt', *Journal of Personality and Social Psychology*, Vol. 83, No. 1, 2002, pp. 138-159.

50 *See* Tangney et al. 2007.

51 *See, e.g.*, P. Velotti et al., 'Faces of Shame: Implications for Self-Esteem, Emotion Regulation, Aggression, and Well-Being', *The Journal of Psychology*, Vol. 151, No. 2, 2017, pp. 171-184.

52 J.P. Tangney, J. Stewing & L. Hafez, 'Shame, Guilt and Remorse: Implications for Offender Populations', *The Journal of Forensic Psychiatry & Psychology*, Vol. 22, No. 5, 2011, pp. 706-723; J. Stewing et al., 'Shaming, Blaming, and Maiming: Functional Links Among the Moral Emotions, Externalization of Blame, and Aggression', *Journal of Research in Personality*, Vol. 44, No. 1, 2010, pp. 91-102.

53 *See supra* note 47.

54 Tangney et al. 2011.

55 *Id.*

and negative in shame.[56] Empathy is considered the core of moral and prosocial behavior. It can be defined as a multi-dimensional socio-affective process consisting of 'gaining information about the internal affective representations of others,'[57] eliciting vicarious emotional responses. Although the exact role of empathy – and of its components –[58] in prosocial behavior is debated,[59] evidence supports the claim that empathy does have an overall bearing on prosocial behavior.[60] Especially concerning other individuals, empathy promotes caregiving behavior, and it also leads to aversions to violence.[61]

Admittedly, how and why people appraise the very same morally salient situation with different emotions and consequently different behavioral responses depends on a variety of socio-environmental factors, including personal histories, environmental influences, and cultural backgrounds. These factors reportedly trigger and mediate emotional responses in morally salient situations. Research has revealed that specific social, economic, and environmental factors (e.g., secure attachments, positive social engagement, exposure to positive environments, and social acceptance) are essential to the development and maintenance of the socio-emotional competencies that are linked to morality and prosocial behavior.[62] Notably, studies have documented a positive relationship between these factors and the development and functioning of key brain areas that are involved in the experience of adaptive moral emotions, as well as adaptive emotion processing and regulation.[63] Thus, cross-disciplinary evidence backs the idea that positive social, environmental stimuli and emotional support can (re)shape brain circuits that correlate socio-emotional competencies implicated in morality and prosocial behavior, with beneficial and enduring effects on

56 *See, e.g.*, J. P. Tangney, 'Moral Affect: The Good, The Bad, and The Ugly', *Journal of Personality and Social Psychology*, Vol. 61, No. 4, 1991, pp. 598-607.

57 *See* M.H. Davis, 'Measuring Individual Differences in Empathy: Evidence for a Multidimensional Approach', *Journal of Personality and Social Psychology*, Vol. 44, 1983, pp. 113-126.

58 See G. Ugazio, J. Majdandžić & C. Lamm, 'Are Empathy and Morality Linked? Insights from Moral Psychology, Social and Decision Neuroscience, and Philosophy', in H. Maibom (Ed.), Empathy and Morality, Oxford, Oxford University Press, 2014, pp. 155-171.

59 J. Decety & J. M. Cowell, 'Friends or Foes: Is Empathy Necessary for Moral Behavior?', *Perspectives on Psychological Science*, Vol. 9, 2015, pp. 525-537.

60 J. Zaki, *Empathy is a Moral Force, in* K. Gray & J. Graham (Eds.), *Atlas of Moral Psychology*, New York, Guildford Press 2018, pp. 49-58.

61 J. Decety & J. M. Cowell, 'Empathy, Justice, and Moral Behavior', *AJOB Neuroscience*, Vol. 6, 2015, pp. 3-14.

62 E.H. Telzer et al., 'Social Influence on Positive Youth Development: A Developmental Neuroscience Perspective', *Advances in Child Development and Behavior*, Vol. 54, 2018, pp. 215-258.

63 L. Cozolino, *Neuroscience of Human Relationships: Attachment and the Developing Social Brain* 2nd edn, W.W. Norton & Company, New York 2014.

social functioning. This perspective is also consistent with studies on factors related to crime desistance.[64]

5 Emotions, the Social Environment, and Violence

Empirical work has further contextualized the critical roles of emotions and emotion-related skills in moral and social behavior within violent behavior in healthy populations. While psychological work has widely analyzed the specific relationships between specific social emotions and violence, neuroscientific research has mostly focused on analyzing how negative socio-environmental factors affect individuals' neurobiology and, as a consequence, how such neurobiological effects may lead to maladaptive emotional responses and behavioral outcomes, including violent behaviors. Thus, while there is no definitive neurobiology of violence, research from social neuroscience has been shedding light on the mutual relationship between the social environment and neurobiology, further clarifying the mechanisms that may increase the risk of engaging in aggressive and violent conduct.

From a psychological perspective, a wide body of literature has inquired into the connections between emotions and violence. One influential formulation of emotions and violence is that of James Gilligan, a psychiatrist from New York University who worked for many years with perpetrators of violent crimes in supermax prisons in Massachusetts. Gilligan places overwhelming shame, poor self-esteem, and humiliation at the center of his psychodynamic formulation of violence.[65] He holds that perpetrators with serious histories of violence live with unacknowledged (or repressed) overwhelming feelings of shame, humiliation, low self-esteem and low self-respect that usually originate in a series of negative environmental, developmental, and cultural factors, including child abuse, physical violence, exposure to violence, social rejection, low attachment, neglect, and abandonment. However, Gilligan has argued that for shame to produce violence, several other preconditions must be met.[66] First, the situational circumstances present at the time of the violent crime must have diminished or neutralized guilt and empathy feelings the person would otherwise have felt. Second, the individual must have perceived him- or herself as lacking sufficient nonviolent means by which to save or restore his or her self-esteem, such as employment, education, or high socio-economic status.

64 *See, e.g.*, P. Giordano, R.D. Schroeder & S.A. Cernkovich, 'Emotions and Crime Over the Life Course: A Neo-meadian Perspective on Criminal Continuity and Change', *American Journal of Sociology*, Vol. 112, 2007, pp. 1603-1661; B. Weaver, *Offending and the Importance of Social Relations*, 1st edn, Routledge, 2016.

65 *See, e.g.*, J. Gilligan, *Violence: Reflections on a National Epidemic*, Putnam, New York 1996, pp. 103-114.

66 *Id.*, pp. 111-114.

The adversive role of shame, as an emotive risk factor of violence, has found traction in the psychological and criminological literature. For instance, in their agentic and systematic theory of violence, Scheff and Retzinger[67] posit that violence is the outcome of a 'vicious circle' including alienation, unacknowledged or repressed shame, and anger. Specifically, when an individual does not acknowledge being hurt by a rejection, as is the case with unacknowledged shame, then this emotion becomes redirected as anger toward the self and others.[68] According to Scheff and Retzinger, this condition leads to humiliated fury and, ultimately, to disrespectful, violent reactions.[69]

Other studies have likewise qualified anger and violence as (mal)adaptive responses to shame. For instance, based on prior research findings across the literature, Elison et al.[70] have interestingly suggested a psychobiological chain linking shame to anger and aggression via the experience of social pain, namely the painful feeling an individual experiences in response to the threats of social rejection or social exclusion.[71] The authors have qualified shame as an adaptive response to, or a strategy for coping with the threats of social exclusion. When people experience shame feelings, this experience is both physically and emotionally painful. Physical and emotional pain elicit anger and aggression. Thus, the authors have suggested that anger expressed through aggression is a (mal)adaptive coping strategy or psychological defense for handling shame.

Social psychology and social neuroscience studies have provided accounts of maladaptive emotional responses and violence that suggest that unhealthy social factors (e.g., emotional neglect)[72] and experiences of traumatic life events (e.g., physical abuse or exposure to violence)[73] may predispose an individual to maladaptive action tendencies and socio-affective

67 T. J. Scheff & S. M. Retzinger, *Emotions and Violence: Shame and Rage in Destructive Conflicts*, Lexington Books, Lexington 1991.

68 *Id.*

69 *See also* P. Fonagy, 'The Developmental Roots of Violence in the Failure of Mentalization', *in* F. Pfäfflin & G. Adshead (Eds.), *A Matter of Security the Application of Attachment Theory to Forensic Psychiatry and Psychotherapy*, London, J. Kingsley Publishers, 2003, p. 42 ("[t]he act of violence ... is rarely one of blind rage. Rather, it is a desperate attempt to protect the fragile self against the onslaught of shame, mostly innocently triggered by another.").

70 J. Elison, C. Garofali, & P. Velotti, 'Shame and Aggression: Theoretical Considerations', *Aggression and Violent Behavior*, Vol. 19, 2014, pp. 447-453.

71 *See, e.g.*, N. Einseberg, 'The Neural Bases of Social Pain: Evidence for Shared Representations with Physical Pain', *Psychosomatic Medicine*, Vol. 74, 2012, pp. 126-135.

72 A. N. Schore, 'Early Relational Trauma, Disorganized Attachment, and the Development of a Predisposition to Violence', *in* Daniel Siegel and Marion Solomon (Eds.), *Healing trauma: Attachment, Mind, Body, and Brain*, New York, W.W. Norton & Company 2003, pp. 107–167.

73 C. Smith & T. P. Thornberry, 'The Relationship Between Childhood Maltreatment and Adolescent Involvement in Delinquency', *Criminology*, Vol. 33, 1995, pp. 451-481; C. S. Widom, 'Does Violence Beget Violence? A Critical Examination of the Literature', *Psychological Bulletin*, Vol. 106, 1989, pp. 3-28; A. E. Wall

dysfunctions, including low self-regulation and low emotion regulation, blunted affect and lack of impulse control.[74] For instance, several neuroscientific studies have investigated the relationship between cortisol levels (i.e., biological stress response) and chronic environmental stressors and violence – especially in adolescence and young adulthood.[75]

In principle, these studies have suggested that the presence of chronic stressors and a lack of emotional and social support with which to mitigate the effects of such stressors, produce adversive and dysregulating outcomes on the individual's biological stress response with long-term negative effects on the brain, mental health and social behavior.[76] For instance, exposure to violence and contextual stressors has been associated with elevated cortisol levels and hyperresponsivity to threats in the long term. This chronic or long-lasting hyperresponsivity to threats seems to explain why people (especially youth) living in violent communities may experience 'pathological adaptations,' including a desensitization to violence.[77] Likewise, abuse, trauma, and maltreatment are also associated with elevated cortisol levels in both adolescents and adults.[78] Importantly, chronic stress has been shown to alter physiological brain function in the long term, especially in several brain regions such as the hippocampus, amygdala, and various regions of the prefrontal cortex (PFC).[79] Dysfunctions in these brain regions have been found to negatively affect moral reasoning

---

& R. P. Barth, 'Aggressive and Delinquent Behavior of Maltreated Adolescents: Risk Factors and Gender Differences', *Stress, Trauma, & Crisis*, Vol. 8, No. 1, 2005, pp. 1-24.

74 Sociological research converges on the same conclusion: social contexts can influence one's dispositions and motivations to experience specific moral feelings in given situations, and drive behavior accordingly. *See, e.g.*, C. Haney, C. Banks, & P. Zimbardo, 'Interpersonal Dynamics in A Simulated Prison', *Journal of Criminology and Penology*, Vol. 1, No. 1, 1973, pp. 69-97 (indicating that given certain circumstances, the "situation" can induce ordinary people to commit destructive deeds). *See also* K. Matzuda et al., 'Gang Membership and Adherence to the "Code of the Street"', *Justice Quarterly*, Vol. 30, No. 3, 2013, pp. 440-468 (explaining that "the code of the street can lead to gang violence by producing anticipated shame for not standing up for oneself or demanding respect"); C. Melde & F.A. Esbensen, 'Gang Membership as a Turning Point in the Life Course', *Criminology*, Vol. 49, 2011, pp. 513-552 (finding that gang membership may reduce anticipated guilt among adolescents. This finding suggests that the gang may provide situational contexts and/or normative standards that diminish or neutralize anticipated guilt and increase the use of neutralizations toward violence among its members).

75 *See, e.g.*, S. M. Ayer et al., 'Exposure to Violence Predicting Cortisol Response During Adolescence and Early Adulthood: Understanding Moderating Factors', *Journal of Youth Adolescence*, Vol. 43, No. 7, 2014, pp. 1066–1079.

76 *Id.*

77 *See* J. Garbarino, C.P. Bradshaw, J.A. Vorrasi, 'Mitigating the Effects of Gun Violence on Children and Youth', *The Future of Children*, Vol. 12, 2002, pp. 73–85.

78 E. McCrory, S. A. De Brito, & E. Viding, 'The Neurobiology and Genetics of Maltreatment and Adversity', *Journal of Child Psychology and Psychiatry*, Vol. 51, 2010, pp. 1079–1095.

79 *See, e.g.*, K. Fone & M. V. Porkess, 'Behavioural and Neurochemical Effects of Post-weaning Social Isolation in Rodents – Relevance to Developmental Neuropsychiatric Disorders', *Neuroscience & Biobehavioral Review*, Vol. 32, 2008, pp. 1087-1102; J. D. Bremner, 'Traumatic Stress: Effects on the Brain', *Dialogues in Clinical Neuroscience*, Vol. 8, 2006, pp. 445-461.

and social functioning, and to increase the risk of engaging in criminal behaviors, especially those involving aggression and violence.[80]

Overall, empirical research suggests that the underpinnings of violence are multifactorial, including socioeconomic, cultural and psychological components. Notably, empirical research suggests that most violence is not a matter of individual pathology. Most violence is created. Inequity drives violence. Lack of opportunity drives violence. On the individual level, violence is driven by shame, anger, social isolation and rejection, traumas, and an inability to meet one's economic needs. And, like so many conditions known all too well by public health professionals, violence itself drives violence.

6 Neuroscientific Research in (Forensic) Clinical Populations

Neuroscientific studies performed with (forensic) clinical populations have provided additional support that certain emotions and socio-affective functions help to protect against violence. While a direct link between the brain, mental illness, and violence is 'scientifically contestable and epistemologically untenable,'[81] neuroscientific studies have begun to highlight structural and functional alterations that underpin abnormal mental processes deemed as risk factors of aggressive and violent conduct, including – but not limited to – poor self-regulation, poor emotion regulation and deficient emotional responsiveness. Structural and functional imaging studies have indicated complex brain networks involved in each of these socio-affective mental processes. Abnormal neural responses to emotionally salient cues, particularly cues of threat and distress, have been implicated in a wide array of psychiatric conditions. Notably, abnormal neural responses

80 *See* C. Nee & Z. Verhnam, 'Expertise and Its Contribution to the Notion of Protective Factors in Offender Rehabilitation and Desistance', *Aggression and Violent Behavior*, Vol. 32, 2017, pp. 37–44 (claiming that "[t]he chaotic and impoverished background of most offenders is unlikely to offer the neurological prerequisites desired to foster cognitive, behavioural and interpersonal competencies. Sufficient nutrition, rest, a stimulating and loving environment; ample opportunity to observe prosocial be- haviour; consistent rewards for the incremental development of self-regulation and empathy for others; a childhood free from physical violence and access to toxic substances; are not the typical context of the child more likely to become an offender. These prerequisites of emotion regulation, impulse control and empathy are often sadly lacking.").

81 Amanda Pustilnik, 'Violence on the Brain: A Critique of Neuroscience in Criminal Law', *Wake Forest Law Review*, Vol. 44, 2009, pp. 183-237, p.184. Admittedly, one risk of studying the neurobiology of violence by mostly considering forensic clinical samples is to conceptualise proneness to violence as an innate biological predisposition, while violence most commonly forms under the influence of shaping social forces.

involved in the expression and regulation of emotions have been reported in schizophrenia,[82] psychopathy,[83] post-traumatic stress disorder,[84] and borderline personality disorder.[85]

Self-regulation has been defined as

> people's capacity to focus on long-term goals and resist temptation and impulses for immediate gratification. . . . As such, self-regulation involves the ability to alter thoughts, actions, and emotions in a way that serves goal striving, whether the goal is set by the self, the society or both.[86]

On the other hand, deficits in self-regulation have been associated with increased impulsiveness, or poor emotional control in response to salient stimuli.[87]

Much of what is known about the neural substrates of self-regulation comes from lesion studies in clinical populations. Various cortical and subcortical regions have been implicated in self-regulation. Among the most replicated brain regions involved in self-regulation are the ventromedial prefrontal cortex (VmPFC) and the anterior cingulate cortex[88] – both of which are critical in emotional processing, as well as in behavioral motivation and regulation. As Heatherton has suggested, damage to the VmPFC may cause a deficiency in incorporating feedback from others and social norms to make appropriate behavioral choices in social contexts, resulting in social disinhibition and inappropriate approach behavior toward other individuals.[89] Thus, damage to these brain areas has been associated with an array of dysfunctions, including the incapacity to regulate social, affective and appetitive behaviors, which may also result in aggressive and antisocial conduct. Importantly, studies on VmPFC patients have suggested that most patients appear to be fully

82 *See, e.g.*, S. Ruiz, N. Birbaumer, & R. Sitaram, 'Abnormal Neural Connectivity in Schizophrenia and fMRI-Brain-Computer Interface as a Potential Therapeutic Approach', *Frontiers in Psychiatry*, Vol. 4, 2013, pp. 1-14.

83 *See, e.g.*, J.L. Müller et al., 'Abnormalities in Emotion Processing within Cortical and Subcortical Regions in Criminal Psychopaths: Evidence from a Functional Magnetic Resonance Imaging Study Using Pictures with Emotional Content', *Biological Psychiatry, 2003*, Vol. 54, pp. 152-162.

84 *See, e.g.*, J. E. Sherin, 'Post-traumatic Stress Disorder: The Neurobiological Impact of Psychological Trauma', *Dialogues in Clinical Neuroscience*, Vol. 13, No. 3, pp. 263-278.

85 *See, e.g.*, H.W. Koenigsberg et al., 'Neural Correlates of Emotion Processing in Borderline Personality Disorder', *Psychiatry Research*, Vol. 172, No. 3, 2009, pp. 192-199.

86 L. Lazarus et al., 'The Roles of Impulsivity, Self- regulation, and Emotion Regulation in the Experience of Self-disgust', *Motivation & Emotion*, Vol. 43, 2019, p. 147.

87 T.F. Heatheron, 'Neuroscience of Self- and Self-Regulation', *Annual Review of Psychology*, Vol. 62, No. 1, 2011, pp. 363-390.

88 *Id.*

89 *Id.*

aware of the impropriety of their actions. Nevertheless, they are unable to control their dysfunctional behavior.[90]

Additional support for this perspective emerges from studies on neuropsychiatric forensic populations. These studies have implied that those who show a lack of insight into their own behavior are less inhibited regarding violating the rights of others. For instance, injury to the VmPFC and the ACC has been linked to the onset of reckless and antisocial behavior without remorse.[91] Importantly, as one study has highlighted, 'without the restraint of intuitive moral emotions and self-other conjoining . . . patients may not be able to deter an impulse to act in an unacceptable manner, even as they know right and wrong and understand the nature of their acts.'[92]

Emotion dysregulation (i.e., the incapacity to exert control over one's emotional responses to external stimuli) is another risk factor of violent behavior,[93] as well as an important subject of clinical research in affective neuroscience. Studies on emotion dysregulation have primarily focused on breakdowns in the amygdala-PFC circuit. Studies on patients with mood disorders, including depression, borderline personality disorder and post-traumatic stress disorder, have suggested exaggerated activation of the amygdala in response to emotional stimuli and reduced activation of cortical regions such as the VmPFC.[94] Taken together, these findings on dysfunctional amygdala-PFC circuitry in mood disorders highlight the importance of emotion regulation for psychological well-being and social functioning.

As for deficient emotional responsiveness, the vast majority of neuroscientific studies have focused on the thorny category of psychopathy. In a widely cited review article, Raine and

---

90 *See, e.g.*, A. Damasio, *Descartes' Error: Reason, Emotion, and the Human Brain*, Penguin Books, New York 1994, pp. 36-58; A. Bechara et al., 'Insensitivity to Future Consequences Following Damage to Human Prefrontal Cortex', *Cognition*, Vol. 50, 1994, pp. 7-15; A. Bechara, D. Tranel, & H. Damasio, 'Characterization of the Decision-Making of Patients with Ventromedial Prefrontal Cortex Lesions', *Brain*, Vol. 123, 2000, pp. 2189-2202.

91 M. Koenigs, *The Role of Prefrontal Cortex in Psychopathy*, Reviews in the Neurosciences, Vol. 23, No. 3, 2012, pp. 253-262.

92 M. F. Mendez, 'The Neurobiology of Moral Behavior: Review and Neuropsychiatric Implications', *CNS Spectrums*, Vol. 14, No. 11, 2009, pp. 608-620.

93 *See, e.g.*, T. Roberton, M. Daffern, & R.S. Bucks, 'Maladaptive Emotion Regulation and Aggression in Adult Offenders', *Psychology, Crime, & Law*, Vol. 20, 2014, pp. 933-954; K. Long et al., 'The Role of Emotion Regulation in the Relations between Psychopathy Factors and Impulsive and Premeditated Aggression', *Personality Disorders: Theory, Research, and Treatment*, Vol. 5, 2014, pp. 390-396.

94 For a meta-analysis of these studies, *see* J. Hiser & M. Koenigs, 'The Multifaceted Role of the Ventromedial Prefrontal Cortex in Emotion, Decision Making, Social Cognition, and Psychopathology', *Biological Psychiatry*, Vol. 83, 2018, pp. 638-647.

Yang[95] integrated literature on moral decision-making and antisocial behavior with a focus on psychopathy. Interestingly, the study found that the key brain areas that are either structurally or functionally impaired in patients diagnosed with psychopathy (e.g., the VmPFC or the amygdala) are the same as those forming the socio-emotional circuitry of the brain network involved in moral judgments. Impairments in these brain areas seem to be associated with the affective/interpersonal factors of psychopathy (also called Factor 1 of the Psychopathy Checklist-Revised [PCL-R]),[96] and seem to explain why patients affected by this type of disorder show severe deficits in empathic concern, callousness or emotional flatness, as well as deficiencies in using emotional information to regulate their behavior and respond to other individuals' distress. Another recent study by Espinoza et al.[97] has furthermore suggested that the affective/interpersonal symptoms of psychopathy (Factor 1) are associated with aberrant connectivity in multiple brain networks, including paralimbic regions, while no significant functional network associations were found with Factor 2 of the PCL-R (antisocial, lifestyle)[98] and total PCL-R scores. This finding appears to support the conclusion that the severe moral deficits in psychopathy are correlated by severe abnormalities in socio-emotional brain circuits that have links with moral and prosocial behavior.

Importantly, individuals with psychopathy do seem to retain a cognitive understanding of moral and legal wrongs.[99] However, as one study has suggested,[100] psychopaths treat the word 'wrong' in a purely conventional way, as if it simply means 'prohibited by local authorities'. This means that even if psychopaths are capable of *propositionally* distinguishing rightness from wrongness, and therefore of knowing the moral meaning of an action, they tend to make socially poor or immoral decisions because they are unable to generate the feelings that guide adaptive decision-making in healthy individuals. Although psychopathy represents less than 1% of the general population and the 15%-20% of the forensic population,[101] neuroscientific research on psychopathy has become the main vehicle to

95 A. Raine & Y. Yang, 'Neural Foundations to Moral Reasoning and Antisocial Behavior', *Social Cognitive Affective Neuroscience*, Vol. 1, No. 3, 2009, pp. 203-213.

96 R. D. Hare, *The Hare Psychopathy Checklist-Revised*, Multi-Health Systems, Toronto, 1991.

97 F.A. Espinoza et al., 'Aberrant Functional Network Connectivity in Psychopathy from a Large (N=985) Sample', *Human Brain Mapping*, Vol. 39, No. 6, 2018, pp. 2624-2634.

98 Hare 1991.

99 N. Levy, 'The Responsibility of the Psychopath Revisited', *Philosophy, Psychiatry & Psychology*, Vol. 129, 2007, p. 132 (claiming that psychopaths know their actions "are widely perceived to be wrong . . . they are unable to grasp the distinctive nature and significance of their wrongness")

100 R.J. Blair, 'A Cognitive Developmental Approach to Morality: Investigating the Psychopath', *Cognition*, Vol. 57, 1995, pp. 1-29.

101 K. Kiehl & M. Hoffman, 'The Criminal Psychopath: History, Neuroscience, Treatment, and Economics, Jurimetrics', 51, 2001, pp. 355-397.

suggest that deficits in emotional responsiveness is another key risk factor for moral decision-making and prosocial behavior, as well as a risk factor for antisocial violent conduct.

As I mentioned in the beginning of this section, mental illness per se typically does not cause violence. On the contrary, mediating contextual factors should be considered when analyzing this relationship. As Sivier has suggested,[102] the susceptibility to aggression and violence also depends on the psychopathological context. For instance, in the context of post-traumatic stress disorder, aggressive acts normally occur when triggered by cues that evoke the original trauma. For people with borderline personality disorder – which is characterized by extreme emotional sensitivity and dysregulation – impulsive or reactive aggression often occurs when an individual is presented with a provocation in an interpersonal context. Therefore, violence does not originate in mental disorders per se, nor are mental disorders sufficient to explain a violent episode. Rather, it is important to also account for the context in which the violent episode occurs to fully comprehend its nature and, possibly, to understand whether the episode may be linked to the individual's pathological condition.

Overall, neuroscientific research on clinical populations has confirmed the relevance of emotional faculties in morally adaptive action tendencies and social functioning. Even more importantly, these studies have suggested a dissociation between socio-affective dysfunction and cognitive understanding in producing morally adaptive social behavior. Notably, socio-affective impairments may well compromise moral and social functioning, even when the cognitive faculties of knowledge and understanding are intact.

The complexity of the multiple factors underlying violence, including by individuals with mental illness, entails several legally relevant questions. For instance, what does it mean for an individual to know of what he or she is doing when he or she commits violence? Should the individual simply possess a cognitive awareness of his or her violent actions? Or must the individual also have the capacity to affectively appreciate how his or her violent conduct impacts others? And what does it mean to be capable of being in control of one's violent impulses? Are there degrees of control that the law should recognize if the individual, while possessing the ability to understand the meaning of a course of action, lacks the capacity to apply such understanding to the current situation?

---

102 L. Sivier, 'Neurobiology of Aggression and Violence', *American Journal of Psychiatry*, Vol. 165, No. 4, pp. 429-442.

These questions are critical and worthy of an in-depth exploration in future research. In the remainder of this chapter, I suggest several ways by which these issues could potentially be addressed in criminal law discussions.

7 Implications for Criminal Law

Behavioral and neuroscientific studies on emotions, social behavior and violence provide some challenging information for criminal law and justice. First, emotions and emotion-related skills are key factors for adaptive moral and social behavior. Second, dysfunctional emotional responses to social demands increase the risk of aggressive or violent behavior. Third, emotional responses to social demands are mediated by socio-environmental influences. Fourth, adversive social factors including social exclusion and rejection promote rather than prevent violence.

This general set of questions leads to further and more criminal-violence-specific ones. 1) Could the advances in (neuro)scientific research on emotions and social behavior influence the operation of criminal law pertaining to the culpability of people who engage in criminal violence? 2) Could the (neuro)scientific advances regarding emotions and social behavior change the current punitive approach to violence?

7.1 *Culpability*

The previously illustrated (neuro)scientific insights into emotions, social factors and violence contribute to an understanding of criminal violence that is more complex than what it is commonly assumed in criminal law and lay views. This suggested complexity has led several authors to ask whether and how the law could incorporate such knowledge to revise the orthodox canons of culpability for perpetrators of violent crimes.[103] The answer to this question is, *prima facie*, certainly negative. First and most importantly, the empirical evidence and knowledge about the neuropsychological dynamics and mechanisms correlated with specific types of behaviors (e.g., violent behaviors) are not sufficient per se to have an influence on normative parameters of culpability.[104] On the contrary, supporting nor-

103 *See, e.g.*, P. Sasso, 'Implementing the Death Penalty: The Moral Implications of Recent Advances in Neuropsychology', *Cardozo Law Review*, Vol. 29, 2007, pp. 765-818.

104 *See, e.g.*, C. Campbell, 'The Neurobiology of Violence: Science and Law', *in* S. Richmond, G. Rees, & S. Edwards (Eds.), *I Know What You're Thinking: Brain Imaging and Mental Privacy*, Oxford, Oxford University Press, 2012, p. 145 (arguing that "under the rules for 'insanity' in most common law jurisdictions the requirement that the defendant either did not 'know' the 'nature and quality' of their actions per se, or that their actions were 'legally wrong', would *not* seem to be such as to allow for a lack of 'feeling' of

mative arguments are necessary to legitimize the potential use of such insights to induce any normative change to the parameters of culpability for these behavioral categories.

Second, criminal culpability is a general paradigm. As such, it not only concerns violent crimes, but also *all* criminally relevant behaviors. Thus, an analysis of the potential implications of neuropsychological knowledge about violence regarding criminal culpability must be preceded by an analysis of the impact of neuropsychological insights into emotions and socio-environmental influences on the general tenets of criminal culpability.

The possible inclusion of emotions, and social factors, within culpability assessments is not a new topic in Western legal debates.[105] Notably, this issue has been in the center of long-standing debates between subjectivist and objectivist stances in substantive criminal law.[106] As Sasso has reported,[107] subjectivist legal scholars have provided a variety of normative definitions of the relevant emotion-related capacities an individual must possess to qualify as a full moral agent including 1) the capacity to care for the interests of other humans; 2) the capacity to engage in the moral evaluation of one's self and experience moral emotions such as guilt, remorse and resentment; 3) the capacity to internalize the normative expectations of others; 4) the capacity to identify oneself as a participant in the community's blaming practices; and 5) the capacity to control one's conduct to the extent necessary to act in accordance with one's moral judgments.

The combination of these insights and the above illustrated empirical insights into the relevance of emotions and social factors in understanding moral and antisocial behavior lays the foundation for two main critiques of the current (purely) mental foundations of culpability. The first critique concerns an overreliance on cognitive faculties in culpability ascriptions. The essential claim is that moral decisions and behavior emerge from an integrated core of intertwined (cognitive and emotional) functions wherein emotions are key determinants of the decision to act either in accordance with or in breach of the normative requirements. Thus, as Sasso has observed,

morality to be sufficient for the defence to hold. Hence, the oft repeated complaint that insanity is inadequate as a defence in that it allows only for defects of cognition and not defects of emotion, or of emotional regulation. In this context, new neuroscience information of the sort described by Raine et al. is irrelevant, because the law essentially defines it to be so").

105 *See, e.g.*, J. Horder, 'Cognition, Emotion and Criminal Culpability', *Law Quarterly Review*, Vol. 106, 1990, pp.469-486; S. Pillsbury, *Judging Evil: Rethinking the Law of Murder and Manslaughter*, New York University Press, New York 1998; P. Arenella, 'Convicting the Morally Blameless: Reassessing the Relationship between Legal and Moral Accountabiliy', *UCLA Law Review*, Vol. 39, No. 6, 1992, pp. 1511-1622.

106 G. Fletcher, *Rethinking Criminal Law*, Little Brown, Boston 1978.

107 Sasso 2007, pp. 774-775.

> a *full* moral agent must possess not only the necessary cognitive foundation to understand moral norms on an intellectual level . . . but also the capacity to emotionally appreciate and understand moral norms, e.g., self-identify with moral norms and be vulnerable to feelings of guilt and remorse when he fails to conform his conduct in accordance with them. …Moreover, emotional knowledge is critical to the declarative recall of socially relevant facts … to ensure adequate social behavior in real-time and circumstances.[108]

The second consequential critique concerns the abstract construct of criminal wrongdoing that underlies culpability ascriptions. Several scholars support the view that crime should not be addressed as simply as a discrete species of wrongdoing that is perpetrated against the law of the state. More broadly, crime should be viewed and addressed as a negative interpersonal interaction, a 'violation of people and [social] relationships'.[109] If one acknowledges this more comprehensive relational account of crime, then a cognitivist account of culpability appears to reflect only a partial understanding of the relevant mechanisms that contribute to an individual's decision to do wrong and violate a social relationship in a particular situation. Thus, assessing whether an account of a rational moral agent's attributes is based on a defensible vision of humans as social beings requires criminal law to assign more prominence to the (mental) dynamics that actually and critically contribute to adaptive social behavior in morally relevant contexts. Because the emotional experience in a particular social context or interpersonal situation is pivotal to the individual's decision to violate the law, whether criminal law provides an accurate and just inquiry into the commission of offences warrants consideration.

In view of this critique, perhaps the notion of culpability could more accurately be expanded and grounded in *situated*[110] decision-making instead in abstract decision-making. That is, culpability could be 'situated' in all relevant factors that determine an individual's deliberation regarding whether to engage in wrongdoing on a particular occasion. Accordingly, such an evaluation of culpability should not be limited to an inquiry into cognitive states and faculties at the time of the offence, but should also examine the situation that gave rise to the experience of given emotions, the appropriateness of an individual's behavioral response to those emotions in that particular instance and the invididual's capacity to appropriately emotionally respond to that situation.

---

108 *Id.*, p. 776.

109 Howard Zehr, *Changing Lenses: Restorative Justice for Our Times*, 25th Anniversary edn., Herald Press, Harrisonbourg (VA) 2015, pp. 184-188.

110 *Cf.* A. Norrie, 'Practical Reasoning and Criminal Responsibility: A Jurisprudential Approach', *in* D. B. Cornish & R. V. Clarke (Eds.), *The Reasoning Criminal: Rational Choice Perspectives on Offending*, New York, Routledge, 2014, pp. 217-230.

A deeper contextualization of criminal choices and behaviors within further relevant dynamics that support decision-making and behavior in morally salient situations conditions culpability on a *holistic* judgement[111] of the agent's (capacity for) rational moral agency. With a more holistic lens regarding culpable choices, the notion of culpability could ultimately embrace further elements *in addition to* the current prototypically cognitive ones, including the agent's *capacity to emotionally appreciate* the moral significance of his or her action to comply with applicable norms on a particular occasion (e.g., the agent's capacity to emotionally respond to morally salient stimuli like the harm suffered by the victim) as well as the agent's *unjustifiable* feeling of disregard for a *fair* opportunity[112] to avoid wrongdoing on that particular occasion. Including further mental factors within the general notion of culpability may entail several consequences at the doctrinal level. These consequences may include a more in-depth evaluation of motives for *mens rea* purposes; a re-analysis of the relationship between justifications such as self-defense and *mens rea*, a more dimensional evaluation of the perpetrator's mental capacities at the time of the offence; a more in-depth evaluation of the potential influence of the social environment, including the individual's personal history and social background, on the perpetrator's choice and behavior. Due to space constraints, I cannot explore in depth the doctrinal corollaries that would follow from the proposed holistic paradigm of culpability. There is substantial complexity to a normative argument of how and why substantive criminal law could revise the parameters of culpability to increase the prominence of the socio-emotional dimension of wrongdoers. Such an argument requires a careful and detailed scholarly endeavor, which I have undertaken in other works.[113]

Overall, the promotion of a doctrinal debate around a paradigm shift in culpability standards in view of the (neuro)science of emotions and socio-environmental influences may encourage criminal law scholars to rethink orthodox perspectives on substantive criminal law in the light of the empirical knowledge. If the criminal law is to retain its humanity, it cannot ignore the complexities of the human brain and its relationship with the social environment, as they bear on an individual's capacity for moral agency and, hence, on his or her culpability.

---

111 *Cf.* K. Kesser Ferzan 2007.

112 *Cf.* D. O. Brink & D. K. Nelkin 2013.

113 F. Coppola, *The Emotional Brain and The Guilty Mind: A Novel Paradigm of Criminal Culpability*, Hart Publishing, Oxford (forthcoming); F. Coppola, 'Motus Animi in Mente Insana: An Emotion-Oriented Paradigm of Legal Insanity Informed by the Neuroscience of Moral Judgments and Decision-Making', *The Journal of Criminal Law and Criminology*, Vol. 109, No. 1, 2019, pp. 1-68.

7.2 *Punishment*

Less popular in neurolegal debates – but yet more concrete – is the specific contribution of the above illustrated body of (neuro)scientific information to a rethinking of criminal justice responses to people who have commited violent crimes, belonging to either non-clinical or clinical populations.

While different justice systems adopt diverse conceptions and applications of punishment – ranging from more prototypically retributive to more prototypically rehabilitative ones – criminal violence generally calls for more severe and restrictive punitive responses, which often include more intense security regimes characterized by restricted living conditions, periods of isolation, and limited access to benefits and social activities.[114]

Contrary to the popular belief that violence should be dealt with via punitiveness and restriction, numerous empirical studies have consistently shown that restrictive and isolating punitive treatments appear to precipitate or exacerbate the same psychological risk factors of violence.[115] Specifically, this research suggests that excessively restrictive and tendentially exclusionary punitive measures not only risk promoting or aggravating the same negative feelings that have been associated with violence (e.g., shame, humiliation, low self-esteem, low-self-respect, anger and hostility),[116] but they also demotivate moral feelings that are positively associated with prosocial behavior. In other words, by stimulating the same negative feelings that are positively associated with violence, exclusionary and punitive approaches to violence risk creating a vicious cycle of negative emotions that is not only psychologically damaging but is also counterproductive.

However, several authors[117] have suggested that responses to people who have engaged in violent acts should be designed to decrease maladaptive feelings of shame and encourage emotions that inhibit violence toward others, such as self-respect, self-esteem, empathy with the suffering of others, as well as feelings of guilt and remorse over impulses to harm

114 *See supra* note 30.

115 *See, e.g.*, J. Gilligan, 'Punishment and Violence: Is Criminal Law Based on a Huge Mistake?', *Social Research*, Vol. 67, pp. 745-772; Craig Haney, 'The Psychological Impact of Incarceration: Implications for Post-Prison Adjustment', *in* J. Travis & M. Waul (Eds.), *Prisoners Once Removed The Impact of Incarceration and Reentry on Children, Families, and Communities*, Washington, D.C., The Urban Institute Press, 2003, pp. 33-66; P. Scharff Smith, 'The Effects of Solitary Confinement on Prison Inmates: A Brief History and Review of the Literature', *Crime & Justice*, Vol. 34, 2006, pp. 441-528; S. Hulley, B. Crewe, & S. Wright, 'Re-examining the Problems of Long-term Imprisonment', *The British Journal of Criminology*, Vol. 56, No. 4, 2016, pp. 769-792; J. Meijers et al. 'Reduced Self-Control After 3 Months of Imprisonment: A Pilot Study', *Frontiers in Psychology*, Vol. 9, 2018.

116 Gilligan, *id.*

117 Gilligan, *id.*

others. Because such feelings are best created in inclusionary and stimulating environments, programs should feature a wide range of socially rehabilitative strategies in community-like settings or therapeutic communities, to help perpetrators to overcome their (often profound) feelings of rejection, exclusion and humiliation and to empower them to value positive aspects of their social identity and act in prosocial ways through dialogue, cooperation and acceptance.[118]

Importantly, these psychological insights find support in brain-based studies that have begun exploring – though indirectly – the generalized negative impact of the prison environment[119] and, specifically, of particularly harsh correctional practices such as solitary confinement,[120] on the brain and behavior. Collectively, these studies have suggested that both overcrowded and isolating prison environments may precipitate or aggravate specific neurobiological alterations, which, in their turn, may fuel specific risk factors for antisocial behavior, such as emotion dysregulation or blunted affect. Consequently, such environments may stimulate maladaptive patterns of behavior, especially in 'individuals who are chronic offenders, where existing neurobiological vulnerabilities are intensified in settings of confinement and segregation.'[121]

Overall, while empirical evidence per se cannot challenge certain theoretical approaches to punishment, at the same time, insights into the social brain and behavior may suggest a revision of ordinary ways of conceiving of restrictive and exclusionary punishment as an effective response to crime and, especially, violent crime. Rather, such insights may support socio-rehabilitative strategies, which give more space to less restrictive and more inclusionary strategies including restorative justice-based processes, education, job-training and re-entry programs designed to help perpetrators to effectively reintegrate into their communities.

Granted, this kind of evidence may imply different consequences for different legal systems adopting diverse conceptions and applications of punishment. For instance, the consequences of this body of knowledge may be particularly significant in systems like that of the United States, which endorses an understanding of retribution that has become fused

---

118 J. Gilligan & B. Lee, 'Beyond the Prison Paradigm: From Provoking Violence to Preventing It by Creating Anti-prisons (Residential Colleges and Therapeutic Communities)', *Annals of the New York Academy of Science*, Vol. 1036, 2004, pp. 300-324.

119 A. Baskin-Sommers & K. Fontaneau, 'Correctional Change Through Neuroscience', *Fordham Law Review*, Vol. 85, pp. 423-436.

120 *See, e.g.*, Scharff Smith 2006; T.A. Kupers, *Solitary: The Inside Story of Supermax Isolation and How We Can Abolish It*, University of California Press, Oakland, California 2017.

121 Baskin-Sommers & Fontaneau 2016, p. 428.

with harsh punitiveness, suffering and social revenge, especially for violent perpetrators. On the other hand, in countries that adopt a theoretical model of punishment that aims for resocialization, such as the continental European ones, these studies could strengthen their rehabilitative ideal and encourage alternative ways of dealing with violence, including restorative-justice-based practices.

Admittedly, the issue of how to deal with specific classes of perpetrators with a stronger rehabilitation approach remains open. Evidence on how to deal with people suffering from specific socio-affective personality disorders – notably, psychopathy – needs to be more solid. Research on alternatives to regular incarceration for this particular popolation should remain a central tenet of ongoing and future research initiatives.

8 Conclusion

I conclude this chapter by emphasizing the comprehensive and multidimensional meaning of its title, *Bringing (the right) feelings back*. The potential of social and affective neuroscience, coupled with studies from social and personality psychology, in supporting a different legal approach to criminal violence does not simply entail acknowledging and valuing the socio-affective dimension of perpetrators in culpability attributions or in justice responses. More broadly, the potential of this body of empirical knowledge is to change the lenses through which criminal law and justice systems view and address criminal violence.

Notably, this body of knowledge could contribute to humanizing violence in the legal and public eye, with society no longer viewing violence as symptomatic of dangerous wickedness, but rather as symptomatic of the universal human fallibility, which too often hides profound and unresolved trauma. A stronger sensitivity on the part of criminal law and justice systems to preponderant factors of violent behaviors may lead to a rethinking of how violence is adjudicated and addressed, and ultimately lead to responses that do not rely on social rejection and exclusion as ways of challenging violent wrongdoing. Importantly, a greater humanization of violence may lead criminal law and justice to acknowledge and value an individual's capacity for positive change, something inherent to each human, including those who commit the worst and most harmful acts. Ultimately, it may lead to effective responses to violence that actually prevent it rather than aggravate or redistribute it.

Admittedly, whether and how this body of scientific knowledge may be incorporated in legal standards and practices represent a complex interdisciplinary challenge. Only a strong synergy among legal scholars, psychologists, neuroscientists, sociologists, and psychiatrists can bring meaningful change to complex issues like the prevention and reduction of criminal violence. While I acknowledge the ambition of this long-term project, I also believe it is worth attempting.

References

American Law Institute, Model Penal Code, 1962

Anyagwe, C., *Criminal Law: The General Part*, Langaa RPCIG, 2015

Arenella, P., 'Convicting the Morally Blameless: Reassessing the Relationship between Legal and Moral Accountabiliy', *UCLA Law Review*, Vol. 39, No. 6, 1992, pp. 1511-1622

Askar, P.J. & Kenny D.T., 'Views from the Inside: Young Offenders' Subjective Experiences of Incarceration', *International Journal of Offender Therapy and Comparative Criminology*, Vol. 52, 2008, pp. 584-597

Ayer, S. M., Heinze, J.E., Miller, A.L., Stoddard, S.A. & Zimmerman, M.A., 'Exposure to Violence Predicting Cortisol Response During Adolescence and Early Adulthood: Understanding Moderating Factors', *Journal of Youth Adolescence*, Vol. 43, No. 7, 2014, pp. 1066–1079

Bandes, S., 'Remorse and Criminal Justice', *Emotion Review*, Vol. 8, N.1, 2016, pp. 14-19

Baskin-Sommers, A. & Fontaneau, K., 'Correctional Change Through Neuroscience', *Fordham Law Review*, Vol. 85, pp.423-436

Baumeister, R.F., Stillwell, A.M. & Heatherton, T.F., 'Guilt: An Interpersonal Approach', *Psychological Bulletin*, Vol. 115, No. 2, 1994, pp. 243-267

Bechara, A., Damasio, A.R., Damasio, H., & Anderson, S.W., 'Insensitivity to Future Consequences Following Damage to Human Prefrontal Cortex', *Cognition*, Vol. 50, 1994, pp. 7-15

Bechara, A., Tranel, D., & Damasio, H., 'Characterization of the Decision-Making of Patients with Ventromedial Prefrontal Cortex Lesions', *Brain*, Vol. 123, 2000, pp. 2189-2202

Bibas, S., *The Machinery of Criminal Justice*, New York: Oxford University Press, 2012

Blair, R.J, 'A Cognitive Developmental Approach to Morality: Investigating the Psychopath', *Cognition*, Vol. 57, 1995, pp. 1-29

Blair, R. J. & Fowler, K., 'Moral Emotions and Moral Reasoning from the Perspective of Affective Cognitive Neuroscience: A Selective Review', *European Journal of Developmental Science*, Vol. 2, 2008, pp. 303-323

Bogert, C., 'How the Media Help Drive Harsh Criminal Justice Policies', *Los Angeles Times*, 31 May, 2019

Bremner, J. D., 'Traumatic Stress: Effects on the Brain', *Dialogues in Clinical Neuroscience*, Vol. 8, 2006, pp. 445-461

Brink, D.O. & Nelkin D.K. (2013). 'Fairness and the Architecture of Responsibility', *in* D. Shoemaker (Ed.), *Oxford Studies in Agency and Responsibility* Vol. 1, New York: Oxford University Press, pp. 284-313

Brown, B., I Thought It Was Just Me (But It Isn't): Making the Journey from 'What Will People Think?' to 'I Am Enough', New York: Gotham Books, 2007

Campbell, C. (2012). 'The Neurobiology of Violence: Science and Law', *in* S. Richmond, G. Rees, & S. Edwards (Eds.), *I Know What You're Thinking: Brain Imaging and Mental Privacy*, Oxford: Oxford University Press, pp. 139-154

Claessen, J., Forgiveness in Criminal Law Through Incorporating Restorative Mediation, Oisterwijk: Wolf Legal Publishers, 2017

Coppola, F., 'Motus Animi in Mente Insana: An Emotion-Oriented Paradigm of Legal Insanity Informed by the Neuroscience of Moral Judgments and Decision-Making', *The Journal of Criminal Law and Criminology*, Vol. 109, No. 1, 2019, pp. 1-68

Coppola, F., The Emotional Brain and The Guilty Mind: A Novel Paradigm of Criminal Culpability, London: Hart Publishing, forthcoming

Coricelli, G., Dolan, R.J. & Sirigu, A., 'Brain, Emotion, and Decision-Making: The Paradigmatic Example of Regret', *Trends in Cognitive Science*, Vol. 11, pp. 258-265

Cozolino, L., Neuroscience of Human Relationships: Attachment and the Developing Social Brain (2nd ed.), New York: W.W. Norton & Company, 2014

Damasio, A., Descartes' Error: Reason, Emotion, and the Human Brain, New York: Penguin Books, 1994

Damasio, A., The Feeling of What Happens: Body and Emotions in The Making of Consciousness, San Diego: Harcourt Trade, 1999

Davidson, R., 'Cognitive Neuroscience Needs Affective Neuroscience (and Vice Versa)', *Brain and Cognition*, Vol. 42, 2000, pp. 89-92

Davis, M. H., 'Measuring Individual Differences in Empathy: Evidence for a Multidimensional Approach', *Journal of Personality and Social Psychology*, Vol. 44, 1983, pp. 113-126

Decety, J. & Cowell, J. M., 'Empathy, Justice, and Moral Behavior', *AJOB Neuroscience*, Vol. 6, 2015, pp. 3-14

Decety, J. & Cowell, J. M., 'Friends or Foes: Is Empathy Necessary for Moral Behavior?', *Perspectives on Psychological Science*, Vol. 9, 2015, pp. 525-537

Duff, R.A., *Trials and Punishments*, Cambridge: Cambridge University Press, 1986

Duff, R.A., 'Choice, Character, and Criminal Liability', *Law & Philosophy*, Vol. 12, No. 4, 1993, pp. 345-383

Dowler, K., 'Media Consumption and Public Attitudes Toward Crime and Justice: The Relationship Between Fear of Crime, Punitive Attitudes and Perceived Political Effectiveness', *Journal of Criminal Justice and Popular Culture*, Vol. 10, No. 2, 2009, pp. 109-126

Eisenberg, N., Eggum, N. & Di Giunta, L., 'Empathy-related Responding: Associations with Prosocial Behavior, Aggression, and Intergroup Relations', *Social Issues Policy Review*, Vol. 4, No. 1, 2010, pp. 143-180

Ekman, P. (1999). 'Basic Emotions', *in* T. Dalgleish & M. J. Power (Eds.), *Handbook of Cognition and Emotion*, New York: John Wiley & Sons Ltd., pp. 45-60

Einseberg, N., 'The Neural Bases of Social Pain: Evidence for Shared Representations with Physical Pain', *Psychosomatic Medicine*, Vol. 74, 2012, pp. 126-135

Elison, J., Garofali, C. & Velotti, P., 'Shame and Aggression: Theoretical Considerations', *Aggression and Violent Behavior*, Vol. 19, 2014, pp. 447-453

Espinoza, F.A. et al., 'Aberrant Functional Network Connectivity in Psychopathy from a Large (N=985) Sample', *Human Brain Mapping*, Vol. 39, No. 6, 2018, pp. 2624-2634

Faqir, R., 'The Philosophy of Punishment: A Study to the History of Classical and Positive Schools of Penology', 1 *Forensic Research & Criminology International Journal*, Vol. 1, No. 6, 2015, 1-8

Ferguson, R., 'Violence, Crime, and Violent Crime', *International Journal of Conflict and Violence*, Vol. 3, N.1, 2009, pp. 23-29

Finkel, N. & Parrot G., *Emotions & Culpability: How the Law is At Odds with Psychology, Jurors, and Itself*, Washington D.C.: American Psychological Association, 2006

Fletcher, G., *Rethinking Criminal Law*, Boston: Little Brown, 1978

Fonagy, P. (2003). 'The Developmental Roots of Violence in the Failure of Mentalization', *in* F. Pfäfflin & G. Adshead (Eds.), *A Matter of Security the Application of Attachment Theory to Forensic Psychiatry and Psychotherapy*, London, J. Kingsley Publishers, pp. 13-56

Fone, K. & Porkess, M. V., 'Behavioural and Neurochemical Effects of Post-weaning Social Isolation in Rodents – Relevance to Developmental Neuropsychiatric Disorders', *Neuroscience & Biobehavioral Review*, Vol. 32, 2008, pp. 1087-1102

Fridja, N.H. (2004). 'Emotions and Actions', *in* A. Manstead, N. Fridja & A. Fisher (Eds), *Feelings and Emotions*, Cambridge: Cambridge University Press, pp. 158-173

Gabriel, U. & Greve, W., 'The Psychology of Fear of Crime: Conceptual and Methodological Perspectives', *British Journal of Criminology*, Vol. 43, No. 3, 2003, pp. 600-614

Garbarino, J., Bradshaw, C.P. & Vorrasi, J.A., 'Mitigating the Effects of Gun Violence on Children and Youth', *The Future of Children*, Vol. 12, 2002, pp. 73-85

Garland, D., *The Culture of Control: Crime and Social Order in Contemporary Society*, New York: Oxford University Press 2001

Gilligan, J. *Violence: Reflections on a National Epidemic*, New York: Putnam, 1996

Gilligan, J., 'Punishment and Violence: Is Criminal Law Based on a Huge Mistake?', *Social Research*, Vol. 67, 2000, pp. 745-772

Gilligan, J. & Lee, B., 'Beyond the Prison Paradigm: From Provoking Violence to Preventing It by Creating Anti-prisons (Residential Colleges and Therapeutic Communities), *Annals of the New York Academy of Science*, Vol. 1036, 2004, pp. 300-324

Giordano, P., Schroeder, R.D. & Cernkovich, S.A., 'Emotions and Crime Over the Life Course: A Neo-meadian Perspective on Criminal Continuity and Change', *American Journal of Sociology*, Vol. 112, 2007, pp. 1603-1661

Haidt, J. (2003). 'The Moral Emotions', *in* R. Davidson, K. Scherer, & H. Hill Goldsmith (Eds.), *Handbook of Affective Sciences*, New York: Oxford University Press, pp. 852-870

Haney, C., Banks, C. & Zimbardo, P., 'Interpersonal Dynamics in A Simulated Prison', *Journal of Criminology and Penology*, Vol. 1, No. 1, 1973, 69-97

Haney, C. (2003). 'The Psychological Impact of Incarceration: Implications for Post-Prison Adjustment', *in* J. Travis & M. Waul (Eds.), *Prisoners Once Removed the Impact of Incarceration and Reentry on Children, Families, and Communities*, Washington, D.C.: The Urban Institute Press, pp. 33-66

Heatheron T.F., 'Neuroscience of Self- and Self-Regulation', *Annual Review of Psychology*, Vol. 62, No. 1, 2011, pp. 363-390

Hare, R.D., The Hare Psychopathy Checklist-Revised, Toronto: Multi-Health Systems, 1991

Harris, N., 'Reassessing the Dimensionality of Moral Emotions, *British Journal of Psychology*, Vol. 94, No. 4, 2003, pp. 457-473

Hart, H.L.A., Punishment and Responsibility: Essays in the Philosophy of Law, Oxford: Oxford University Press, 1967

Hiser, J. & Koenigs, M., 'The Multifaceted Role of the Ventromedial Prefrontal Cortex in Emotion, Decision Making, Social Cognition, and Psychopathology', *Biological Psychiatry*, Vol. 83, 2018, pp. 638-647

Horder, J., 'Cognition, Emotion and Criminal Culpability', *Law Quarterly Review*, Vol. 106, 1990, pp.469-486

Hulley, S., Crewe, B., & Wright, S., 'Re-examining the Problems of Long-term Imprisonment', *The British Journal of Criminology*, Vol. 56, No. 4, 2016, pp. 769-792

Husak, D., '"Broad" Culpability and the Retributivist Dream', *Ohio State Journal of Criminal Law*, Vol. 9, 2012, pp. 449-485

Johnson, C.L. (2013). 'The Effects of Imprisonment', *in* F. Cullen & P. Wilcox (Eds.), *The Oxford Handbook of Criminological Theory and Criminal Justice*, New York: Oxford University Press, pp. 672-690

Kalmoe, N., 'Yes, Political Rhetoric Can Incite Violence', *Politico Magazine*, 30 October, 2018

Keiler, J. & Roef, D. (Eds.), *Comparative Concepts of Criminal Law* 2nd edn, Cambridge: Intersentia, 2016

Kesser Ferzan, K., 'Holistic Culpability', *Cardozo Law Review*, Vol. 28, N. 6, 2007, pp. 2523-2543

Kiehl, K & Hoffman, M., 'The Criminal Psychopath: History, Neuroscience, Treatment, and Economics, Jurimetrics', 51, 2001, pp. 355-397

Koenigs, M., *The Role of Prefrontal Cortex in Psychopathy*, Reviews in the Neurosciences, Vol. 23, No. 3, 2012, pp. 253-262

Koenigsberg, H.W. et al., 'Neural Correlates of Emotion Processing in Borderline Personality Disorder', *Psychiatry Research*, Vol. 172, No. 3, 2009, pp. 192-199

Kupers, T.A., *Solitary: The Inside Story of Supermax Isolation and How We Can Abolish It*, Oakland, California: University of California Press, 2017

Lazarus, L., Ypsilianti, A., Powell, P., & Overton, P.G., 'The Roles of Impulsivity, Self-regulation, and Emotion Regulation in the Experience of Self-disgust', *Motivation & Emotion*, Vol. 43, 2019, pp. 145-158

Lebowitz, M. S. & Dovidio, J. F., 'Implications of Emotion Regulation Strategies for Empathic Concern, Social Attitudes, and Helping Behavior', Emotion, Vol. 15, 2015, pp. 187-194

Levenson, R.W., 'The Interpersonal Functions of Emotions', *Cognition and Emotion*, Vol. 13, No. 5, 1999, pp. 481-504

Levy, N. 'The Responsibility of the Psychopath Revisited', *Philosophy, Psychiatry & Psychology*, Vol. 129, 2007, pp. 129-138

Lippke, R., 'Retribution and Incarceration', *Public Affairs Quarterly*, Vol. 17, 2003, pp. 29-48

Long, K., Felton, J.W., Lilienfeld, S.O., & Lejuez, C. W., 'The Role of Emotion Regulation in the Relations between Psychopathy Factors and Impulsive and Premeditated Aggression', *Personality Disorders: Theory, Research, and Treatment*, Vol. 5, 2014, pp. 390-396

Matzuda, K., Melde, C., Taylor, T.J., Freng, A. & Esbensen, F.A., 'Gang Membership and Adherence to the "Code of the Street"', *Justice Quarterly*, Vol. 30, No. 3, 2013, pp. 440-468

McCrory, E., De Brito, S. A. & Viding, E., 'The Neurobiology and Genetics of Maltreatment and Adversity', *Journal of Child Psychology and Psychiatry*, Vol. 51, 2010, pp. 1079–1095

Meijers, J., Harte J.M., Meynen G., Cuijpers P., Scherder E.J.A., 'Reduced Self-Control After 3 Months of Imprisonment: A Pilot Study', *Frontiers in Psychology*, Vol. 9, 2018

Melde, C. & Esbensen, F.A., 'Gang Membership as a Turning Point in the Life Course', *Criminology*, Vol. 49, 2011, pp. 513-552

Mendez, M. F., 'The Neurobiology of Moral Behavior: Review and Neuropsychiatric Implications', *CNS Spectrums*, Vol. 14, No. 11, 2009, pp. 608-620

Moors, A., Ellsworth, P.C., Scherer, K.R. & Fridja, N.H., 'Appraisal Theories of Emotion: State of the Art and Future Development', *Emotion Review*, Vol. 5, pp. 119-124

Morse, S.J., 'Reason, Result, and Criminal Responsibility', *University of Illinois Law Review*, 2004, pp. 363-444

Müller, J.L. et al., 'Abnormalities in Emotion Processing within Cortical and Subcortical Regions in Criminal Psychopaths: Evidence from a Functional Magnetic Resonance Imaging Study Using Pictures with Emotional Content', Biological Psychiatry, 2003, Vol. 54, pp. 152-162

Nee, C. & Verhnam, Z., 'Expertise and Its Contribution to the Notion of Protective Factors in Offender Rehabilitation and Desistance, Aggression and Violent Behavior, Vol. 32, 2017, pp. 37-44

Norrie, A. (2014). 'Practical Reasoning and Criminal Responsibility: A Jurisprudential Approach', *in* D. B. Cornish & R. V. Clarke (Eds.), *The Reasoning Criminal: Rational Choice Perspectives on Offending*, New York: Routledge, pp. 217-230

Nussbaum, M., *Women and Human Development*, New York: Cambridge University Press, 2000

Okon-Singer, H., Hendler, T., Pessoa, L. & Shackman, A.J., 'The Neurobiology of Emotion–Cognition Interactions: *Fundamental Questions and Strategies for Future Research'*, *Frontiers in Human Neuroscience*, Vol. 9, 2015, pp. 1-14

Pascual, L., Rodriguez, P. & Gallardo-Pujol, D., 'How does Morality Work in the Brain?', *Frontiers in Integrative Neuroscience*, Vol. 1, 2013, pp. 1-8

Pillsbury, S., Judging Evil: Rethinking the Law of Murder and Manslaughter, New York: New York University Press, 1998

Pillsbury, S., 'Emotions and Criminal Punishment in Theory and Practice', 2016, http://emotionresearcher.com/emotion-and-criminal-punishment-in principle-and-in-practice/

Preckel, K. & Singer, T., 'On the Interaction of Social Affect and Social Cognition: Empathy, Compassion, and Theory of Mind', *Current Opinion in Behavioral Science*, Vol. 19, 2018, pp. 1-6

Pustilnik, A., 'Violence on the Brain: A Critique of Neuroscience in Criminal Law', *Wake Forest Law Review*, Vol. 44, 2009, pp. 183-237

Raine, A. & Yang, Y., 'Neural Foundations to Moral Reasoning and Antisocial Behavior', *Social Cognitive Affective Neuroscience*, Vol. 1, N. 3, 2009, pp. 203-213

Ristroph, A., 'Criminal Law in the Shadow of Violence', *Alabama Law Review*, Vol. 62, No. 3, 2011, pp. 570-621

Roberton, T., Daffern, M. & Bucks, R.S., 'Maladaptive Emotion Regulation and Aggression in Adult Offenders', *Psychology, Crime, & Law*, Vol. 20, 2014, pp. 933-954

Ruiz, S., Birbaumer, N. & Sitaram, R., 'Abnormal Neural Connectivity in Schizophrenia and fMRI-Brain-Computer Interface as a Potential Therapeutic Approach', *Frontiers in Psychiatry*, Vol. 4, 2013, pp. 1-14

Sabini, J. & Silver, M., 'In Defense of Shame: Shame in the Context of Guilt and Embarrassment', *Journal for the Theory of Social Behavior*, Vol. 27, No. 1, 2001, pp. 1-15

Sasso, P., 'Implementing the Death Penalty: The Moral Implications of Recent Advances in Neuropsychology', *Cardozo Law Review*, Vol. 29, 2007, pp. 765-818

Scharff, Smith P., 'The Effects of Solitary Confinement on Prison Inmates: A Brief History and Review of the Literature', *Crime & Justice*, Vol. 34, 2006, pp. 441-528

Scheff, T. J. & Retzinger, S. M., *Emotions and Violence: Shame and Rage in Destructive Conflicts*, Lexington: Lexington Books, 1991

Schnittker, J.A., 'Enduring Stigma: The Long-term Effects of Incarceration on Health', *Journal of Health and Social Behavior*, Vol. 48, 2007, pp. 115-130

Schore, A. N. (2003). 'Early Relational Trauma, Disorganized Attachment, and the Development of a Predisposition to Violence', *in* Daniel Siegel and Marion Solomon (Eds.), *Healing trauma: Attachment, Mind, Body, and Brain*, New York: W.W. Norton & Company, pp. 107–167

Sherin, J. E., 'Post-traumatic Stress Disorder: The Neurobiological Impact of Psychological Trauma', *Dialogues in Clinical Neuroscience*, Vol. 13, No. 3, pp. 263-278

Sivier, L., 'Neurobiology of Aggression and Violence', *American Journal of Psychiatry*, Vol. 165, No. 4, pp. 429-442

Smith, C. & Thornberry, T. P., 'The Relationship Between Childhood Maltreatment and Adolescent Involvement in Delinquency', *Criminology*, Vol. 33, 1995, pp. 451-481

Smith, R.H., Webster, M., Gerrod Parrott, W., Eyre, H.L., 'The Role of Public Exposure in Moral and Nonmoral Shame and Guilt', *Journal of Personality and Social Psychology*, Vol. 83, No. 1, 2002, pp. 138-159

Stewing, J., Tangney, J.P., Heigel, C., Harty, L., McCloskey, L. 'Shaming, Blaming, and Maiming: Functional Links Among the Moral Emotions, Externalization of Blame, and Aggression', *Journal of Research in Personality*, Vol. 44, No. 1, 2010, pp. 91-102

Stolk, S., 'A Sophisticated Beast? On the Construction of an 'Ideal' Perpetrator in the Opening Statements of International Criminal Trials', *European Journal of International Law*, Vol. 29, No. 3, pp. 677-701

Tangney, J. P., 'Moral Affect: The Good, The Bad, and The Ugly', *Journal of Personality and Social Psychology*, Vol. 61, No. 4, 1991, pp. 598-607

Tangney, J.P., Stewing, J. & Mashek, D.J., 'Moral Emotions and Moral Behavior', *Annual Review of Psychology*, Vol. 58, 2007, pp. 345-372

Tangney, J.P., Stewing, J. & Hafez, L., 'Shame, Guilt and Remorse: Implications for Offender Populations', *The Journal of Forensic Psychiatry & Psychology*, Vol. 22, No. 5, 2011, pp. 706-723

Telzer, E.H., van Hoorn, J., Rogers, C.R., Do, K.T., 'Social Influence on Positive Youth Development: A Developmental Neuroscience Perspective', *Advances in Child Development and Behavior*, Vol. 54, 2018, pp. 215-258

Ugazio, G., Majdandžić, J. & Lamm, C. (2014). 'Are Empathy and Morality Linked? Insights from Moral Psychology, Social and Decision Neuroscience, and Philosophy', *in* H. Maibom (Ed.), *Empathy and Morality*, Oxford: Oxford University Press, pp. 155-171

Velotti, P., Garofalo, C., Bottazzi, F. & Caretti, V., 'Faces of Shame: Implications for Self-Esteem, Emotion Regulation, Aggression, and Well-Being', *The Journal of Psychology*, Vol. 151, No. 2, 2017, pp. 171-184

Wall, A.E. & Barth, R.P., 'Aggressive and Delinquent Behavior of Maltreated Adolescents: Risk Factors and Gender Differences', *Stress, Trauma, & Crisis*, Vol. 8, No. 1, 2005, pp. 1-24

Ward, B.H., 'Sentencing Without Remorse', *Loyola University Chicago Law Journal*, Vol. 38, No. 1, 2006, pp. 131-167

Weaver, B., *Offending and the Importance of Social Relations* (1st ed.), Routledge, 2016

Widom, C. S., 'Does Violence Beget Violence? A Critical Examination of the Literature', *Psychological Bulletin*, Vol. 106, 1989, pp. 3-28

Woodall, J., Dixey R., & South J., 'Control and Choice in English Prisons: Developing Health-promoting Prisons, *Health Promotion International*, Vol. 29, N.3, 2013, pp. 474-482

Zaki, J. (2018). *Empathy is a Moral Force, in* K. Gray & J. Graham (Eds.), *Atlas of Moral Psychology*, New York: Guildford Press, pp. 49-58

Zehr, H., *Changing Lenses: Restorative Justice for Our Times* (25th Anniversary ed.), Harrisonbourg (VA), Herald Press, 2015, pp. 184-188

5 The Relevance of Free Will, Rationality, and Aristotle for Legal Insanity

G. Meynen

1 Introduction

Legal insanity is an element of many criminal law systems, including the vast majority of US jurisdictions and almost all countries in the European Union.[1]

Insanity means, briefly, that a crime has been committed, but that the offender is excused because of the presence of a mental illness at the time of the crime, usually a severe mental illness.[2] The defense has led to many debates, and continues to do so. According to Mackay, "Perhaps more than any other area of the criminal law, the insanity defence generates heated discussion and debate."[3] One of the issues under debate concerns the fundamental question: why do we *need* the defense? Quoting Slobogin, one could answer: 'A person with severe mental disability, like the person who acts in self - defense or who causes harm accidentally, does not deserve the moral condemnation associated with criminal punishment.'[4] But then the follow-up question arises: what is it that makes certain people suffering from a mental illness not appropriate candidates for desert?

In this chapter, I will critically consider two common answers to this question. The first answer is that a mental disorder may result in *lack of free will*; the second answer cites that

---

1 Sweden is an exception. *See* R.J. Simon & H. Ahn-Redding, *The Insanity Defense, the World Over*, Lexington Books, Lanham Maryland 2006, and on Europe *see also* H.J. Salize & H. Dressing (Eds.), *Placement and Treatment of Mentally Disordered Offenders. Legislation and Practice in the European Union*, Pabst, Lengerich, 2005; M. van der Wolf & H. van Marle, 'Legal Approaches to Criminal Responsibility of Mentally Disordered Offenders in Europe', *in* K. Goethals (Ed.), *Forensic Psychiatry and Psychology in Europe*, Springer, New York 2018.

2 Often, but not always, a specific type of impact of the disorder is also required, *see* the next sections.

3 R.D. Mackay, *Mental Condition Defences in the Criminal Law*, Clarendon Press, Oxford 1995, p. 73. In the same vein, Slobogin writes "[t]he insanity defense is perhaps the most widely discussed doctrine in criminal law", C. Slobogin, 'Introduction to This Special Issue: The Characteristics of Insanity and the Insanity Evaluation Process', *Behavioral Sciences and the Law*, Vol. 36, No. 3, 2018, pp. 271-275.

4 Slobogin 2018, p. 272.

mental illness may undermine one's *rationality*.[5] The larger part of this chapter will be concerned with the concept of free will (Section 2), rather than rationality (Section 3). After considering both answers, I will propose an alternative normative framework for insanity, based on Aristotle's influential account of responsibility (Section 4). I will also discuss two problems with this framework, one conceptual and one practical problem. In Section 5, conclusions will be drawn.

2 Lack of Free Will as the Justification of Legal Insanity

2.1 Free Will and Debates Surrounding It

Many authors have argued that a lack of free will as a result of psychopathology explains the exculpation of mentally disordered defendants. For instance, James Gilligan considers free will central to insanity: "The insanity defense is based on the assumptions that with the exception of the insane, everyone possesses free will and the ability to distinguish right from wrong."[6] A similar opinion is expressed by Leue, Salize and Dressing in a book on treatment of mentally ill offenders in the European Union: "The idea that offenders suffering from a mental disorder must primarily be considered as ill and should therefore be exempted from punishment is of considerable antiquity, dating back to ancient Greek and Roman sources. It is grounded in the concept that human beings have free will and are able to differentiate and choose intentionally between right and wrong or good and evil."[7] And later in the same volume, one can read: "To assess mentally disturbed offenders differently from suspects whose mental abilities are not disturbed is a practice based on the assumption that mental disorders significantly affect a person's ability to exercise free will and to control their actions."[8] In the Netherlands, Mooij has emphasized the foundational

5 For a discussion of the topics of this chapter, *see also* G. Meynen, *Legal Insanity. Explorations in Psychiatry, Law, and Ethics*, Springer, New York 2016, in particular Chapter 4, 'Lack of free will and irrationality', on which the arguments that will follow are partially based.

6 J. Gilligan, 'A Modest Proposal to Universalize the Insanity Defense and Replace Prisons and Punishment With Treatment and Education', *International Journal of Applied Psychoanalytic Studies*, Vol. 12, No. 2, 2015, p. 134 (abstract).

7 A. Leue, H.J. Salize & H. Dressing, 'Criminal Responsibility', *in* H.J. Salize & H. Dressing (Eds.), *Placement and Treatment of Mentally Disordered Offenders. Legislation and Practice in the European Union*, Pabst, Lengerich 2005. *See* W. Sinnott-Armstrong & K. Levy, 'Insanity Defenses', *in* J. Deigh & D. Dolinko (Eds.), *The Oxford Handbook of Philosophy of Criminal Law*, Oxford University Press, New York 2011, for consequentialist arguments in favor of the insanity defense, having to do with, deterrence and the fact that, when sentenced to prison, the disorder could deteriorate and the person could become (even) more dangerous.

8 H. Dressing *et al.*, 'Legal Frameworks and Key Concepts', *in* H.J. Salize & H. Dressing (Eds.), *Placement and Treatment of Mentally Disordered Offenders. Legislation and Practice in the European Union*, Papst, Lengerich, 2005; id., p. 62.

relevance of free will for legal insanity.[9] Many more examples of a similar view could be given and Morse rightfully notes that "people will often say that a defendant who acted under duress or who was legally insane lacked free will."[10] The idea that lack of free will is crucial to exculpation has also philosophical backup; in moral philosophy it is not uncommon at all to think there is a deep connection between free will and responsibility: "In philosophical thought, free will is closely associated with moral responsibility."[11] From this perspective, it is unsurprising that regarding a ground for exculpation – which insanity is – people tend to refer to free will.

But there are problems with this justification. First, one should note that whereas insanity is an area of intense debate in criminal law, free will is an area of intense debate in philosophy; the philosophical disputes about free will have been raging for centuries.[12] In this section, I will consider this 'free will problem' in philosophy. Of note, challenges to free will are derived or motivated by other disciplines, in particular: physics, neuroscience, and psychology. I will conclude that given the controversies surrounding free will, it is not an attractive concept to justify the insanity defense.

Traditionally, at least in Western philosophy, the main problem of free will concerns its (in)compatibility with determinism, the idea that there are no alternative possibilities and that, in other words, the future is fixed. For centuries, it was a theological issue, rooted in the apparent incompatibility of free will and divine foreknowledge. Since, according to the church, God's knowledge did not only cover the past and present, but also the future, all future human actions were determined by his knowledge. In other words, the fact that God knew everything that would ever happen, seriously threatened any room for free will and free action.[13] Humans could only do what God already knew that they would do. Now, how could a just God punish people for their deeds if they were determined to do as they did (as a result of God's own omniscience)? For centuries, this was a core problem in theology and philosophy.

A second form of determinism concerns physics, more specifically the laws of physics. These laws, in combination with the current state of the universe, would determine the state of the universe at any future moment in time. Note, that it is not required that such

9 A.W.M. Mooij, *Toerekeningsvatbaarheid. Over Handelingsvrijheid*, Boom, Amsterdam 2004.

10 S.J. Morse, 'The Non-Problem of Free Will in Forensic Psychiatry and Psychology', *Behavioral Sciences and the Law*, Vol. 25, No. 2, 2007, p. 211. Even though Morse himself emphatically disagrees, see later in this chapter.

11 A.R. Mele, *Free: Why Science Hasn't Disproved Free Will*, Oxford University Press, Oxford 2014, p. 6.

12 R. Kane, *A Contemporary Introduction to Free Will*, Oxford University Press, New York 2005; Mele 2014.

13 Kane 2005.

a future state would also be predictable. It may well be that we lack the information or computational power to accurately foresee future events, but they are determined nevertheless. All events occur as a result of cause-effect relations, whose character is enshrined in the laws of nature. For Kant such a world was theoretically – at the level of pure reason – incompatible with free will.[14] Only on a practical level, meanwhile, the two are, in his view, compatible.

Still, physics not only teaches us that the world is determined. A highly influential physics theory – quantum mechanics – presupposes, according to its most popular interpretation, that at the fundamental level of elementary particles, the world is not determined; randomness rules. Such randomness does not appear to help free will at all, because a random action would not count as a free action. If my arm goes up randomly, that does not seem to be a free action.[15] On the contrary, one could argue, because on such an account, our actions cannot even be determined by our wills, because they are purely random.

Now how seriously can we take determinism if an extremely successful theory in physics – quantum mechanics – presupposes such indeterminism. Honderich has formulated two replies: first, how to interpret quantum mechanics is still an issue of debate. Dutch physicist and noble prize laureate 't Hooft,[16] for instance, favors a deterministic interpretation of quantum mechanics. Secondly, even if the behavior of elementary particles would be random, this need not be true for larger objects, such as brains.[17] Another response is that other sciences – other than physics – have shown that our behavior is determined.[18]

One such science is neuroscience. Arguably, the most famous study in discussions on free will and neuroscience is the Libet experiment.[19] In 1983, Libet and his colleagues reported that, at group level, just about 150 ms before we move our wrist, we become aware of that

14 I. Kant, *Critique of Pure Reason*, The Cambridge Edition of the Works of Immanuel Kant, Cambridge University Press, Cambridge/New York 1998.

15 *See, however*, R. Kane, *The Oxford Handbook of Free Will*, 2nd edn., Oxford University Press, Oxford/New York 2011 and J. R. Searle, *Freedom and Neurobiology: Reflections on Free Will, Language, and Political Power*, Columbia University Press, New York 2007.

16 Interview with 't Hooft in Physics Today. https://physicstoday.scitation.org/do/10.1063/PT.6.4.20170711a/full/. The matter itself is beyond my expertise, therefore I won't refer to the scientific papers. But for those interested and able, *see* G. 't Hooft, 'A mathematical theory for deterministic quantum mechanics', *Journal of Physics: Conference Series*, Vol. 67, Article Id. 012015, 2007.

17 T. Honderich, 'Determinism as True, Compatibilism and Incompatibilism as False, and the Real Problem Will', *in* R. Kane (Ed.), *The Oxford Handbook of Free Will*, Oxford University Press, Oxford 2002.

18 Kane 2005.

19 B. Libet *et al.*, 'Time of Conscious Intention to Act in Relation to Onset of Cerebral Activity (Readiness-Potential). The Unconscious Initiation of a Freely Voluntary Act', *Brain*, Vol. 106, No. 3, 1983, pp. 623-643; B. Libet, 'Do We Have Free Will?', *Journal of Consciousness Studies*, Vol. 6, No. 8–9, 1999, pp. 47-57.

movement (that we are about to make). But already half a second, so hundreds of milliseconds earlier, a characteristic electrophysiological signal was recorded, the so-called *readiness potential*. Libet and coworkers concluded that the brain 'decides' about our actions even before we become aware of them. Others have downplayed the relevance of the findings for the free will debate because of methodological concerns.[20] A central uncertainty regarding the Libet experiment is whether the (start of the) readiness potential is causally related to the action.[21]

Another line of research concerns psychological studies that were elegantly reviewed by Daniel Wegner in a thought-provoking argument claiming that free will is an illusion.[22] Various strands of psychological research show that people sometimes attribute certain events to themselves – "I did this" – while this was not the case. So, people may take credit for an action that is not actually theirs. And people may even provide reasons for actions that *could not have been the real* reasons for their actions. Such people apparently 'confabulate' their reasons *after* the act, Wegner concludes based on various experiments.

The debate on the implications of scientific findings for the free will debate continues, and one could say that the 'jury is still out' on the extent to which science leaves room for free will.[23] In fact, two issues can be distinguished: firstly, what does the neuroscience results actually show? Secondly, what does this mean for free will? The first question basically focusses on the strengths and weaknesses of the neuroscientific experiments, while the second issue is more philosophical as it takes into account the consequences for various philosophical *positions* on free will.

Basically, there are three philosophical positions on the compatibility of free will and determinism: hard determinism, compatibilism and libertarianism. Hard determinists

20 Mele 2014; J.A. Radder & G. Meynen, 'Does the Brain "Initiate" Freely Willed Processes? A Philosophy of Science Critique of Libet-Type Experiments and Their Interpretation', *Theory and Psychology*, Vol. 23, No. 1, 2013, pp. 3-21; J.F. Kihlstrom, 'Time to Lay the Libet Experiment to Rest: Commentary on Papanicolaou', *Psychology of Consciousness: Theory, Research, and Practice*, Vol. 4, No. 3, 2017, pp. 324-329.

21 S. Armstrong, M.V. Sale, & R. Cunnington, 'Neural Oscillations and the Initiation of Voluntary Movement', *Frontiers in Psychology*, Vol. 9, No. 2509, 2018.

22 He did not only build his case, however, on psychological data, also on neurobiological findings and some psychopathological research D.M. Wegner, *The Illusion of Conscious Will*, The MIT Press, Cambridge Massachusetts 2002. *See* A.R. Mele, 'Free Will, Moral Responsibility, and Scientific Epiphenomenalism', *Frontiers in Psychology*, Vol. 9, No. 2536, 2018 on both Weger's and Libet's challenge to free will. Mele concludes: "The scientific work and arguments I have discussed here leave ample room for moral responsibility and free will."

23 R. Vieira da Cunha & J.B. Relvas, '"Who's Afraid of the Big Bad Neuroscience?" Neuroscience's Impact on Our Notions of Self and Free Will', *in* J. Leefmann & E. Hildt (Eds.), *The Human Sciences after the Decade of the Brain*, Academic Press, Cambridge Massachusetts 2017, pp. 21-44.

believe that determinism exists and that it is incompatible with free will. Neuroscientific data confirming determinism bolster their position. Compatibilists, meanwhile, hold that free will is compatible with determinism. But compatibilists have different views on *why* free will and determinism are compatible. Some of these views may come under attack because of neuroscientific of psychological studies. Suppose that one holds that, even in a deterministic world, we are responsible for actions, just as long as our actions are *guided by our reasons*. Then, it may well be problematic when Wegner argues that the reasons we provide for our actions are mere confabulations. In other words, compatibilists provide disparate arguments why they feel that free will and determinism are compatible, and these arguments may be vulnerable to different scientific findings.[24] Libertarians form the third group, and they hold that we have free will and that it is incompatible with determinism. Clearly, if neuroscience would show that our actions are determined, libertarians have a problem. A very interesting, but less common, fourth position is hard incompatibilism. Hard incompatibilists holds that both determinism and (quantum mechanics-type) indeterminism are incompatible with free will. Derk Pereboom has developed this position.[25] So, either way, free will is impossible.

Finally, let us consider a strictly philosophical argument against free will, that does not rely on the incompatibility of free will and (in)determinism, but follows another line of thought. Galen Strawson contends that the concept of free will would require something that comes down to *causa sui*. He writes:

> When one acts, one acts in the way one does because of the way one is. So to be truly morally responsible for one's actions, one would have to be truly responsible for the way one is: one would have to be *causa sui*, or the cause of oneself, at least in certain crucial mental respects. But nothing can be *causa sui* – nothing can be the ultimate cause of itself in any respect. So nothing can be truly morally responsible.[26]

24 For instance, some endorse the reasons-responsive view J.M. Fischer & M. Ravizza, *Responsibility and Control: A Theory of Moral Responsibility*, Cambridge University Press, New York 1998, in which reasons – and responsiveness to them – are central (see main text). In that case, psychological and neuroscientific findings (allegedly) showing that our reasons are confabulations may undermine one's position. Others have a more classical compatibilist view that holds that one is free just as long as one is not hampered by (external) obstacles or impediments. This argument is less (directly) vulnerable to the (alledged) finding that reasons are mere confabulations, because it focusses on the absense of obstacles rather than relying on the responsiveness to reasons.

25 D. Pereboom, *Free Will, Agency, and Meaning in Life*, Oxford University Press, Oxford/New York 2014; D. Pereboom, *Living without Free Will*, Cambridge University Press, Cambridge 2001.

26 Quote taken from the Article Summary of G. Strawson, 'Free Will', *in Routledge Encyclopedia of Philosophy (online)*, 2011. *See also* G. Strawson, 'The Impossibility of Moral Responsibility', *Philosophical Studies: An International Journal for Philosophy in the Analytic Tradition*, Vol. 75, No. 1/2, 1994, pp. 5-24.

Consequently, neither determinism nor indeterminism will be able to help free will, because the concept is in itself flawed; it requires something that is not on offer: being the cause of oneself. In order to be responsible for my decision now, I would have to be the cause of its cause. But to be truly responsible, I would also have to be the cause of the cause of that cause, and so on – which implies an infinite regress. Strawson therefore rejects free will and responsibility.

So far, I have merely sketched some of the debates and positions on free will, focusing on one problem: the *existence* of free will (mainly whether it is possible in a deterministic world). But, indirectly, the related problem of the *definition* of free will, also emerged. For instance, should it be defined in terms of alternative possibilities, then determinism is a serious problem. But if free will is conceived of in terms of reasons for actions, it is susceptible to findings that show that humans merely confabulate. And evidently, there are many disagreements about the definition of free will as well.

I conclude that the many *controversies* surrounding free will provide a good reason not to use this concept to justify legal insanity. Now, let us consider the *relevance* of free will to legal insanity. This will give us a second reason not to cite (lack of) free will as the rational for the insanity defense.

2.2 *Free Will and Standards of Legal Insanity*

Stephen Morse forcefully rejects the view that legal insanity should be understood and justified in terms of 'a lack of free will'.[27] He argues that no relevant legal doctrine (in the US) refers to free will. Let us, at least in part, follow a similar approach in order to evaluate the relevance of free will for legal insanity.[28] First, the two standards used in most US states – M'Naghten[29] and the Model Penal Code test – will be considered, not only for their own sake, but also because many other legal systems have similar tests.[30] Furthermore, these tests appear to have been most often studied, so our findings could be related to this body of research.[31] Even though the approach in this section is analogous to Morse's, the results will be somewhat different from his.

27 Morse 2007.

28 Obviously, there are different ways to analyse the importance of free will for the justification of the insanity defense, and looking at the legal standards is just one of them, but it will be my approach in what follows.

29 Used in most (approx. 38) US states, C.L. Scott & P.J. Resnick, 'Forensic Psychiatry', *in* S. Fatemi & P. Clayton (Eds.), *The Medical Basis of Psychiatry*, Springer, New York 2016, pp. 799-808.

30 Simon & Ahn-Redding 2006.

31 "The majority of insanity research has taken place in jurisdictions that adopt either the M'Naghten test or the American Law Institute (ALI), 1962 test, or variants thereof." B.O. Gardner, D.C. Murrie, & N. Torres,

Arguably, the most influential legal standard or criterion for insanity is the M'Naghten rule:

> At the time of committing the act, the party accused was laboring under such a defect of reason, from disease of the mind, as not to know the nature and quality of the act he was doing; or if he did know it, that he did not know what he was doing was wrong.[32]

The Rule was the result of a case, concerning Daniel M'Naghten, who believed that there was a conspicary against him, in which the Prime Minister, Sir Robert Peel, played a role. M'Naghten, therefore, tried to assassinate the Prime Minister, but he accidentally killed his secretary, Edward Drummond, instead. M'Naghten was acquitted because of insanity. The verdict was followed by such a fierce debate that the House of Lords asked the judiciary to provide a criterion for legal insanity, resulting in what became known as the M'Naghten Rule.[33] Apart from the disease requirement, there is one central issue in this insanity criterion: *knowledge*. The entire defense is about what the defendant *knew*, to which I will refer as an epistemic standard. Perhaps, it is unsurprising that the Judges came up with such an epistemic criterion since the defendant was *deluded*. "Delusions," according to the DSM-5, "are fixed beliefs that are not amenable to change in light of conflicting evidence."[34] It is clear that delusions are *epistemic* phenomena.

Let us now look at the standard from the perspective of free will. Above, the intricate question about the compatibility of free will and determinism was discussed, and the fact that diverging views about free will exist, was emphasized. But let us now try to find some 'common ground' regarding the notion of free will. Tim O'Connor starts the entry on free will in the *Stanford Encyclopedia of Philosophy* as follows:

> The term 'free will' has emerged over the past two millennia as the canonical designator for a significant kind of *control* over one's actions. Questions concerning the nature and existence of this kind of control (*e.g.*, does it require and do we have the freedom to do otherwise or the power of self-determination?), and what its true significance is (is it necessary for moral responsibility

---

'Insanity Findings and Evaluation Practices: A State - Wide Review of Court - Ordered Reports', *Behavioral Sciences and the Law*, Vol. 36, 2018, pp. 303-316.

32 *M'Naghten's Case*, 10 Cl. & Fin. 200, 8 Eng. Rep. 718 (H.L. 1843).

33 D.N. Robinson, *Wild Beasts & Idle Humours: The Insanity Defense from Antiquity to the Present*, Harvard University Press, Cambridge Massachusetts 1996.

34 American Psychiatric Association, *Diagnostic and Statistical Manual of Mental Disorders: Dsm-5*, 5th edn, American Psychiatric Association, Arlington Virginia 2013.

> or human dignity?) have been taken up in every period of Western philosophy and by many of the most important philosophical figures, such as Plato, Aristotle, Augustine, Aquinas, Descartes, and Kant. (...) As should be clear from this short discussion of the history of the idea of free will, free will has traditionally been conceived of as a kind of power to control one's choices and actions.[35]

Control is, apparently, central to the notion of free will. In the same line, Michael McKenna and Derk Pereboom, prominent philosophers of free will, propose the following definition of free will: "*Free will* is the unique ability of persons to excercise the strongest sense of control over their actions necessary for moral responsibility."[36] The common denominator regarding free will appears to be: control.[37] This is not only true for philosophy. According to Baumeister and Monroe, who have taken an empirical and psychological approach to (beliefs about) free will, this is in agreement with how "ordinary people typically understand free will: as making choices, acting on one's own, controlling one's behavior to conform to social rules, and pursuing delayed rewards over time."[38] They also write from an historical perspective: "Free will can thus be understood as form of volition (action control) that evolved to enable people to live in cultural societies."[39]

It is important to realize that control is different from epistemic issues. In fact, usually two conditions are considered required for responsibility, as formulated by Fernando Rudy-Hiller:

> Philosophers usually acknowledge two individually necessary and jointly sufficient conditions for a person to be morally responsible for an action, *i.e.*, susceptible to be praised or blamed for it: a *control* condition (also called freedom condition) and an *epistemic* condition (also called knowledge, cognitive, or mental condition). Philosophers usually acknowledge two individually necessary and jointly sufficient conditions for a person to be morally responsible for an

35 T. O'Connor, 'Free Will', *in* E.N. Zalta (Ed.), *Stanford Encyclopedia of Philosophy*, 2018.

36 M. McKenna & D. Pereboom, *Free Will: A Contemporary Introduction*, Routledge, New York 2016, p. 6. They also ask the question: "Why is it common to characterize free will as a kind of control, specifically in relation to moral responsibility?" McKenna & Pereboom 2016, p. 6.

37 This notion can be further analyzed as consisting of two components: "When an agent exercises free will over her choices and actions, her choices and actions are *up to her*. But up to her in what sense? As should be clear from our historical survey, two common (and compatible) answers are: (i) up to her in the sense that she is able to choose otherwise, or at minimum that she is able not to choose or act as she does, and (ii) up to her in the sense that she is the source of her action." O'Connor 2018.

38 R.F Baumeister & A.E. Monroe, 'Chapter One - Recent Research on Free Will: Conceptualizations, Beliefs, and Processes', *in* J.M. Olson & M.P. Zanna (Eds.), *Advances in Experimental Social Psychology*, Vol. 50, Elsevier, Amsterdam 2014, pp. 1-52.

39 Baumeister & Monroe 2014, taken from the abstract.

> action, *i.e.*, susceptible to be praised or blamed for it: a control condition (also called freedom condition) and an epistemic condition (also called knowledge, cognitive, or mental condition)

In other words, free will is related to the control requirement, not with the epistemic condition for responsibility.

Based on this analysis, it can be concluded that the M'Naghten rule does not rely on the concept of free will, but on the concept of knowledge, and, more specifically, on the exculpating powers of lack thereof (ignorance). Consequently, free will does not provide the rational or justification for the most influential criterion of insanity in the Western world, the M'Nagthen rule.

However, not all US states use the M'Naghten rule. A considerable number of states[40] has the Model Penal Code (American Law Institute 1985) test, according to which,

> a person is not responsible for criminal conduct if at the time of such conduct as a result of mental disease or defect he lacks substantial capacity either to appreciate the criminality (wrongfulness) of his conduct or to conform his conduct to the requirements of the law.

Whilst the first part of this insanity test covers an epistemic issue (albeit more narrow than M'Naghten), the second part refers to behavioral control. Many legal systems use such a control prong in their standard (often together with an epistemic part). Now, as became clear in the above-mentioned quotes, the element of control *is* related to free will. Accordingly, as far as jurisdictions have a control prong, free will could be relevant as a rational for the defense. Yet, one has to be a bit careful, because the term control, even though apparently intimately related to free will, is not *identical* to free will. Free will appears to be a *particular* form of control, and its specific nature is topic of debate. For instance, should this control be understood in having alternative possibilities, or being responsive to reason, etcetera (see section 2.1)?

Free will, in sum, does not have *prima facie* relevance for the M'Naghten Rule, the most influential standard for insanity. Meanwhile, it could well be relevant to the Model Penal Code test, but *only* to the control part of it.

40 Four US states do not have an insanity defense.

The corollary of this section is that free will provides a rational for the control prong at best – not for the epistemic condition. Moreover, it is controversial (both its definition and existence), and it is therefore unlikely that using it as the justification of the defense really helps to clarify the matter.

3 Lack of Rationality as the Justification of Legal Insanity

According to Morse, free will is not foundational to legal insanity. In his view, "nonculpable irrationality is the underlying basis for the insanity defense."[41] He (2000, p. 253) explains this idea as follows:

> The law's concept of responsibility follows from its view of the person and the nature of law itself. Unless human beings are rational creatures who can understand the applicable rules and standards, and can conform to those legal requirements through intentional action, the law would be powerless to affect human behavior. (…) Indeed, it is my claim that lack of the general capacity for rationality explains precisely those cases, such as infancy or certain instances of severe mental disorder or dementia, in which the law now excuses agents or finds them not competent to perform some task.[42]

Carl Elliott, a bioethicist, has a similar view on the justification of legal insanity: 'The most straightforward condition for moral responsibility, and one that is often put forward in the criminal law, is rationality.'[43]

But how helpful is irrationality as a justification of the insanity defense? One should note, first of all, that 'rationality' has an advantage over the concept of free will. Whereas many people have doubts about – or plainly deny – the existence of free will, nobody seems to deny that people are – at least sometimes – rational creatures. So, in that sense, rationality is less problematic than free will.

---

41 S.J. Morse, 'Excusing and the New Excuse Defenses: A Legal and Conceptual Review', *Crime and Justice*, Vol. 23, 1998, p. 335.

42 S.J. Morse, 'Rationality and Responsibility', *Southern California Law Review*, Vol. 74, 2000, p. 253. Morse considers the *M'Naghten Rule* to be a rationality standard for legal insanity. M'Naghten Rule: "At the time of committing the act, the party accused was laboring under such a defect of reason, from disease of the mind, as not to know the nature and quality of the act he was doing; or if he did know it, that he did not know what he was doing was wrong." *M'Naghten's Case*, 10 Cl. & Fin. 200, 8 Eng. Rep. 718 (H.L. 1843).

43 C. Elliott, *The Rules of Insanity: Moral Responsibility and the Mentally Ill Offender*, State University of New York Press, Albany 1996, p. 109.

But what does rationality mean? Here lies the difficulty. The term rationality features in many debates. In one such a debate, on rationality in health care, Djulbegovic and Elqayam discuss its 'many faces', providing a 'list of major theories and models of rationality of relevance to medical decision-making'.[44] From this list it becomes clear that rationality has lots of different meanings. They state: "Fundamentally, we argue that what is 'rational' behaviour under one rationality theory may be irrational under the other theory" (2017, p. 920). So, there is substantial disagreement about what rationality amounts to.[45]

According to Jon Elster, an authority on rationality, the standard view of rationality states that

> rational choice is defined in terms of the relations among action, desires, beliefs and information. Minimally, rational-choice theory must tell the agents how best to realize their desires, given their beliefs. Furthermore, the theory must prescribe which beliefs it is rational for the agents to hold, given their evidence or information.[46]

Let us now consider the question – just like regarding free will above – to what extent this notion of rationality is reflected in in the legal standard.

The first thing to note is that rationality as a term is not mentioned in the M'Naghten rule. One could say that the notion 'reason' refers to rationality, but it is important to realize that this term is filled in by the knowledge – "...*as* not to know..." – component. But, on a

44 B. Djulbegovic & S. Elqayam, 'Many Faces of Rationality: Implications of the Great Rationality Debate for Clinical Decision-Making', *Journal of Evaluation in Clinical Practice*, Vol. 23, No. 5, 2017, pp. 915-922.

45 *See also* S.P. Garvey, 'Agency and Insanity', *Buffulo Law Review*, Vol. 66, No. 1, 2018, pp. 123-191, who recently argued that there are two 'irrationality' views regarding legal insanity: "Enter the irrationality theory. The theory's champions naturally agree that irrationality is somehow the touchstone of insanity, but their accounts differ in detail and nuance, making it hard to tell exactly what the theory stands for. Maybe it would be better to talk about irrationality theories, which bear a familial resemblance to one another, but differing in important ways."

46 J. Elster, 'Interpretation and Rational Choice', *Occasion: Interdisciplinary Studies in the Humanities*, Vol. 1, No. 1, 2009. He goes on stating: "Needless to say, a belief may be rational and yet false. Finally, since rational agents cannot always simply limit themselves to the evidence already at hand, the theory must tell them how much new information to acquire before they form the beliefs on which they can base a decision." *See also* Stone on Elster: ""We want," Elster declares, "to be rational" (Elster 1989b, 28). By this he means that people want their behavior to be governed by three optimizing operations. To satisfy these operations, they must act so as best to realize their preferences, given their beliefs. They must also adopt the best beliefs, given the information they have. And they must gather the best amount of information, given their beliefs and preferences (*i.e.* no large expenditures of energy in search of information regarding trivial decisions). An agent who performs these three operations successfully is to that extent a rational agent", P. Stone, 'Rationality, Intelligibility, and Interpretation', *Occasion: Interdisciplinary Studies in the Humanities*, Vol. 1, No. 1, 2009.

deeper level, could M'Naghten be somehow related to this standard view of rationality? The rule does not appear to be linked to the first part: the rule does not address what people should do *given* their beliefs. But the rule could be considered a rationality criterion as far as it concerns beliefs that are 'irrational' for the person to hold. One could argue that if a person is deluded that person does not rationally revise her knowledge/beliefs in view of other information that contradicts the contents of the delusion. In this – indirect – sense, M'Naghten can be considered related to rationality, even though rationality is not explicitly mentioned. In any case, epistemic issues *are* a concern both to rationality and to M'Naghten. Consequently, in my view, M'Naghten is – albeit somewhat loosely – related to Elster's notion of rationality.

But it is also important to recognize that M'Naghten does *not* articulate the question whether the defendant has realized his goals *given* his beliefs. It does not state: if the action was irrational given the person's beliefs, he is insane. In fact, an act that is irrational in view of a person's beliefs could rather be connected to *control*.[47] For example, a person who cannot control his impulses may act irrationally in the sense that he acts against his own views, or not in line with them. He takes alcohol even though he believes he should not, or he reacts aggressively, whereas he does not believe that aggression is the right course of action.[48] The Model Penal Code's control prong can cover a situation in which a person acts against his own beliefs, for instance, as a result of a commanding voice. A defendant who hears a commanding voice he cannot but obey may perform a delinquent action that is completely contrary to his own beliefs. Such a defendant can be exculpated based on the Model Penal Code's control prong: the command undermined the defendant's own behavioral control; he could no longer act in line with his own beliefs. In that way, it covers more of rationality than the M'Naghten Rule.[49]

Confusingly, however, sometimes, the epistemic component is referred to as the rationality component: "The current criminal law governing insanity acknowledges that some criminal defendants are not responsible for their actions due to a lack of rationality, meaning the defendant lacks the capacity to appreciate the nature or wrongfulness of their acts."[50] And M'Naghten is then considered a rationality standard: "In the United Kingdom, insanity is

47 Baumeister & Monroe 2014, p. 40 interestingly, but in view of our analysis unsurprisingly, make a connection between free will, control and rational choice: "If there is indeed such a thing as a free will, then it would have to be found in both self-control and rational choice."

48 *See also* Elster 2009: "Some of them appeal to irrationality, in terms of weakness of will or clinical depression."

49 *See* on this matter, but from a somewhat different angle, Meynen 2016.

50 R.K Helm, S.J. Ceci & K.A. Burd, 'Unpacking Insanity Defence Standards: An Experimental Study of Rationality and Control Tests in Criminal Law', *The European Journal of Psychology Applied to Legal Context*, Vol. 8, No. 2, 2016, pp. 63-68.

currently decided based on rationality only (The McNaughten Rule)"[51] Based on our analysis, however, it would be better to consider the Model Penal Code a rationality standard as it covers more of rationality than M'Naghten.

But there is another issue with the term rationality that needs to be addressed. Up till now it was assumed that we as humans are rational in our decisions – but are we? Is it not human to be irrational from time to time and is it not the case that we sometimes act irrational, stupid, etcetera? Also Elster acknowledges that humans are not so rational. As Stone writes about Elster:

> Elster firmly believes that the interpretation of human behavior could not be carried out without a theory of rationality. At the same time, however, he also believes that actual human beings are frequently irrational; indeed, he has amassed an extensive and growing catalogue of the irrationalities people *routinely* display.[52]

Louis Charland, in a debate about decision-making competency in healthcare, seems to go a step further. He asks the question whether Star Trek's Mr. Spock, who was strictly rational, is actually 'mentally competent'.[53] The idea in Charland's paper is that strict rational decision-making – without the influence of emotions – may not amount to *competent* decision-making. Put a bit differently, not being strictly 'rational' can actually be good for decision-making.[54] So one may be tempted to ask: how can the term irrationality help to explain exculpation due to mental illness, if irrationality – on some interpretation of the term – is essentially part of the human condition in general and if not being strictly rational may actually be 'good' for decision-making?

---

51 Helm, Ceci & Burd 2016.

52 Stone 2009 (emphasis added).

53 Charland writes: "Spock is a pure "cognizer." He is basically incapable of experiencing emotion. The creators of Star Trek would have us believe that Spock, a being more or less without the capacity for emotion, can make practical as well as theoretical decisions. He can reason theoretically like a computer, such as when he calculates planetary orbits and destinations, and he can reason practically, such as when he ducks in the face of a projectile thrown by an angry alien. As we shall see, Spock is an item of science fiction in more than one way. However, there is nothing fictional about the ideal he represents. It is the ideal of "pure reason" we find in philosophical thinkers such as Kant. I shall later argue that a pure cognizer such as Spock is incapable of practical reasoning in several crucial respects." L.C. Charland, 'Mr. Spock Mentally Competent? Competence to Consent and Emotion', *Philosophy, Psychiatry, and Psychology*, Vol. 5, No. 1, 1998, pp. 67-81.

54 But this also depends on one's definition of rationality of course and this is something Charland himself addresses as well.

In conclusion, in a way, rationality is related to both standards, at least on our interpretation, in which it covers both an epistemic and a control component. Meanwhile, there are many views of rationality, and what is rational on one definition, may not be rational on the other. That, in my view, makes it less helpful as a concept to straightforwardly explain and justify the insanity defense.[55]

4 ARISTOTLE'S MODEL AND ITS LEGAL APPLICATION

4.1 *The Aristotelean Components of Responsibility*

As discussed in the previous sections, both concepts, free will and rationality, have theoretical value, but neither of them offers a satisfactory, straightforward explanation and justification of legal insanity. Could there be a more direct way to justify the insanity defense? I endorse a model that can be considered an Aristotelean framework for legal insanity, and that was already introduced earlier, in section 2.2 (without mentioning Aristotle).[56] This contains two elements: a control element and an epistemic component. This simple framework is not only reflected in moral philosophy, but also in the law, as Moore (1984, p. 221) states:

> In criminal law, as in morals, two general sorts of conditions excuse: ignorance that is not itself culpable, and compulsion.... These two moral excuses are as old as Aristotle and are embodied in contemporary criminal law. (...) It is these two traditionally excusing conditions that have been adapted by lawyers and judges as they have added criteria to legal insanity beyond the requirement that an accused must be mentally ill.[57]

And both elements can also be recognized in Slobogin's words about the rational for legal insanity:

55 Elliott 1996, p. 109 himself has acknowledged that the ambiguities surrounding the notion of rationality are problematic: "Unfortunately, however, the notion of rationality is complex and vague enough to make its practical interpretation rather puzzling, and as a consequence, it is particularly difficult to use as a criterion for moral responsibility." Morse 2002, p. 1064 however, has a different opinion: "Lack of capacity for rationality is almost always the most *straightforward* explanation of why we colloquially say that some people cannot control themselves when they experience intense desires." (emphasis added).

56 *See* Aristotle, *The Nicomachean Ethics*, Oxford World's Classics, Oxford University Press, Oxford 2009, Nicomachean Ethics, Book III.

57 M.S. Moore, *Law and Psychiatry: Rethinking the Relationship*, Cambridge University Press, Cambridge 1984. And he adds that M'Naghten reflects the first.

> The most fundamental reason for retaining the insanity defense is the belief that impairment caused by mental disability can sometimes render an offender blameless, either because the person does not realize a crime is being committed or because, despite that realization, the person cannot control the relevant behavior.[58]

The Aristotelian model not only provides a justification for the Model Penal Code's epistemic and control prong. The two components can also be found in many[59] other insanity standards, for instance, in Germany[60] and in Italy. Article 88 of the Italian Penal Code reads:

> A person who committed a criminal act is not considered responsible if at the time of the commission of the criminal act he was *incapable of understanding the significance of his act or control his conduct*, by reason of insanity.[61]

In fact, according to Van der Wolf and Van Marle (2018, p. 41), in "current European provisions, it is common to find both a test for cognition and volition or control."[62] And also in China, the two components are reflected in article 18 of the criminal law:

> A mentally ill person who causes dangerous consequences at a time when he is *unable to recognize or unable to control* his own conduct is not to bear criminal responsibility after being established through accreditation of legal procedures; but his family or guardian shall be ordered to subject him to strict

58 Slobogin 2018, pp. 271-272.

59 An exception is Norway where the mere *presence* of psychosis at the time of the crime is sufficient for legal insanity (Norwegian Penal Code), *see* I. Melle, 'The Breivik Case and What Psychiatrists Can Learn from It', *World Psychiatry*, Vol. 12, No. 1, 2013, pp. 16-21; J. Bijlsma, 'A New Interpretation of the Modern Two-Pronged Tests for Insanity: Why Legal Insanity Should Not Be a Status Defense', *Netherlands Journal of Legal Philosophy*, Vol. 47, No. 1, 2018, pp. 29-48.

60 Para. 20 Strafgeseztbuch, Schuldunfähigkeit wegen seelischer Störungen, Germany.

61 S. Ferracuti & P. Roma, 'Models of Care for Mentally Disordered Prisoners in Italy', *International Journal of Mental Health*, Vol. 37, No. 4, 2008, p. 84 (emphasis added).

62 Van der Wolf & Van Marle 2018. Sometimes the M'Naghten rule is considered a to be a cognitive standard. However, I prefer the term 'epistemic', because it is more precise and directly related to the notions of ignorance and knowledge. Cognition, meanhwile, can be interpreted in such a way that control becomes part of it. *See, e.g.*, G. Tsimploulis *et al.*, 'Schizophrenia and Criminal Responsibility: A Systematic Review', *Journal of Nervous Mental Disorders*, Vol. 206, No. 5, 2018, pp. 370-377 who use the term 'cognition' as related to executive functioning (which in the literature is also considered central to self-control, *see* J. Meijers *et al.*, 'Reduced Self-Control after 3 Months of Imprisonment; a Pilot Study', *Frontiers in Psychology*, Vol. 9, No. 69, 2018. Then, the line between cognition and control is blurring.

> surveillance and arrange for his medical treatment. When necessary, he will be given compulsory medical treatment by the government.[63]

Even though in the Netherlands no formal criterion for legal insanity has been defined, both epistemic issues and control issues are taken into account by behavioral experts and the courts.[64] In my view, the dual model of responsibility offers a straightforward and accurate justification of legal insanity – at least given the approach followed in this chapter. It not only explains the insanity defense, it also enables us to understand how free will and rationality *are* relevant to legal insanity: free will is relevant due to its connection with the control prong, while rationality is relevant as long as it is interpreted as consisting of a control and an epistemic component.

In fact, the dual model not only *justifies* the insanity defense, it also entails a *prescription* regarding its structure: the insanity standard should contain both elements. In other words, if one accepts the Aristotelean model as a justification, this implies that the model's components should be reflected in the legal insanity criterion.

Yet, legal insanity is a practical concept, it functions in criminal law, and in the end, it has to be applied in the courtroom. The application of this Aristotelean model in criminal law may still generate further questions – and they need to be addressed. In the remainder of this section, I will discuss two important issues regarding these elements, one concerning the interpretation of the epistemic component and the other concerning the reliability of the control element in legal practice.

4.2 The Epistemic Component Should Be Interpreted in the Moral Sense

Hallevy describes the problem regarding the interpretation of epistemic element as follows:

> The key term 'wrong', which refers to the criminal prohibition, was not easily interpreted after M'Naghten. It was asked whether it refers to the *legal* or to the *moral* meaning of the prohibition. For example, the offender who sets fire to a brothel under the delusion that he is commanded by God to do so in order to advance his redemption, he is fully aware of the criminal prohibition against setting the fire. The offender understands that his conduct is legally prohibited,

63 L. Zhao & G. Ferguson, 'Understanding China's Mental Illness Defense', *The Journal of Forensic Psychiatry & Psychology*, Vol. 24, No. 5, 2013, p. 639 (emphasis added).

64 J. Bijlsma, *Stoornis En Strafuitsluiting. Op Zoek Naar Een Toetsingskader Voor Ontoerekenbaarheid*, Wolf Legal Publishers, Oisterwijk 2016.

> but he considers it to be morally commendable. The M'Naghten rules did not explicitly interpret which type of 'wrong' the court must address: the legal or the moral one. English common law preferred the legal meaning over the moral one, and American courts have left the decision to the jury, so that at times the wrong is legal and at others it is moral.[65]

So, there is discussion about the nature of the wrongness: legal or moral. But, we may ask ourselves: how *should* it be interpreted? I believe that the above-mentioned example illustrates that it should be interpreted as moral wrongness because that better covers the exculpating effects of mental illness. Clearly, mental disorders may change our beliefs about what is legally wrong and what is not legally wrong. For instance, a person may delusionally believe that he is attacked by his colleague and act to his defense, under the impression that his act is legally justified as self-defense. In fact, persecutory delusions are the most common type of delusion, "*i.e.*, belief that one is going to be harmed, harassed, and so forth by an individual, organization, or other group".[66] And one can imagine that at some point people who have such a delusion may feel they are justified to act against the 'persecutors'.

But in other cases, a delusion may not lead to the conviction that one's action is legally justified. Rather, the person's deluded beliefs may 'override' the legal considerations, as in the scenario mentioned by Hallevy. In fact, in my view, such 'overriding' cases particularly concern delusions that involve God, divine commands, Satan, demons – more generally: the supernatural – and/or considerations about the afterlife. Another example of this type would be a mother who becomes depressed and later also psychotic after giving birth to her child. At some point she believes a demon is going to take her child to hell unless she kills it, because then it will go to heaven. The mother, tragically, believes she does something morally good for her child, even though she knows that this act is legally wrong. In my view, such a tragedy should be covered by legal insanity.[67]

---

65 G. Hallevy, *The Matrix of Insanity in Modern Criminal Law*, Springer, New York 2015 (references omitted, emphasis added).

66 American Psychiatric Association 2013, p. 87.

67 On this matter *see also* S.L.T.J. Ligthart, T. Kooijmans & G. Meynen, 'Een Juridisch Criterium Voor De Ontoerekeningsvatbaarheid: Een Uitspraak Van Het Gerechtshof Den Haag Geanalyseerd', *Delikt en Delinkwent*, Vol. 1, No. 9, 2018, pp. 101-110. They describe a Dutch case in which the Court of appeal used a criterion in which knowledge of the legal wrongness was a component (in Dutch crimianl law, no criterion for insanity has been defined). Referring to another Dutch case, in which a mother who killed her daughter to safe her from satanists was considered insane, the authors argued for the moral interpretation of the 'wrongness' element. S.J. Morse, 'Legal Insanity in the Age of Neuroscience', *in* S. Moratti & D. Patterson (Eds.), *Legal Insanity and the Brain. Science, Law, and European Courts*, Hart Publishing, Oxford 2016, p. 257 supports the moral interpretation for similar reasons: "To the extent that an outcome might turn on

Notably, in general, the moral interpretation also works in cases of self-defense, as self-defense is not only legally but also morally justified. Therefore, in practice, the moral interpretation is the broader interpretation.

Finally, one could object: does this not create a situation in which everyone who believes that he is morally right can get away with a crime? Well, we should remind ourselves that the insanity criteria only apply as far as that belief was *the result of a (severe) mental illness.* So, not every extremist is excused.

4.3 *The Control Prong Should Be Included*

An important argument against the M'Naghten Rule, is that it is too narrow. As Scott and Resnick put it, "This test, sometimes referred to as the 'right or wrong test' has been criticized because it is limited to the defendant's awareness of his acts as compared to his ability to *control* his behavior due to mental illness."[68] Given the Aristotelean model, this criticism is very understandable. Yet, not everybody is convinced that a control prong should be added. Regarding the control element, Morse argues

> I am an opponent of control tests because I have not encountered a convincing conceptual account of an independent lack of control and an operational definition of such an incapacity that would permit expert or lay testimony to resolve whether a defendant had such a problem. I readily concede that lack of control may be an independent type of incapacity that should mitigate or excuse responsibility, but until a good conceptual and operational account of lack of control is provided, I prefer to limit the insanity defence to cognitive tests.[69]

How to respond to this line of criticism regarding the control prong?

First of all, it is important to note that our analysis of the notion of free will, of the notion of rationality, and of the Aristotelian model *all* show the relevance of the control element.

---

moral versus legal wrong, the former should be preferred because it is more action guiding and provides a better fit with the underlying rationale for the defence."

68 Scott & Resnick 2016, p. 804, (emphasis added). *See also* A.W. Norrie, *Crime, Reason and History: A Critical Introduction to Criminal Law*, 3rd edn, Cambridge University Press, Cambridge 2014, p. 247: "The Royal Commission (1949-1953)... described the M'Naghten test as 'obsolete and misleading', for insanity 'does not only, or primarily affect the cognitive or intellectual faculities, but affects the whole personality of the patient, including both the will and the emotions.' An insane person, they added, may both know the nature and quality of the act and that it is wrong by law, but yet commit it as a result of mental disease. The M'Naghten rules, 170 year old and still going strong, steadfastly refuse to countenance such a possibility."

69 Morse 2016, p. 259.

This provides a strong and fundamental argument for including a control element. Furthermore, (self-)control is a term that is commonly used throughout psychiatry, neuroscience and (neuro)psychology, not only in research but also in clinical practice.[70] This is not only true for impulse-control (spectrum) disorders,[71] but also for self-control problems that may arise in a range of conditions, varying from manic episodes to frontotemporal dementia. Control is also reflected in criminal law as a central issue[72] and juries and courts frequently decide about the extent to which certain events – *e.g.*, traffic accidents – were under the defendant's control.[73] Consequently, I ask the rhetorical question: Why would a term that is commonly used in philosophy, in law, and in psychiatry, suddenly be 'not good enough' as an element for the insanity defense – where the three disciplines meet?

Therefore, the law should make it possible that if the jury or judge conclude that, based on medical expertise, it has been established that the defendant, as a result of a mental illness, could not sufficiently control his behavior, the defendant can be considered insane. The judgement, in other words, can, in my view, be on the judge or jury, based on behavioral expert testimony.[74] Arguably, the most important condition that deserves, at least in some cases, exculpation, concerns the commanding voice that cannot be disobeyed. It may be difficult to accept that such voices actually exist, until one encounters a patient who, as a result of such voices, has seriously harmed himself, for instance taking his own eyesight. Even though such cases are rare, the law should provide the opportunity to exculpate people who acted delinquently based on command hallucinations – the control prong provides such a possibility.

5 Conclusion

In this chapter, I set out to examine the relevance of free will and rationality for justifying and understanding the insanity defense. It turned out that, rather than free will and rationality, the Aristotelean model for responsibility offers a straightforward way to explain the insanity defense. Mental disorders may have profound effects on our knowledge as

---

70 *See, for example*, Meijers *et al.* 2018; J.B. Li, S. Salcuni & E. Delvecchio, 'Meaning in Life, Self-Control and Psychological Distress among Adolescents: A Cross-National Study', *Psychiatry Research*, Vol. 272, 2018, pp. 122-129; K. Smith, 'Sex and Drugs and Self-Control: How the Teen Brain Navigates Risk', *Nature*, Vol. 554, No. 7693, 2018, pp. 426-428.

71 American Psychiatric Association 2013.

72 See Moore quote *supra*.

73 And clearly, the court may also take into account whether a defendant was coerced to do something.

74 Empirical research on the control prong also does not suggests that it leads to many more insanity verdicts, *see* S. Penney, 'Impulse Control and Criminal Responsibility: Lessons from Neuroscience', *International Journal of Law and Psychiatry*, Vol. 35, No. 2, 2012, pp. 99-103.

well as on behavioural control, which constitute the two elements of Aristotle's account of responsibility. Meanwhile, some have argued against the control prong as a criterion for insanity, for it would be too theoretically unclear and too difficult to operationalize. In response to this objection, I have argued that since the term control is commonly used in the behavioral sciences, in moral philosophy, as well as in criminal law, it should be good enough for legal insanity, where the three disciplines meet.

The dual model, notably, is not in conflict with rationality as a foundation of insanity, on the contrary: the two prongs are directly related to a common interpretation of rationality. Neither is the model in conflict with free will as a foundation of insanity; control is conceptually connected to free will. Yet, the significant advantage of the Aristotelian model is that it is less ambiguous than the notion of rationality and less narrow and controversial than free will. Therefore, it is much clearer what the notion entails, not only in law, but also in forensic practice. Clarity is of the essence, as it will help to ensure intelligibility, applicability and equality before the law.

In fact, the twofold model not only explains and justifies the insanity defense, but it also entails a prescription regarding its structure: the insanity criterion should contain both elements.

Within the context of legal insanity, the interpretation of the knowledge component is crucial. I have argued for the 'moral' interpretation. In practice, the 'legal' interpretation often works well for cases in which the (deluded) defendant wrongly believed that she was attacked – so, instances of self-defense against an imagined attacker. But in other cases, in which, *e.g.*, the supernatural and the afterlife play a role, the delusion may somehow 'override' a person's legal considerations. These may be cases in which a mother kills her newborn baby, not as an act of self defence against the baby, but to protect the baby from the devil or from eternal damnation – so, paradoxically, to safe the victim. It should also be possible to qualify defendants in such tragic cases as legally insane.

References

American Psychiatric Association, *Diagnostic and Statistical Manual of Mental Disorders: Dsm-5*, 5th edn, American Psychiatric Association, Arlington Virginia 2013.

Aristotle, *The Nicomachean Ethics*, Oxford World's Classics, Oxford University Press, Oxford/New York 2009.

Armstrong, S., Sale, M.V. & Cunnington, R., 'Neural Oscillations and the Initiation of Voluntary Movement', *Frontiers in Psychology*, Vol. 9, No. 2509, 2018.

Baumeister, R.F. & Monroe, A.E., 'Chapter One – Recent Research on Free Will: Conceptualizations, Beliefs, and Processes', *in* J.M. Olson & M.P. Zanna (Eds.), *Advances in Experimental Social Psychology*, Vol. 50, Elsevier, Amsterdam 2014, pp. 1-52.

Bijlsma, J., *Stoornis En Strafuitsluiting. Op Zoek Naar Een Toetsingskader Voor Ontoerekenbaarheid*, Wolf Legal Publishers, Oisterwijk 2016.

Bijlsma, J., 'A New Interpretation of the Modern Two-Pronged Tests for Insanity: Why Legal Insanity Should Not Be a Status Defense', *Netherlands Journal of Legal Philosophy*, Vol. 47, No. 1, 2018, pp. 29-48.

Charland, L.C., 'Mr. Spock Mentally Competent? Competence to Consent and Emotion', *Philosophy, Psychiatry, and Psychology*, Vol. 5, No. 1, 1998, pp. 67-81.

Djulbegovic, B. & Elqayam, S., 'Many Faces of Rationality: Implications of the Great Rationality Debate for Clinical Decision-Making', *Journal of Evaluation in Clinical Practice*, Vol. 23, No. 5, pp. 915-922.

Dressing, H. *et al.*, 'Legal Frameworks and Key Concepts', *in* H.J. Salize & H. Dressing (Eds.), *Placement and Treatment of Mentally Disordered Offenders. Legislation and Practice in the European Union*, Papst, Lengerich 2005, pp. 54-63.

Elliott, C., *The Rules of Insanity: Moral Responsibility and the Mentally Ill Offender*, State University of New York Press, Albany 1996.

Elster, J., 'Interpretation and Rational Choice', *Occasion: Interdisciplinary Studies in the Humanities*, Vol. 1, No. 1, 2009.

Ferracuti, S., & Roma, P., 'Models of Care for Mentally Disordered Prisoners in Italy', *International Journal of Mental Health*, Vol. 37, No. 4, 2008, pp. 71-87.

Fischer, J.M. & Ravizza, M., *Responsibility and Control: A Theory of Moral Responsibility*, Cambridge University Press, Cambridge/New York 1998.

Gardner, B.O., Murrie, D.C. & Torres, N., 'Insanity Findings and Evaluation Practices: A State - Wide Review of Court - Ordered Reports', *Behavioral Sciences and the Law*, Vol. 36, 2018, pp. 303-316.

Garvey, S.P., 'Agency and Insanity', *Buffulo Law Review*, Vol. 66, No. 1, 2018, pp. 123-191, 2018.

Gilligan, J., 'A Modest Proposal to Universalize the Insanity Defense and Replace Prisons and Punishment With Treatment and Education', *International Journal of Applied Psychoanalytic Studies*, Vol. 12, No. 2, 2015, pp. 134–152.

Hallevy, G., *The Matrix of Insanity in Modern Criminal Law*, Springer, New York 2015.

Helm, K., Ceci, S.J. & Burd, K.A., 'Unpacking Insanity Defence Standards: An Experimental Study of Rationality and Control Tests in Criminal Law', *The European Journal of Psychology Applied to Legal Context*, Vol. 8, No. 2, 2016, pp. 63-68.

Honderich, T., 'Determinism as True, Compatibilism and Incompatibilism as False, and the Real Problem Will', *in* R. Kane (Ed.), *The Oxford Handbook of Free Will*, Oxford University Press, Oxford 2002.

Kane, R., *A Contemporary Introduction to Free Will*, Oxford University Press, New York 2005.

Kane, R., *The Oxford Handbook of Free Will*, 2nd ed., Oxford University Press, Oxford/New York 2011.

Kant, I., *Critique of Pure Reason*, The Cambridge Edition of the Works of Immanuel Kant, Cambridge University Press, Cambridge/New York 1998.

Kihlstrom, J.F., 'Time to Lay the Libet Experiment to Rest: Commentary on Papanicolaou', *Psychology of Consciousness: Theory, Research, and Practice*, Vol. 4, No. 3, 2017, pp. 324-329.

Leue, A., Salize, H.J. & Dressing, H., 'Criminal Responsibility', *in* H.J. Salize & H. Dressing (Eds.), *Placement and Treatment of Mentally Disordered Offenders. Legislation and Practice in the European Union*, Papst, Lengerich 2005, pp. 23-28.

Li, J.B., Salcuni, S. & Delvecchio, E., 'Meaning in Life, Self-Control and Psychological Distress among Adolescents: A Cross-National Study', *Psychiatry Research*, Vol. 272, 2018, pp. 122-129.

Libet, B., 'Do We Have Free Will?', *Journal of Consciousness Studies*, Vol. 6, No. 8–9, 1999, pp. 47-57.

Libet, B. *et al.*, 'Time of Conscious Intention to Act in Relation to Onset of Cerebral Activity (Readiness-Potential). The Unconscious Initiation of a Freely Voluntary Act', *Brain*, Vol. 106, No. 3, 1983, pp. 623-642.

Ligthart, S.L.T.J., Kooijmans, T., Meynen, G., 'Een Juridisch Criterium Voor De Ontoerekeningsvatbaarheid: Een Uitspraak Van Het Gerechtshof Den Haag Geanalyseerd', *Delikt en Delinkwent*, Vol. 1, No. 9, 2018, pp. 101-110.

Mackay, R.D., *Mental Condition Defences in the Criminal Law*, Clarendon Press, Oxford 1995.

McKenna, M. & Pereboom, D., *Free Will: A Contemporary Introduction*, Routledge, New York 2016.

Meijers, J. *et al.*, 'Reduced Self-Control after 3 Months of Imprisonment; a Pilot Study', *Frontiers in Psychology*, Vol. 9, No. 69, 2018.

Mele, A.R., 'Free Will, Moral Responsibility, and Scientific Epiphenomenalism', *Frontiers in Psychology*, Vol. 9, No. 2536, 2018.

Mele, A.R., *Free: Why Science Hasn't Disproved Free Will*, Oxford University Press, Oxford 2014.

Melle, I., 'The Breivik Case and What Psychiatrists Can Learn from It', *World Psychiatry*, Vol. 12, No. 1, 2013, pp. 16-21.

Meynen, G., *Legal Insanity. Explorations in Psychiatry, Law, and Ethics*, Springer, New York 2016.

Mooij, A.W.M., *Toerekeningsvatbaarheid. Over Handelingsvrijheid*, Boom, Amsterdam 2004.

Moore, M.S., *Law and Psychiatry: Rethinking the Relationship*, New York: Cambridge University Press, Cambridge/New York 1984.

Morse, S.J., 'Excusing and the New Excuse Defenses: A Legal and Conceptual Review', *Crime and Justice*, Vol. 23, 1998, pp. 329-406.

Morse, S.J., 'Legal Insanity in the Age of Neuroscience', *in* S. Moratti & D. Patterson, Legal Insanity and the Brain. Science, Law, and European Courts, Hart Publishing, Oxford 2016.

Morse, S.J., 'The Non-Problem of Free Will in Forensic Psychiatry and Psychology', *Behavioral Sciences and the Law*, Vol. 25, No. 2, 2007, pp. 203-220.

Morse, S.J., 'Rationality and Responsibility', *Southern California Law Review*, Vol. 74, 2000, pp. 251-268.

Norrie, A.W., *Crime, Reason and History: A Critical Introduction to Criminal Law. Third Edition*, 3rd edn, Cambridge University Press, Cambridge 2014.

O'Connor, T., 'Free Will', *in* E.N. Zalta (Ed.), *Stanford Encyclopedia of Philosophy*, 2018.

Penney, S., 'Impulse Control and Criminal Responsibility: Lessons from Neuroscience', *International Journal of Law and Psychiatry*, Vol. 35, No. 2, 2012, pp. 99-103.

Pereboom, D., *Free Will, Agency, and Meaning in Life*, Oxford University Press, Oxford/New York 2014.

Pereboom, D., *Living without Free Will*, Cambridge University Press, Cambridge/New York 2001.

Radder, J.A., Meynen, G., 'Does the Brain "Initiate" Freely Willed Processes? A Philosophy of Science Critique of Libet-Type Experiments and Their Interpretation', *Theory and Psychology*, Vol. 23, No. 1, 2013, pp. 3-21.

Robinson, D.N., *Wild Beasts & Idle Humours: The Insanity Defense from Antiquity to the Present*, Harvard University Press, Cambridge Massachusetts 1996.

Rudy-Hiller, F. 'The Epistemic Condition for Moral Responsibility', *in* E.N. Zalta (Ed.), *Stanford Encyclopedia of Philosophy*, 2018.

Salize, H.J. & Dressing, H. (Eds.), *Placement and Treatment of Mentally Disordered Offenders. Legislation and Practice in the European Union*, Papst, Lengerich 2005.

Scott, C.L. & Resnick, P.J., 'Forensic Psychiatry', *in* S. Fatemi & P. Clayton (Eds.), *The Medical Basis of Psychiatry*, Springer, New York 2016, pp. 799-808.

Searle, J.R. *Freedom and Neurobiology: Reflections on Free Will, Language, and Political Power*, Columbia University Press, New York 2007.

Simon, R.J. & Ahn-Redding, H., *The Insanity Defense, the World Over*, Lexington Books, Lanham Maryland 2006.

Sinnott-Armstrong, W. & Levy, K., 'Insanity Defenses', *in* J. Deigh & D. Dolinko, *The Oxford Handbook of Philosophy of Criminal Law*, Oxford University Press, New York 2011.

Slobogin, C., 'Introduction to This Special Issue: The Characteristics of Insanity and the Insanity Evaluation Process',.*Behavioral Sciences and the Law*, Vol. 36, No. 3, 2018, pp. 271-275.

Smith, K., 'Sex and Drugs and Self-Control: How the Teen Brain Navigates Risk', *Nature*, Vol. 554, No. 7693, 2018, pp. 426-428.

Stone, P., 'Rationality, Intelligibility, and Interpretation', *Occasion: Interdisciplinary Studies in the Humanities*, Vol. 1, No. 1, 2009.

Strawson, G., 'Free Will', *Routledge Encyclopedia of Philosophy (online)*, 2011.

Strawson, G., 'The Impossibility of Moral Responsibility', *Philosophical Studies: An International Journal for Philosophy in the Analytic Tradition*, Vol. 75, No. 1/2 1994, pp. 5-24.

't Hooft, G., 'A mathematical theory for deterministic quantum mechanics', *Journal of Physics: Conference Series*, Vol. 67, Article Id. 012015, 2007.

Tsimploulis, G. *et al.*, 'Schizophrenia and Criminal Responsibility: A Systematic Review', *Journal of Nervous Mental Disorders*, Vol. 206, No. 5, 2018, pp. 370-377.

Vieira da Cunha, R. & Relvas, J.B., '"Who's Afraid of the Big Bad Neuroscience?" Neuroscience's Impact on Our Notions of Self and Free Will', *in* J. Leefmann & E. Hildt (Eds.), *The Human Sciences after the Decade of the Brain*, Springer, New York 2017, pp. 21-44.

Wegner, D.M., *The Illusion of Conscious Will*, The MIT Press, Cambridge Massachusetts 2002.

Van der Wolf, M. & Van Marle, H., 'Legal Approaches to Criminal Responsibility of Mentally Disordered Offenders in Europe', *in* K. Goethals (Ed.), *Forensic Psychiatry and Psychology in Europe*, Springer, New York 2018.

Zhao, L. & Ferguson, G., 'Understanding China's Mental Illness Defense', *The Journal of Forensic Psychiatry & Psychology*, Vol. 24, No. 5, 2013, pp. 634-567.

6 Coercive Forensic Neuroimaging and the Prohibition of Ill-Treatment (Article 3 ECHR)[1]

S. Ligthart

1 Introduction

While modern scientific technologies play an important role in the fight against crime, the Grand Chamber of the European Court of Human Rights considers that 'any state claiming a pioneer role in the development of new technologies bears special responsibility for striking the right balance.'[2]

Besides the United States and Australia,[3] European countries like Slovenia, England and Wales and the Netherlands fulfil such a pioneer role in using neuroscientific technologies and information in criminal law.[4] In the Netherlands for instance, the public database for case law, which only publishes a small proportion of the total number of criminal cases,[5] shows that neuroscientific information has already been used in 207 criminal cases between

1 The findings that are presented in this chapter are derived from the author's current PhD project and build on S.L.T.J. Ligthart, 'Coercive neuroimaging technologies in criminal law in Europe: Exploring the implications for the prohibition of ill-treatment (article 3 ECHR)', in L.S. Reins (Ed.), *Regulating new technologies in uncertain times*, Springer 2019.

2 ECtHR (GC) 4 December 2008, appl.nos. 30562/04 and 30566/04 (*S. & Marper/UK*), paras. 105 and 110.

3 N.A. Farahany, 'Neuroscience and behavioral genetics in US criminal law: an empirical analysis', *Journal of Law and the Biosciences*, Vol. 2, 2015, pp. 485-509; L.M. Gaudet & G.E. Marchant, 'Under the Rader: Neuroimaging Evidence in the Criminal Courtroom', *Drake Law Review*, 2016, pp. 577-661; A. Alimardani & J. Chin, 'Neurolaw in Australia: The Use of Neuroscience in Australian Criminal Proceedings', *Neuroethics*, 2019, https://doi.org/10.1007/s12152-018-09395-z. And to some extent Canada: J. Chandler, 'The use of neuroscientific evidence in Canadian criminal proceedings', *Journal of Law and the Biosciences*, Vol. 2, 2015, pp. 550-557.

4 M. Hafner, 'Judging homicide defendants by their brains: an empirical study on the use of neuroscience in homicide trials in Slovenia', *Journal of Law and the Biosciences* 2019, pp. 1-29, https://doi.org/10.1093/jlb/lsz006; P. Catley & L. Claydon, 'The use of neuroscientific evidence in the courtroom by those accused of criminal offenses in England and Wales', *Journal of Law and the Biosciences*, Vol. 2, 2015, pp. 510-549; C.H. de Kogel & E.J.M.C. Westgeest, 'Neuroscientific and behavioral genetic information in criminal cases in the Netherlands', *Journal of Law and the Biosciences*, Vol. 2, 2015, pp. 580-605.

5 www.rechtspraak.nl.

2000 and 2012.[6] Furthermore, the Dutch Ministry of Justice and Security initiated research on the possibilities of neuroscientific applications in prison settings.[7] According to the State Secretary of Justice and Security, such applications are promising regarding forensic diagnostics and risk assessment.[8] These examples illustrate the interest for the contribution of neuroscience to criminal law. Not only by legal and neuroscientific scholars, but also by policymakers, judges and other legal practitioners. The possibilities and challenges of neuroscience for criminal law are also discussed in other European countries like Belgium, France and Italy.[9]

This interest for the contribution of neuroscience to criminal justice in Europe underlines the importance of the Grand Chamber's consideration, to strike the right balance between the use of new technologies on the one hand, and the protection of (human) rights on the other. This is particularly important regarding a much debated issue in the neurolegal discussion: the use of *coercive* neuroimaging in criminal justice ('coercive forensic neuroimaging').

Neuroimaging could be helpful to answering crucial legal questions in criminal justice. If a defendant or prisoner refuses cooperation, the public prosecutor or prison director may wish to apply neuroimaging *against the person's will*. However, *coercive* forensic neuroimaging raises fundamental theoretical and legal questions regarding the European Convention on Human Rights (ECHR).[10] One of these questions is how coercive neuroimaging in criminal law relates to the prohibition of torture, inhuman and degrading treatment and punishment ('ill-treatment', Article 3 ECHR).[11] Because this question (and comparable questions regarding the US legal system[12]) received only few attention yet, I examine the

6 De Kogel & Westgeest 2015.

7 L. Cornet et al., Neurowetenschappelijke toepassingen in de jeugdstrafrechtketen, WODC, The Hague 2016.

8 *Kamerstukken II* 2016/17, 36937, 20.

9 S. Moratti & D. Patterson (Eds.), *Legal Insanity and the Brain: Science, Law and European Courts*, Hart Publishing, Portland 2016, pp. 77-110.

10 E. Rusconi & T. Mitchener-Nissen, 'Prospects of functional magnetic resonance imaging as lie detector', *Frontiers in Human Neuroscience*, 2013, doi: 10.3389/fnhum.2013.00594; J.C. Bublitz, 'Freedom of Thought in the Age of Neuroscience', *ARSP* 2014, Vol. 100, pp. 1-25; R. Encinas de Muñagorri & C. Saas, 'France. Is the Evidence Too Cerebral to Be Cartesian?', *in* S. Moratti & D. Patterson (Eds.), *Legal Insanity and the Brain: Science, Law and European Courts*, Hart Publishing, Portland 2016, pp. 77-110; G. Meynen, 'Legal Insanity and Neurolaw in the Netherlands', *in* S. Moratti & D. Patterson (Eds.), *Legal Insanity and the Brain: Science, Law and European Courts*, Hart Publishing, Portland 2016, pp. 137-168; D.A.G. van Toor DAG, *Het schuldige geheugen? Een onderzoek naar het gebruik van hersenonderzoek als opsporingsmethode in het licht van de eisen van instrumentaliteit en rechtsbescherming*, Wolters Kluwer, Deventer 2017.

11 Ligthart 2019.

12 S.K. Thompson, 'The Legality of the Use of Psychiatric Neuroimaging in Intelligence Interrogation', *Cornell Law Review* 2005, Vol. 90, pp. 1601-1638.

legal implications of coercive forensic neuroimaging in light of Article 3 ECHR in this chapter.

The outline of this chapter is as follows. Section 2 briefly mentions four neuroimaging applications and the way in which they could contribute to materializing the aims of criminal law. Section 3 differentiates between two types of coercion and explains their practical and legal relevance. Section 4 concisely describes the meaning and scope of the prohibition of ill-treatment ex Article 3 ECHR and exposes the legal questions that coercive neuroimaging raises in this context. In Section 5, I examine the legal conditions for coercive forensic neuroimaging in light of Article 3 ECHR. The results of this analysis are discussed in section 6.

2 Forensic Neuroimaging

Neuroimaging technologies are, to some extent, able to provide insight into our brains and their activity. The literature generally distinguishes structural and functional neuroimaging.[13] Structural imaging technologies, like MRI and CT,[14] reflect the biological structures of the brain. They reflect *brain anatomy*.[15] Functional neuroimaging, on the contrary, provides information about how the brain is active while it functions. These technologies reflect *brain activity*.[16] Examples are fMRI, EEG, PET and SPECT.[17]

Both structural and functional neuroimaging obtain information from someone's brain. This information could be relevant in a forensic context.[18] Much research has been done regarding possible legal applications of these neuroimaging technologies. I focus on four categories of neuroimaging applications that can obtain particular brain-related information and could therefore contribute to answering central questions of criminal law:[19]

13 S. Richmond, 'Introduction', *in* S. Richmond, S. Rees & S.J.L. Edwards (Eds.), *I know what you're thinking: Brain imaging and mental privacy*, Oxford University Press, London 2012, pp. 1-10.

14 Magnetic resonance imaging and computerized tomography.

15 A.L. Roskies, 'Brain Imaging Techniques', *in* S.L. Morse, A.L. Roskies (Eds.), *A primer on criminal law and neuroscience*, Oxford University Press, New York 2013, pp. 37-74, at p. 37.

16 Id., p. 66.

17 Functional magnetic resonance imaging, electroencephalography, positron emission tomography and Single-photon emission computed tomography.

18 De Kogel & Westgeest 2015, pp. 580-605; Farahany 2015, pp. 485-509.

1. brain-based lie detection;[20]
2. brain-based memory detection;[21]
3. diagnostic neuroimaging and[22]
4. neuroimaging to predict future dangerousness ('neuroprediction').[23]

Besides these four categories, more potential legal applications of neuroimaging are conceivable, such as pain detection and real-time mindreading.[24] However, these applications are still in very early experimental stages. Much more research must be done before they could actually contribute to criminal justice. The four applications mentioned above are scientifically further developed, and their results have already been offered in (different) legal procedures.[25] Notice, however, that the line of argument in this chapter could also apply *mutatis mutandis* to the use of other coercive neuroimaging applications.

The four neuroimaging applications mentioned above can, each in their own way, be very helpful to answering crucial questions of criminal law, generally regarding guilt, legal responsibility and the risk of future dangerousness.[26] Note that most of these applications are still in an experimental stage – despite the fact that they have already been offered in legal procedures. Especially regarding lie and memory detection, more field research has

19 For a brief discussion of these categories, *see* Ligthart 2019.

20 M.J. Farah *et al.*, 'Functional MRI-based lie detection: scientific and societal challenges', *Nature Reviews Neuroscience*, Vol. 15, 2014, pp. 123-131.

21 J.P. Rosenfeld (Ed.), *Detecting Concealed Information and Deception: Recent Developments*, Academic Press, London 2018.

22 J.R. Simpson (Ed.), *Neuroimaging in Forensic Psychiatry: From the Clinic to the Courtroom*, Willey-Blackwell, Chichester 2012.

23 A.L. Glenn & A. Raine, 'Neurocriminology: Implications for the Punishment, Prediction and Prevention of Criminal Behaviour', *Nature Reviews Neuroscience*, Vol. 15, 2014, pp. 54-63; E. Aharoni *et al.*, 'Neuroprediction of future rearrest', *PNAS*, Vol. 110, 2013, pp. 6223-6228.

24 K.R. Davis *et al.*, 'Brain imaging tests for chronic pain: medical, legal and ethical issues and recommendations', *Nature Reviews Neurology*, Vol. 13, 2017, pp. 624-638; M.A. Just *et al.*, 'Machine learning of neural representations of suicide and emotion concepts identifies suicidal youth', *Nature Human Behaviour*, Vol. 1, 2012, pp. 911-919.

25 A. Giridharadas, 'India's use of brain scans in courts dismays critics', *New York Times*, 15 September 2008; S. Pardo & D. Patterson, *Minds, Brains, and Law. The Conceptual Foundations of Law and Neuroscience*, Oxford University Press, New York 2015, pp. 86-91; De Kogel & Westgeest 2015.

26 H.T. Greely, 'Mind Reading, Neuroscience, and the Law', *in* S.J. Morse & A.L. Roskies (Eds.), *A Primer on Criminal Law and Neuroscience*, Oxford University Press, New York 2013, pp. 120-149, at pp. 124-127; G. Meynen, 'Forensic psychiatry and neurolaw: Description, developments and debates', *International Journal of Law and Psychiatry*, 2018, doi: 10.1016/j.ijlp.2018.04.005; Rosenfeld 2018; B. Verschuere & E.H. Meijer, 'What's on Your Mind? Recent Advances in Memory Detection Using the Concealed information Test', *European Psychologist*, Vol. 19, 2014, pp. 162-171; T. Nadelhoffer *et al.*, 'Neuroprediction, Violence, and the Law: Setting the Stage', *Neuroethics*, Vol. 5, 2012, pp. 67-99.

to be done before they can be used in (forensic) practice.[27] An important current limitation of these tests, for instance, is that the subject can manipulate the imaging results with mental or physical actions (countermeasures), like moving his tongue or recalling emotional memories.[28] This limitation applies, to some extent, also to diagnostic neuroimaging and neuroprediction. After all, neuroimaging data are useless if the subject only moves a few millimetres with his head.[29]

Although several important scientific hurdles have yet to be taken, an important task of neurolaw scholars is to anticipate coming developments and consider potential legal implications of the (coercive) use of these applications in criminal law, before they actually arrive in court.[30] In the following section, I concisely discuss two types of coercion and explain their (legal) relevance regarding coercive forensic neuroimaging.

3 Coercion: Two Types and Their (Legal) Relevance

In Ligthart 2019, I conceptualized two types of coercion with which forensic neuroimaging can be applied: 1) physical coercion and 2) legal coercion.[31] In this section I briefly discuss both types and their practical and legal relevance.[32]

Physical coercion contains the use of *physical force* in order to accomplish a primary goal. For instance, if a defendant refuses to cooperate with neuroimaging, he can be physically secured in a way that most movements are impossible, which could, in some cases, enable

27 J.B. Meixner Jr., 'Admissibility and Constitutional Issues of the Concealed Information Test in American Courts: An Update', *in* J.P. Rosenfeld (Ed.), *Detecting Concealed Information and Deception: Recent Developments*, Academic Press, London 2018, pp. 405-430, at pp. 420-422; A.D. Wagner *et al.*, 'fMRI and Lie Detection: A Knowledge Brief of the MacArthur Foundation Research Network on Law and Neuroscience', MacArthur Foundation, 2016; E.H. Meijer *et al.*, 'Deception detection with behavioral, autonomic, and neural measures: Conceptual and methodological considerations that warrant modesty', *Psychophysiology*, Vol. 53, 2016, pp. 593-604.

28 J.P. Rosenfeld *et al.*, 'Simple, effective countermeasures to P300-based tests of detection of concealed information', *Psychophysiology*, Vol. 41, 2004, pp. 205-219, at pp. 205-219; Wagner *et al.* 2016; N. Kanwisher, 'The Use of fMRI in Lie Detection: What Has Been Shown and What Has Not', *in* E. Bizzi *et al.* (Eds.), *Using Imaging to Identify Deceit. Scientific and Ethical Questions*, American Academic of Arts and Sciences, Cambridge 2009, p. 12.

29 *Cf.* Kanwisher 2009, p. 12.

30 T. Nadelhoffer T & W. Sinnott-Armstrong, 'Neurolaw and Neuroprediction: Potential Promises and Perils', *Philosophy Compass*, Vol. 7, 2012, pp. 631-642, at p. 634; M. Ienca & R. Andorno, 'Towards new human rights in the age of neuroscience and neurotechnology', *Life Sciences, Society and Policy*, Vol. 13, 2017, pp. 2-27, at p. 5.

31 Ligthart 2019. *Cf.* Pardo & Patterson 2015, p. 153.

32 For a more comprehensive discussion, *see* Ligthart 2019.

the examiner to accomplish the neuroimaging assessment.[33] Another possibility is the use of chemical fixation, *i.e.* forcible administration of medication for the purpose of controlling.[34]

Legal coercion does not require physical force in order to accomplish the ultimate goal. Instead, the intended result is achieved through a *decision* of the person concerned. That decision has, however, been influenced by a legal threat to any non-cooperative person. Such a threat could be direct or rather indirect, formulated as an offer. Regarding neuroimaging, the law could for instance consider non-cooperation as a criminal offence (direct threat). Another possibility is that the law requires particular neuroimaging results as *conditio sine qua non* for bail, parole or probation.[35] This can be qualified as an indirect threat, because the law then implies that non-cooperation will result in rejection of any request for bail, parole or probation.

The distinction between these two types of coercion is relevant, both in a practical and legal way. The practical relevance is that some (functional) neuroimaging applications require the subject to do something, and can therefore only be applied successfully with legal coercion.[36] For instance, some neuroimaging applications require the subject to perform a task, like pressing a yes-or-no-button in the context of lie detection. Other applications, like some types of memory detection,[37] require the subject to observe presented stimuli *attentively*.[38] Compelling a subject to adequately perform certain tasks with physical force is hard to imagine. Moreover, the results of several neuroimaging applications can be manipulated by the subject through moving his tongue or recalling emotional events. Preventing such countermeasures with physical force seems impossible. However, if such countermeasures can be detected, the use of it can be threatened with legal consequences.[39] Such a legal threat could make the subject decide to omit manipulative measures.

33 Van Toor 2017, p. 433; Thompson 2005, p. 1631.

34 CPT, 'Means of restraint in psychiatric establishments for adults' (Revised CPT standards) (CPT/Inf(2017)6), Strasbourg.

35 *Cf.* G. Meynen, 'Brain-based mind reading in forensic psychiatry: exploring possibilities and perils', *Journal of Law and the Biosciences*, Vol. 4, pp. 311-329, at p. 326.

36 *Cf.* A.L. Roskies, 'Mind Reading, Lie Detection, and Privacy', *in* J. Clausen & N. Levy (Eds.), *Handbook of Neuroethics*,.Springer, Dordrecht 2015, pp. 679-695, at p. 684.

37 Like the concealed information test.

38 J.P. Rosenfeld *et al.*, 'The Complex Trial Protocol (CTP): a new, countermeasure-resistant, accurate, P300-based method for detection of concealed information', *Psychophysiology*, Vol. 45, 2008, pp. 906-919, at p. 906; T.W. Picton, 'The P300 wave of the human event-related potential', *Journal of Clinical Neurophysiology*, Vol. 9, 1992, pp. 456-479, at p. 456.

39 J.P. Rosenfeld *et al.*, 'Review of recent studies and issues regarding the P300-based complex trial protocol for detection of concealed information', *International Journal of Psychophysiology*, Vol. 90, 2013, pp. 118-134, at p. 120-121.

From a human rights perspective, the legal relevance of differentiating physical from legal coercion is twofold. Firstly, contrary to legal coercion, physical coercion implies an (additional) intrusion with a person's body and could therefore result in an interference with (or violation of) the right to respect for one's bodily (and/or mental) integrity.[40] Secondly, regarding legal coercion, the person concerned *decides* to cooperate with neuroimaging: in a certain way, he then *consents* with it. If a person consents with governmental actions, the question arises to which extent human rights still protect the person's interests.[41] For instance, free and informed consent for a medical intervention can avoid state liability under article 3 ECHR.[42] An important question, however, is whether one's consent is free enough to avert state liability, if it is given under a certain legal pressure, like potential criminal liability or rejection of a parole request.[43]

In the following section I discuss the meaning and scope of the prohibition of ill-treatment (Article 3 ECHR) and illustrate how coercive forensic neuroimaging raises issues in this context.

4 ARTICLE 3 ECHR AND COERCIVE FORENSIC NEUROIMAGING

According to Article 3 ECHR, 'No one shall be subjected to torture or to inhuman or degrading treatment or punishment.' This prohibition is absolute, which means that derogation of it will never be justified, neither in times of war or other public emergencies (Article 15(2) ECHR), nor in the context of fighting terrorism and organized crime, or saving lives.[44] So, if a particular treatment falls within the scope of this prohibition, it will therefore violate Article 3 ECHR.

Whether a specific treatment falls within the scope of the prohibition of ill-treatment is relative and depends on all circumstances of a particular case, like the duration, purpose, intention and motivation of the treatment, its physical and mental effects and, in some

40 *E.g.* ECtHR 18 October 2012, appl.no. 37679/08 (*Bureš v. Czech Republic*); ECtHR 31 May 2016, appl.no. 29106/13 (*Coman/Romania*).

41 W. Buelens, C. Herijgers & S. Illegems, 'The View of the European Court of Human Rights on Competent Patients' Right of Informed Consent. Research in the Light of Article 3 and 8 of the European Convention on Human Rights', *European Journal of Health Law*, Vol. 23, 2016, pp. 481-509.

42 ECtHR 3 October 2008, appl.no. 35228/03 (*Bogumil v. Portugal*), para. 71.

43 *See* Section 5.

44 ECtHR (GC) 25 September 1997, appl.no. 23178/94 (*Aydin v. Turkey*), para. 81; ECtHR (GC) 26 July 1999, appl.no. 25803/94 (*Selmouni v. France*), para. 95; ECtHR (GC) 1 June 2010, appl.no. 22978/05 (*Gäfgen v. Germany*), para. 107.

cases, the sex, age and health of the victim.[45] Taking all relevant circumstances into consideration, the treatment must attain a *minimum level of severity* in order to count as a violation of Article 3 ECHR. This means that the degree of suffering and humiliation must in any event go beyond the unavoidable element of suffering or humiliation connected with a given form of legitimate treatment or punishment.[46]

If a treatment attains a minimum level of severity and therefore falls within the scope of Article 3 ECHR, it can subsequently be qualified as torture, inhuman or degrading. In this regard, torture is considered to be the most severe form of ill-treatment. Degrading treatments form the lowest grade. Citing the Court's Grand Chamber, these three types of ill-treatment contain the following. *Torture* is "a deliberate inhuman treatment causing very serious and cruel suffering."[47] A treatment is *inhuman* if it was "premeditated, was applied for hours at a stretch and caused either actual bodily injury or intense physical or mental suffering."[48] Finally, a treatment is considered to be *degrading* if it "humiliates or debases an individual, showing a lack of respect for, or diminishing, his or her human dignity, or when it arouses feelings of fear, anguish or inferiority capable of breaking an individual's moral and physical resistance."[49]

These definitions may not immediately be associated with the use of neuroimaging technologies like (f)MRI, EEG and PET, which are broadly used in day-to-day medical practice. However, there is an important difference between neuroimaging in medical practice on the one hand, and in criminal justice on the other. In a medical setting, subjects usually participate voluntarily with neuroimaging because it is in their best interest, for instance to localize and subsequently treat a brain tumour. In the context of criminal justice, however, neuroimaging could contribute to a criminal conviction (*e.g.* lie- and memory detection), justify compulsory treatment (*e.g.* diagnostic neuroimaging) or legitimize the rejection of a parole request (*e.g.* neuroprediction). So in criminal justice, neuroimaging

45 ECtHR (GC) 1 June 2010, appl.no. 22978/05 (*Gäfgen v. Germany*), para. 88. The Court approaches the ECHR as a living instrument, and interprets it in light of the present-day conditions (ECtHR 25 April 1978, appl.no. 5856/72 (*Tyrer/UK*), para. 31). As a result, the minimum level of severity has been lowered by the Court in recent years (Harris DJ et al., *Harris O'Boyle & Warbrick: Law of the European Convention on Human Rights*, New York: Oxford University Press 2014, p. 237). In this regard, S.L.T.J. Ligthart, T. Kooijmans & G. Meynen, 'Neurotests in de Nederlandse strafrechts- pleging: een verkenning van juridische mogelijkheden en uitdagingen', *Delikt en Delinkwent*, Vol. 8, 2017, pp. 579-603, suggest that neuropsychological research findings could also influence the threshold of Article 3 ECHR.

46 ECtHR 18 January 1978, appl.no. 5310/71 (*Ireland v. UK*), para. 163.

47 ECtHR (GC) 25 September 1997, appl.no. 23178/94 (*Aydin v. Turkey*), para. 82.

48 ECtHR (GC) 21 January 2011, appl.no. 30696/09 (*M.M.S. v. Belgium and Greece*), para. 220.

49 ECtHR (GC) 17 July 2014, appl.nos. 32541/08 and 43441/08 (*Svinarenko and Slyadnev v. Russia*), para. 115. In this regard, it may be sufficient if the victim is (only) humiliated in his own eyes, provided that a minimum level of severity is attained: ECtHR 25 April 1978, appl.no. 5856/72 (*Tyrer v. UK*), paras. 30-32.

will not always be in favour of the subject's best interest. Consequently, not every person would be very likely to cooperate voluntarily. Is such cases, the authorities could apply neuroimaging coercively, *i.e. against the person's will.*

Such coercive use of neuroimaging technologies could interfere with the subject's physical and/or mental integrity, and therefore raise issues under the prohibition of ill-treatment.[50] Imagine, for instance, that a prison director wants to examine a detainee's brain using a CT scan, in order to determine whether he suffers from a specific brain abnormality and therefore poses a (higher) risk of future dangerousness. A CT scan requires injection of contrast liquid into the bloodstream of the subject, which is physically intrusive. Furthermore, CT exposes the subject to a certain amount to radiation and could therefore (however not significantly) increase the risk of cancer.[51] If the detainee refuses cooperation, the prison authorities could compel the CT scan using a security bed, head fixation strap or intramuscular injection of sedatives. Especially if the subject resists such a treatment, it could result in physical harm and/or (mental) suffering. Does such a treatment show a lack of respect for human dignity? Could it arouse feelings of fear, anguish or inferiority and break the subject's moral or physical resistance? Could it cause great distress and physical suffering which attains a minimum level of severity?[52] And, finally, to what extent would it be relevant if no physical force is used, but the detainee is told that non-cooperation will result in rejection of any probation request? Fundamental questions like these arise regarding coercive forensic neuroimaging in the context of the prohibition of ill-treatment. These questions are examined in the following section.

5 Coercive Forensic Neuroimaging in Light of Article 3 ECHR

5.1 *Introduction*

In the former section I briefly described the meaning and scope of the prohibition of ill-treatment and illustrated the legal questions that arise regarding coercive forensic neuroimaging in light of Article 3 ECHR. In this section I examine the main question of this chapter – how coercive forensic neuroimaging relates to the prohibition of ill-treatment. For this I use a research method that has been explored in Ligthart 2019. The first step of

---

50 *Cf.* Thompson 2005; Rusconi & Mitchener-Nissen 2013, p. 8.

51 S.E. Rushing, D.A. Pryma & D.D. Langleben, 'PET and SPECT', *in* J.R. Simpson (Ed.), *Neuroimaging in Forensic Psychiatry: From the Clinic to the Courtroom*, Willey-Blackwell, Chichester 2012, pp. 3-26, at pp. 7-8.

52 *Cf.* ECtHR 19 February 2015, appl.no. 75450/12 (*M.S. v. Croatia (No. 2)*); ECtHR18 October 2012, appl.no. 37679/08 (*Bureš v. Czech Republic*).

this method is creating an analogy between 'coercive forensic neuroimaging' on the one hand, and, on the other hand, treatments about which case law does already exist in the context of Article 3 ECHR (Section 5.2). The second step is determining the conditions that the ECHR sets for comparable treatments in light of the prohibition of ill-treatment (Section 5.3). Finally, I apply these conditions to coercive forensic neuroimaging (Section 5.4).

5.2 *An Analogy*

Because this chapter deals with the legal implications of coercive neuroimaging in light of Article 3 ECHR, the analogy has to focus on those aspects of a treatment that are relevant in the context of Article 3 ECHR. For the ultimate judgement about the prohibition of ill-treatment, the Court pays attention to many factors, of which three typical characteristics of a treatment itself: 1) the nature and method of the treatment,[53] 2) its purpose[54] and 3) the manner in which it was carried out.[55] Therefore, the analogy focusses on these three characteristics of coercive forensic neuroimaging.[56]

The nature, method and purpose of coercive forensic neuroimaging are in a relevant way comparable with the nature, method and purpose of 'a compulsory medical procedure to obtain evidence of a crime'. The Grand Chamber describes this latter treatment as follows:

> [A] medical procedure in defiance of the will of a suspect in order to obtain from him or her evidence of his or her involvement in the commission of a criminal offence.[57]

According to this definition, the method, nature and purpose of this treatment contain respectively the use of a *medical procedure, in defiance of the person's will* in order to *obtain evidence from the person about his involvement in a crime.* Neuroimaging technologies are, basically, also medical procedures, which are mostly used in medical practice, for instance to diagnose epilepsy (EEG), localize a tumour (MRI) or obtain information about bone

53 ECtHR (GC) 26 October 2000, appl.no. 30210/96 (*Kudła v. Poland*), para. 91; ECtHR 10 October 2001, appl.no. 33394/96 (*Price v. VK*), para. 21-30; ECtHR 18 January 1978, appl.no. 5310/71 (*Ireland v. VK*), para. 163.

54 ECtHR (GC) 1 June 2010, appl.no. 22978/05 (*Gäfgen v. Germany*), para. 88; ECtHR27 November 2003, appl.no. 65436/01 (*Hénaf v. France*), paras. 47-60.

55 ECtHR (GC) 11 July 2006, appl.no. 54810/00 (*Jalloh v. Germany*), para. 82; ECtHR 5 April 2005, appl.no. 54825/00 (*Nevmerzhitsky v. Ukraine*), paras. 94 and 97.

56 *See*, for a more comprehensive analysis, Ligthart 2019.

57 ECtHR (GC) 11 July 2006, appl.no. 54810/00 (*Jalloh v. Germany*), para. 70. *Cf.* ECtHR 13 May 2008, appl.no. 52515/99 (*Juhnke v. Turkey*), para. 72; ECtHR 3 May 2012, appl.no. 23880/05 (*Salikhov v. Russia*), para. 73.

fractures (CT).[58] If such a technology is applied *coercively*, it can also be defined as a medical procedure in defiance of the person's will. Furthermore, as outlined in Section 2, the purpose of forensic neuroimaging is obtaining information from someone's brain, regarding guilt, legal responsibility or a risk of future criminal behaviour. In other words, forensic neuroimaging also aims to obtaining information from a person about his involvement in a (future) crime. So, basically, the nature, method and purpose of coercive forensic neuroimaging are, to a relevant extent, comparable with those of a compulsory medical procedure to obtain evidence of a crime. Consequently, case law of the ECtHR regarding the latter treatment could be helpful to examine the legal implications of coercive forensic neuroimaging in light of Article 3 ECHR.

The manner in which coercive forensic neuroimaging is carried out, depends on the type of coercion that will be used. *Physical coercion* consists of two characterizing aspects: 1) physical force, 2) which accomplishes a primary goal. Both aspects are also reflected in case law of the Court regarding the use of measures of restraint, like 'fixation beds' and chemical fixation (physical force), which measures are used to preventing a person of causing damage, absconding, suppressing evidence, or to realizing a medical intervention (accomplishing a primary goal).[59] So, basically, both neuroimaging with physical coercion and the use of measures of restraint, contain physical force, which accomplishes a primary goal.

Legal coercion, on the other hand, consists of two different characterizing components: 1) a legal treat to non-cooperative subjects 2) which could enforce the intended result, by making the subject decide to cooperate. Both components are also reflected in case law regarding the use of sanctioning as an instrument of pressure, for instance by threatening with disciplinary penalties (legal threat) in order to make prisoners supply urine samples (enforcement of intended result).[60] So, depending on the type of coercion that will be used, the manner in which coercive forensic neuroimaging is carried out, is comparable with the use of measures of restraint or sanctioning as an instrument of pressure. Therefore, case law of the ECtHR regarding these comparable forms of coercion, could provide helpful insights for examining the legal implications of coercive forensic neuroimaging in light of Article 3 ECHR.

58 *Cf.* T. Greely & A.D. Wagner, *Reference Guide on Neuroscience*, National Academies Press/Federal Judicial Centre, Washington D.C. 2011, pp. 763-765, 768 and 772.

59 *E.g.* ECtHR 31 May 2016, appl.no. 29106/13 (*Coman v. Romania*), para. 14, 38-40; ECtHR 29 September 2005, appl.no. 24919/03 (*Mathew v. The Netherlands*), para. 180; ECtHR 24 September 1992, appl.no. 10533/83 (*Herczegfalvy v. Austria*), para. 81.

60 ECtHR 11 October 2005, appl.no. 60682/00 (*Young v. UK*).

In sum, I argue that, in the context of Article 3 ECHR, coercive forensic neuroimaging is, to a relevant extent,[61] comparable with the use of a compulsory medical procedure to obtain evidence of a crime. Of course, there can also be clear differences, to which I also pay attention in the analyses below. In the following sections I determine the legal conditions for compulsory medical procedures to obtain evidence (Section 5.3), which I subsequently apply to coercive forensic neuroimaging (Section 5.4).

5.3 *Compulsory Medical Procedures to Obtain Evidence and Article 3 ECHR*

The prohibition of ill-treatment does not as such prohibit recourse to a forcible medical intervention that assists in the investigation of an offence. However, any resource to a compulsory medical intervention must be convincingly justified on the facts of a particular case.[62] According to the Court, "any interference with a person's physical integrity carried out with the aim of obtaining evidence must be the subject of rigorous scrutiny, with the following factors being of particular importance":[63]

- the extent to which the forcible medical intervention was necessary to obtain the evidence;
- the health risks for the subject;
- the manner in which the procedure was carried out and the physical pain and (mental) suffering it caused;
- the degree of medical supervision and
- the actual effects on the subject's health.

In light of all the circumstances of the individual case, the intervention must not attain a minimum level of severity that would bring it within the scope of Article 3 ECHR.[64] Let us consider these factors a bit more in-depth below.

61 *I.e.* regarding the three relevant characteristics of a treatment in the context of Article 3 ECHR.

62 ECtHR (GC) 11 July 2006, appl.no. 54810/00 (*Jalloh v. Germany*), paras. 70-71; ECtHR 3 May 2012, appl.no. 23880/05 (*Salikhov v. Russia*), paras. 73-74; ECtHR 13 May 2008, appl.no. 52515/99 (*Juhnke v. Turkey*), para. 72.

63 ECtHR 3 May 2012, appl.no. 23880/05 (*Salikhov v. Russia*), para. 75; ECtHR (GC) 11 July 2006, appl.no. 54810/00 (*Jalloh v. Germany*), paras. 71-76; ECtHR 3 October 2008, appl.no. 35228/03 (*Bogumil v. Portugal*), para. 70.

64 ECtHR 3 May 2012, appl.no. 23880/05 (*Salikhov v. Russia*), para. 75; ECtHR (GC) 11 July 2006, appl.no. 54810/00 (*Jalloh v. Germany*), paras. 71-76.

Factor 1. Necessity

The factor of necessity consists of two components: proportionality and subsidiarity. Regarding *proportionality*, due regard must be had to the seriousness of the offence in issue.[65] For instance, in the case of *Jalloh v. Germany*, a small street dealer was caught for selling drugs. When the police arrested the dealer, he swallowed a package of cocaine. In order to obtain this piece of evidence, the authorities forcibly administered emetics to the dealer.[66] With regard to the necessity of this compulsory medical intervention, the Court noted that drug trafficking is a serious offence. However, this particular case concerned only a small street dealer (the obtained cocaine amounted only 0.2182 grams). The minor importance of this offence was, according to the Court, also reflected in the relative low sentence (a six-month suspended prison sentence and probation).[67] On the contrary, in *Salikhov v. Russia*, the police forcibly clipped the fingernails of a suspect of rape, and attempted to take a blood sample. Regarding the necessity, the Court considered rape a serious offence, to which states have a positive obligation to enact legislation which provides effective investigation, prosecution and punishment.[68]

The legitimacy of taking the principle of proportionality (and thus the severity of the crime) into considering in the context of Article 3 ECHR, has been disputed.[69] For instance, in his concurring opinion in *Jalloh v. Germany*, Judge Bratza could not accept that the gravity of the offence should be regarded as a relevant factor in determining whether a particular treatment violates Article 3 ECHR.[70] According to Bratza, the absolute character of the prohibition of ill-treatment does not allow for balancing the victim's conduct and public interests against the use of a treatment that (initially) attains a minimum level of severity: the threshold of Article 3 ECHR should not change according to the gravity of the offence.

However, the way in which the Court uses the principle of proportionality (and the gravity of the offence) does, in my view, not disrespect the absolute character of the prohibition of ill-treatment. In fact, the only thing the Court has ruled, is that the (dis)proportionality of an intervention is relevant for the question whether that intervention is necessary. If the intervention is not necessary, that could contribute to attaining a minimum level of

---

65 ECtHR (GC) 11 July 2006, appl.no. 54810/00 (*Jalloh v. Germany*), para. 71; ECtHR 3 May 2012, appl.no. 23880/05 (*Salikhov v. Russia*), para. 73.

66 Via a tube through his nose, into his stomach and, additionally, with an injection: ECtHR (GC) 11 July 2006, appl.no. 54810/00 (*Jalloh v. Germany*), para. 13.

67 ECtHR (GC) 11 July 2006, appl.no. 54810/00 (*Jalloh v. Germany*), para. 77.

68 ECtHR 3 May 2012, appl.no. 23880/05 (*Salikhov v.* Russia), para. 76.

69 *See e.g.* ECtHR (GC) 11 July 2006, appl.no. 54810/00 (*Jalloh v. Germany*), Concurring opinion of Judge Bratza; Dissenting opinion of Judges Wildhaber and Caflisch; Joint dissenting opinion of Judges Ress, Pellonpää and Šikuta.

70 ECtHR (GC) 11 July 2006, appl.no. 54810/00 (*Jalloh v. Germany*), Concurring opinion of Judge Bratza.

severity. However, the Court has not ruled that, if a treatment initially falls within the scope of Article 3 ECHR, a violation can nevertheless be avoided if the treatment is proportionate in light of the gravity of the offence.[71] Therefore, I favour the interpretation of Van Kempen, according to whom the principle of proportionality works in this context only in one way.[72] If a treatment itself is not severe enough to attain a minimum level of severity, the disproportionality of it can nevertheless 'push' the treatment within the scope of Article 3 ECHR. However, if the treatment *does* already attain a minimum level of severity, the gravity of the offence cannot 'pull the treatment out' of the scope of Article 3 ECHR. This interpretation relates well with the absolute character of the prohibition of ill-treatment: any treatment that attains a minimum level of severity is prohibited, irrespective of the victim's conduct and the nature of the offence concerned.[73]

As regard to *subsidiarity*, the authorities must demonstrate that they took into consideration alternative, less intrusive methods of recovering the evidence.[74] For instance, in *Jalloh v. Germany* the Grand Chamber was not satisfied that the forcible administration of emetics was indispensable to obtain the evidence, because the authorities could simply have waited for the drugs to leave the applicant's body via the natural way.[75] In *Salikhov v. Russia*, the applicant initially demonstrated willingness to cooperate with the police demands. However, the police favoured (brute) force instead, which was, according to the Court, not essential to obtain the evidence and constituted a violation of Article 3 ECHR.[76] Whether material could or should be obtained with alternative, less intrusive methods, the nature of the material seems relevant:

> The purpose of the medical intervention was the collection of biological samples which could be later examined for traces of the victim's blood or epithelial cells. Such traces being by their nature fragile and perishable, time was of the essence and the procedures had to be carried out urgently.[77]

71 *E.g.* ECtHR 3 May 2012, appl.no. 23880/05 (*Salikhov v. Russia*), para. 80-81: despite the gravity of the offence, the compulsory medical intervention violated a\Article 3 ECHR.

72 Van Kempen, comment to ECtHR (GC) 11 July 2006, appl.no. 54810/00 (*Jalloh v. Germany*), *NJCM-Bulletin* 2007/3, p. 365-366.

73 ECtHR (GC) 1 June 2010, appl.no. 22978/05 (*Gäfgen v. Germany*), para. 107.

74 ECtHR (GC) 11 July 2006, appl.no. 54810/00 (*Jalloh v. Germany*), para. 71; ECtHR 3 May 2012, appl.no. 23880/05 (*Salikhov/Russia*), para. 73.

75 ECtHR (GC) 11 July 2006, appl.no. 54810/00 (*Jalloh v. Germany*), para. 77.

76 ECtHR 3 May 2012, appl.no. 23880/05 (*Salikhov v. Russia*), paras. 77-81.

77 Id., para. 76.

Apparently, the fragile and perishable nature of the material can require urgent collection. This implies that, in such cases, less intrusive methods are not necessarily preferred, if they are more time-consuming than another, more intrusive method.

Factor 2. Health risks

A compulsory medical intervention should not entail any risks of lasting detriment to a subject's health.[78] In *Jalloh v. Germany* the Court was not satisfied that the forcible administration of emetics, which appeared to be lethal in two earlier cases, entailed merely negligible health risks. Apparently, some negligible health risks might be permissible, real health risks are not. In establishing health risks, the Court takes different factors into consideration, like whether the procedure has caused harm in other cases, a statement of a medical specialist, and the fact that other member states refrain from the particular procedure, which suggests that it is considered to pose health risks.[79]

Factor 3. Manner in which it was carried out

The manner in which a person is subjected to a compulsory medical procedure in order to retrieve evidence from him, must not attain a minimum level of severity. In particular, account has to be taken of whether the procedure caused serious physical pain or suffering.[80] It is noteworthy that the use of a physically non-intrusive method could nevertheless reach a minimum level of severity, because of the type or degree of coercion that is used. In *Bureš v. Czech Republic*, for instance, the applicant had been restrained to a hospital bed in a sobering-up centre during subsequent time periods, together for almost four hours. According to the Court, the use of this measure of restraint must have caused great distress and physical suffering, was inhuman and violated Article 3 ECHR.[81] Nevertheless, using measures of restraint is not by definition prohibited under Article 3 ECHR, if they are imposed in connection with a lawful arrest or detention and does not entail the use of force, or public exposure, exceeding what is reasonably necessary.[82] The measure must, however, not be disproportionate, having regard to the specific facts of the case.[83]

78 ECtHR (GC) 11 July 2006, appl.no. 54810/00 (*Jalloh v. Germany*), para. 71; ECtHR 3 May 2012, appl.no. 23880/05 (*Salikhov v. Russia*), para. 73.

79 ECtHR (GC) 11 July 2006, appl.no. 54810/00 (*Jalloh v. Germany*), para. 77.

80 ECtHR (GC) 11 July 2006, appl.no. 54810/00 (*Jalloh v. Germany*), para. 72; ECtHR 3 May 2012, appl.no. 23880/05 (*Salikhov v. Russia*), para. 73.

81 ECtHR 18 October 2012, appl.no. 37679/08 (*Bureš v. Czech Republic*), paras. 88-90 and 106. *Cf.* ECtHR 19 February 2015, appl.no. 75450/12 (*M.S./Croatia (No. 2)*), para. 102.

82 ECtHR (GC) 17 July 2014, appl.nos. 32541/08 and 43441/08 (*Svinarenko and Slyadnev v. Russia*), para. 117.

83 ECtHR 27 November 2003, appl.no. 65436/01 (*Hénaf v. France*), para. 56. *Cf.* ECtHR 18 October 2012, appl.no. 37679/08 (*Bureš v. Czech Republic*), para. 94.

Factors 4 and 5. Medical supervision and actual health effects

Regarding medical supervision, it is relevant whether a compulsory medical procedure was ordered and administered by a medical specialist and whether the person concerned was placed under constant medical supervision.[84] Furthermore, it is important to obtain an adequate anamnesis of the applicant's health status prior to the compulsory procedure, in order to ascertain whether his health might be at risk if the procedure will be applied against his will.[85] A final relevant factor is whether the compulsory medical procedure actually causes any aggravation of the subject's health, and has lasting consequences in this regard.[86]

5.4 *Coercive Forensic Neuroimaging and Article 3 ECHR*

In the former section I discussed the legal implications of the use of compulsory medical interventions to obtain evidence of a crime in light of Article 3 ECHR. In Section 5.2, we saw that coercive forensic neuroimaging is, in the context of Article 3 ECHR, in a relevant way comparable with a compulsory medical intervention to obtain evidence of a crime. Therefore, in this section I examine the legal implications of coercive forensic neuroimaging in light of Article 3 ECHR, using the case law as discussed above.

In the previous section we saw that coercive medical procedures to obtain certain forensic information, are not as such prohibited under Article 3 ECHR. However, any interference with a person's physical integrity in order to obtain evidence must be subjected to rigorous scrutiny, and in this regard, the five factors discussed above are of particular importance. On the one hand, one can argue that neuroimaging is, in principle, not physically intrusive (provided that injection of contrast liquid is not required), does therefore not interfere with a person's physical integrity, as a consequence of which there is no reason to assume that the five factors discussed above are of particular importance in this context. After all, unlike taking blood, clipping finger nails and administering emetics, neuroimaging obtains information from the subject without entering or touching his body. It only observes the subject's brain from an external perspective.[87]

---

84 ECtHR (GC) 11 July 2006, appl.no. 54810/00 (*Jalloh v. Germany*), para. 73; ECtHR 3 May 2012, appl.no. 23880/05 (*Salikhov/Russia*), paras. 73 and 79; ECtHR 3 October 2008, appl.no. 35228/03 (*Bogumil v. Portugal*), para. 70.

85 ECtHR (GC) 11 July 2006, appl.no. 54810/00 (*Jalloh v. Germany*), para. 80.

86 Id., paras. 74 and 91; ECtHR 3 May 2012, appl.no. 23880/05 (*Salikhov v. Russia*), para. 73; ECtHR 3 October 2008, appl.no. 35228/03 (*Bogumil v. Portugal*), para. 70.

87 Pardo & Patterson 2015, p. 156.

However, this line of reasoning is, in my view, not very persuasive. First, in the context of Article 8 ECHR, the Court has ruled repeatedly that any coercive medical intervention interferes with the subject's physical integrity – even if it is 'of minor importance'.[88] This means that any coercive medical intervention interferes with one's physical integrity, such as taking saliva,[89] supplying urine samples[90] and, more important, coercively applying X-ray.[91] While these specific interventions did not attain a minimum level of severity, and were therefore considered under Article 8 ECHR,[92] it does not affect the fact that these compulsory medical interventions, including a coerced X-ray, interfere with a person's physical integrity. Consequently, coercive neuroimaging, being a coercive medical procedure, does also interfere with the subject's physical integrity.[93] Therefore, the five factors discussed above are of particular importance regarding coercive forensic neuroimaging in light of the prohibition of ill-treatment. Moreover, if neuroimaging is applied with *physical coercion*, that will result in an additional interference with one's bodily integrity.

Secondly, the Court considers the five factors highly important *in connection with the particularly intrusive nature* of the medical procedure concerned.[94] While neuroimaging is not intrusive in a physical way, it could be considered to be intrusive in the sense that it intrudes into someone's mental life.[95] In this connection, the five factors can also be considered to be particularly important for the ultimate judgement about coercive neuroimaging in light of Article 3 ECHR.

In sum, I argue that coercive forensic neuroimaging, as a compulsory medical intervention, interferes with the subject's physical integrity. Furthermore, such a treatment can be considered as mentally intrusive. Consequently, in order to examine how coercive forensic neuroimaging relates with Article 3 ECHR, the following factors are particularly important:
- the extent to which coercive forensic neuroimaging is necessary to obtain the information;
- the health risks for the subject;

---

88 *E.g.* ECtHR 15 May 2018, appl.no. 41079/16 (*Caruana v. Malta*), para. 26; ECtHR 19 December 2013, appl.no. 45872/06 (*Yuriy Volkov v. Ukraine*), para. 84; ECtHR 3 July 2012, appl.no. 34806/04 (*X. v. Finland*), para. 212; ECtHR 13 May 2008, appl.no. 52515/99 (*Juhnke v. Turkey*), paras. 71 and 76.
89 ECtHR 15 May 2018, appl.no. 41079/16 (*Caruana v. Malta*).
90 ECtHR 11 October 2005, appl.no. 60682/00 (*Young v. UK*).
91 ECHR 10 December 1984, appl.no. 10435/83 (*Acmanne and others v. Belgium*).
92 *Cf.* ECtHR 22 July 2003, appl.no. 24209/94 (*Y.F. v. Turkey*), para. 71.
93 Depending on its severity in a particular case, it could fall within the scope of Article 3 or 8 ECHR.
94 ECtHR (GC) 11 July 2006, appl.no. 54810/00 (*Jalloh v. Germany*), para. 71; ECtHR 3 May 2012, appl.no. 23880/05 (*Salikhov v. Russia*), para. 73.
95 R. Brownsword, 'Regulating brain imaging: Questions of privacy, informed consent, and human dignity', *in* S. Richmond, S. Rees, S.J.L. Edwards (Eds.), *I know what you're thinking: Brain imaging and mental privacy*, Oxford University Press, London 2012, pp. 223-244, at p. 223.

- the manner in which the neuroimaging procedure is carried out and the physical pain and (mental) suffering it causes;
- the degree of medical supervision and
- the actual effects on the subject's health.

Factor 1. Necessity: proportionality and subsidiarity
Neuroimaging technologies like (f)MRI, EEG and MEG[96] are not, or only slightly physically intrusive. Therefore, presumably, regardless the minor severity of an offence in a particular case, these technologies would not easily lead to disproportionality. Some technologies, like PET and SPECT, are a bit more intrusive, because they require injection of radioactive contrast liquid into the subject's bloodstream.[97] They could therefore require a more severe crime in order to avoid disproportionality.

With regard to subsidiarity, alternative, less intrusive methods should prevail over coercive forensic neuroimaging. For instance, if the results of a recent neuroimaging application could be acquired from a hospital, coercive neuroimaging will not meet with the requirement of subsidiarity. Furthermore, the nature of the information that a neuroimaging application obtains, is relevant in this context. If the information is fragile and/or perishable, a quick neuroimaging assessment could prevail over a more time consuming, but less intrusive method.

Regarding diagnostic neuroimaging and neuroprediction, the nature of the information will probably not give rise to the need of urgent collection. These applications obtain information about brain features that, in principle, will not change considerably or disappear in a (relative) short time period. For instance, brain damage, a tumour or inactivity of a particular brain area are, in general, structural by nature: they continue to exist over time. If a defendant, for instance, suffered from a damaged prefrontal cortex at the time of the offence, this can, in principle, be detected today, tomorrow and next month with neuroimaging. The same applies *mutatis mutandis* to brain-based lie detection. According to the assumption, specific brain areas are activated more than others if the subject tells a lie.[98] For this, it is in principle irrelevant whether the subject lies today, tomorrow or next month. Deliberately providing false information would activate those specific brain areas each time, which can be detected with neuroimaging. Of course, after a certain period of time the subject can forget some aspects of a former event, or remember them wrongfully.

96 Magnetoencephalography.
97 Rushing, Pryma & Langleben 2012, pp. 6-8.
98 Farah *et al.* 2014.

However, in such cases, the subject does not *deliberately* provide false statements and is therefore not lying.[99]

In the context of brain-based memory detection, however, parts of the information to obtain could be perishable and therefore require urgent collection. After all, by forgetting information, certain aspects of a particular event disappear from one's memory. Indeed, research shows that the detection of recognition of *peripheral* aspects of a mock crime (like a painting on a wall of the crime scene), is less accurate after one or two weeks than the detection of recognition of central aspects of the same crime (like the stolen ring).[100] Furthermore, in order to determine whether a subject recognizes a crime related object accurately, no crime related information should be leaked to innocent subjects.[101] After all, if crime related information leaks, an 'innocent' subject could recognize leaked crime related stimuli, which would wrongfully imply that he knows something about the crime concerned. In order to overcome the risk of forgotten and leaked information, urgent application of memory detection is desirable.[102] Therefore, in the context of subsidiarity, quick brain-based memory detection could, under certain circumstances, prevail over alternative, less intrusive but more time consuming methods.

Factor 2. Health risks

In general, neuroimaging technologies do not entail any (significant) health risks for the subject. However, the individualized health risks of a specific neuroimaging application depend on the technology that is used, together with all personal circumstances of the subject. For instance, while (f)MRI does in general not pose any health risks, it could be risky for persons with metal objects in their body, a pacemaker or claustrophobia.[103]

Furthermore, some technologies expose the subject to some extent to radiation. The doses of radiation of a brain scan with PET entail approximately 1 milisievert (mSv), with CT

---

99 *Cf.* Pardo & Patterson 2015, pp. 81, 100 and 108-110; N. Lisofsky *et al.*, 'Investigating socio-cognitive processes in deception: A quantitative meta-analysis of neuroimaging studies', *Neuropsychologia* 2014. 61, p. 113.

100 Rosenfeld *et al.* 2013, p. 123; X. Hu & J.P. Rosenfeld, 'Combining the P300-complex trial-based concealed information test and the reaction time-based autobiographical implicit association test in concealed memory detection', *Psychophysiology*, Vol. 49, 2012, pp. 1090-1100, at p. 1097.

101 M.T. Bradley *et al.*, 'Leakage of information to innocent suspects', *in* B. Verschuere, G. Ben-Shakhar & E. Meije (Eds.), *Memory detection: Theory and application of the Concealed Information Test*, Cambridge University Press, New York 2011, pp. 187-199; H. Meijers *et al.*, 'Memory detection with the Concealed Information Test: A meta analysis of skin conductance, respiration, heart rate, and P300 data', *Psychophysiology*, 2014, 51(9), p. 897.

102 *Cf.* Van Toor 2017, pp. 84-87.

103 T. Brown & E. Murphy, 'Through a Scanner Darkly: Functional Neuroimaging as Evidence of a Criminal Defendant's Past Mental States', *Stanford Law Review* 2010, 62, p. 1138.

2 mSv and with SPECT 6,9 mSv.[104] In principle, these doses pose no significant health risks. According to Rushing, Pryma and Langleben:

> Doses of radiation below 1 Sv [=1000 mSv] are unlikely to produce any immediate detectable changes in humans, though they have risk of inducing mutations which may lead or predispose to cancer formation at a later time.[105]

According to Eugene, a widely used figure is a 5% excess risk of death from cancer with a 1000 mSv dose.[106] This means for instance that a CT scan of the brain increases the subject's risk to die from cancer with, on average, 0,01%. The individualized risk will however depend on personal circumstances, like sex and age.[107] So, an important medical question is which health risks exist from radiation exposure through different neuroimaging applications, regarding different subgroups of subjects. The subsequent legal/political question then would be, which health risks we want to accept in order to answer different legal questions of criminal justice. The Dutch legislator, for instance, decided not to allow the use of CT in order to investigate a defendant's body, because of its relative high dose of radiation exposure (unlike X-ray, which is permitted).[108]

Factor 3. Manner in which coercive forensic neuroimaging is carried out

The manner in which coercive forensic neuroimaging is carried out, depends on the type of coercion that is used. Below, I discuss forensic neuroimaging with legal and physical coercion.

Legal coercion does not entail any form of physical force. Instead, in this context the subject decides to cooperate with a neuroimaging assessment, which assessment in itself does, in principle, not cause any (severe) physical and mental pain or suffering. An fMRI scan may be noisy and unpleasant, and the injection of contrast liquid could be annoying. Nevertheless, these (short) treatments are not expected to cause a degree of suffering that attains a minimum level of severity.[109] Furthermore, neuroimaging technologies like (f)MRI, EEG and CT, which are broadly used in day-to-day medical practice, without physical force, will usually not result in severe feelings of fear or humiliation, nor will they disrespect

---

104 Rushing, Pryma & Langleben 2012, p. 7; www.radiologyinfo.org, search for 'Radiation Dose in X-Ray and CT Exams'.

105 Rushing, Pryma & Langleben 2012, p. 7.

106 C. Eugene, 'Radiation Risk From Medical Imaging', *Mayo Clinic Proceedings*, Vol. 85, 2012, pp. 1142-1146, at p. 1144.

107 Rushing, Pryma & Langleben 2012, p. 8.

108 *Kamerstukken II* 1999/00, 26 983, nr. 3, p. 18. Besides, CT was thought to be too expensive.

109 *Cf.* Thompson 2005, pp. 1624-1625.

one's human dignity.[110] In general, I think that the use of forensic neuroimaging without physical force will in principle not entail a degree of suffering or humiliation that goes beyond the unavoidable element of suffering or humiliation connected with a legitimate (medical) form of neuroimaging assessments. After all, for the degree of pain and suffering that a neuroimaging technology *an sich* causes, it is in principle immaterial whether that technology is used for medical or forensic purposes.[111] Regarding coercive memory detection, however, a nuance is noteworthy. In this context the subject *must* observe the presented stimuli attentively. The mental impact of this application depends on the content of the presented stimuli. For instance, if the subject is obliged to observe pictures of a brutally murdered victim, or images of child pornography (in order to investigate whether he recognizes crime related images), it is not unthinkable that such an examination could arouse feelings of anguish, fear or inferiority – especially if the subject has ever been a victim of a comparable crime.

As we discussed in Section 3, if neuroimaging is applied with legal coercion, the subject *decides* to cooperate. To some extent he then *consents* with the neuroimaging application. Informed consent can, under certain circumstances, avert state liability under article 3 ECHR.[112] An important requirement for valid consent in this context is that the decision is *voluntary*,[113] which raises questions in the context of legally *coerced* neuroimaging.

Generally, voluntariness can be operationalized as the (degree of) control that an individual has over his own behaviour.[114] In the context of informed consent, a decision cannot be considered to be voluntary if the decision was influenced by coercion consisting of a *threat*.[115] A threat can be defined as a proposal that worsens the recipient's situation,

110 *Cf.* B. Holley, 'It's All in Your Head: Neurotechnological Lie Detection and the Fourth and Fifth Amendments', *Developments in Mental Health Law*, Vol. 28, 2009, pp. 1-23, at p. 21.

111 *E.g.* diagnosing epilepsy vs. detecting memories (EEG).

112 ECtHR 3 October 2008, appl.no. 35228/03 (Bogumil/Portugal), para. 71: "Si en effet il y a eu consentement éclairé, comme l'allègue le Gouvernement, aucune question ne se pose sous l'angle de l'article 3 de la Convention." Cf. ECHR 2 March 1983, appl.no. 9974/82 (X. v. Denmark), p. 284; Buelens, Herijgers & Illegems 2016, p. 503.

113 ECtHR 8 November 2011, appl.no. 18968/07 (*V.C. v. Slovakia*), para. 112. *Cf.* ECtHR 13 May 2008, appl.no. 52515/99 (*Juhnke v. Turkey*), para. 76; Buelens, Herijgers & Illegems 2016, p. 484.

114 M. Nelson *et al.*, 'The Concept of Voluntary Consent', *The American Journal of Bioethics*, Vol. 11, 2011, pp. 6-16, at p. 7; E. Wall, 'Voluntary Action', *Philosophia*, Vol. 28, 2001, pp. 127-136, at p. 130.

115 N. Eyal, 'Informed Consent', *in* E.N. Zalta (Ed.), *Stanford Encyclopaedia of Philosophy*, Fall 2012 edn., para. 5.1; Nelson *et al.* 2011, p. 8; T.L. Beauchamp & J.F. Childress, *Principles of Biomedical Ethics*, Oxford University Press, New York 2009, pp. 132-134; J. McGregor, 'Bargaining Advantages and Coercion in the Market', *Philosophy Research Archives*, XIV, 1988-89, pp. 23-50, at p. 46; D. Beyleveld & R. Brownsword, *Consent in the Law*, Hart Publishing, Portland 2007, pp. 131-132 and 138.

compared with a relevant baseline position before the proposal.[116] As McGregor puts it: 'generally a threat is a proposal which projects evil consequences or a sanction for non-compliance.'[117] The classic example of a threat is the following proposal: 'Your money or your life!' The individual's baseline position before this proposal, included both his money *and* his life. After the proposal, the individual's situation is worsened: now he can only keep his money *or* his life.[118] Contrary to threats, *offers* do not worsen the recipients' situation, and therefore do, in principle, not affect the voluntariness of decisions.[119] An example of an offer is the proposal of a pharmacist that offers a life-saving drug to an individual, in exchange for a sum of money.

In determining the validity of a person's consent to cooperate with legally coerced forensic neuroimaging, the voluntariness of his decision must be examined For this, the character of the government's proposal should be analysed: if it contains a threat, the subject's decision cannot be free, his consent will be invalid and can therefore not avert a violation of article 3 ECHR.

If legal coercion consists of a *direct* threat to non-cooperation with neuroimaging, *e.g.* with a fine or other forms of punishment, the choice of the subject to cooperate can clearly not be held to be voluntary. Imagine, for instance, that a public prosecutor does the following proposal to a defendant (based on a legal provision): "You cooperate with neuroprediction, or I will prosecute you for refusing to do so." This proposal clearly worsens the defendant's situation: before, he was neither prosecuted for any refusal, nor had he to undergo neuroprediction. After the proposal, his options are limited: he will either be prosecuted or undergoes neuroprediction. Consequently, his decision will not be voluntary and his consent invalid,[120] which can therefore not avoid state liability under Article 3 ECHR.

---

116 S. Anderson, 'Coercion', in E.N. Zalta (red.), *The Stanford Encyclopedia of Philosophy* (Winter 2017 Edition), para 2.2; J.W. Berg *et al.*, *Informed Consent: Legal Theory and Clinical Practice*, Oxford University Press, New York 2001, pp. 67-68; A. Wertheimer, 'A Philosophical Examination of Coercion for Mental Health', *Behavioral Sciences and the Law*, Vol. 11, 1993, pp. 239-258, at p. 244; R. Nozick, 'Coercion' *in* S. Morgenbesser, P. Suppes & M. White (Eds.), *Philosophy, Science, and Method*, St. Martin's Press, New York 1969, pp. 440-472, at p. 447.

117 McGregor 1988-89, p. 36.

118 Berg 2001, pp. 67-68; Anderson 2017, para 2.2; Beauchamp & Childress 2009, pp. 132-134; Wertheimer 1993, pp. 244-244.

119 G. Szmukler & P.S. Appelbaum, 'Treatment pressures, leverage, coercion, and compulsion in mental health care', *Journal of Medical Health*, Vol. 17, 2008, pp. 233-244, at p. 236; Wertheimer 1993, p. 244; Nozick 1969, p. 447.

120 *Cf.* ECtHR 11 October 2005, appl.no. 60682/00 (*Young v. UK*); ECtHR 5 January 2006, appl.no. 2352/02 (*Schmidt v. Germany*).

However, if a proposal to cooperate with forensic neuroimaging is formulated as an offer, things become more complicated.[121] Imagine for instance that a prison director proposes the following to an inmate: "You may go on parole, if you cooperate with neuroprediction." In principle, this proposal is an offer, not a threat, because it does not worsen the inmate's baseline position. After all, before the proposal he could not go on parole, after the proposal he can choose: stay in prison (without neuroimaging) or leave a few years earlier (with neuroimaging). No matter what he decides, he will never be worse off than before the director's proposal. Therefore, his decision can, in principle, be considered to be voluntary. If the other requirements of informed consent are also satisfied with, the inmate's consent could avoid a violation of Article 3 ECHR.

However, different scholars have argued that under certain circumstances a (coercive) offer can also result in an *in*voluntary decision.[122] According to McGregor, this is the case if the weaker recipient of an offer is in miserable circumstances with no other options, and the stronger proposer takes advantage of that situation.[123] In such situations of power imbalance and dependency, an *offer that you cannot refuse* is nothing more but just a rephrased threat.[124] Similarly, Beecher argues that such offers cannot result in valid consent:

> [T]he prospect of an award of extreme benefit to the subject such as a great reduction in time of imprisonment or parole on pardon could constitute a bribe greater than the human spirit could be expected to support, with clear violation of the necessary requirements of the principle of consent.[125]

Furthermore, Zimmerman argues that offers confine the possibilities of free decision-making, if the proposer has influenced the baseline situation of the recipient.[126] He illustrates this with the following example: "If *P* throws *Q* into the water and then offers to save *Q*

121 *Cf.* J. Pugh, 'Coercion and the Neurocorrective Offer', *in* D. Birks & T. Douglas (Eds.), *Treatment for crime: philosophical essays on neurointerventions in criminal justice*, Oxford University Press, Oxford 2018, pp. 94-115.

122 *E.g.* D. Zimmerman, 'Coercive Wage Offers', *Philosophy & Public Affairs*, Vol. 10, 1981, pp. 121-145; J. McGregor, 'Undue Influence as Coercive Offer in Clinical Trials', *in* D.A. Reidy & W.J. Riker (Eds.), *Coercion and the State*, Springer Science + Business Media B.V., Dordrecht 2008, pp. 45-59; D. Lyons, 'Welcome Threats and Coercive Offers', *Philosophy*, Vol. 50, 1975, pp. 425-436; P. Westen, '"Freedom" and "Coercion" – Virtue Words and Vice Words', *Duke Law Journal*, Vol. 34, 1985, pp. 541-593.

123 McGregor 2008, p. 52.

124 Id, p. 51; McGregor 1988-89, p. 34.

125 H.K. Beecher, 'Some fallacies and errors in the application of the principle of consent in human experimentation', *Clinical Pharmacology and Therapeutics*, Vol. 3, 1962, pp. 141-145, at p. 145.

126 Zimmerman 1981, p. 132.

(where he can do so at relatively little cost to himself) only if *Q* promises to give him his life savings afterwards, the offer is coercive and the promise void."[127]

Power imbalance and dependency are common in criminal justice: individuals in custody and prison, for instance, are to a great extent dependent of decisions of prison directors, public prosecutors and judges. Furthermore, it is mostly due to the public prosecutor and judge, that one finds himself in custody or prison. Therefore, it can be argued that offers such as "You may go on parole, if you cooperate with neuroprediction", nevertheless hamper voluntariness, hinder valid informed consent and therefore cannot avoid violation of Article 3 ECHR.[128]

The ECtHR seems to follow a comparable line of argument and adopts an approach similar to those of McGregor and Zimmerman. For instance, in *Y.F. v. Turkey*, regarding a consented gynaecological examination during detention, the Court considered that one "could not have been expected to resist submitting to such an examination in view of her vulnerability at the hands of the authorities who exercised complete control over her throughout her detention."[129] According to Buelens, Herijgers and Illegems, there seems to be a factual presumption in the Court's reasoning, that detainees cannot give free consent.[130] I doubt whether this will always be true regarding every single consenting decision. Nevertheless, I do agree that in situations of power imbalance and dependency, like in prison, the voluntariness of consenting decisions should be examined closely.[131]

Physical coercion could, in some cases, be helpful to accomplish a neuroimaging assessment while the subject resists. By physically or chemically restraining a resisting subject, neuroimaging can be applied despite the subject's non-cooperation.[132] It is however noteworthy that not every neuroimaging application can be successfully applied with physical coercion. If he must perform a task or observe stimuli attentively, physical coercion will not be very helpful. Furthermore, in preventing countermeasures, like recalling emotional memories and moving one's tongue, physical force will be useless.

According to the Grand Chamber, measures of restraint do not usually give rise to an issue under Article 3 ECHR, if they have been imposed in connection with lawful arrest or

127 Id, pp. 134, 137-138.
128 Note that in the context of Article 6 ECHR, other rules apply regarding a 'knowing and intelligent waiver'.
129 ECtHR 22 July 2003, appl.no. 24209/94 (*Y.F. v. Turkey*), para. 34. *See also* ECtHR 13 May 2008, appl.no. 52515/99 (*Juhnke v. Turkey*), para. 76.
130 Buelens, Herijgers & Illegems 2016, p. 506.
131 Id., p. 484.
132 Van Toor 2017, p. 433; Thompson 2005, p. 1631.

detention and do not entail the use of (additional) force, or public exposure, exceeding what is reasonably considered necessary in the circumstances.[133] Forensic neuroimaging can be applied during lawful custody, a prison sentence or detention under an entrustment order. However, any recourse to physical force towards a person deprived of his liberty, which has not been made strictly necessary by his own behavior, diminishes human dignity and will in principle violate Article 3 ECHR.[134] Regarding the necessity of such restraint, the Grand Chamber states:

> In this regard, it is of importance for instance whether there is reason to believe that the person concerned would resist arrest or try to abscond or cause injury or damage or *suppress evidence.*[135]

It can be argued that, for instance, a defendant who resists a neuroimaging application, which could reveal information about his involvement in a (future) crime, is in a way suppressing evidence, which could legitimize some measures of restraint. However, having regard to the specific facts of the case,[136] such measures must not be disproportionate.[137] Therefore, it is also relevant which specific measure of restraint will be used, and how intrusive that measure is. Neuroimaging requires the subject to lie still. Consequently, a resisting subject should be secured in a way that most movements are impossible, comparable with the use of a restraint bed. Such measures are, according to the Court, "usually perceived by those who have experienced it as traumatic, impossible to forget, capable of causing physical injury, humiliating and disappointing."[138] In order not to be disproportionate, such measures should therefore have a compelling reason. Note however that if physical coercion itself attains a minimum level of severity,[139] the presumed proportionality of it cannot avoid a violation of the *absolute* prohibition of ill-treatment.

Finally, confinement to a restraint bed, without medical reasons, should rarely be applied for more than a few hours.[140] Having regard to the limited duration of neuroimaging assessments, this requirement will not be very problematic.

---

133 ECtHR (GC) 17 July 2014, appl.nos. 32541/08 and 43441/08 (*Svinarenko and Slyadnev v. Russia*), para. 117.

134 ECtHR (GC) 28 September 2015, appl.no. 23380/09 (*Bouyid/Belgium*), para. 88.

135 ECtHR (GC) 17 July 2014, appl.nos. 32541/08 and 43441/08 (*Svinarenko and Slyadnev v. Russia*), para. 117 (emphasis added).

136 ECtHR 20 January 2011, appl.no. 891/05 (*Kashavelov v. Bulgaria*), para. 38.

137 ECtHR 27 November 2003, appl.no. 65436/01 (*Hénaf v. France*), para. 56.

138 ECtHR 19 February 2015, appl.no. 75450/12 (*M.S. v. Croatia (No. 2)*), para. 102.

139 *E.g.* ECtHR 13 February 2014, appl.no. 66393/10 (*Tali v. Estonia*), para. 81-82; ECtHR 18 October 2012, appl.no. 37679/08 (*Bureš v. Czech Republic*), paras. 88-90; ECtHR 31 March 2009, appl.no. 14612/02 (*Wiktorko v. Poland*), paras. 55-57.

140 ECtHR 29 May 2012, appl.nos. 16563/08, 40841/08, 8192/10 and 18656/10 (*Julin v. Estonia*), para. 127. *Cf.* ECtHR 13 February 2014, appl.no. 66393/10 (*Tali v. Estonia*), paras. 81-82.

Factors 4 and 5. Medical supervision and actual health effects

In *Jalloh v. Germany* it was the public prosecutor who ordered the compulsory medical intervention. The applicant was taken to a hospital, where a doctor executed the procedure. Approximately one hour later, the same doctor examined the applicant and declared him fit for detention.[141] The Court did not criticise this allocation of competences.[142] This suggests that, in the context of Article 3 ECHR, it could be permitted if a public prosecutor orders coercive neuroimaging, which is carried out by a medical specialist,[143] who simultaneously supervises the procedure. However, in deducing such general rules from specific cases, we should be cautious. Case law of the ECtHR focusses on the specific questions of a particular case, in light of all the specific facts and circumstances. So, although the Court did not criticise the allocation of competences in *Jalloh v. Germany*, it is not a proven fact that such an allocation will always be permitted, regarding any coercive forensic neuroimaging assessment.

Furthermore, in *Jalloh v. Germany* the Court was not satisfied with the way in which the applicant's health risks were ascertained prior the medical procedure.[144] Such a prior medical examination is also of great importance regarding coercive neuroimaging. Depending on one's personal circumstances, different contraindications can object to specific neuroimaging technologies. For instance, intra-uterine devices, pacemakers and implanted insulin pumps, are contraindications for (f)MRI, whereas pregnancy pleads against technologies that expose the subject to radioactivity, like PET, SPECT and CT. Furthermore, if the subject suffers from claustrophobia or obesities, an open (f)MRI could desirable.

Finally, whether coercive neuroimaging causes actual derogation of the subject's health, can only be determined afterwards. This makes it even more important to assess the individualized health risks in each case very carefully, prior the neuroimaging assessment.

6 CONCLUSION

In the former sections I argued that coercive forensic neuroimaging is, in the context of Article 3 ECHR, to a relevant extent comparable with compulsory medical interventions to obtain evidence of a crime. I examined the legal conditions that follow from Article 3

141 ECtHR (GC) 11 July 2006, appl.no. 54810/00 (*Jalloh v. Germany*), paras. 11-12.
142 Id., para. 80.
143 Like a (behavioural) neurologist, (neuro)psychologist or psychiatrist: De Kogel & Westgeest 2015, p. 602; Ligthart, Kooijmans & Meynen 2017, pp. 602-603.
144 ECtHR (GC) 11 July 2006, appl.no. 54810/00 (*Jalloh v. Germany*), para. 80.

ECHR for this comparable treatment, and applied them to coercive forensic neuroimaging. Yet, one last question remains to be answered: how does coercive forensic neuroimaging relate to the prohibition of ill-treatment ex Article 3 ECHR?

The answer is a typical legal one: it depends. Whether coercive forensic neuroimaging attains a minimum level of severity, depends on all relevant circumstance of the case, with particular regard to the five factors discussed in the previous section. For instance, if the information can be acquired through less intrusive methods; coercive neuroimaging is disproportionate to the crime concerned; or the subject shows willingness to cooperate, *coercive* neuroimaging will not meet with the requirement of necessity.

Additionally, a neuroimaging technology, like (f)MRI, can be harmless for person A, but lethal for B (who carries metal objects in his body). Furthermore, whether coercive neuroimaging is necessary, entails health risks, or causes pain or suffering, depends to a large extent on the type of coercion that will be used. With legal coercion, no additional interferences with the subject's physical integrity take place. Because neuroimaging itself is, in principle, not or only slightly physically intrusive, the risk that neuroimaging with legal coercion causes severe pain or suffering, is limited. In addition, with legal coercion the subject consents with neuroimaging, which could, depending on the relevant circumstances avert a violation of Article 3 ECHR.

Contrary to legal coercion, physical coercion does imply additional physical force. Restraining a resistant person could enable a successful neuroimaging application,[145] which can be justified, *e.g.* to prevent a defendant from suppressing evidence. However, in a specific case, such measures can cause great distress and suffering, which could violate article 3 ECHR.[146]

Altogether, to answer the central question of this chapter, all specific facts and circumstances of the particular case are essential. Therefore, it is difficult to determine concrete conditions under which coercive forensic neuroimaging will not violate the prohibition of ill-treatment. Nevertheless, the five factors that were discussed in this chapter, are a helpful guideline for implementing coercive neuroimaging in criminal law systems in Europe. Taking into account these factors and considerations, pioneering member states must strike a right

145 Physical force is however useless if the subject must perform a task, observe stimuli attentively or in order to prevent countermeasures.

146 *See e.g.* ECtHR 18 October 2012, appl.no. 37679/08 (*Bureš v. Czech Republic*), paras. 88-90; ECtHR 13 February 2014, appl.no. 66393/10 (*Tali v. Estonia*), paras. 81-82.

balance between using new neuroscientific technologies and respecting the prohibition of ill-treatment.

References

Aharoni, E. *et al.*, 'Neuroprediction of future rearrest', *PNAS*, Vol. 110, pp. 6223-6228.

Alimardani, A. & Chin., J., 'Neurolaw in Australia: The Use of Neuroscience in Australian Criminal Proceedings', *Neuroethics*, 2019, https://doi.org/10.1007/s12152-018-09395-z.

Anderson, S., 'Coercion', *in* E.N. Zalta (Ed.), *The Stanford Encyclopaedia of Philosophy*, Winter 2017 edn).

Beauchamp, T.L. & Childress, J.F., *Principles of Biomedical Ethics*, Oxford University Press, New York 2009.

Beecher, H.K., 'Some fallacies and errors in the application of the principle of consent in human experimentation,' *Clinical Pharmacology and Therapeutics*, Vol. 3, 1962, pp. 141-145.

Berg, J.W. *et al.*, *Informed Consent: Legal Theory and Clinical Practice*, Oxford University Press, New York 2001.

Beyleveld, D. & Brownsword, R., *Consent in the Law*, Hart Publishing, Portland 2007.

Brown, T. & Murphy, E., 'Through a Scanner Darkly: Functional Neuroimaging as Evidence of a Criminal Defendant's Past Mental States', *Stanford Law Review*, Vol. 62, 2010, pp. 119-1208.

Bublitz, J.C., 'Freedom of Thought in the Age of Neuroscience', *ARSP*, Vol. 100, 2014, pp. 1-25.

Buelens, W., Herijgers, C. & Illegems, S., 'The View of the European Court of Human Rights on Competent Patients' Right of Informed Consent. Research in the Light of Article 3 and 8 of the European Convention on Human Rights', *European Journal of Health Law*, Vol. 23, 2016, pp. 481-509.

Bradley, M.T. *et al.*, 'Leakage of information to innocent suspects', *in* B. Verschuere, G. Ben-Shakhar & E. Meijer (Eds.), *Memory detection: Theory and application of the Concealed Information Test*, Cambridge University Press, New York 2011, pp. 187-199.

Brown, T. & Murphy, E. 'Through a Scanner Darkly: Functional Neuroimaging as Evidence of a Criminal Defendant's Past Mental States', *Stanford Law Review* 2010, 62, pp. 119-1208.

Brownsword, R., 'Regulating brain imaging: Questions of privacy, informed consent, and human dignity', *in* S. Richmond, S. Rees & S.J.L. Edwards (Eds.), *I know what you're thinking: Brain imaging and mental privacy*, Oxford University Press, Croydon 2012, pp. 223-244.

Catley, P. & Claydon, L., 'The use of neuroscientific evidence in the courtroom by those accused of criminal offenses in England and Wales', *Journal of Law and the Biosciences*, Vol. 2, 2015, pp. 510-549.

Chandler, J., 'The use of neuroscientific evidence in Canadian criminal proceedings', *Journal of Law and the Biosciences*, Vol. 2, pp. 550-557.

Cornet, L. *et al.*, *Neurowetenschappelijke toepassingen in de jeugdstrafrechtketen*, WODC, The Hague 2016.

CPT, 'Means of restraint in psychiatric establishments for adults' (Revised CPT standards) (CPT/Inf(2017)6), Strasbourg.

Davis, K.R. *et al.*, 'Brain imaging tests for chronic pain: medical, legal and ethical issues and recommendations', *Nature Reviews Neurology*, Vol. 13, 2017, pp. 624-638.

Encinas de Muñagorri, R. & Saas, C., 'France. Is the Evidence Too Cerebral to Be Cartesian?', *in* S. Moratti & D. Patterson (Eds.), *Legal Insanity and the Brain: Science, Law and European Courts*, Hart Publishing, Portland 2016, pp. 77-110.

Eugene, C., 'Radiation Risk From Medical Imaging', *Mayo Clinic Proceedings*, Vol. 85, pp. 1142-1146.

Eyal, N., 'Informed Consent', *in* E.N. Zalta (Ed.), *Stanford Encyclopaedia of Philosophy*, Fall 2012 edn.

Farah, M.J. *et al.*, 'Functional MRI-based lie detection: scientific and societal challenges' *Nature Reviews Neuroscience*, Vol. 15, 2014, pp. 123-131.

Farahany, N.A., 'Neuroscience and behavioral genetics in US criminal law: an empirical analysis', *Journal of Law and the Biosciences*, Vol. 2, 2015, pp. 485-509.

Ford, E. & Aggerwal, N., 'Neuroethics of Functional Neuroimaging in the Courtroom', *in* J.R. Simpson (Eds.), *Neuroimaging in Forensic Psychiatry. From Clinic to the Courtroom*, Wiley-Blackwell, Chichester 2012, pp. 325-340.

Gaudet, L.M. & Marchant, G.E., 'Under the Rader: Neuroimaging Evidence in the Criminal Courtroom', *Drake Law Review*, 2016, pp. 577-661.

Giridharadas, A., 'India's use of brain scans in courts dismays critics', *New York Times*, 15 September 2008.

Glenn, A.L. & Raine, A., 'Neurocriminology: Implications for the Punishment, Prediction and Prevention of Criminal Behaviour', *Nature Reviews Neuroscience*, Vol. 15, 2014, pp. 54-63.

Greely, H.T., 'Mind Reading, Neuroscience, and the Law', *in* S.J. Morse & A.L. Roskies (Eds.), *A Primer on Criminal Law and Neuroscience*, Oxford University Press, New York 2013, pp. 120-149.

Greely, T. & Wagner, A.D., *Reference Guide on Neuroscience*, National Academies Press/Federal Judicial Centre, Washington D.C. 2011.

Hafner M, 'Judging homicide defendants by their brains: an empirical study on the use of neuroscience in homicide trials in Slovenia', *Journal of Law and the Biosciences* 2019, pp. 1-29, https://doi.org/10.1093/jlb/lsz006.

Harris DJ et al., *Harris O'Boyle & Warbrick: Law of the European Convention on Human Rights*, New York: Oxford University Press 2014.

Holley B., 'It's All in Your Head: Neurotechnological Lie Detection and the Fourth and Fifth Amendments', *Developments in Mental Health Law*, Vol. 28, 2009, pp. 1-23.

Hu, X. & Rosenfeld, J.P., 'Combining the P300-complex trial-based concealed information test and the reaction time-based autobiographical implicit association test in concealed memory detection', *Psychophysiology*, Vol. 49, 2012, pp. 1090-1100.

Ienca, M. & Andorno, R., 'Towards new human rights in the age of neuroscience and neurotechnology', *Life Sciences, Society and Policy*, Vol. 13, 2017, pp. 2-27.

Just, M.A. *et al.*, 'Machine learning of neural representations of suicide and emotion concepts identifies suicidal youth', *Nature Human Behavior*, Vol. 1, 2012, pp. 911-919.

Kanwisher, N., 'The Use of fMRI in Lie Detection: What Has Been Shown and What Has Not', *in* E. Bizzi *et al.* (Eds.), *Using Imaging to Identify Deceit. Scientific and Ethical Questions*, American Academic of Arts and Sciences, Cambridge 2009.

Kelly, B.D., 'Brain imaging in clinical psychiatry: Why?, *in* S. Richmond, S. Rees & S.J.L. Edwards (Eds.) *I know what you're thinking: Brain imaging and mental privacy*, Oxford University Press, London 2012, pp. 111-121.

De Kogel, C.H. & Westgeest, E.J.M.C., 'Neuroscientific and behavioral genetic information in criminal cases in the Netherlands', *Journal of Law and the Biosciences*, Vol. 2, 2015, pp. 580-605.

Ligthart, S.L.T.J., 'Coercive neuroimaging technologies in criminal law in Europe: Exploring the implications for the prohibition of ill-treatment (article 3 ECHR)', *in* L.S. Reins (Ed.), *Regulating new technologies in uncertain times*, Springer 2019.

Ligthart, S.L.T.J., Kooijmans, T. & Meynen, G., 'Neurotests in de Nederlandse strafrechtspleging: een verkenning van juridische mogelijkheden en uitdagingen', *Delikt en Delinkwent*, Vol. 8 2017, pp. 579-603.

Ligthart, S.L.T.J. *et al.*, 'Prison and the brain: Neuropsychological research in light of the European Convention on Human Rights', *New Journal of European Criminal Law*, Vol 10(3) 2019, pp. 287-300 .

Lisofsky, N. et al., 'Investigating socio-cognitive processes in deception: A quantitative meta-analysis of neuroimaging studies', *Neuropsychologia* 2014. 61, p. 113-122.

Lyons, D., 'Welcome Threats and Coercive Offers', *Philosophy*, Vol. 50, 1975, pp. 425-436.

McGregor, J., 'Bargaining Advantages and Coercion in the Market', *Philosophy Research Archives*, XIV, 1988-89, pp. 23-50.

McGregor, J., 'Undue Influence as Coercive Offer in Clinical Trials', *in* D.A. Reidy & W.J. Riker (Eds.), *Coercion and the State*, Springer Science + Business Media B.V., Dordrecht 2008, pp. 45-59.

Meijer, H. *et al.*, 'Memory detection with the Concealed Information Test: A meta analysis of skin conductance, respiration, heart rate, and P300 data', *Psychophysiology*, 2014, 51(9), p. 879-904.

Meijer, E.H. *et al.*, 'Deception detection with behavioral, autonomic, and neural measures: Conceptual and methodological considerations that warrant modesty', *Psychophysiology*, Vol. 53, 2016, pp. 593-604.

Meixner Jr., J.B., 'Admissibility and Constitutional Issues of the Concealed Information Test in American Courts: An Update', *in* J.P. Rosenfeld (Ed.), *Detecting Concealed Information and Deception: Recent Developments*, Academic Press, London 2018, pp. 405-430.

Meynen, G., 'Legal Insanity and Neurolaw in the Netherlands, *in* S. MorattI & D. Patterson (Eds.), *Legal Insanity and the Brain: Science, Law and European Courts*, Hart Publishing, Portland 2016 pp. 137-168.

Meynen, G., 'Brain-based mind reading in forensic psychiatry: exploring possibilities and perils', *Journal of Law and the Biosciences*, Vol. 4, 2017, pp. 311-329.

Meynen, G., 'Forensic psychiatry and neurolaw: Description, developments and debates', *International Journal of Law and Psychiatry*, 2018, doi: 10.1016/j.ijlp.2018.04.005.

Nadelhoffer, T. & Sinnott-Armstrong, W., 'Neurolaw and Neuroprediction: Potential Promises and Perils', *Philosophy Compass*, Vol. 7, 2012, pp. 631-642.

Nadelhoffer, T. *et al.*, 'Neuroprediction, Violence, and the Law: Setting the Stage', *Neuroethics*, Vol. 5, 2012, pp. 67-99.

Nelson, M. *et al.*, 'The Concept of Voluntary Consent', *The American Journal of Bioethics*, Vol. 11, 2011, pp. 6-16.

Nozick, R., 'Coercion' *in* S. Morgenbesser, P. Suppes & M. White (Eds.), *Philosophy, Science, and Method*, St. Martin's Press, New York 1969, pp. 440-472.

Pardo, S. & Patterson, D., *Minds, Brains, and Law. The Conceptual Foundations of Law and Neuroscience*, Oxford University Press, New York 2015.

Picton, T.W., 'The P300 wave of the human event-related potential', *Journal of Clinical Neurophysiology*, Vol. 9, 1992, pp. 456-479.

Pugh, J., 'Coercion and the Neurocorrective Offer', *in* D. Birks & T. Douglas (Eds.), *Treatment for crime: philosophical essays on neurointerventions in criminal justice*, Oxford University Press 2018, pp. 94-115.

Richmond, S., 'Introduction', *in* S. Richmond, S. Rees & S.J.L. Edwards (Eds.), *I know what you're thinking: Brain imaging and mental privacy*, Oxford University Press, London 2012, pp. 1-10.

Rosenfeld, J.P. (Ed.), *Detecting Concealed Information and Deception: Recent Developments*, Academic Press, London 2018.

Rosenfeld, J.P. *et al.*, 'Simple, effective countermeasures to P300-based tests of detection of concealed information', *Psychophysiology*, Vol. 41, 2004, pp. 205-219.

Rosenfeld, J.P. *et al.*, 'The Complex Trial Protocol (CTP): a new, countermeasure-resistant, accurate, P300-based method for detection of concealed information', *Psychophysiology*, Vol. 45, 2008, pp. 906-919.

Rosenfeld, J.P. *et al.*, 'Review of recent studies and issues regarding the P300-based complex trial protocol for detection of concealed information', *International Journal of Psychophysiology*, Vol. 90, 2013, pp. 118-134.

Roskies, A.L., 'Brain Imaging Techniques', *in* S.L. Morse & A.L. Roskies (Eds.), *A primer on criminal law and neuroscience*, Oxford University Press, New Yok 2013, pp. 37-74.

Roskies, A.L., 'Mind Reading, Lie Detection, and Privacy', *in* J. Clausen & N. Levy (Eds.), *Handbook of Neuroethics*, Springer, Dordrecht 2015, pp. 679-695.

Rusconi, E. & Mitchener-Nissen, T., 'Prospects of functional magnetic resonance imaging as lie detector', *Frontiers in Human Neuroscience*, 2013, doi: 10.3389/fnhum.2013.00594.

Rushing, S.E., Pryma, D.A. & Langleben, D.D., 'PET and SPECT', *in* J.R. Simpson (Ed.), *Neuroimaging in Forensic Psychiatry: From the Clinic to the Courtroom*, Willey-Blackwell, Chichester 2012, pp. 3-26.

Simpson, J.R. (Ed.), *Neuroimaging in Forensic Psychiatry: From the Clinic to the Courtroom*, Willey-Blackwell, Chichester 2012.

Szmukler, G. & Appelbaum, P.S., 'Treatment pressures, leverage, coercion, and compulsion in mental health care', *Journal of Medical Health*, Vol. 17, 2008, pp. 233-244.

Thompson, S.K., 'The Legality of the Use of Psychiatric Neuroimaging in Intelligence Interrogation', *Cornell Law Review*, Vol. 90, 2005, pp. 1601-1638.

Van Toor, D.A.G., *Het schuldige geheugen? Een onderzoek naar het gebruik van hersenonderzoek als opsporingsmethode in het licht van de eisen van instrumentaliteit en rechtsbescherming*, Wolters Kluwer, Deventer 2017.

Verschuere, B. & Meijer, E.H., 'What's on Your Mind? Recent Advances in Memory Detection Using the Concealed information Test', *European Psychologist*, Vol. 19 2014, pp. 162-171.

Wagner, A.D. *et al.*, 'fMRI and Lie Detection: A Knowledge Brief of the MacArthur Foundation Research Network on Law and Neuroscience', MacArthur Foundation, 2016.

Wall, E., 'Voluntary Action', *Philosophia*, Vol. 28, 2001, pp. 127-136.

Wertheimer, A., 'A Philosophical Examination of Coercion for Mental Health', *Behavioral Sciences and the Law*, Vol. 11, 1993, pp. 239-258.

Westen, P., '"Freedom" and "Coercion" - Virtue Words and Vice Words', *Duke Law Journal*, Vol. 34, 1985, pp. 541-593.

Witzel, J., 'Implications of Neuroimaging for Dangerousness Assessment', *in* J.R. Simpson (Ed.), *Neuroimaging in Forensic Psychiatry. From Clinic to the Courtroom*, Wiley-Blackwell, Chichester 2012, pp. 195-200.

Zimmerman, D., 'Coercive Wage Offers', *Philosophy & Public Affairs*, Vol. 10 1981, pp. 121-145.

7 Personality Change, Criminal Responsibility and Diminished Capacity

P. Catley

1 Free Will and Responsibility

> Clearly free will is a prerequisite for moral agency, and for society to run smoothly, we all need to believe that we are in full control of our actions. [...] Is it reasonable, however, to posit that some people are more free than others?[1]

The neuroscientifically plausible view that free will is an illusion[2] runs contrary to the law's assumption that it is, at least normally, appropriate to hold individuals responsible for their actions. Just as Mobbs *et al* argue that 'for society to run smoothly, we all need to believe that we are in full control of our actions', so for the law. The law presumes that individuals have free will, that they could choose to act otherwise and hence that it is right to hold them responsible for their actions. The courts operate under the assumption that normally people are in control of their actions. English law[3] does acknowledge certain exceptions including insanity, duress, diminished responsibility and loss of self-control.[4] It also sets an age requirement before attributing criminal responsibility. However, in general the assumption of the law is that people are responsible for and can/should be held to account for their actions.

One need not challenge society's and the law's fundamental belief in free will to question whether there are circumstances where an individual may be more or less free. However, English law operates on a binary divide: individuals are either responsible or they are not.

1 D. Mobbs *et al.*, 'Law, Responsibility, and the Brain', *PLOS Biology*, Vol. 5, No. 4, 2007, https://doi.org/10.1371/journal.pbio.0050103.

2 For the implications of this for the law, *see*: J. Greene & J. Cohen, 'For the law, neuroscience changes nothing and everything', *Philosophical Transactions of the Royal Society of London*, Vol. 359, No. 1451, 2004, pp. 1775-1785. I explore this more fully in P. Catley, 'The Future of Neurolaw', *European Journal of Current Legal issues*, Vol. 22, No. 2, 2016, http://webjcli.org/article/view/487/651.

3 Throughout for convenience the term English law will be used to cover the law of England and Wales.

4 Insanity and diminished responsibility are discussed later in this chapter. The defence of duress normally applies where a person feels compelled to act through fear of death or personal injury. The loss of control defence was introduced by s. 54 of the Coroners and Justice Act 2009. It is a partial defence reducing a conviction for murder to one for manslaughter. It replaced the provocation defence.

There is generally no gradation. This contrasts, for example, to the approach to criminal offences in the Netherlands where a five-point scale operates in assessing criminal responsibility.[5] In England gradations of responsibility may be relevant for sentencing following conviction in a criminal trial, but they are generally not relevant to determinations of guilt or innocence.

As science gains a greater understanding of the working of the human brain, society is gaining new and clearer insights into why we behave as we do. It is important that the law keeps abreast of these changes. In England, and much of the common law world, the legal definition of insanity is based on the medico-scientific knowledge of 1843[6] and the test of unfitness to plead is based on the state of scientific understanding in 1836.[7] When expert witnesses are called to give evidence on such important issues, the courts should not be asking them to apply tests based on outdated science.

This chapter will explore situations where changes in the brain are associated with changes in personality that are manifested in changes in behaviour. It will focus primarily on situations where that changed behaviour is criminal, but will also touch on other behaviour that has unfortunate implications for the individuals concerned and their friends and families. Before looking at how the criminal law responds and how it should respond to changed personality claimed to arise from changes in the brain, three famous cases of personality change will be examined. These will illustrate some of the possible causes of major personality changes, the issues that may arise and how behaviour may change over time. These lead into an examination of five cases where English courts and tribunals have faced defendants whose behaviour has been significantly altered by brain injury/disease. The limitations of the English criminal law defences of insanity, automatism and diminished responsibility will be explored, as will the Law Commission's proposal for a new defence of not criminally responsible by reason of a recognised medical condition. The chapter will conclude with a plea for a new partial defence based on diminished capacity.

5 In the Netherlands five degrees of responsibility are recognised: complete responsibility, slightly diminished, diminished, severely diminished and total absence of responsibility. *See* D. Vinkers *et al.*, 'The relationship between mental disorders and different types of crime', *Criminal Behaviour and Mental Health*, Vol. 21, No. 5, 2011, pp. 307-320 and L. Claydon, 'Are there lessons to be learned from a more scientific approach to mental condition defences', *International Journal of Law and Psychiatry*, Vol. 35, No. 2, 2012, pp. 88-98.

6 *Daniel M'Naghten's Case* (1843) 10 Cl & Fin 200.

7 *R v. Pritchard* (1836) 7 C & P 303.

2 PERSONALITY CHANGE: THE CLASSIC CASE

Phineas Gage is probably the most famous example of a person's personality being changed by a traumatic head injury. Indeed, he has been described as 'neuroscience's most famous patient'[8] and it has been estimated that his case appears in 60% of introductory psychology textbooks.[9] Gage was working on the American railroad in 1848 when he suffered his injury. The exact facts of his accident are unclear, but what is well established is that an explosion drove a 3 feet 7 inch, 13¼ pound tamping iron that he was using through his skull and brain. The tamping iron landed many yards away. Gage amazingly survived.

The classic versions of his case emphasise the changes to Gage's character. Kean summarises these accounts neatly: 'Gage's frontal lobes got pulped, he transformed from a clean-cut, virtuous foreman into a dirty, scary, sociopathic drifter.'[10] Damasio *et al.* write about how Gage:

> remained as able-bodied and appeared to be as intelligent as before the accident; he had no impairment of movement or speech; new learning was intact, and neither memory nor intelligence in the conventional sense had been affected. On the other hand, he had become irreverent and capricious. His respect for the social conventions by which he once abided had vanished. His abundant profanity offended those around him. Perhaps most troubling, he had taken leave of his sense of responsibility. He could not be trusted to honor his commitments. His employers had deemed him 'the most efficient and capable' man in their 'employ' but now had to dismiss him. In the words of his physician, 'the equilibrium or balance, so to speak, between his intellectual faculty and animal propensities' had been destroyed.[11]

These accounts of personality change stem largely from the account of the second doctor to see Gage on the day of his fateful accident. Dr John Harlow wrote about his patient both

8 S. Kean, 'Phineas Gage, Neuroscience's Most Famous Patient', *Slate*, 2014.

9 M. Macmillan, 'Restoring Phineas Gage: a 150th retrospective', *Journal of the History of the Neurosciences*, Vol. 9, No. 1, 2000, pp. 46-66.

10 Kean, *supra* n. 8.

11 H. Damasio *et al.*, 'The Return of Phineas Gage: Clues About the Brain from The Skull of a Famous Patient', *Science*, Vol. 264, No. 5162, 1994, pp. 1102-1105, at p. 1102.

shortly after the accident[12] and twenty years later.[13] It was Harlow who referred to Gage's friends and acquaintances viewing him as being 'no longer Gage.'[14]

Harlow's later account, informed by examining Gage's skull after death,[15] was that the damage to the frontal parts of the brain caused the changed behaviour.[16] This view was supported by the physiologist David Ferrier ten years later.[17] More than a century later examination of Gage's skull were conducted using modern neuroscientific techniques. It was concluded that the areas of the brain likely to have been affected were 'the ventromedial region of both frontal lobes': areas responsible for 'rational decision-making and the processing of emotion.'[18] A later study[19] identified the damage as being focussed on the left frontal cortex. Importantly, this study also looked at the fibre pathways between areas of the brain, concluding that

> the impact on measures of network connectedness between directly affected and other brain areas was profound, widespread, and a probable contributor to both the reported acute as well as long-term behavioral changes.[20]

3 Personality Change: A Modern Classic

The short account[21] by Burns and Swerdlow of a forty-year old American teacher whose behaviour changed markedly has attracted extensive interest from lawyers, ethicists, psy-

12 J.M. Harlow, 'Passage of an iron rod through the head', *Boston Medical and Surgical Journal*, Vol. 39, No. 20, 1848, pp. 389-393.

13 J.M. Harlow, 'Recovery from the passage of an iron bar through the head', *Publications Massachusetts Medical Society*, Vol. 2, No. 3, 1868, pp. 327-347. A copy of this 1868 presentation published in Boston in 1869 is available at: https://archive.org/details/66210360R.nlm.nih.gov/page/n3.

14 Id., p. 14 of the 1868 publication *supra* n. 13. For the passage from which Damasio *et al.*'s quote is largely drawn, *see* pp. 13-14 of the 1869 publication. *See also* K. O'Driscoll & J.P. Leach, '"No longer Gage": an iron bar through the head. Early observations of personality change after injury to the prefrontal cortex', *British Medical Journal (Clinical Research Edition)*, Vol. 317, No. 7174, 1998, pp. 1673-1674.

15 Phineas Gage died in 1860. At Dr Harlow's suggestion, his family disinterred Gage's body and recovered his skull.

16 Harlow, *supra* n. 13, p. 19 of the 1869 publication.

17 D. Ferrier, 'The Goulstonian Lectures on the localisation of cerebral diseases', *British Medical Journal*, Vol. 1, 1878, pp. 443-447.

18 Damasio *et al.*, *supra* n. 11, p. 1102.

19 J.D. van Horn *et al.*, 'Mapping Connectivity Damage in the Case of Phineas Gage', *PLOS ONE*, Vol. 7, No. 5, 2012.

20 Id., p. 1.

21 J.M. Burns & R.H. Swerdlow, 'Right Orbitofrontal Tumor with Pedophilia Symptom and Constructional Apraxia Sign', *Archives of Neurology*, Vol. 60, 2003, pp. 437-440.

chiatrists and psychologists.[22] In this case the man started to develop an interest in child pornography, started visiting prostitutes and then began to make sexual advances towards his pre-pubescent step daughter. The step daughter told her mother, the mother reported the matter to the police and the man was convicted of child molestation. He was sentenced to attend a rehabilitation clinic for sex addiction with the threat of jail if he refused or failed to complete the programme successfully. Although he wanted to avoid jail, he could not resist the urge to solicit sexual favours from the staff and from fellow patients. The evening before he was due to be sentenced to prison, he was taken to hospital complaining of a headache. By this stage he was also walking with a wide gait and appeared unconcerned when he urinated on himself. When tested he was unable to write a legible sentence or draw a clock face, but his verbal and memory skills seemed unaffected. He was found to have a large brain tumour; when this was resected, he was able to walk normally and recovered control of his bladder. He was sent back and completed the treatment course. Seven months later he returned to live with his wife and step daughter. About three months after returning home he started secretly collecting pornography once more, three months later he complained of severe headaches and was readmitted to hospital where it was found that the tumour had regrown. The tumour was removed and his behaviour reverted to what it had been originally. It is very hard to argue that there was no correlation between the tumour and his behaviour. Burns and Swerdlow comment that:

The orbitofrontal cortex is involved in the regulation of social behavior. Lesions acquired very early in life impede social- and moral-knowledge acquisition, which may result in poor judgment, reduced impulse control and sociopathy. A similar acquired sociopathy occurs with adult-onset damage, but previously established moral development is preserved. Nevertheless, poor impulse regulation leads to bad judgment and sociopathic behaviour.[23]

They conclude that 'Our patient could not refrain from acting on his pedophilia despite the awareness that this behaviour was inappropriate.'[24]

22 *See for example*: N. Farahany, 'Law and Behavioural Morality', *Nomos*, Vol. 52, 2012, pp. 115-165; W. Glannon, 'The Limitations and Potential of Neuroimaging in the Criminal Law', *Journal of Ethics*, Vol. 18, No. 2, 2014, pp. 153-170; O. Goodenough & M. Tucker, 'Law and Cognitive Neuroscience', *Annual Review of Law and Social Science*, Vol. 6, 2010, pp. 61-92; G. Meynen, *Legal Insanity: explorations in Psychiatry, Law and Ethics*, Springer, New York 2016; and S.J. Morse, 'Neuroimaging Evidence in Law: A Plea for Modesty and Relevance', *in* J. R. Simpson (Ed.), *Neuroimaging in Forensic Psychiatry: From the Clinic to the Courtroom*, Wiley-Blackwell, Chichester 2012.

23 Burns & Swerdlow, *supra* n. 21, pp. 438-439.

24 Id., p. 440.

Looking back to the initial quote from Mobbs *et al.*, the tumour patient we have just been considering would certainly seem to fall within the class of people who, in terms of controlling their behaviour, are less free than others.

4 Linking Brain Injuries with Criminality

Charles Whitman was another individual with a brain tumour. Whitman's tumour was found to be in the region of the amygdala – an area of the brain involved *inter alia* with emotion regulation, damage to the area potentially leading the person to act without worrying about the consequences.[25] Whitman first killed his wife and his mother then went to the University of Texas in Austin and from the university tower shot 16 people dead and wounded a further 32.[26] The Travis County Grand Jury concluded that the tumour 'undoubtedly caused him much pain and possibly contributed to his insane actions.'[27]

A subsequent investigation into the killings noted that 'abnormal aggressive behavior may be a manifestation of organic brain disease.'[28] However, the investigation concluded that 'the application of existing knowledge of organic brain function does not enable us to explain the actions of Whitman'.[29] That was 1966. Whitman never stood trial, so the courts never had to determine the cause(s) of his actions. He had been shot dead in the Texas University Tower by a police marksman. In a note left after he killed his mother, Whitman had written:

> I do not really understand myself these days. I am supposed to be an average reasonable and intelligent young man. However, lately (I cannot recall when it started) I have been a victim of many unusual and irrational thoughts. These thoughts constantly recur, and it requires a tremendous mental effort to concentrate on useful and progressive tasks.

---

25 K.J. Reddy, K.R. Menon & U.G. Hunjan, 'Neurobiological Aspects of Violent and Criminal Behaviour: Deficits in Frontal Lobe Function and Neurotransmitter', *International Journal of Criminal Justice Sciences*, Vol. 13, No. 1, pp. 44-54.

26 J.M. Blomberg *et al.*, 'Report to the Governor, Medical Aspects, Charles J Whitman Catastrophe', *8 September 1966, p. 5 of the* Findings and Recommendations, available at: http://alt.cimedia.com/statesman/specialreports/whitman/findings.pdf.

27 The News and Courier, *'Jury Blames Tumor For Killings'.* August 5, 1966. p. 9 available at: https://archive.is/20130124173937/http://news.google.com/newspapers?id=6FlJAAAAIBAJ&sjid=KQoNAAAAIBAJ&pg=804,861969&dq/.

28 Blomberg *et al.*, *supra* n. 26, p. 8.

29 Id.

In the note Whitman went on to talk about his 'overwhelming violent impulses' and how he had been 'fighting my mental turmoil alone, and seemingly to no avail.' He mentions 'tremendous headaches' and linked to these headaches made a plea that: 'After my death I wish that an autopsy would be performed on me to see if there is any visible physical disorder.'[30] There was an autopsy. It was this autopsy that discovered the tumour. The findings were examined in depth. The initial investigation was conducted by a pathologist.[31] He dismissed the possibility of a link between the tumour and the killings, but his evidence failed to persuade the Grand Jury. The second investigation involved 32 experts drawn from a wide range of disciplines including neuropathology, mental health, psychiatry, forensic pathology, psychology, functional behavioural problems, psychopathy and at least four tumour specialists.[32] This second investigation was the one that concluded that whilst 'abnormal aggressive behavior may be a manifestation of organic brain disease' existing knowledge as to how the brain works was not sufficient to explain whether the tumour caused Whitman to act as he did.

In the three cases just examined the courts did not have to determine responsibility for the behaviour. Whilst Phineas Gage's behaviour was viewed as problematic and led *inter alia* to his employer dispensing with his services, it was not criminal. The 40-year old step father did not argue at trial that the tumour caused his behaviour because at the time of his trial he did not know that he had a brain tumour.[33] Charles Whitman did not stand trial, as he had been shot dead. Although a Grand Jury was called to look into the shootings and a team of experts reported to the Governor on the cause of the shootings, there was no investigation as to Whitman's criminal responsibility for his acts. The next section will examine a couple of English cases where criminal (and civil) responsibility has been an issue following acts which were claimed only to have occurred because of personality changing events.

5 Personality Change and Responsibility: Two Contrasting Cases

Christopher Meah suffered severe head injuries when the car in which he was a rear seat passenger hit a tree. His brain injuries were likened 'to the sort of damage which could be

---

30 All quotes from the first page of letter written by Charles Whitman on 31 July 1966, shortly after he had killed his wife and his mother; but before he went to the University of Texas and commenced his shooting spree. The letter is available at http://alt.cimedia.com/statesman/specialreports/whitman/letter.pdf.

31 Dr Colomon de Chenar.

32 The list of experts and their specialisms is on pages 1-4 of the report *supra* n. 26.

33 Burns & Swerdlow's account (*supra* n. 21) does not include the court's reasons for sending him back to the rehabilitation course. Presumably the court considered the tumour relevant in deciding to send him back to the rehabilitiation course, rather than sentencing him to imprisonment.

caused deliberately in the course of carrying out a leucotomy'.[34] Kerrie Gray was a passenger on a small train which collided with a larger high-speed train. In the accident 31 people were killed and over 500 were injured.[35] Gray suffered only minor physical injuries, but suffered post-traumatic stress disorder (PTSD) and depression as a result of the accident. The personalities of both Meah and Gray changed after their respective accidents. Both Meah and Gray went on to commit criminal offences which expert witnesses said they would not have committed but for their accident. There the similarities end.

Before his accident Christopher Meah had committed a string of criminal offences. However, these were of a different type and seriousness to those he committed later. His early criminal history involved theft, driving offences, house breaking, burglary and one offence of assaulting a police officer. Additionally, his medical record identified a number of fights in which he had been involved and in which he had sustained injuries.[36] He also admitted that he had been using drugs for the three years prior to the accident and was typically drinking 15 – 20 pints of beer plus spirits each week. Meah had not done well at school and perhaps given what has just been outlined it was unsurprising that he had not managed to keep any job for long, and had spent significant periods out of work.[37]

Gray, on the other hand, had pursued a law-abiding life. Prior to the train crash, he was employed by a local authority and he was in a long-term relationship. His life was described by one judge as 'relatively uneventful';[38] it certainly did not indicate that he was likely to go on to commit a very serious criminal offence. Following the accident, Gray

> became withdrawn, was liable to angry outbursts and shunned physical contact – which naturally put a strain on his relationship with his partner. He began drinking heavily. [...] his attendance [at work] became irregular, due to various manifestations of PTSD. He changed jobs. [...] he found coping with work increasingly difficult.[39]

22 months after the accident Gray was driving when a drunk stumbled into the road causing Gray to brake. The drunk then punched the windows of Gray's car. Gray got out.

---

34 *Meah v. McCreamer* [1985] 1 All ER 367, p. 380.

35 Gray v. Thames Trains and others [2009] UKHL 33 [20] – [21].

36 In most of these fights Meah appears to have been the victim. However, in at least one he was the aggressor. In this fight he was provoked by someone who was the other side of a plate glass window. He attempted to head butt the person through the window and as a result cut his own head.

37 For fuller details of Meah's life before the accident *see* Woolf J's judgment *supra* n. 34, particularly pp. 373-374.

38 Gray v. Thames Trains and others supra n. 35 per Lord Hoffman [21].

39 Id. Lord Hoffman [57].

He later said that he was reminded of the rail crash.[40] There was a scuffle between Gray and the drunk which was broken up by passers-by. Gray then drove to the home of his girlfriend's parents, got a knife and drove back to look for the drunk. He found him and killed him by stabbing him several times.

Gray was charged with murder. Two experts, one for the defence and one for the prosecution, both agreed that at the time of the killing Gray was suffering from PTSD. Gray's plea of guilty to manslaughter on the grounds of diminished responsibility was accepted by the prosecution. He was sentenced to an indefinite hospital detention order.[41]

As Lord Brown said later in the House of Lords:

> I have the greatest sympathy for this Respondent. Truly his life has been a tragedy. For forty years a decent and law-abiding citizen, now, consequent on severe psychological trauma sustained in the Ladbroke Grove rail crash, subject to hospital and restraint orders following conviction for manslaughter. But for his injuries it is inconceivable that the Respondent would ever have killed anyone.[42]

Christopher Meah elicited less sympathy, and was treated more harshly by the criminal law. As noted earlier, Meah had not been a decent, law abiding member of society prior to the car crash in which he sustained severe head injuries. The accident did however change him. His former wife and his subsequent girlfriend, with whom he had a child, both noted a 'very marked change in his behaviour'.[43] He became more aggressive, more sexually demanding and more callous.

Three and a half years after the car crash Meah sexually assaulted and maliciously wounded a woman. The same day he sexually assaulted another woman. Seven months later, whilst on bail in respect of the first two offences, Meah raped and maliciously wounded a third woman. For these offences he was sentenced to life imprisonment – the maximum sentence available to the court.

40 Gray v. Thames Trains and another [2008] EWCA Civ 713 [7].
41 Pursuant to Sections 37 and 41 of the Mental Health Act 1983.
42 Gray v. Thames Trains and others supra n. 35 per Lord Brown [89].
43 Meah v. McCreamer, supra n. 34, p. 375.

Four expert witnesses called to give evidence at a subsequent civil trial[44] all agreed that Meah's personality had altered as a result of the head injuries sustained in the car crash. However, they were divided when it came to the question as to whether or not the brain damage could be said to have caused the offending behaviour.

Summarising Dr Roberts' evidence with regard to the injuries suffered by Meah, Woolf J. said that Dr Roberts

> had no doubt head injuries of this kind can make persons more aggressive and more psychopathic, and he was not prepared to say that the injury played no part at all. He agreed that the injury could have had a disinhibiting effect and he said he was quite prepared to accept that the behaviour of the plaintiff had changed after the accident. It did, however, remain his view that you could not, on the balance of probabilities, relate the attacks to the injury and say but for the injuries the attacks would not have occurred.[45]

Dr Leigh initially thought the time lapse between the accident and the offences was critical.[46] However, under cross-examination and in light of the evidence of Meah's former partners he accepted that if their accounts were accurate it was 'more likely that the accident was connected with the attacks.'[47]

The other two experts believed that Meah would not have committed the offences had he not suffered the head injury. Dr Noble stated of Meah that: 'He is just the sort of person who is likely to react very badly to frontal damage and in particular to display abnormal sexual behaviour, aggressiveness or antisocial conduct.'[48] In Dr Noble's view the injury removed the inhibitions which would otherwise have restrained Meah's conduct. Hence the brain damage could be said to be responsible for his actions. Dr Gooddy was similarly persuaded that on the balance of probabilities the offence would not have occurred but for the brain damage sustained in the car crash. Dr Gooddy described Meah as a psychopath

44 Meah brought a civil action for damages against the insurers of the car in which he had had been travelling. He sought damages for not just pain and suffering and loss or earnings, but also for being imprisoned for crimes which he would not have committed, but for the accident. Meah was successful in his action. Subsequent caselaw has upheld the principle that a claimant cannot profit from his own wrongdoing - *ex turpi causa non oritur actio* – so future similar civil actions for compensation for committing a crime would be very unlikely to succeed.

45 Meah v. McCreamer, supra n. 34, p. 381.

46 In his report he had stated: 'The fact that 3.5 years had gone by before Mr Meah was involved in this serious anti-social behaviour ... suggests that the frontal lobe damage, itself, was not responsible for this serious anti-social behaviour.' *Meah v. McCreamer, supra* n. 34, p. 382.

47 Id.

48 Id., p. 380.

and in relation to the injury he had suffered he said that he was 'the worst possible person to sustain an injury of this kind' as the lack of inhibition arising from the effects of the injury exaggerated his tendencies and made him more likely to put them into effect.[49]

If we refer back again to the initial quote from Mobbs *et al.*, Meah is clearly in less control of his actions following the accident than he was prior to the accident. The same is true of Gray. However, Gray had a partial defence. Following the acceptance of Gray's plea of diminished responsibility, the trial judge chose a sentence which reflected the fact that he might respond better to treatment in hospital rather than detention in prison. Meah was not treated in the same manner. He was sentenced to life imprisonment and detained as a Category A prisoner – a designation reserved for the most dangerous prisoners. Arguably, given the extreme seriousness of his offences and his dangerous disinhibited violent behaviour this was appropriate; yet possibly it did not reflect his blameworthiness. Meah was not able to claim diminished responsibility as the partial defence only applies to a charge of murder. He was not insane, he knew the nature and quality of his acts and he knew that what he did was legally wrong.[50] He was also probably not treatable; as Dr Gooddy said 'He will never be the same man again'.[51] Meah illustrates a problem for the law: the person who because of a brain injury is less blameworthy, but more dangerous.

6 THREE MORE ENGLISH CASES

Graham Worrall worked for British Rail as a technician. According to Worrall's account, whilst working for the railway he suffered a severe electric shock which rendered him unconscious for over half an hour, he was then treated in hospital for shock and burns. Worrall claimed that the shock changed his personality. Almost exactly two years after the incident, Worrall committed a serious sexual offence against a prostitute. Nine months later he committed a similar offence against another prostitute. He was convicted and sentenced to six years imprisonment for the two offences. At a subsequent trial[52] medical evidence was provided; this was summarised in the statement of claim:

---

49 Id., p. 381.

50 *Infra* n. 79 and accompanying text.

51 *Meah v. McCreamer,* supra note 34, p. 380.

52 *Worrall v. British Railways Board* (unreported) All England Official Transcripts (1997-2008) (judgment 29 April 1999). In this case Worrall sued his former employers for loss of earnings and pension rights arising from their negligence. The British Railways Board had dismissed Worrall when he was sentenced to imprisonment. The Board accepted that they had been negligent, but disputed the extent of his injuries and argued (successfully) that for public policy reasons (*see supra* n. 44) that they were not liable to compensate Worrall for losses that had arisen as a result of his criminal acts.

> As will appear from the medical reports the plaintiff suffered serious psychological effects and/or neurological damage and by reason of the same his personality changed so that he committed criminal offences and was in prison for six years ... for two offences of buggery committed against working prostitutes in 1986. The criminal behaviour was caused by the plaintiff's injuries and their secondary psychological and psychiatric effects.[53]

At trial Worrall had not argued that his criminal behaviour had been caused by the accident.[54] However, as with Meah, even if the causal link had been accepted it is hard to see how under the current law it would have affected the determination of guilt. As it was not a murder charge the partial defence of diminished responsibility was not available to him. Additionally, there was no suggestion that he was unfit to plead and no suggestion that he was insane. If his argument was accepted then it might possibly have affected sentence, but again as with Meah, the effect might simply have led to him being viewed by the sentencing judge as more dangerous – therefore potentially leading to a longer sentence on the basis that the public needed to be protected from such a dangerous offender.

Derek Chisnall was a successful solicitor until he fell from his horse. It was a serious accident. He stopped breathing and had to be resuscitated. He suffered cerebral damage and his personality changed. Nevertheless, Chisnall continued in practice. However, he found it difficult to manage his large practice. He failed to file accounts, withdrew money from client's accounts and used it for his own purposes. The shortfall in client accounts amounted to at least £697,600. The Solicitors Disciplinary Tribunal referred to a psychiatric report that found:

> because of his disturbed emotional state and impaired executive functions (reasoning, judgment, memory and concentration), the respondent had been unable to carry out the tasks entrusted to him by his clients to the best of his ability; such indolent behaviour and lack of concern in an otherwise diligent and reliable person was undoubtedly the consequence of brain damage.[55]

Normally a solicitor who had acted as Derek Chisnall had acted would have been struck off. However, the Tribunal took the view that this was an exceptional case. They accepted that he was liable for what he had done, but emphasised that this was not the same as being

53 Id.

54 At trial Worrall had argued that he had not committed the offences and had presented alibi evidence that he was elsewhere. This was not believed by the jury.

55 P. Niekerk, 'Solicitors Disciplinary Tribunal – Re Derek John Arthur Chisnall (decision 4525)', *Law Society's Gazette*, Vol. 87, No. 48, 1990.

culpable. Chisnall's psychiatric report had said that it was difficult to give a prognosis as to recovery. In his particular case they decided to spare him the 'ignominy' of being struck off, but in order to protect the public they decided that he should be suspended for life, but with the express provision that the suspension might be brought to an end if he was shown once more to be fit to practice. Whilst not a determination of criminal responsibility, the approach of the Solicitors Disciplinary Tribunal is interesting for the sympathetic manner in which the case was assessed and the way the outcome could be altered if Chisnall recovered.

Trevor Hayes was a criminal with a brain tumour. Prior to October 2010 he had committed a number of relatively minor crimes of dishonesty: theft, fraud, deception as well as a number of motoring offences. He had one conviction for violence, actual bodily harm, for which he had been fined. In October 2010 his style of offending changed. Between October 2010 and January 2011, he committed four firearms offences,[56] three robberies and one offence of arson. He pleaded guilty and was sentenced to an indeterminate sentence of imprisonment for public protection (IPP)[57] coupled with a sentence of 15 years imprisonment. IPPs were introduced to protect the public from serious offenders whose crimes did not merit a life sentence. Prisoners subject to IPPs have to first complete their tariff sentence, in Hayes' case 15 years, then became eligible to apply for release. They will only be released if the Parole Board is satisfied that their continued detention is no longer necessary in order to protect the public. If released a former IPP prisoner will be on supervised licence for at least 10 years. IPPs proved very contentious and following a review were abolished in 2012.[58] However, abolition was not retrospective, so prisoners already subject to such sentences remained subject to them.

Hayes' tumour was only discovered after he had been convicted and sentenced. His tumour was described as having grown to 'enormous size'.[59]

> The MRI scan prior to operation confirmed the presence of a large tumour compressing the brain and stretching from the middle of the frontal lobe into the parietal lobe. It had eroded the vault of the skull and was seen to be protruding through the skull plate itself.[60]

56 Two offences of possession of a firearm with intent to cause fear of violence and two offences of having a firearm with intent to commit an indictable offence (robbery).

57 IPP stands for Imprisonment for Public Protection. IPPs were introduced in 2005 pursuant to the Criminal Justice Act 2003.

58 Legal Aid, Sentencing and Punishment of Offenders Act 2012 s. 123.

59 *R v. Trevor Raymond Hayes* [2013] EWCA Crim 897 [23].

60 Id.

Hayes appealed against his sentence. There was evidence that his later offending behaviour was out of character; his original pre-sentence report had noted that the escalation in his offending behaviour had been 'wholly unexpected by those who had been supervising him in the community.'[61] There was also evidence that some of Hayes' behaviour whilst preparing for and committing the offences was odd. He wore the same high visibility jacket whilst committing all the serious offences in the three-month period. He had visited the bank where he committed an armed robbery several times in the week preceding the offence. He wore a balaclava when committing all the offences, but, when robbing the bank, he took it off despite the presence of CCTV cameras. He pointed a sawn-off shotgun at a man and demanded the keys to the man's van, but when given the keys he then returned them. His previous lower level offending had not been marked by such eccentric actions.

Dr Fenwick, a consultant neuropsychiatrist, gave evidence at Hayes' appeal that:

> [t]here is medical evidence that Mr Hayes has had a meningioma which has been growing for at least the last ten years. This tumour reached an unusually large size and will certainly have compromised his cognitive functioning and his mental states. There is little doubt that he had an abnormality of mind at the time of the offences in 2010 and that this abnormality of mind significantly impaired his judgment, his understanding and his insight into his own behaviour. He had never used a gun before or employed threatening behaviour. These, together with the impulsiveness, the other features of these crimes, discussed above, and the personality changes noticed by those close to him, would suggest that the tumour had a significant effect on his behaviour and mental state ... Although it is never possible to be 100% certain, I do feel that the characteristics of the offences point to the abnormal mental state which had developed due to his tumour, and in consequence, had there been no tumour he would not have behaved in the way that he did. I would have expected him to continue with his previous career of petty thieving ... but not to embark on the use of firearms and direct personal threats of violence.[62]

The operation to remove the tumour was only partially successful; not all of it was removed and it was considered very likely that it would regrow. However, the evidence from the medical staff and prison officers indicated that he 'showed no evidence of aggressive or impulsive outbursts, and nothing to suggest he would again be a danger to the public.'[63]

61 Id. [15].
62 Id. [26].
63 Id. – quoted from Dr Fenwick's report.

The Court of Appeal was satisfied by Dr. Fenwick's evidence that, following the removal of the tumour, Hayes no longer presented a risk of serious harm to the public and that therefore 'in these highly exceptional circumstances'[64] the IPP should be set aside. Additionally, the minimum sentence was reduced from 15 years to 11 years because of the tumour evidence.

7 Interim Conclusions from the English Cases

English courts and tribunals have been ready to accept that behaviour may change as a result of brain injury,[65] brain disease[66] or even the effect of traumatic events on brain functioning.[67] They have also accepted that brain injury and brain disease can affect responsibility[68] and future risk.[69] Expert evidence has been accepted pointing to reduced impulse control,[70] aggressive behaviour[71] and poor judgment.[72]

In the cases there has been a need to show changed behaviour. In Meah's case this was not just the offences, but also the evidence of his post-injury callous behaviour towards his sexual partners. In Gray's case there was evidence of his work and relationship problems. Trevor Hayes was able to introduce evidence that not only was his behaviour whilst committing his later offences bizarre, but in addition after most of the tumour was removed his behaviour was not perceived as presenting a danger to the public. In addition to the evidence of behaviour there was expert evidence that injury had been suffered and that the behavioural change could be linked to that injury. The experts were in agreement in Gray's case, but there was some division in the case of Meah.

The ability of English courts and tribunals to handle the evidence of personality change is interesting and shows a variety of approaches. In Gray's case it led to the prosecution accepting a plea of guilty to a lesser charge and the imposition of a sentence aimed more at rehabilitation than punishment, but still with a clear focus on public protection. In

64 Id. [30].
65 *E.g.* Christopher Meah and Derek Chisnall.
66 *E.g.* Trevor Hayes.
67 *E.g.* Kerrie Gray.
68 Kerrie Gray's plea of diminished responsibility was accepted. Derek Chisnall's liability for breaches of the Solicitor's Rules was explicitly differentiated from his culpability for his acts.
69 Christopher Meah's brain injury made him more dangerous. Trevor Hayes' brain tumour was linked to his more violent behaviour, but the partially successful treatment of his tumour together with his subsequent behaviour led to him being viewed as less dangerous.
70 *E.g.* Christopher Meah and Kerrie Gray.
71 *E.g.* Christopher Meah, Kerrie Gray and Trevor Hayes.
72 *E.g.* Christopher Meah, Kerrie Gray, Derek Chisnall and Trevor Hayes.

Chisnall's case the approach could be seen to be similar. The tribunal protected society by stopping Chisnall from practicing as a solicitor, but held open the possibility that, if he recovered, he could be allowed to return to practice. Evidence of Hayes' tumour and the impact it had on his behaviour led to a reduced sentence. The removal of the indeterminate element of his sentence could be seen as significant, but the reduction of the tariff sentence from 15 years to 11 years could be seen as a relatively marginal reduction. If one sees criminal sentencing as primarily linked to the offence, then this reduction might seem unwarranted. If one sees it as linked to the blameworthiness of the behaviour then the four-year reduction may seem insufficient. The criminal court that sentenced Meah saw a very dangerous violent offender with little in the way of impulse control and sentenced him to the maximum available sentence. In Worrall's case, the defendant did not claim at his criminal trial that his criminal behaviour had been caused by the neurological damage and psychological effects which had changed his personality. He instead claimed not to have carried out the attacks and to have been elsewhere at the time. We can surmise why he did not advance the personality-change-based arguments, but we cannot know the reason.[73]

8 INADEQUACY OF ENGLISH LAW

As a result of brain injury, brain disease or psychological changes following traumatic events some people are less able to control their behaviour. This can lead to their coming before the criminal courts. The defence of diminished responsibility could potentially apply to many of the cases we have been considering, except that it is limited to murder.[74] The lack of a general partial defence akin to the partial defence of diminished responsibility

73 Perhaps he thought he had a better chance of acquittal if he claimed to have been elsewhere. Perhaps he genuinely was elsewhere and his conviction was a miscarriage of justice. Perhaps the neurological damage and psychological damage affected his memory. Perhaps he didn't really believe in the personality-change argument, but only later brought it up to pursue an action for negligence against his former employer. Or perhaps he realised from the precedent of *Meah* that in determinations of guilt for crimes other than murder evidence of brain-injury-induced criminal behaviour offers no defence and can lead courts to focus on the perceived dangerousness of the offender and the risk of reoffending.

74 The reason why it exists as a defence for murder is the mandatory life sentence that applies under English law for those convicted of murder. The defence of diminished responsibility is only a partial defence: it reduces a conviction for murder to one for manslaughter. Whilst the maximum sentence for manslaughter is life imprisonment, this is not a mandatory sentence. The courts have the discretion to impose a more appropriate sentence. Arguably this means that for other offences where there is discretion as to sentence there is no need for a defence along the lines of the diminished responsibility defence. However, diminished responsibility has two further advantages. Firstly, in terms of fair labelling of criminal behaviour – the offender who successfully pleads diminished responsibility is not labelled a murderer. Secondly, and perhaps most importantly, the defence will, if the plea is not accepted by the prosecution, be tested in court.

is a serious lacuna that should be remedied. As the following discussion will show, automatism and insanity do not fill the gap.

8.1 Automatism

From a defendant's perspective, automatism[75] is the more attractive mental condition defence as it leads to acquittal: an accused who succeeds with a plea of automatism walks free from court. However, automatism must be from an external cause.[76] In *Charlson* the accused who was suffering from a brain tumour succeeded in a claim of automatism; however subsequent case law means this decision is unlikely to be followed.[77] PTSD on the other hand might, depending on the facts, be viewed, as automatism.[78] However, the authority for this proposition, *R v. T* is not the decision of an appellate court and therefore in the English system of precedent is less significant. Additionally, the cause of the PTSD in *R v. T* had happened only three days prior to the defendant's criminal act – a very different scenario than that in *Gray*, where a year that elapsed between the train crash and Gray stabbing to death the person who had stepped in front of his car. Whilst an automatism verdict might be attractive to the defendant, it is worrying from the perspective of public

---

75 Automatism in this context is being differentiated from insane automatism. A finding of insane automatism leads to the same disposal options as the special verdict of not guilty by reason of insanity. Automatism is also sometimes referred to as non-insane automatism or sane automatism to differentiate it more clearly from insane automatism.

76 English law distinguishes internal causes leading to a finding of insane automatism (insanity) and external causes leading to a finding of automatism. This leads to the strange result that an accused who commits a crime having taken insulin and suffering a hypoglycaemic episode will be acquitted, unless fault attaches to the taking of the insulin. An accused who commits a crime having failed to take insulin and then suffered a hyperglycaemic episode will be found to be insane.

77 In *R v. Charlson* [1955] 1 WLR 317, Charlson was suffering from a cerebral tumour which led him to act 'as an automaton without any real knowledge of what he was doing'. He succeeded in his defence of automatism. However, in *R v. Kemp* Kemp who was suffering from arteriosclerosis which had caused a congestion of blood on the brain was found to be suffering from a 'disease of the mind'. Devlin J. held 'In my judgment the condition of the brain is irrelevant and so is the question of whether the condition of the mind is curable or incurable, transitory or permanent.' [1957] 1 QB 399 at 407. The issue came before the House of Lords in *Bratty v. Attorney General for Northern Ireland* where Lord Denning approved *Kemp* and stated that 'it seems to me that any mental disorder which has manifested itself in violence and is prone to recur is a disease of the mind. At any rate it is the sort of disease for which a person should be detained in hospital rather than given an unqualified acquittal.' per Lord Denning *Bratty v. Attorney General for Northern Ireland* [1963] AC 386, p. 412. In the Law Commission's 2013 Discussion Paper *Criminal Liability: Insanity and Automatism* they noted that Charlson should under the current law not have succeeded on the basis of sane automatism, but should have been found to be insane (p. 93).

78 In *R v. T* [1990] Crim LR 256 a defendant who committed a robbery whilst suffering from PTSD as a result of having been raped was able to claim sane automatism. Similarly, though not an automatism case, in *R v. Huckerby* a security guard who was convicted of conspiracy to rob was allowed an appeal because he had not been able to show expert evidence that could have supported his contention that his PTSD, depression and acute stress disorder explained his failure to activate the alarm and a tracking device.

protection. If a person, who acts violently or in some other criminal manner because of for example PTSD or a brain tumour, is able to plead automatism successfully and as a result walks free, then the public are not protected. It may be appropriate to view the defendant as having been less blameworthy, but the needs of society at large also require consideration.

8.2 *Insanity*

The defence of insanity might appear a likely defence for those representing defendants with abnormal brain functioning of the kinds we have been considering in this chapter. However, the defence as developed through caselaw is unlikely to apply to many such defendants. The test of insanity as applied in the English courts dates back to 1843:

> to establish a defence on the ground of insanity, it must be clearly proved that, at the time of the committing of the act, the party accused was labouring under such a defect of reason, from disease of the mind, as not to know the nature and quality of the act he was doing; or, if he did know it, that he did not know he was doing what was wrong.[79]

The elements of this test likely to present the greatest difficulty to defendants such as those we have been considering are those found in the final part. The first element – the 'defect of reason' – potentially applies in all the cases we have examined. The head injuries, brain tumours and PTSD all led to defective reasoning in the form of poor judgment, aggressive reactions and impulsiveness. The archaic term 'disease of the mind' has been interpreted by the courts widely. Brain tumours almost certainly fall within the phrase.[80] Whether brain injuries and psychological responses to traumatic events fit neatly within its ambit is more problematic. PTSD is a psychological state rather than a disease.[81] Personality-changing brain injuries, such as those suffered by Meah, would similarly not normally be labelled by the medical profession as diseases of the mind or even the brain. However, both fall within the ambit set out by Lord Denning in the House of Lords in *Bratty v.*

---

79 *Daniel M'Naghten's Case* (1843) 10 Cl & Fin 200. It is taken from the guidance given by the senior judges to Parliament (the House of Lords) following the finding that Daniel M'Naghten was 'not guilty being insane' of the murder of Edward Drummond. Drummond was the Prime Minister Sir Robert Peel's Private Secretary and the killing was generally viewed as an attempt to kill the Prime Minister. Lord Tindal CJ responded on behalf of the majority of the senior judges and explained the common law defence of insanity. The quotation comes from Lord Tindal's explanation.

80 Though note the earlier discussion of *R v Charlson supra* n. 77 where a brain tumour led to a successful plea of automatism.

81 As noted above *supra* n. 78 PTSD has in one reported case led to a finding of automatism.

Attorney General for Northern Ireland 'that any mental disorder which has manifested itself in violence and is prone to recur is a disease of the mind.'[82] This very wide definition would include Meah's head injury, Gray's PTSD and Hayes' tumour.

However, the final alternative limbs of needing to show that as a result the defendant either did not 'know the nature and quality' of the act or did not know what was being done was legally wrong[83] would appear to rule out all our examples. The American teacher described by Burns and Swerdlow appears to have known what he was doing when he made sexual advances towards his step daughter. Trevor Hayes appears to have known what he was doing, even though he behaved oddly while committing his offences. The same applies in the other criminal cases. Possibly by the time the American teacher was making sexual approaches to staff and people on the course he had ceased to know what he was doing, but his more general knowledge that what he was doing was wrong does not seem to have been eradicated.[84] Even Charles Whitman, whose actions were described as 'insane' by the Travis County Grand Jury, would not seem to satisfy the requirements of the English insanity defence as he appears to have known what he was doing and known that it was legally wrong.

8.3 *Other Defences*

There are other general defences which some defendants might be able to use, but these commonly will not apply in the sort of cases we have been considering. For example, a defendant fearing a violent attack can act in self-defence, even if the belief of imminent attack is mistaken and unreasonable. Possibly a brain condition might lead to a defendant holding an honest, but mistaken and unreasonable belief either about the threat and/or the level of violent defence that was reasonable in the circumstances. There is guidance from the Ministry of Justice that indicates that self-defence is to be judged subjectively.[85] However, in *R v. Martin* the Court of Appeal indicated that in assessing self-defence the

82 Attorney General for Northern Ireland v. Bratty supra n. 77, p. 412.

83 In *R v. Windle* [1952] 2 QB 826 it was held that the term 'wrong' in the *M'Naghten* test meant 'legally wrong' rather than for example morally wrong.

84 Burns & Swerdlow note that when on the training programme: "Our patient could not refrain from acting on his pedophilia despite the awareness that this behaviour was inappropriate." *Supra* n. 21, p. 440

85 Ministry of Justice Circular 2010/13 para 25 relates to the test in the loss of control defence and states that: "in common with the complete defence of self-defence, this is a subjective test. The defendant does not need to prove that his or her fear was reasonable; the jury need only be convinced that the fear was genuine." The loss of control defence was introduced by the Coroners and Justice Act 2009 (*supra* n. 4). The new defence replaced the provocation defence and like diminished responsibility has the effect, if successfully pleaded, of reducing murder to manslaughter.

court could take into account physical characteristics, but should only take into account psychiatric characteristics in exceptional circumstances.[86] [87]

9 Towards a Better Approach

9.1 *Is the Medical Condition Linked to the Behaviour?*

In framing the law, one should differentiate between defendants who have a medical condition which is linked to their criminal behaviour and those whose medical condition is not linked. In the case of Kerrie Gray the expert witnesses were agreed that he would not have killed had he not suffered PTSD. In Christopher Meah's case the experts were not all in agreement, but the judge found the expert evidence that he would not have committed the crimes but for his head injury more persuasive. The disciplinary tribunal in Derek Chisnall's case were persuaded that his misuse of client money would not have arisen but for the head injury sustained when he fell from his horse.[88] In these three cases there was evidence not just that the individual was suffering from a medical condition which could lead to the sort of behaviour that had been shown by the defendant, but also that in other ways the individual's behaviour had changed.

9.2 *Was the Medical Condition an Operative Factor at the Time of the Act?*

In Whitman's case the Governor's expert panel, whilst acknowledging that organic brain disease could lead to abnormal aggressive behaviour, was unable to determine definitively whether the tumour explained the killings. The argument that it might have been in his case, was however, arguably stronger than in the case of Graham Worrall. Whitman definitely had a tumour, he had suspected that there might be something wrong with him and

86 "We would accept that the jury are entitled to take into account in relation to self-defence the physical characteristics of the defendant. However, we would not agree that it is appropriate, except in exceptional circumstances which would make the evidence especially probative, in deciding whether excessive force has been used to take into account whether the defendant is suffering from some psychiatric condition." *R v. Martin (Anthony)* [2001] EWCA Crim 2245 [67]. In Martin's appeal there was also discussion as to whether psychiatric evidence could be relevant to the question of whether he honestly believed that he needed to defend himself [68] – [74], but on the facts the Court of Appeal considered that the question of Martin's honest belief had already been fully explored at trial.

87 Arguably a brain tumour or a brain injury might be seen as physical, whereas PTSD might be seen as psychiatric.

88 In the other cases this was not an issue which the courts were called upon to determine.

wrote of his concerns about 'the overwhelming violent urges'[89] that he could not explain or understand. Worrall, on the other hand, claimed to have been knocked unconscious for 30 minutes by a severe electric shock and that subsequently as a result of his injuries he had to take time off work, but the evidence from the hospital which he attended[90] and the evidence of his employer[91] did not support his account. In framing the law, the aim should be to determine whether the medical condition was a factor at the time of the offence.

9.3 *What Part Did Other Factors Play?*

There may be other factors at play which could offer alternative explanations. It was noted that Derek Chisnall had been drinking more following his accident. Kerrie Gray had similarly been drinking more and had consumed alcohol on the night on which he committed his crime. It was also reported that he had recently split up from his girlfriend.[92] The victims of the first two attacks by Christopher Meah reported that at the time of the offences Meah appeared high on drink or drugs.[93] However, these alternative explanations may be linked to the medical condition and/or might not have been causally linked to the offence. Derek Chisnall's drinking could have been exacerbated by the problems he found in maintaining his solicitor's practice, just as the problems of managing his practice could have been exacerbated by the drinking. His head injury may have adversely affected his judgement on these matters. Expert evidence linked the problems in Gray's relationship with his PTSD; so whilst the relationship problems may have affected his equilibrium on the night of the killing, this could still be linked back to the PTSD. There is no suggestion in the case report that he was drunk or that his drinking had led to his violent reaction. Meah's drinking and drug taking may have made him more aggressive and less inhibited, but so may the head injury. In his case the drinking and drug taking were not out of line with his behaviour prior to his accident, but the vicious sexual assaults were – so again the head injury could be seen as linked to the criminal acts, at least on the balance of probabilities. It is contended that the medically explained personality change should be a factor in explaining the behaviour, not that it should necessarily be the only factor.

89 *Supra* n. 30.

90 The hospital record noted that Graham Worrall blood pressure and pulse had been checked and then simply noted: 'Had an electric shock. Didn't feel it at all. Walked in. No cut. No blackouts. Reassured.' *Worrall v. British Railways Board supra* n. 52.

91 According to his employer's records he had not taken time off following the accident. He had subsequently taken time off, but this was for reasons unconnected with the accident.

92 A. Fresco, 'Rail Crash Survivor became a Killer', *The Times*, 4 March 2003; the Court of Appeal report merely refers to the deterioration of their relationship *supra* n. 40 [7].

93 Meah v. McCreamer supra n. 34, pp. 376-377.

9.4 *Lack of Control*

According to Burns and Swerdlow the teacher 'could not refrain from acting on his pedophilia despite the awareness that this behaviour was inappropriate'.[94] Such an individual would seem significantly less blameworthy, than an individual who acted in the same way, but from choice. However, it is not necessarily the case that earlier in the development of the tumour the same defendant was as blameless. When he was surreptitiously visiting prostitutes and viewing pornography was he more in control? The fact that he concealed his actions suggests a degree of control that seems absent later. Yet, it is not necessarily that simple, the fact that he was aware that his behaviour was inappropriate may not mean that he could in fact control it – possibly he could conceal it, but not control it.

Other defendants could be in the position that it was extremely difficult, though not necessarily impossible to control their impulses.[95] If such a defendant succumbs to the impulses she may not be as blameless as the defendant facing an irresistible impulse, but she is still arguably less blameworthy than a defendant who has free choice.

9.5 *A Possible Reform*

Currently English law has no defence of irresistible impulse,[96] however, if implemented, the Law Commission's proposal to reform the law of insanity and automatism would introduce one. The Law Commission propose a new defence of 'not criminally responsible by reason of a recognised medical condition'.

> The party seeking to raise the new defence must adduce expert evidence that at the time of the alleged offence the defendant wholly lacked the capacity:
> (i) rationally to form a judgment about the relevant conduct or circumstances;
> (ii) to understand the wrongfulness of what he or she is charged with having done; or

94 Burns & Swerdlow, *supra* n. 21, p. 440.

95 *E.g.* Whitman wrote of 'overwhelming violent impulses' and of being 'a victim of many unusual and irrational thoughts. These thoughts constantly recur, and it requires a tremendous mental effort to concentrate on useful and progressive tasks'. *Supra* n. 30.

96 Some jurisdictions have such a defence *e.g.* Ireland *The People (Attorney General) v Hayes* (30 Nov 1967) (unreported). Approved in *Doyle v Wicklow County Council* [1973] IESC 1, [1974] IR 55.

(iii) to control his or her physical acts in relation to the relevant conduct or circumstances as a result of a qualifying recognised medical condition.[97]

The proposed defence would replace the existing insanity defence and cover some cases currently falling within automatism. A person who successfully pleads the new defence could be sentenced to a hospital order (with or without a restriction of liberty order), a supervision order or could receive an absolute discharge.[98] Such a defence would potentially provide a defence for the teacher unable to prevent himself from making sexual advances whilst on the rehabilitation course as he arguably 'wholly lacked the capacity' 'to control his physical acts' as a result of the tumour (a recognised medical condition). However, the bar is set very high – to avail herself of the defence a defendant must 'wholly' lack capacity – diminished capacity is not enough. The way in which it is proposed that the new defence should be structured means that defendants who are in that grey area where it is unclear whether their capacity is wholly lacking or not may get the benefit of any reasonable doubt.

> We provisionally propose that if sufficient evidence is adduced on which, in the opinion of the court, a properly directed jury could reasonably conclude that the defence might apply, the defence should be left to the tribunal of fact to consider. The prosecution then bears the burden of disproving the defence beyond reasonable doubt.[99]

However, as noted above, the proposed new defence would not cater for the defendant who simply had diminished capacity. This is a real problem as many of the cases we have been considering are cases of diminished capacity.

9.6 DIMINISHED RESPONSIBILITY

Section 2 of the Homicide Act 1957 sets out the partial defence of diminished responsibility:

> (1) A person ('D') who kills or is a party to the killing of another is not to be convicted of murder if D was suffering from an abnormality of mental functioning which –
> (a) arose from a recognised medical condition,

97 Law Commission, 'Criminal Liability: Insanity and Automatism', 2013, p. 193, Proposal 3.

98 Id., p. 194, Proposal 10. These are similar possible outcomes to those currently available under English law for an individual found not guilty by reason of insanity in the Crown Court.

99 Id., p. 193, Proposal 6.

> (b) substantially impaired D's ability to do one or more of the things mentioned in subsection (1A), and
> (c) provides an explanation for D's acts and omissions in doing or being a party to the killing.
> (1A) Those things are –
> (a) to understand the nature of D's conduct;
> (b) to form a rational judgment;
> (c) to exercise self-control.
> (1B) For the purposes of subsection (1)(c), an abnormality of mental functioning provides an explanation for D's conduct if it causes, or is a significant contributory factor in causing, D to carry out that conduct.[100]

There are similarities between the diminished responsibility defence and the proposed defence of not criminally responsible by reason of a recognised medical condition. Both have to be based on a 'recognised medical condition' and both relate to rationality, understanding and self-control. There are however significant differences. Diminished responsibility applies only to murder: it is a partial defence reducing a conviction for murder to one for manslaughter. It applies where the defendant's ability is 'substantially impaired' whereas the Law Commission's proposed new defence is generally applicable, leads to a special not guilty verdict and requires that the defendant 'wholly' lacks capacity.

9.7 *A Better Option: A General Diminished Capacity Defence*

Whilst the diminished responsibility defence could be extended to become a general defence; there would be problems with this approach. Its operation relies upon an underlying lesser offence – this works for murder, but would potentially require the creation of a host of lesser offences that would apply if diminished responsibility was successfully argued. A better option would be to create a new partial defence based on the proposed 'not criminally responsible by reason of a recognised medical condition' defence to cover cases of substantial impairment. Replacing the word 'wholly' with 'substantially' as used in the diminished responsibility defence could provide a workable option.[101] This defence

100 As amended by s. 52 of the Coroners and Justice Act 2009.

101 The term 'substantially impaired' as used in s. 2 (1) of the Homicide Act has been the subject of case law see particularly *R v. Golds* [2016] UKSC 61. In *Golds*, Lord Hughes giving the unanimous decision of the Supreme Court stated at [44]:

1. Ordinarily in a murder trial where diminished responsibility is in issue the judge need not direct the jury beyond the terms of the statute and should not attempt to define the meaning of "substantially". Experience has shown that the issue of its correct interpretation is unlikely to arise in many cases. The jury should normally be given to understand that the expression is an ordinary English word, that it

would then apply where a defendant substantially lacked capacity; the wording of the new defence otherwise being identical to that proposed by the Law Commission for their new defence.

The new defence would recognise that there is not a simple bifurcated division between defendants who have capacity and those who lack capacity. It would allow for recognition of a middle area where capacity is substantially lacking. This overcomes one problem noted by the Law Commission:

> it is simply not possible to determine scientifically the difference between an impulse which has not been resisted and an impulse which could not be resisted, either in a person who is clinically sane or a person who has a psychiatric illness.[102]

This diminished capacity defence would note that some blameworthiness was still attached to the defendant, but that it was less than that attaching to a defendant with full capacity. The idea of a diminished capacity defence has been argued for by others, notably Stephen Morse.[103] It has advantages over simply viewing the issue as going to mitigation. As Morse explained:

> Although partial responsibility can in principle be fully considered at sentencing, this method suffers from substantial defects. First and most important, sentencing is a matter of discretion. Judges may refuse to give reduced rationality its

---

imports a question of degree, and that whether in the case before it the impairment can properly be described as substantial is for it to resolve.

2. If, however, the jury has been introduced to the question of whether any impairment beyond the merely trivial will suffice, or if it has been introduced to the concept of a spectrum between the greater than trivial and the total, the judge should explain that whilst the impairment must indeed pass the merely trivial before it need be considered, it is not the law that any impairment beyond the trivial will suffice. The judge should likewise make this clear if a risk arises that the jury might misunderstand the import of the expression; whether this risk arises or not is a judgment to be arrived at by the trial judge who is charged with overseeing the dynamics of the trial. Diminished responsibility involves an impairment of one or more of the abilities listed in the statute to an extent which the jury judges to be substantial, and which it is satisfied significantly contributed to his committing the offence. Illustrative expressions of the sense of the word may be employed so long as the jury is given clearly to understand that no single synonym is to be substituted for the statutory word.

This approach of giving the words their normal meaning and providing where necessary illustrative examples would appear a useful starting point for interpreting the term 'substantially impaired' if used in a diminished capacity defence.

102 P. Shea, 'M'Naghten Revisited – Back to the Future?', *Current Issues in Criminal Justice*, Vol. 12, No. 3, 2000, p. 357 quoted by the Law Commission, p. 64 at 4.51.

103 See S.J. Morse, 'Diminished Rationality, Diminished Responsibility', *Ohio State Journal of Criminal Law*, Vol. 289, No. 1, 2003, pp. 289-308.

> just mitigating force, and there may be wide disparities among judges sentencing similarly situated defendants. Judges, like all members of a society, have some implicit or explicit 'theory' of responsibility and how it should guide punishment. Judges' responsibility theories will also differ substantially. There is no guarantee that any individual judge's theory will be consonant with what the legislature or other more representative groups would agree is fair, and thus, the judge's mitigation decision may not comport with community norms. Moreover, mitigating primarily at sentencing removes this important culpability determination from the highly visible trial stage, at which the community's representative – the jury – makes the decision, and relegates it to the comparatively low visibility sentencing proceeding. Our criminal justice system has a preference for making crucial culpability determinations that affect punishment at trial. Partial responsibility is an explicitly normative judgment that should be made, therefore, by the community's representatives at the guilt phase, and not by judges at sentencing.[104]

The importance of leaving culpability decisions to the jury is illustrated by one of the earliest recorded personality-change-based defences. In 1874 Eadweard Muybridge was charged with the murder of his wife's lover. His defence counsel argued in his opening speech that:

> We shall prove that years ago, the prisoner was thrown from a stage, receiving a concussion of the brain, which turned his head from black to gray in three days and has never been the same since.[105]

The jury rejected the defence despite evidence from friends and acquaintances as to how his character had changed following the stagecoach accident.[106]

9.8 *Comparison with Morse's Proposed Defence*

In his 2003 work Morse proposes that his proposed general partial defence of guilty but partially responsible (GPR) would apply 'if, at the time of the crime, the defendant suffered from substantially diminished rationality for which the defendant was not responsible and

104 Id., pp. 298-299 (references to footnotes in the original omitted).

105 A. Shimamura 'Muybridge in Motion: Travels in Art, Psychology and Neurology, *History of Photography*, Vol. 26, No. 4, 2002, pp. 341-350.

106 Muybridge was however acquitted on the grounds that killing one's wife's lover was justifiable homicide. Muybridge subsequently achieved fame for his photographs of animals and people in motion.

which substantially affected the defendant's criminal conduct.'[107] There is much to commend in the idea of a general partial defence, the requirement for substantial diminution and substantial effect and the exclusion of the defence where it arises from the defendant's prior fault. However, whilst recognising the merits of Morse's proposed defence, it has some limitations.

Morse focusses on 'substantially diminished rationality' whereas my proposed variant of the Law Commission's proposed new defence covers diminished rationality, understanding and control. In cases such as those of Meah, Gray, Whitman and the American teacher, whilst rationality may have been affected, the most obvious impairment relates to impulse control. As Penney concludes having reviewed the neuroscientific literature "it is empirically true that a person can understand the wrongfulness of an act yet be powerless to refrain from committing it."[108] He later comments: "science does suggest that some people, in some situations, may find it next to impossible to control their behavior, even if they know it is wrong."[109]

In one way, Morse's proposed defence is considerably wider than the one which I propose. Mine requires that the defence stems from a recognised medical condition,[110] Morse's has no such requirement. There may be circumstances where a deserving defendant will have impaired capacity which can't be linked to a recognised medical condition – in my proposal that would simply go to mitigation. In the current political climate, a medically based partial defence would, I believe, be more likely to be politically acceptable than a potentially much wider defence.

Morse proposes that sentencing should be reduced for GPR defendants. He builds on the Federal Sentencing Guidelines' provisions[111] and proposes a fixed sentence reduction for GPR,[112] which would be inversely linked to the seriousness of the crime.[113] This has the merit of consistency, but in treating all cases the same it is incapable of adjustment to

107 *Supra* n. 103, p. 300.

108 S. Penney, 'Impulse Control and Criminal Responsibility: Lessons from Neuroscience', *International Journal of Law and Psychiatry* Vol. 35, No. 2, 2012, pp. 99-103 and 99.

109 Id., p. 100.

110 The Law Commission's proposed defence requires supporting reports from two experts and I see no reason not to follow this for my proposed partial defence.

111 Morse cites the U.S. Sentencing Guidelines Manual 2002 para. 5K2.13 provision that sentence should be reduced if a "significantly reduced mental capacity . . . contributed to the commission of the offense." The 2018 Manual para. 5K2.13 provides that: 'A downward departure may be warranted if (1) the defendant committed the offense while suffering from a significantly reduced mental capacity; and (2) the significantly reduced mental capacity contributed substantially to the commission of the offense.'

112 Morse, *supra* n. 103, p. 303.

113 In other words, the sentence reduction would be greater for less serious offences.

particular circumstances. I would propose that where the court has been satisfied that the partial defence applies the sentencing judge should have to explicitly address the impact of the finding of partial responsibility on sentence. This would force the judge to explain the impact in the particular case. In some cases, such as a treatable brain tumour, this could lead to a much-reduced sentence as not only might it be thought that the defendant's blameworthiness was substantially reduced, but it might also be considered that her future dangerousness following treatment was minimal. In other cases, notwithstanding a finding of partial responsibility, a judge might conclude that the defendant would continue to pose a serious danger to the public and that therefore a lengthy sentence remains warranted. In an ideal world, the creation of this new defence would coincide with the development of innovative new sentencing options. The Solicitors' Disciplinary Tribunal demonstrated a novel approach in Chisnall's case. This fitted their view of the need for public protection, the defendant's blameworthiness and the possibility of recovery. Recovery is possible not just in brain tumour cases. The traditional image of Phineas Gage after his accident as a 'dirty, scary, sociopathic drifter'[114] appears only to have been temporary; later in life he held down a responsible job in Chile as a long-distance stagecoach driver.[115] Van Horn *et al's* analysis of Gage's injuries[116] noted the impact on connections within the brain; greater understanding of the brain's ability to recreate networks[117] suggest that whilst these may have profound impact in the short term, in the longer term in some cases new neural networks may develop. Similarly, counselling may have a very positive impact for some patients suffering from PTSD.[118]

10 Conclusion

A general partial diminished capacity defence would avoid the stigma of the insanity defence and avoid the risk to the public of an automatism finding attaching to dangerous individuals. It would complement the Law Commission's proposed 'not criminally responsible by reason of a recognised medical condition', providing a way of marking out reduced blameworthiness where a defendant's capacity for rationality, knowledge or control

114 Kean, *supra* n. 8.

115 *See*: M.B. Macmillan, *An Odd Kind of Fame: Stories of Phineas Gage*, The MIT Press, Cambridge Massachusetts 2000.

116 Van Horn *et al.*, supra n. 19.

117 *See e.g.* R.J. Nudo, 'Recovery after Brain Injury: Mechanisms and Principles', *Frontiers in Human Neuroscience*, Vol. 23, No. 887, 2013.

118 *See e.g.* E.B. Foa, 'Psychological Processes related to Recovery from a Trauma and an Effective Treatment for PTSD, *Annals of the New York Academy of Sciences*, Vol. 821, No. 1, 1997, pp. 410-424; R.A. Bryant, 'Psychological Interventions for Trauma Exposure and PTSD', In D.J. Stein, M.J. Friedman & C. Blanco (Eds), *Post-Traumatic Stress Disorder*, Wiley-Blackwell, Hoboken NJ, 2011.

when committing a crime is substantially impaired. The burden of proof could be framed in the same way as the Law Commission proposal – placing an evidential burden on the defence and requiring the support of a minimum of two expert witnesses. Once this evidential burden had been cleared it would then be for the prosecution to prove beyond doubt that the defence did not apply. Where the defence is found to apply a verdict of guilty but only partially responsible by reason of a recognised medical condition would be returned and the judge when sentencing would have to explain how the finding had impacted on the sentence imposed.[119]

119 This chapter was first submitted in March 2019 and is based on a paper first given in Maastricht in April 2018. Subsequent to the submission of the first draft of this chapter the Sentencing Council for England and Wales announced a consultation (see: www.sentencingcouncil.org.uk/consultations/sentencing-offenders-with-mental-health-conditions-or-disorders-consultation/) on draft sentencing guidelines for offenders with mental health conditions or disorders. At the time of submitting this final version of the chapter that consultation is still open. Whilst the proposals (see: www.sentencingcouncil.org.uk/offences/magistrates-court/item/sentencing-offenders-with-mental-health-conditions-or-disorders-for-consultation-only/) are generally to be welcomed they suffer from the weaknesses identified by Morse (*supra* n. 103) in that they would keep the crucial culpability assessments away from the trial stage where they could be determined by the jury and would keep them relegated to the relatively less visible sentencing stage. Time will tell whether these new sentencing guidelines are implemented, but, even if they are, they will not negate the need for a new partial defence of diminished capacity.

References

Blomberg, J.M. *et al.*, 'Report to the Governor, Medical Aspects, Charles J Whitman Catastrophe', 8 September 1966, available at: http://alt.cimedia.com/statesman/specialreports/whitman/findings.pdf.

Bryant, R.A., 'Psychological Interventions for Trauma Exposure and PTSD', In D.J. Stein, M.J. Friedman & C. Blanco (Eds), *Post-Traumatic Stress Disorder*, Wiley-Blackwell, Hoboken NJ, 2011.

Burns, J.M. & Swerdlow, R.H., 'Right Orbitofrontal Tumor with Pedophilia Symptom and Constructional Apraxia Sign', *Archives of Neurology*, Vol. 60, 2003, pp. 437-440.

Catley, P., 'The Future of Neurolaw', *European Journal of Current Legal issues*, Vol. 22, No. 2, 2016, http://webjcli.org/article/view/487/651.

Claydon, L., 'Are there lessons to be learned from a more scientific approach to mental condition defences', *International Journal of Law and Psychiatry*, Vol. 35, No. 2, 2012, pp. 88-98.

Damasio, H. *et al.*, 'The Return of Phineas Gage: Clues About the Brain from The Skull of a Famous Patient', *Science*, Vol. 264, No. 5162, 1994, pp. 1102-1105.

Farahany, N., 'Law and Behavioural Morality', *Nomos*, Vol. 52, 2012, pp. 115-165.

Ferrier, D., 'The Goulstonian Lectures on the localisation of cerebral diseases', *British Medical Journal*, Vol. 1, 1878, pp. 443-447.

Foa, E.B., 'Psychological Processes related to Recovery from a Trauma and an Effective Treatment for PTSD, *Annals of the New York Academy of Sciences*, Vol. 821, No. 1, 1997, pp. 410-424.

Fresco, A., 'Rail Crash Survivor became a Killer', *The Times*, 4 March 2003.

Glannon, W., 'The Limitations and Potential of Neuroimaging in the Criminal Law', *Journal of Ethics*, Vol. 18, No. 2, 2014, pp. 153-170.

Goodenough, O. & Tucker, M., 'Law and Cognitive Neuroscience', *Annual Review of Law and Social Science*, Vol. 6, 2010, pp. 61-92.

Greene, J. & Cohen, J., 'For the law, neuroscience changes nothing and everything', *Philosophical Transactions of the Royal Society of London*, Vol. 359, No. 1451, 2004, pp. 1775-1785.

Harlow, J.M., 'Passage of an iron rod through the head', *Boston Medical and Surgical Journal*, Vol. 39, No. 20, 1848, pp. 389-393.

Harlow, J.M., 'Recovery from the passage of an iron bar through the head', *Publications Massachusetts Medical Society*, Vol. 2, No. 3, 1868, pp. 327-347.

Van Horn, J.D. *et al.*, 'Mapping Connectivity Damage in the Case of Phineas Gage', *PLOS ONE*, Vol. 7, No. 5, 2012.

Kean, S., 'Phineas Gage, Neuroscience's Most Famous Patient', *Slate*, 2014.

Macmillan, M., 'Restoring Phineas Gage: a 150th retrospective', *Journal of the History of the Neurosciences*, Vol. 9, No. 1, 2000, pp. 46-66.

Macmillan, M.B., *An Odd Kind of Fame: Stories of Phineas Gage*, The MIT Press, Cambridge Massachusetts 2000.

Meynen, G., *Legal Insanity: explorations in Psychiatry, Law and Ethics*, Springer, New York 2016.

Mobbs, D. *et al.*, 'Law, Responsibility, and the Brain', *PLOS Biology*, Vol. 5, No. 4, 2007, https://doi.org/10.1371/journal.pbio.0050103.

Morse, S.J., 'Diminished Rationality, Diminished Responsibility', *Ohio State Journal of Criminal Law*, 2003, pp. 289-308.

Morse, S.J., 'Neuroimaging Evidence in Law: A Plea for Modesty and Relevance', *in* J. R. Simpson (Ed.), *Neuroimaging in Forensic Psychiatry: From the Clinic to the Courtroom*, Wiley-Blackwell, Chichester 2012.

Niekerk, P., 'Solicitors Disciplinary Tribunal – Re Derek John Arthur Chisnall (decision 4525)', *Law Society's Gazette*, Vol. 87, No. 48, 1990.

Nudo, R.J., 'Recovery after Brain Injury: Mechanisms and Principles', *Frontiers in Human Neuroscience*, Vol. 23, No. 887, 2013.

O'Driscoll, K. & Leach, J.P., '"No longer Gage": an iron bar through the head. Early observations of personality change after injury to the prefrontal cortex', *British Medical Journal (Clinical Research Edition)*, Vol. 317, No. 7174, 1998, pp. 1673-1674.

Reddy, K.J., Menon, K.R. & Hunjan, U.G., 'Neurobiological Aspects of Violent and Criminal Behaviour: Deficits in Frontal Lobe Function and Neurotransmitter', *International Journal of Criminal Justice Sciences*, Vol. 13, No. 1, pp. 44-54.

Shea, P., 'M'Naghten Revisited – Back to the Future?', *Current Issues in Criminal Justice*, Vol. 12, No. 3, 2000, pp. 347-362.

Shimamura, A., 'Muybridge in Motion: Travels in Art, Psychology and Neurology', *History of Photography*, Vol. 26, No. 4, 2002, pp. 341-350.

Vinkers, D. *et al.*, 'The relationship between mental disorders and different types of crime', *Criminal Behaviour and Mental Health*, Vol. 21, No. 5, 2011, pp. 307-320.

8 Addiction, Capacities and Criminal Responsibility – A Comparative Analysis

A. Goldberg & D. Roef

1 Introduction

Addiction and criminal law frequently cross paths: alcohol or drugs abuse affects over 50 per cent of the prison population.[1] Without diverging the discussion as to the cause of this criminogenic development, it is highly relevant to address how current criminal justice systems process addicted offenders and whether this is in line with the scientific knowledge of the condition. Addiction surely impacts health and behaviour immensely and consequently could be a factor worth considering for the law. In fact, the legal relevancy of addiction may be discussed in three ways: on a theoretical-conceptual level, on a practical level regarding individual assessment and by influencing or informing criminal policy.

First, the role of addiction is relevant when considering the current criminal law doctrines and concepts in general. Particularly the insanity defence, or its civil law counterpart of non-accountability and non-culpability,[2] seem intuitively most relevant for addicts, because it applies, albeit somewhat differently per jurisdiction, to defendants with mental disorders which may influence their responsibility. Therefore, a doctrinal discussion involves the question of whether the current legal standards for the insanity defence are sufficiently capable of addressing addicted offenders. Second, within such a doctrinal framework, the question arises whether the individual capacities of the defendant (or lack thereof) can be accurately assessed. When confronted with an addicted defendant, judges may wonder, for instance, whether this particular individual is legally insane due to the consequences

---

1 C.J. Mumola & J.C. Karberg, Drug Use and Dependence, State and Federal Prisoners, 2004, 2006, p. 1.

2 For reasons of readability, from now on the common law term 'insanity defence' is also used to denote its civil law equivalents of 'non-accountability' (*ontoerekenbaarheid* in the Netherlands) and 'non-culpability' (*Schuldunfähigkeit* in Germany). Similarly, we will use the term 'diminished responsibility' when refering to its civil law counterparts of diminished accountability and diminished culpability, being well aware that, although these two notions have a similar function, they are not identical. The Dutch concept of non-accountability emphazises that the insanity defence is essentially a question of 'legal attribution' thereby reflecting the normative character of this excuse. The German notion of non-culpability, on the other hand, stresses much more the excusing effect of the defence, *i.e.* the negation of the blameworthiness of the offender. *See also*: J. Blomsma & D. Roef, 'Justifications and Excuses' *in* J. Keiler and D. Roef (Eds.), *Comparative Concepts of Criminal Law* 3rd edn, Intersentia, Cambridge 2019, p. 243.

of addiction on the individual's capacities.[3] Third, criminal policies may also benefit from research on neuroscience and addiction. Scientific evidence may influence and inform policy-making regarding the way criminal law ought to apply to addicts. This has happened before to other categories of offenders; consider, for instance, how neuroscience has affected juvenile criminal policy and responsibility practices.[4] This shows that neuroscience can contribute to overall criminal policy and can perhaps shape addiction policy in a similar fashion. This paper concerns the first question and relates to the possible doctrinal qualification of addicted offenders. In what way does addiction diminish certain capacities that are central in assessing criminal responsibility? Alternatively put, which legal insanity standards seem to be best equipped to assess the (degrees of) responsibility of the addicted offender?

In answering this question, it is first necessary to elaborate on the conceptualization of addiction, particularly from a capacitarian perspective. Unfortunately, there is no consensus regarding the conceptualization of addiction, and hence, it is debated to what extent the addicted individual is really incapacitated. The so-called 'addiction-debate' sparks controversy and evolves around two models: the choice model (CM) and the brain disease model (BDM). Addiction may shape cognitive, volitional and affective capacities, but these two models differ fundamentally in their view on the nature of incapacitation. As such, the consequences in terms of the insanity defence differ depending on the view adopted.

Arguably, there are potentially also other ways to negate or diminish criminal responsibility, such as duress. However, we chose to focus solely on the insanity defence as this excuse is most appropriate for addiction-related cases. Moreover, this defence relates most directly to a capacitarian discussion that is central in both the scientific addiction debate and criminal law doctrines. Given this specific focus, we refrain from discussing the separate problem of prior fault (*culpa in causa, actio libera in causa*), but will only illustrate its importance when discussing some relevant case law.

---

3 N.A. Vincent, 'On the Relevance of Neuroscience to Criminal Responsibility', *Criminal Law and Philosophy*, Vol. 4, 2010, pp. 88-90.

4 Over the last decades, robust brain science has influenced the age of criminal responsibility and adolescent criminal law, particularly by demonstrating the underdeveloped brain and associated lack of capacities. In the US, this led to the abolishment of capital punishment for individuals under the age of 18 (*Roper v. Simmons*), to the abolishment of life without parole for individuals under 18 for all crimes except homicide (*Graham v. Florida*) and eventually also for homicide cases (*Miller v. Alabama*). In the Netherlands, neuroscience helped shape the new 2014 adolescent criminal law, which allows adolescents between the ages of 18 and 23 to be sentenced according to juvenile criminal law. *See also*: C.S. Barendregt & A.M. van der Laan, 'Neuroscientific Insights and the Dutch Adolescent Criminal Law: A brief report', *Journal of Criminal Justice*, 2018.

The structure of the paper is as follows. We start with a critical assessment of addiction-related capacities in light of the aforementioned models. Next, we discuss the requirements for the insanity defence in order to evaluate how they are applied to addiction-related cases. We adopt a comparative legal approach by addressing three jurisdictions, *i.e.*, the common law system of England and Wales, and the civil law systems of Germany, and the Netherlands. We end the paper with some concluding remarks.

2 A Capacitarian Approach to Addiction

Before we clarify the legal relevance of the (neuro)scientific addiction debate, we have to remind ourselves that the notion of criminal responsibility concentrates on normative questions such as blameworthiness, whereas scientists primarily address explanatory and descriptive matters on the causes of behaviour. However, finding social, psychological or neurological causes of addiction is in itself not that relevant, or at least not sufficient for establishing excusing conditions in the law. Assuming that causation in itself already excuses criminal behaviour constitutes, in the words of Morse, the so-called fundamental psycholegal error. This is the error of thinking that if we find a cause for the choices an actor makes, the actor is excused. This would imply, especially in the light of any deterministic world view, that no one could be held responsible because all our behaviour can be understood as being caused by factors beyond our ultimate control. At least *de lege lata* in its current theoretical foundations and practices, criminal law does not incorporate such a general view that causation excuses.[5] This means that in order for addiction to have an excusing effect, whether it is qualified as a brain disease or not, still needs to be related to certain normative criteria that ground criminal responsibility. If not in terms of causation, in which way can the science of addiction then contribute to matters of responsibility? Arguably, the affected capacities, rather than causation, are considered most important in determining responsibility.[6] In its foundations, the law is clearly based on a capactarian view on responsibility and not on the principle of causation.[7] Depending on the type and degree of incapacitation, the law may adjust the individual's criminal responsibility, and science can offer insights on the workings of these capacities.

5 This is solely an 'internalist' argument against the idea that causation excuses. It is because our legal doctrines (but also our moral practices) are currently not theoretically based on this idea that we qualify it as a psycholegal 'error'. Arguably, we may still need an 'externalist' argument, probably based on a compatibilist moral philosophy, to defend the thesis that causation does not excuse. *See*: M. Moore, 'Stephen Morse on the Fundamental Psycho-Legal Error', *Criminal Law and Philosophy*, Vol. 1, 2016, p. 48-59.

6 Vincent 2010, p. 84.

7 *See also*: R. Dworkin, *Justice for Hedgehogs*, The Belknap Press of Harvard University Press, Cambridge 2011, p. 227-248.

There is a consensus that three kinds of capacities are relevant to both moral and legal responsibility.[8] First, a cognitive capacity, which involves rationality and knowledge, is deemed necessary in order to understand the nature of one's behaviour and when and why criminal behaviour is morally or legally wrong.[9] Second, a volitional capacity, *i.e.* the ability to control oneself, is relevant in order to resist impulses and act accordingly.[10] Lastly, and often most controversial, is the capacity for emotion, also referred to as an affective capacity. Such a capacity enables individuals not only rationally to understand why certain behaviour is undesirable but also to experience and appreciate them as wrong.[11] These three types of mental capacities are highly relevant for both the theoretical foundations and practical assessment of criminal responsibility; even if the law does not refer to these capacities explicitly, they are implicitly present.[12] To illustrate, many jurisdictions incorporate a requirement for certain capacities through assessing mental disorders, most notably and controversially when the defence is one of insanity.[13] It is, therefore, a worthwhile endeavour to opt for a capacitarian approach, that is, to address addiction in terms of (impaired) capacities in order to assess whether this is in line with the law's requirements for responsibility.

Addressing addiction-impaired capacities, however, is controversial due to the debate surrounding the conceptualization of addiction. Fuelled by two main models, there is disagreement regarding the foundation of what causes and constitutes addiction. The brain disease model (BDM) and the choice model (CM) both directly oppose each other.[14] Importantly, other models and theories exist, but the addiction debate seems to centre on these two.[15] This in itself is interesting, since these two models clearly represent opposite ends on a spectrum, and a more multi-dimensional model could be useful to encompass not just these specific insights, but also a broader view on addiction.[16] Nonetheless, this paper focusses on the BDM and the CM and does not discuss the lack of diversity in the addiction debate. As the name suggests, the BDM has a strong neuroscientific focus and relies heavily on genetic and brain research to substantiate the view that addiction is, fun-

8 W. Glannon, 'Psychopathy and Responsibility', *Journal of Applied Philosophy*, Vol. 4, 2009, p. 263.
9 A. Duff, 'Legal and Moral Responsibility', *Philosophy Compass*, Vol. 4, 2009, p. 978.
10 Id., p. 978.
11 C. Fine & J. Kennett, 'Mental Impairment, Moral Understanding and Criminal Responsibility: Psychopathy and the Purposes of Punishment', *International Journal of Law and Psychiatry*, Vol. 27, 2004, p. 428.
12 H.L. Maibom, 'The Mad, the Bad, and the Psychopath', *Neuroethics*, Vol. 1, 2008, p. 167.
13 G. Meynen, Legal insanity: Explorations in psychiatry, law, and ethics, Springer, Basel 2016, p. 2.
14 For the BDM, *see* A.I. Leshner, 'Addiction is a Brain Disease, and it Matters', *Science*, Vol. 278, 1997; for the CM, *see* G.M. Heyman, *Addiction: A disorder of choice*, Harvard University Press, Cambridge Massachusetts 2009.
15 S.E. Hyman, 'Addiction: a Disease of Learning and Memory', *American Journal of Psychiatry*, Vol. 162, 2005, p. 1414.
16 M. Lewis, 'Addiction and the Brain: Development, Not Disease', *Neuroethics*, Vol. 10, 2017, p. 8.

damentally, a chronic and relapsing brain disease.[17] Quite the opposite is the CM. By addressing the high rates of natural recovery and the environmental correlates associated with quitting drugs, this model focusses on the consciously willed behaviour of the individual and their autonomy to change this behaviour.[18]

Hence, these three types of capacities and the impairment thereof in addiction may depend on the viewpoint on the nature of addiction. In terms of cognition, addiction arguably does not directly influence the cognitive capacity for rationality. Although it could be relevant in cases of severe intoxication, or drug-induced psychosis, addiction in itself does not alter the individual's sense of reality. Most addicts know that their (criminal) behaviour, for instance, theft for the purpose of financing drug use, is wrongful, harmful or even self-destructive, but they often quite deliberately continuing pursuing it.[19] Consequently, on first sight, there seems to be little disability in terms of rationality. However, studies on decision-making have consistently outlined the deficits amongst addicted populations. The ability for rational decision-making relies heavily on weighing costs and benefits, processes that involve planning and attention.[20] Overseeing long-term consequences with respect to short-term rewards, and dividing your attention according, is an ability that is often diminished in addicts. That means that the individual allocates more attention to behaviour with short-term rewards rather than behaviour associated with long-term consequences.[21] In that sense, decision-making is less rational for those addicted to substances, and consequently, one could consider their cognitive capacities at least somewhat diminished.

In addition, emotion and affect can be considered to play a key role.[22] The experience of emotion, such as feeling 'the high' after taking drugs, is a large motivator to continue using them.[23] Moreover, there are strong correlations between stress, depression and anxiety on the one hand, and addiction on the other. For instance, the commonly accepted stance is that people who are experiencing negative affect, being the experience of negative emotions

17 N.D. Volkow & J.S. Fowler, 'Addiction, a Disease of Compulsion and Drive: Involvement of the Orbitofrontal Cortex', *Cerebral Cortex*, Vol. 10, 2000, p. 318.

18 G.M. Heyman, 'Addiction and Choice: Theory and New Data', *Frontiers in Psychiatry*, Vol. 4, 2013, p. 31.

19 Heyman 2009, p. 99.

20 A. Bechara, 'Decision Making, Impulse Control and Loss of Willpower to Resist Drugs: a Neurocognitive Perspective', *Nature Neuroscience*, Vol. 8, 2005, p. 1458; R.D. Baler & N. D. Volkow, 'Drug Addiction: the Neurobiology of Disrupted Self-control', *Trends in Molecular Medicine*, Vol. 12, 2006, p. 559.

21 Bechara 2005, p. 1458.

22 A. Verdejo-Garcia, L. Clark & B.D. Dunn, 'The Role of Interoception in Addiction: a Critical Review', *Neuroscience and Biobehavioral Reviews*, Vol. 36, 2012, p. 1857.

23 G.L. Clore & J. R. Huntsinger, 'How Emotions Inform Judgment and Regulate Thought', *Trends in Cognitive Sciences*, Vol. 11, 2007, p. 393.

or poor self-esteem, engage in drug use to relieve some of those feelings.[24] This also relates to the high co-occurrence of addiction with other mental disorders, as it suggests that drug use can function as a coping mechanism to manage symptoms.[25] More ambiguous is the addict's actual capacity to experience affect. The perception and reaction to positive emotional stimuli seem to be blunted or reduced in addicts.[26] Conversely, negative stimuli result in a heightened emotional response, for instance in heroin users.[27] This suggests that addicts may not appreciate positive stimuli such as hobbies or relational interactions in the same way as non-users may. Additionally, addicts may experience negative stimuli, for instance, loss of health or money, stronger than healthy individuals may. This could result in a cycle of negative affect, as such negative experiences may trigger a relapse into drug use as a coping mechanism, which often results in negative emotion or poor self-esteem again, and so on. Hence, regarding affective capacities, addiction can affect the way in which stimuli are processed and appreciated, thereby reducing the capacity to value choices and behaviour effectively.

The most vehemently debated capacity in the addiction debate is the addicted individual's volitional capacity. However, regarding this, there is a clear division amongst the CM and the BDM proponents. The latter strongly claim that addicted individuals have virtually uncontrollable cravings, whereas the first believe in free choice, in the sense that it is up to the conscious and willed choice of the individual to start and continue using drugs. It may seem counterintuitive that such a behaviour, which is detrimental for one's wellbeing, is still a product of a conscious and willed decision. However, simply because the behaviour may be (self-)destructive, does not render it involuntary.[28] According to Heyman, first-person experiences of addiction and cravings suggest that there is always an element of control in choosing to consume drugs over the negative consequences. Regardless of individual experiences, many studies address the various problems addicts have with control-related abilities.[29] Inhibition (the act of suppressing pre-motor responses) and

24 J.D. Kassel *et al.*, 'Negative Affect and Addiction', *in* M. al'Absi (Ed.), *Stress and Addiction*, Academic Press, Burlington 2007, p. 172.

25 L. Degenhardt & W. Hall, 'The Relationship between Tobacco Use, Substance-Use Disorders and Mental Health: Results from the National Survey of Mental Health and Well-being', *Nicotine & Tobacco Research*, Vol. 3, 2001, p. 225.

26 F. Aguilar de Arcos *et al.*, 'Experience of Emotions in Substance Abusers Exposed to Images Containing Neutral, Positive, and Negative Affective Stimuli', *Drug and Alcohol Dependence*, Vol. 78, 2005, p. 159.

27 F. Aguilar de Arcos *et al.*, 'Dysregulation of Emotional Response in Current and Abstinent Heroin Users: Negative Heightening and Positive Blunting', *Psychopharmacology*, Vol. 198, 2008, p. 159.

28 Heyman 2009, pp. 100-105.

29 R.Z. Goldstein & N.D. Volkow, 'Dysfunction of the Prefrontal Cortex in Addiction: Neuroimaging Findings and Clinical Implications', *Nature Reviews Neuroscience*, Vol. 12, 2011, p. 652; J.D. Jentsch *et al.*, 'Dissecting Impulsivity and its Relationships to Drug Addictions', *Annals of the New York Academy of Sciences*, Vol.

impulsivity (acting without thinking), both processes inherent to the capacity to exercise control, are continuously shown to be diminished in people with addiction. For instance, individuals with addiction perform poorer on behavioural tasks measuring inhibitory processes compared to non-addicted individuals.[30] In addition, functional brain imaging studies show that there is less activity and functional connectivity in the prefrontal cortex, amongst others, a brain region which plays an important role in inhibitory processes.[31] According to the BDM, this goes to show that addicts experience deficits in volitional capacities. On the contrary, the CM cites research showing the effect of small contingencies on behaviour. By offering addicted individuals vouchers, for instance for the movie theatre, in exchange for abstinence of substances, the majority of them was able to do so. From this, it is inferred that addicts have sufficient control over their actions and, in fact, need little motivation to change their behaviour.[32] Lastly, the CM argues that most addicted individuals recover naturally without any treatment. As such, proponents of this model argue that the consumption of substances and consequently the choice of abstinence is voluntary behaviour.

Notwithstanding the potential volitional incapacity of addicts, one could still argue that an ability to exercise control is not limited to the specific (criminal) behaviour at hand. The so-called concept of diachronic control refers to rational intervals between cravings or substance use. An individual can exercise diachronic control in two ways, by either minimizing the chances of such an 'uncontrolled' moment happening in the first place or by directly taking action against the feelings of diminished control.[33] To use addiction-related examples, the first scenario could refer to avoiding places that create temptation, for instance, taking a different route home in order not to pass by a bar. The second could refer to taking medication or enrol in psychological treatment, which reduces the craving for the drug in general. Both demonstrate that an individual may have lost control during an act, but that the individual could or should have exercised its control diachronically.[34] As such, this is also very much related to the legal concept of prior fault.[35]

1327, 2014; J.L. Smith *et al.*, 'Deficits in Behavioural Inhibition in Substance Abuse and Addiction: a Meta-analysis', *Drug and Alcohol Dependence*, Vol. 145, 2014.

30 Id.

31 Baler & Volkow 2006; A. Zilverstand *et al.*, 'Neuroimaging Impaired Response Inhibition and Salience Attribution in Human Drug Addiction: A Systematic Review', *Neuron*, Vol. 98, 2018, p. 886.

32 Heyman 2009, pp. 105-108.

33 J. Kennett, *Agency and Responsibility: A Common-sense Moral Psychology*, Clarendon Press, Oxford 2001, pp. 134-135.

34 J. Kennett, N.A. Vincent & A. Snoek, 'Drug Addiction and Criminal Responsibility', *in* J. Clausen & N. Levy (Eds.), *Handbook of Neuroethics*, Springer, Dordrecht 2015, pp. 1076-1077.

35 Naturally, there can also be difficulties to exercise diachronic control, due to internal (personal) and external (environmental) barriers. Hence, to merely dismiss volitional incapacity in addicts by referring to diachronic control would be too simplistic. *See also*: id., p. 1077.

By addressing these fundamental differences in the perception of addiction, it almost seems as if the two models describe different phenomena. This may be a relevant observation: Kennett and colleagues suggest a similar explanation for these contradictory findings.[36] Addiction is a highly heterogeneous phenomenon and different explanatory models may cover some vital differences between different types of addiction and severity of the addiction. Arguably, whereas 'hard cases' of addicts exist who have severe difficulty controlling their behaviour, a large group of addicted individuals can be considered to have less severe impairments. This latter group, for instance, would belong to the self-recovery group as well as the group responding well to contingencies.[37]

3 The Insanity Defence Compared: Evaluating a Legal Framework for Addiction

After having established, in a general way, the possible influence of addiction on capacities, in particular, the capacity of control, we now compare the possibilities different legal systems have to address addiction-impaired capacities in criminal law. Using this comparative approach, we address two main issues. First, we discuss the preliminary matter of the exact scope of the insanity defence: does it only negate criminal responsibility, or does it also include the possibility of diminished responsibility? Next and foremost, we address three insanity defences to identify the required (addiction-impaired) capacities for criminal responsibility. We focus on the highly influential M'Naghten rule used in England and Wales, as well as in many other common law systems, before concentrating on two civil law jurisdictions, being Germany and the Netherlands. Based on this doctrinal framework, we discuss how addiction may negate or diminish criminal responsibility in these jurisdictions. As such, the upcoming overview provides neither an exhaustive analysis nor a normative assessment of jurisdictions. Rather it demonstrates a range of possibilities, in order to compare and contextualize how addiction-related criminal behaviour can affect criminal responsibility.

3.1 *Degrees of Criminal Responsibility*

In common law jurisdictions, insanity is an all or nothing defence: a defendant is either fully legally sane or insane.[38] Conversely, most civil law systems allow for different degrees of decreased responsibility due to a mental disorder, applicable to all types of offences.

---

36 Id., pp. 1074-1076.
37 Id.
38 Meynen 2016, p. 161.

Such cases involve a defendant whose required capacities are severely (but not entirely) impaired by the mental disorder. Germany had made this explicit in §§ 20 and 21 German Criminal Code (GCC). They read as follows:

> § 20: Any person who at the time of the commission of the offence is incapable of appreciating the wrongfulness of their actions or of acting in accordance with any such appreciation due to a pathological mental disorder, a profound consciousness disorder, debility or any other serious mental abnormality, shall be deemed to act without guilt.[39]

> § 21: If the capacity of the offender to appreciate the wrongfulness of his actions or to act in accordance with any such appreciation is substantially diminished at the time of the commission of the offence due to one of the reasons indicated in §20, the sentence may be mitigated pursuant to § 49(1).[40]

The Netherlands also accept a diminished responsibility doctrine. Notwithstanding the fact that the Dutch Criminal Code (DCC) does not imply this and the legislator did not envisage it, the Netherlands currently adopts three degrees of responsibility (*toerekenbaarheid*): full responsibility, diminished responsibility and non-responsibility.[41] In the latter case of legal insanity, the defendant will be acquitted and compulsory measures, such as (psychiatric) hospital orders, may be imposed instead of punishment.[42] On the other hand, diminished responsibility does not lead to a full acquittal, since the actor is still considered (somewhat) blameworthy, but instead serves as a mitigating circumstance in the individual's sentence.[43] Consequently, diminished responsible individuals can still be punished in addition to receiving a court-ordered measure.[44]

---

39 Translation our own, but largely based upon the translation by Michael Bohlander of the GCC from www.legislationonline.org, retrieved on 28 January 2019 from www.legislationline.org/download/action/download/id/6115/file/Germany_CC_am2013_en.pdf.

40 Id.

41 Until 2012 the Dutch system accepted an even more fine grained scale of five degrees of responsibility. In addition to the above mentioned three degrees, there was also the possibility of somewhat diminished and severely diminished responsibility. Meynen 2016, p. 162.

42 In the Netherlands according to Article 37 DCC and in Germany according to 64 GCC. *See also* Blomsma & Roef 2019, p. 241.

43 M. Bohlander, *Principles of German Criminal Law*, Hart publishing, Oxford 2009, p. 135.

44 C. Brants, A. Jackson & F. Koenraadt, 'Culpability Compared: Mental Capacity, Criminal Offences and the Role of the Expert in Common Law and Civil Law Jurisdictions', *Journal of International and Comparative Law*, Vol. 3, 2016, p. 411.

This clearly contrasts with England and Wales, which have limited the use of diminished responsibility to homicide cases.[45] According to section 52 of the 2009 Coroners and Justice Act, when the defendant's abilities to understand the nature of one's conduct, to form a rational judgment and to exercise self-control are substantially impaired, the murder charge will be reduced to the less serious one of (voluntary) manslaughter.[46]

In sum, while the common law tradition follows an all or nothing approach, most civil law jurisdictions perceive the insanity defence more as a kind of continuum, which allows the courts to accept different degrees of responsibility. Obviously, this also has consequences for the possible acceptance of addiction as a specific form (and degree) of legal insanity. In light of our analysis of addiction, it seems reasonable to recognise that there are different shades of grey.

As such, we can consider addicted offenders to be *more* or *less* responsible for certain crimes they commit, depending on factors such as the nature of the addiction, the manner of drug use, personal characteristics, such as comorbidity, the criminal offence at hand, the instrumental link between the crime and the addiction, prior fault, etc. This implies that the ideal way of addressing addiction in criminal law should be a matter of degrees. As we will see below, this is exactly the manner in which Germany and the Netherlands deal with addiction-related crimes. It hardly ever happens that addiction leads to a full insanity defence. England and Wales also address addiction primarily as a question of diminished responsibility, but since they consider legal insanity to be a dichotomous concept, and limit diminished responsibility to murder, a more nuanced approach, applicable to all offences, is doctrinally speaking not possible.

3.2 The Common Law (England and Wales) Approach

In order to assess legal insanity, common law jurisdictions employ the M'Naghten rule or variants thereof:

> At the time of committing the act, the party accused was laboring under such a defect of reason, from disease of the mind, as not to know the nature and quality of the act he was doing; or if he did know it, that he did not know what he was doing was wrong.[47]

45 Blomsma & Roef 2019, p. 245.
46 Id., pp. 224-226.
47 [1943] 10 Cl & Fin. 200, 8 Eng. Rep. 718 (HL).

This rule distinguishes two main elements that are relevant in determining legal insanity. First, it states a formal requirement regarding a mental state, namely a pathology ('from disease of the mind'). Second, it addresses the consequences of this pathology: a defect of reason, and hence a lack of knowledge of the nature and quality of her actions. The words reason and knowledge both suggest cognitive capacities and hence on first sight, this rule seems to regard cognitive capacities exclusively.[48] The wording of the rule, as well as this exclusively cognitive lexicon, have resulted in controversies, sparking confusion regarding its scope and applicability.[49]

First, the rule does not specify what constitutes a disease of the mind. Importantly, it is a legal concept, thereby lacking a definition from medical authorities.[50] Addiction, however, does seem to be considered a disease of the mind, at least with regard to diminished responsibility.[51] Second, the psychopathology is exclusively referred to as a defective cognition, thereby excluding non-cognitive disorders that may be equally capable of influencing behaviour.[52] Addiction does not necessarily interfere with an ability to reason and thereby seems not included in the scope of the M'Naghten rule.[53] In other words, the rule excludes certain mental disorders up front, thus limiting its versatility.[54] Moreover, it is debatable whether the type of capacities required to possess 'knowledge of the nature and quality of the act' are merely cognitive.[55]

---

48 R.D. Mackay, 'Righting the wrong? Some Observations on the Second Limb of the M'Naghten Rules', *Criminal Law Review*, Vol. 2, 2009, p. 80.

49 P. Shea, 'M'Naughten Revisited - Back to the Future? The Mental Illness Defence - A psychiatric Perspective', *Current Issues in Criminal Justice*, Vol. 12, 2000, p. 347.

50 B. McSherry, 'Defining what is a 'Disease of the Mind': the Untenability of Current Legal Interpretations', *Journal of Law and Medicine*, Vol. 1, 1993, p. 79; *see also* S. Allnutt, A. Samuels & C. O'Driscoll, 'The Insanity Defence: From Wild Beasts to M'Naghten', *Australasian Psychiatry*, Vol. 15, 2007, p. 294.

51 See for instance the case of *R v. Wood* [2008] 2 Cr. App. R. 34 and *R v. Williams* [2014] 1 Cr. App. R. 23 "In the context of diminished responsibility alcoholism was now regarded as a disease that might fall within the ambit of the Homicide Act 1957 s.2."

52 For example, consider a disorder that does not necessarily influence the person's ability for reason, such as schizophrenia with command hallucinations (*i.e.* mandates that are difficult if not impossible to resist).

53 Meynen 2016, p. 19.

54 Not only is the rule unversatile for that reason, but also because the wording 'to not know' is arguably extreme: it suggests that the individual has to be fully oblivious to reality. Very few psychiatric conditions result in a complete lack of rationality, thereby strongly limiting the rule to very rare if not non-existent cases. The few cases of legal insanity in England and Wales exemplify the strictness of the rule: around 10-17 cases per year successfully invoked the insanity defence, showing how hesitant courts are to grant this defence. *See also* R.D. Mackay, B.J. Mitchell & L. Howe, 'Yet More Facts about the Insanity Defence', *Criminal Law Review*, 2006, p. 400, table 1.

55 There are two possible approaches to deciding whether the act was 'wrongful'. It could convey the capacity of understanding the legal wrongfulness of the behaviour, which would denote the individual's ability to realize that her acts are prohibited. Contrarily, 'wrongfulness' could be interpreted as *moral* wrongfulness rather than a legal one, suggesting something else entirely, as it requires affective capacities. *See also* Mackay, 2009, pp. 80-81.

The implied lack of an exculpatory volitional prong in the M'Naghten rule becomes apparent from case law. A landmark decision, *R v. Kopsch*, addresses this by stating that '[uncontrollable impulses] are not yet part of the criminal law, and it is to be hoped that the time is far distant when it will be made so.'[56] In *Henderson v. Dorset Healthcare* it was additionally outlined that a case of legal insanity is limited to the cognitive capacity to form intent.[57] Consequently, it shows that the insanity defence is unlike to apply to addicted individuals for two reasons. First of all, the all-or-nothing nature of the insanity defence requires such a high threshold of incapacity that solely addiction does not fulfil these standards. Second, regardless of the severity of the incapacitation, addiction appears to affect merely volitional capacities, which is not included in the M'Naghten rule. Hence, more relevant to the addiction debate is the notion of diminished responsibility.

Interestingly, this diminished responsibility defence, reducing a murder sentence to one of manslaughter, does have a volitional prong. Since the 2009 adjustment to the Homicide Act, diminished responsibility can be considered if a mental condition substantially impaired the accused's ability to understand his conduct, form a rational judgment or exercise self-control.[58] Hence, addiction, with its control-related impairments, may be particularly appropriate for invoking diminished responsibility defences. Indeed, this is confirmed by several successful diminished responsibility defences in addicton cases.[59] However, the mere presence of an addiction is not enough: as exemplified in *R v. Bunch*, a three-step process is required. A medical condition is needed, which may be fulfilled by a substance disorder; this medical condition must give rise to an abnormality of mental functioning; and lastly, one of three capacities as mentioned in the Act must be impaired. In this particular case, the defendant could not rely on alcohol dependency, as this was not considered to have led to an abnormality in functioning.[60]

R v. Steward is an interesting example of the influence of the addiction debate despite the lack of a successful diminished responsibility defence.[61] The first expert witness was cited on the following: 'alcohol dependency syndrome, ADS, was incapable of being an abnormality of mind unless the consumption of drink was involuntary. [...]. It may be very, very difficult for someone to resist a drink, but he had never seen a case where it was absolutely impossible to resist.' The second expert witness, however, clearly favoured a

56 [1925] 19 Cr App Rep 50.
57 [2016] EWHC 3275 (QB).
58 Homicide Act 1957 Part 1 s. 2 'Persons suffering from diminished responsibility'.
59 *See, e.g., R v Clive Wood* (2008); *see also R v Stewart* (2009) 2 Cr. App. R. 30; *see also R v Williams* (2013) 1 Cr. App. R. 23 described more thoroughly below.
60 [2013] EWCA Crim 2498.
61 [2009] 2 Cr. App. R. 30.

different approach to addiction. 'In his opinion the applicant's level of alcoholism involved an overpowering desire to drink. His drinking was involuntary. It was an abnormality of mind which impaired the applicant's responsibility for the killing.' Although the diminished responsibility defence was not granted due to the brutality of the offence, the addiction mitigated the sentencing. The appeal case of *R. v Kay*, a schizophrenic who killed under the influence of drugs, also discussed voluntariness.[62] The judge stipulates that diminished responsibility is only possible if the psychosis arose from a recognised medical condition: dependency syndrome would be valid, but voluntary intoxication does not suffice.[63]

In *R v. Wood*, the defendant appealed against the conviction of murder based on his alcoholism.[64] The legal question was one of involuntariness: the court stated that it is inconsistent to regard alcoholism only as a disease when each drink is involuntary. Instead, the court stated that alcoholism can still be used as a mitigating circumstance, despite the fact that some of the defendant's choices were voluntary. Moreover, a murder conviction in *R v. Williams* was also brought before a retrial due to volitional impairment of the defendant's capacities, which had not been properly addressed in the first instance.[65] It was concluded that the court of first instance had not accurately assessed whether addiction led to a 'substantial impairment of the defendant's ability to bring a free and rational mind to bear on what he did' and ought to, therefore, be brought before a jury to be assessed again.

In short, the full insanity defence is rare and restricted to cognitive incapacity, thereby limiting if not fully impeding a successful insanity plea for the addicted offender. However, addiction is still considered a mental defect capable of eliciting a diminished responsibility defence, although this is seldom a successful plea. In addition, the case law shows that the addiction debate is relevant because the courts discuss and apply the different views, especially regarding voluntariness and control, as outlined earlier. Nonetheless, non-homicide offences that are typically motivated by addiction, such as theft or other property offences, cannot be appropriately dealt with due to a lack of a generalized diminished responsibility defence. Obviously, it is still possible to consider the addiction on the sentencing level as a mitigating circumstance. However, from a doctrinal perspective, this is not an ideal solution as it fails to fully incorporate the capacitarian approach of the addiction debate into criminal law.

---

62 For instance, the defence in *R v. Kay* stated the following: "[the defendant's] intoxication was not voluntary because he also had an alcohol and drugs dependency syndrome which combined with schizophrenia, led to an irresistible craving for and/or compulsion to drink and take drugs and prevented him from forming a rational judgment or exercising self-control."

63 [2017] EWCA Crim 647.

64 [2008] 2 Cr. App. R. 30.

65 [2013] 1 Cr. App. R. 23.

3.3 The German Approach

As mentioned earlier, the German system accepts both a full and partial insanity defence. Thereby it acknowledges that criminal responsibility is a matter of degrees and that punishment may be reduced in accordance with the degree of incapacity caused by the mental disorder. According to § 20 GCC, as quoted in full earlier, the offender is excused when due to a pathological mental disorder, a profound consciousness disorder, debility or any other serious mental abnormality, he was incapable of appreciating the wrongfulness of his conduct or of acting in accordance with this appreciation. The two alternatives are generally described as being that the defendant lacks the capacity of insight and restraint.[66] Thus § 20 GCC explicitly includes a volitional prong in the criteria for insanity: the inability to exercise control over one's behaviour.[67] It should, however, be noted that the capacity of restraint is not easily rejected. The threshold is only met when all the defendant's powers could still not bring about motivation to act in conformity with the law.[68]

German case law illustrates that a complete exculpation on the basis of insanity is limited to very extreme cases only. When the mental disorder was not severe enough to excuse the defendant, the individual can nonetheless still rely on the defence of diminished responsibility according to § 21 GCC, if, at the time of the crime, the offender's cognitive or volitional capacities were substantially impaired. It is up to the discretion of the court to decide whether this partial defence, which is applicable to all criminal offences and not just limited (as in common law systems) to murder, will lead to a mitigated punishment.[69] These general rules regarding the insanity defence are also applicable to addiction-related crimes. The medico-legal qualification of the addiction is not very problematic, given the broad categorisation of mental disorders in § 20 GCC: addiction and its physical and psychological consequences are usually considered a pathological mental disorder, or as any other serious mental abnormality.[70] If an addicted offender commits a crime under the direct influence of an acute intoxication he can also be diagnosed as suffering from a pro-

66 *See also*: Bohlander 2009, pp. 131-132.

67 It is interesting to note that the American Model Penal Code as developed by the American Law Institute (1962) has adopted a standard for insanity that is very similar to the civil law approach of Germany. The MPC reads "a person is not responsible for criminal conduct if at the time of such conduct as a result of mental disease or defect he lacks substantial capacity either to appreciate the criminality (wrongfulness) of his conduct or to conform his conduct to the requirement of the law." Although M'Naghten is still the leading insanity rule in the US, a considerable number of states have adopted the Model Penal Code standard or a variant of it, which means that also volitional impairments may have an excusing effect.

68 Blomsma and Roef 2019, p. 243.

69 Id., p. 245.

70 W. Pfister, 'Die Beurteilung der Schuldfähigkeit in der Rechtsprechung des Bundesgerichtshofs', *NStZ-RR*, 2014, p. 194; Streng Münchener Kommentar zum StGb § 20, 2017, nr. 5; H. Sass, R. Erkwoh & A. Rodon, 'Medico-legal aspects of alcohol, drugs and criminality in Germany', *Alcohol and Alcoholism*, 1998, p. 30.

found consciousness disorder, just like non-addicted intoxicated offenders.[71] However, a full insanity defence is only possible in the most severe cases of habitual multiple drug use, polytoxicomania, or cases in which the offender is suffering from comorbid mental disorders in addition to the addiction.[72] Usually, the addiction by itself can only result in a diminished responsibility, which in most cases leads to the imposition of a custodial addiction treatment order, following § 64 GCC.[73]

Obviously, the mere qualification of addiction as a mental disorder is not sufficient to (partially) exculpate the offender. Independently from the precise psychopathological conceptualisation, the German Supreme Court (*Bundesgerichtshof*) has decided that addiction in itself does not constitute a (partial) insanity defence. Additional psychobehavioural and normative requirements have to be fulfilled to demonstrate that the addiction has indeed substantially impaired the mental capacities of the defendant at the time of the crime, particularly the capacity of restraint. In a landmark decision from 1976, the Supreme Court has formulated the following rule which to date has essentially remained unchanged:

> Drug dependency as such does not negate or substantially diminish responsibility (*Schuldfähigkeit*). In case of a drug addict such consequences are only exceptionally given, for example if long-term use of drugs has led to serious personality changes, or when the offender was suffering from serious withdrawal symptoms that drove him to procure drugs by means of a criminal offence, and furthermore when he commits the offence in a state of acute intoxication.[74]

---

71 Consequently, in extreme cases of severe (even voluntary) intoxication, the defendant may be excused according to § 20 GCC, but he may nonetheless still be convicted for the special offence of § 323a GCC (*Raushtat*), which punishes offenders with up to five years of imprisonment when they get seriously intoxicated and commit a crime in that mental state. See about intoxication and criminal responsibility also: Blomsma & Roef 2019, p. 246-250.

72 Eschelbach, *Beck'scher Online-Kommentar StGB*, § 20, nr. 5, retrieved from https://beck-online.beck.de/?vpath=bibdata/komm/BeckOK_StR_25/StGB/cont/beckok.StGB.p20.htm.

73 § 64 GCC reads as follows: "If a person has an addiction to alcohol or other drugs and is convicted of an unlawful act committed while he was intoxicated or as a result of his addiction, or is not convicted only because he has been found to be insane or insanity cannot be excluded on the evidence, the court shall make a custodial addiction treatment order if there is a danger that he will commit future serious unlawful acts as a consequence of his addiction. Such order shall not be made unless ab initio there is a sufficiently certain prospect of success that the person can be healed by way of custodial addiction treatment or that a relapse into addictive behaviour and the commission of serious unlawful acts caused by that addiction can be prevented for a substantial period of time." Translation of the GCC by Michael Bohlander from www.legislationonline.org, retrieved on 28 January 2019 https://www.legislationline.org/download/ action/download/id /6115/file/Germany_CC_am2013_en.pdf.

74 BGH 28 Oktober 1976 – 2 StR 242/76 (translation our own). *See also* the following case law: BGH 6 June 1989 – 5 StR 175/89, NStZ 1989, 430; BGH 10 November 1993 – 2 StR 579/93, StV 1994, p. 303; BGH 4 March 1997 – 1 StR 657/96, NStZ-RR 1997, p. 225; BGH 19 September 2000 – 1 StR 310/00, NStZ 2001, p. 83B; BGH 7 August 2001 – 1 StR 470/00, NJW 2002, p. 150; BGH 17 April 2012 – 1 StR 15/12, NStZ

In recent years, case law and legal doctrine have refined and clarified some of these circumstances that may result in a (partial) exculpation of the addicted offender. For example, it is accepted that the long-term use of hard drugs leads more frequently to serious personality changes and subsequent impairment of the defendant's capacities than an addiction to soft drugs. Case law also classifies the addictive effects of heroin and cocaine as more severe than the effects caused by, for example, amphetamine and cannabis.[75]

From a capacitarian approach to addiction, most illuminating is the explicit reference that serious withdrawal symptoms are capable of diminishing the offender's criminal responsibility. While personality changes and acute intoxication may also affect cognitive capacities, for instance in cases of drug-induced psychosis, the commission of crimes under the compulsive influence of withdrawal symptoms clearly captures a volitional impairment. When addicts shoplift, burgle a house or rob someone to finance their drug use, this potential excusing condition becomes most relevant. Importantly, the Supreme Court has specified that the committed crime must be a property offence directly related to the irresistible impulse caused by the withdrawal symptoms, in order to prevent §§ 20-21 GCC from becoming a loophole. This means that other crimes, such as manslaughter or bodily assault, are excluded.[76] Arguably, these types of crimes could still be (partially) excused if they are committed because of a serious personality change or due to acute intoxication, rather than a volitional impairment. The Supreme Court has additionally stated that the mere financing of one's drug dependency, via illegal means such as theft or drug trafficking, is an insufficient ground for §§20-21 GCC. A mere causal or instrumental link between the offence and the addiction is not enough for a successful defence. Instead, it is required that the property offence is primarily motivated by the uncontrollable desire to counter the withdrawal symptoms, otherwise one can hardly claim a substantial impairment of the capacity of restraint.[77]

Noteworthy is that the Supreme Court has accepted that in exceptional cases the mere 'fear' of serious withdrawal symptoms may already diminish the offender's responsibility,

---

2013, p. 53; BGH 12 March 2013 - 4 StR 42/13, NStZ 2013, p. 519; BGH 20 August 2013 - 5 StR 36/13, NstZ-RR, 2013, p. 346; BGH 18 January 2017 - 2 StR 436/16. *See also*: W. Pfister, 'Drogenkonsum und Strafrecht', *Forens Psychiatr Kriminol*, 2009, p. 257.

75 R. Eschelbach, *Beck'scher Online-Kommentar StGB*, § 20, nr. 5, retrieved from https://beck-online.beck.de/?vpath=bibdata/komm/BeckOK_StR_25/StGB/cont/beckok.StGB.p20.htm.

76 K.R. Maatz, 'Drogenbedingte Verminderung der Schuldfähigkeit – zum gegenwärtigen Stand der Rechtsprechung des Bundesgerichtshofs', *Tagungsband zum XIII. GTFCh-Symposium, 3.-5.4.2003 in Mosbach*, 2013, p.20, retrieved on 25 May 2019 from www.gtfch.org/cms/index.php/en/proceedings/587-gtfch-symposium-2003.

77 Maatz 2013, p. 20.

i.e. when 'he has already experienced this fear before as extremely unpleasant (*grausamst*).'[78] Arguably, this broadens the presence of a volitional impairment considerably, although a close motivational link between the property offence and this withdrawal anxiety must still exist. For instance, the Supreme Court has rejected diminished responsibility in a case where the dominant motive of a heroin addict to commit a robbery was clearly financial, *i.e.* to pay the overdue rent of his apartment. Although he may have been fearful of future withdrawal symptoms, it was not considered a circumstance that substantially impaired his ability to restraint.[79]

To conclude, it is important to note that German law is also unique with respect to the problem of prior fault. The Supreme Court is quite hesitant in accepting the prior fault doctrine. Doing so would entail the risk that addicted offenders are held criminally responsible, not so much for the act they have committed, but for their lifestyle. However, criminal responsibility based on generalized 'lifestyle culpability' (*Lebensführungsschuld*) is considered a violation of the fundamental values and principles of German criminal law. The idea is that the addicted offender should only be blamed and held (diminished) responsible for a concrete criminal offence, and not for being addicted.[80]

3.4 *The Dutch Approach*

Compared with the above-mentioned standards for legal insanity, the Dutch criminal law stands out due to a complete lack of a standard altogether. Article 39 of the DCC specifies:

> Any person who commits an offence for which he cannot be held responsible by reason of mental disease or defect shall not be criminally liable.[81]

As the wording of the article suggests, and contrary to Germany, the Dutch insanity defence does not specify the relevant capacities. Instead, the article merely outlines the requirement of a mental condition, be it impaired development or a pathological disorder of his mental capacities, which leads to legal insanity. Nonetheless, already in the Explanatory Memorandum to article 39 DCC upon introducing the DCC in 1886, the legislator suggested

78 BGH 2 November 2005 – 2 StR 389/05; 17 April 2012 – 1 StR 15/12, NStZ 2013, p. 53. *See also*: Pfister 2014, p. 195.

79 BGH 18 January 2017 – 2 StR 436/16.

80 BGH 15 December 1987 – 1 StR 498/87; BGH 10 June 1998 – 5 StR 89/98, StV 1999, p. 311; BGH 27 January 2004 – 3 StR 479/03, NStZ 2004, p. 495; BGH 16 January 2008 – 3 StR 479/07, NStZ 2008, p. 330; BGH 12 June 2008 – 3 StR 84/08, NStZ 2009, p. 258. *See also* Eschelbach, BeckOK StGB § 20, 2018, nr. 5.

81 Translation of the DCC from www.legislationonline.org, retrieved on 28 January 2019 from https://www.legislationline.org/download/action/download/id/6415/file/Netherlands_CC_am2012_en.pdf

that two capacities are key to criminal responsibility. The legislator envisaged, on the one hand, the freedom of choosing to act or not to act (which may be related to impulse control), and on the other hand, the capacity to distinguish right from wrong. 'No criminal responsibility without accountability of the act to the offender, and no accountability in case either the freedom of acting – choosing between doing or not doing what the law prohibits or requires – is excluded or the offender is in such a state that he cannot realise the unlawfulness of his act and cannot calculate its consequences'.[82] In that respect, the Dutch system is in practice quite similar to the German approach.

The Dutch case law indeed specifies that the impairment of both cognitive and volitional capacities may lead to diminished responsibility.[83] The insanity defence is, however, only accepted when the lack of mental capacities leads to an inability to be aware of the impact and consequences of behaviour, suggesting the prominence of cognitive capacities.[84] Nonetheless, several cases explicitly refer to the ability for control.[85] For instance, insanity was established because the defendant's behaviour was considered 'completely commanded and determined' by their state of mind.[86] This shows that, within a certain theoretical framework, judges are able to employ their own standards in determining legal insanity, which leads to different conclusions and prerequisites on the insanity defence.

Recently, a famous addiction-related case sparked controversy.[87] The defendant attempted to kill his ex-partner and killed her two children while suffering from an amphetamine-induced psychosis. He had a long history of amphetamine addiction, which renders the case interesting in light of the addiction debate rather than only from a voluntary intoxi-

---

82 Quoted in L. Klaming & B-J Koops, 'Neuroscientific Evidence and Criminal Responsibility in the Netherlands', *International Neurolaw*, 2012, p. 8.

83 *See, e.g.*: Hof Leeuwarden 16 September 2010, ECLI: NL:GHLEE:2010:BN7291. "In court, the defendant has indicated that he, at the time of the offence, knew and understood that it was not right to enter the care facility and steal money. However, it has become plausible to the court that the defendant was not fully capable of acting in according with that knowledge" (own translation). *See also*: S.L.T.J. Lighthart, T. Kooijmans & G. Meynen, 'Een juridisch criterium voor ontoerekeningsvatbaarheid: een uitspraak van het Gerechtshof geanalyseerd', *Delikt & Delinkwent*, Vol. 9, 2018, pp. 101-110.

84 Rb Utrecht 3 June 2009, ECLI:NL:RBUTR:2009:BI6218. "The jurisprudence itterates that only cases in which the judge determines that the defendant, due to his pathological disorder, was completely devoid of all insight into the scope of his actions and the potential consequences of those, can be considered a case of full insanity" (own translation). *See also* Hof Leeuwarden 16 September 2010, ECLI:NL:GHLEE:2010:BN7291.

85 J. Bijlsma, Stoornis en Strafuitsluiting: Op Zoek naar een Toetsingskader voor Ontoerekenbaarheid, Wolf Legal Publishers, Oisterwijk 2016, pp. 54-55.

86 Rb Den Haag 25 October 2004, ECLI:NL:RBSGR:2004:AR4526; Rb Amsterdam 30 March 2009, ECLI:NL:RBAMS:2009:BH8888; Rb Den Haag 17 May 2011, ECLI:NL:RBSGR:2011:BQ5165; Rb Den Bosch 29 June 2011, ECLI:NL:RBSHE:2011:BQ9524.

87 Not only due to the discussion on legal insanity, but even more so regarding the discussion on intent and prior fault. However, we chose to focus on the legal insanity controversy in this instance.

cation perspective.[88] Although at first instance, the court did not accept the addiction as the main reason for diminished responsibility, the Court of Appeal decided differently. Following several expert witnesses, the Court concluded that the defendant suffered from 'an autonomous addiction disease' and consequently decided that he was (slightly) diminished responsible. For other reasons, unrelated to this discussion on diminished responsibility, the Supreme Court ordered a retrial. There, the defence argued once more that the defendant suffered from an amphetamine addiction, rendering him incapable to foresee the possibilities of taking more drugs, and hence he ought not to be (fully) blameworthy for the following psychosis.[89] However, the second Court of Appeal decided that the defendant was still responsible for his actions, regardless of the severe volitional consequences of the addiction: only due to a remaining personality disorder (and not because of his addiction) his responsibility is considered to be slightly diminished.[90] This case illustrates how courts may struggle with integrating the defendant's addiction adequately into the law, and even within the same case, lead to widely different conclusions.

In another case, a defendant who experienced a cannabis-induced psychosis was considered legally insane due to the psychosis, which was an unforeseen circumstance of his cannabis use. The Court of Appeal, however, argued that despite this unforeseeability, the defendant was a regular cannabis user and hence knew or should have known that cannabis may affect his psyche negatively. The Supreme Court confirmed this decision, thereby illustrating how low the threshold is for a prior fault reasoning, by attributing effects of drug use to the defendant even in situations where these effects are unforeseeable.[91] Similarly, an offender of aggravated assault who claimed that he was acting out impulsively due to the ingestion of alcohol and medicine, was denied the insanity defence. The Supreme Court upheld this conviction and reasoned that he 'knowingly and willingly accepted the considerable chance that he would lose control over his actions' the moment he used the substances.[92] This again illustrates the extensive acceptance of the prior fault doctrine, which does not just apply to foreseeable criminal acts by the defendants, but to any foreseeable loss of control and consequently the commission of an offence.

88 Hof Leeuwarden 16 April 2007, ECLI:NL:GHLEE:2007:BA3007.

89 Hof Arnhem 17 February 2010, ECLI:NL:GHARN:2010:BL4185.

90 "Despite the fact that the autonomous, seriously addictive qualities of amphetamine have severely affected the defendant's ability to cut down or cease the use of the drug, it can still be concluded that the defendant bears some, albeit very limited, responsibility for becoming psychotic, resulting in the massive break-through of aggressive impulsive as a direct consequence of the psychosis" (own translation).

91 HR 12 February 2008, ECLI:NL:HR:2008:BC3797.

92 HR 14 December 2004, ECLI:NL:HR:2004:AR3226.

It is interesting to note that there are only a few cases with addiction as the main or sole mental condition affecting insanity. Indeed, the most illustrative and elaborate cases are of drug-induced psychosis, predominantly resulting in a prior fault discussion. However, similar to the German approach, withdrawal symptoms can also play a role in Dutch case law.[93] In a manslaughter case, the defendant was considered slightly diminished responsible due to his withdrawal symptoms. These symptoms, in combination with the addiction, resulted in a diminished ability to control his impulses, as contended by both the expert witness and the court.[94]

Unfortunately, in many cases, solely the expert witness discusses the specific role of addiction and/or withdrawal symptoms. Hence, when the court states that it agrees with the expert on the general conclusion, which the court often does, it is impossible to determine what the exact role of addiction or withdrawal was.[95] In many cases, the court's agreement with the full conclusion of the expert makes sense, as the defendant often suffers from comorbid mental disorders: it would be inappropriate to specify this further, in an attempt to find monocausal explanations of the criminal conduct at hand. Perhaps the hesitancy of the courts to explicitly reflect on normative criteria that would allow addiction to be a (partial) defence may also be due to the fact that Article 39 DCC, unlike Germany and England/Wales, lacks any concrete legal standard to begin with. Given the explicit normative nature of the Dutch insanity defence – it is not coincidentally called the excuse of 'non-accountability' – it stands to reason that the context and circumstances of the act, and the personality of the defendant as a whole, determine the attribution of criminal responsibility. As such, if the court does not or cannot specify the role of addiction in its verdict, it remains difficult to generalize on the influence that addiction can have on responsibility.

What these cases illustrate is the difficulty of addressing addiction in isolation of other circumstances and mental conditions, such as psychosis and the prior fault doctrine. Indeed, the prior fault doctrine seems to influence the perception of addiction and the addiction's influence of responsibility strongly. As such, many cases acknowledge the

93 However, there are also cases where withdrawal symptoms are mentioned but do not affect or is not even included in the discussion on insanity or diminished responsibility, such as in Hof Arnhem-Leeuwarden 7 August 2014, ECLI:NL:GHARL:2014:6264 and Rb Zutphen, 10 May 2011, ECLI:NL:RBZUT:2011:BQ 3982.

94 Hof Arnhem, 28 June 2012, ECLI:NL:GHARN:2012:BW9677.

95 Usually, the court merely agrees or disagrees with the full conclusion of the expert, which often contains information on all aspects of the defendant's behaviour and mental state, rather than just an elaboration on the addiction-related capacities. See for instance: Hof 's-Hertogenbosch, 29 February 2016, ECLI:NL:GHSHE:2016:704; Rb Utrecht, 20 May 2010, ECLI:NL:RBUTR:2010:BM8195; Rb Zwolle-Lelystad, 18 November 2011, ECLI:NL:RBZLY:2008:BG5594.

influence and effect of substances and addiction, but disregard these effects in light of the prior fault doctrine. Moreover, without specified capacities that are important in light of determining legal insanity, it could be easier for different courts to reach divergent conclusions in the same case. Nonetheless, addiction does seem to play a role in determining the defence of diminished responsibility.

4 Conclusion

This paper explored, in light of the current addiction debate, how addiction-impaired capacities may influence criminal responsibility, by addressing three jurisdictions. Although the conceptualization of addiction remains a scholarly debate, the law takes the impaired capacities of addicts, especially volitional, into account, mostly by means of a diminished responsibility defence and mitigated sentencing. Our analysis shows that these jurisdictions, despite their particular criteria for the insanity defence, are quite similar in their legal qualification of addiction as a possible excusing condition. Some interesting remarks regarding similarities and differences are worth pointing out.

The common law insanity defence, as defined in the M'Naghten rule, predominantly relates to rationality or cognitive capacities, whilst in comparison, the Netherlands and Germany in addition to cognitive incapacity, also accept volitional impairments. In that respect, it is interesting to note that some scholars have argued that, fundamentally, there may be no need for an additional control prong in the insanity defence, because at least the severe cases of volitional incapacity could potentially be submerged under a cognitive prong. In other words, severely diminished control capacities could potentially be understood as a form of irrationality. Morse, for instance, argues that a volitional element is superfluous in guidelines on legal insanity and contends that the M'Naghten rule can be interpreted in such a way that it allows for cases of volitional incapacity.[96] Relevant to the addiction debate, he explains that the experience of strong, irresistible desires is most commonly a product of irrationality: volitional incapacity is by definition a result of irrationality. Similarly, Penney states, 'a person experiencing an irresistible impulse cannot appreciate the nature and quality of the act' which, of course, refers to the M'Naghten rule requiring an ability to do so.[97] Therefore, despite the sole cognitive focus of the M'Naghten rule, perhaps

96 S.J Morse, 'Uncontrollable Urges and Irrational People', *Virginia Law Review*, Vol. 88, 2002, p. 1064. "No logical or legal reason prevents a court from understanding and interpreting 'control' problems as rationality defects ... Lack of capacity for rationality is almost always the most straightforward explanation of why we colloquially say that some people cannot control themselves when they experience intense desires."

97 S. Penney, 'Irresistible Impulse and the Mental Disorder Defence: The Criminal Code, the Charter and the Neuroscience of Control' *Criminal Law Quarterly*, Vol. 60, 2013, p. 220.

an individual experiencing volitional incapacity can still be considered legally insane, by explaining volitional incapacity as a rationality defect.[98]

However, the current case law does not seem very eager to adopt this proposed strategy of broadening the M'Naghten rule. As Meynen has also pointed out, there is an important inherent limitation in the M'Naghten rule itself.[99] It may be that cognitive capacities entail much more than a mere lack of knowledge, and could include, for instance, the volitional defects as explained by Morse above. However, the M'Naghten rule in its current understanding and application does not seem to support this expanse. Instead of a broad definition of rationality and cognition, the M'Naghten rule explicitly refers to the narrower 'lack of knowledge'. In short, although Morse is right that at least some forms of volitional impairment could be defined as cognitive incapacity, the current 'lack of knowledge' specified by the M'Naghten rule does not allow for this.

Therefore, due to the lack of fit between addiction and the M'Naghten rule, addiction cases ought to resort to a defence of diminished responsibility. Even if the addiction does not negate the capacities in full, it may then still contribute to a mitigated sentence. In fact, for civil law jurisdictions this seems to be the most common way to address addicted defendants. England and Wales, despite a lack of such a generalized defence, also allow diminished responsibility for addiction. In murder cases, this may result in a reduction to voluntary manslaughter, but for other crimes, it is merely a factor considered by the court in determining the most appropriate sentence.

A prominent difference between the jurisdictions is the explicit or implicit role of addiction in the determination of criminal responsibility. Case law from both Germany and England and Wales discuss addiction explicitly: the German Supreme Court even pronounces distinct criteria of the circumstances in which addiction could lead to insanity, or could at least lead to diminished responsibility. Case law even explicitly and often allows for (fear of) withdrawal symptoms, an explicitly addiction-related rather than an intoxication-related condition, to influence responsibility. By contrast, the Dutch courts are not much inclined to specify the specific role of addiction in determining legal insanity. Finally, the German prior fault doctrine seems to be the most lenient out of these three jurisdictions as well.

Arguably, regardless of the possibilities to apply the insanity defence to addiction, there are two final remarks regarding the difficulties of addressing addiction in the law. First of all, in an actual case, it is difficult if not impossible to determine the exact degree in which

98 Morse 2002, p. 1075.
99 Meynen 2016, p. 30.

the addict did not have control over the behaviour. Lord Parker CJ in *R v Byrne* already stated, 'in a case where the abnormality of mind is one which affects the accused's self-control, the step between he did not resist his impulse and he could not resist his impulse is one which is incapable of scientific proof.'[100] Morse argued similarly: 'If or to what degree a person's desire or impulse to act was controllable is not determinable: there is no scientific test to judge whether an impulse was irresistible or simply not resisted.'[101] As such, volitional capacity, albeit theoretically relevant, remains difficult to measure and apply in practice.

A second difficulty relates to the comorbidity associated with addiction. As was illustrated in some of the cases, most offenders who argue for insanity or diminished responsibility do not suffer from addiction solely. Consequently, comorbid personality disorders, drug-induced psychosis, acute intoxication, or other circumstances complicate the analysis of case law. In order to evaluate how addiction as such may play a role in attributing criminal responsibility, the addiction and its psychological and behavioural consequences ought to be discussed in isolation. It is interesting to see that German law seems to give the most attention to this issue, by specifically defining the circumstances and conditions that allow addiction to be at least a partial excuse.

100 [1960] 2 QB 396.

101 S.J. Morse, 'Excusing the Crazy: The Insanity Defense Reconsidered', *Southern California Law Review*, Vol. 58, p. 817.

REFERENCES

Aguilar de Arcos, F. *et al.*, 'Experience of emotions in substance abusers exposed to images containing neutral, positive, and negative affective stimuli,' *Drug and Alcohol Dependence*, Vol. 78, No. 2, 2005, pp. 159-167.

Aguilar de Arcos, F. *et al.*, 'Dysregulation of emotional response in current and abstinent heroin users: Negative heightening and positive blunting', *Psychopharmacology*, Vol. 198, No. 2, 2008, pp. 159-166.

Allnutt, S., Samuels, A. & O'Driscoll, C., 'The insanity defence: From wild beasts to M'Naghten', *Australasian Psychiatry*, Vol. 15, No. 4, 2007, pp. 292-298..

Baler, R.D. & Volkow, N.D., 'Drug addiction: the neurobiology of disrupted self-control', *Trends in Molecular Medicine*, Vol. 12, No. 12, 2007, pp. 559-566

Barendregt, C.S. & van der Laan, A.M., 'Neuroscientific insights and the Dutch adolescent criminal law: A brief report', *Journal of Criminal Justice*, 2018.

Bechara, A., 'Decision making, impulse control and loss of willpower to resist drugs: a neurocognitive perspective', *Nature Neuroscience*, Vol. 8, No. 11, 2005, pp. 1458-1463.

Bijlsma, J., *Stoornis en strafuitsluiting: Op zoek naar een toetsingskader voor ontoereken-baarheid*, Wolf Legal Publishers, Oisterwijk 2016.

Blomsma, J.H. & Roef, D., 'Justifications and excuses', *in* J. Keiler & D. Roef (Eds.), *Comparative Concepts of Criminal Law*, 3rd edn, Intersentia, Cambridge 2019, pp. 207-252.

Bohlander, M., *Principles of German criminal law*, Hart Publishing, Portland Oregon 2009.

Brants, C., Jackson, A. & Koenraadt, F., 'Culpability compared: Mental capacity, criminal offences and the role of the expert in common law and civil law jurisdictions', *Journal of International and Comparative Law*, Vol. 3, No. 2, 2016, pp. 411-440.

Clore, G.L., & Huntsinger, J.R., 'How emotions inform judgment and regulate thought', *Trends in Cognitive Sciences*, Vol. 11, No. 9, 2007, pp. 393-399.

Degenhardt, L. & Hall, W., 'The relationship between tobacco use, substance-use disorders and mental health: results from the National Survey of Mental Health and Well-being', *Nicotine & Tobacco Research*, Vol. 3, No. 3, 2001, pp. 225-234.

Duff, A., 'Legal and moral responsibility', *Philosophy Compass*, Vol. 4, No. 6, 2009, pp. 978-986.

Dworkin, R., *Justice for Hedgehogs*, The Belknap Press of Harvard University Press, Camrbidge 2011.

Fine, C. & Kennett, J., 'Mental impairment, moral understanding and criminal responsibility: Psychopathy and the purposes of punishment', *International Journal of Law and Psychiatry*, Vol. 27, No. 5, 2004, pp. 425-443.

Glannon, W., 'Psychopathy and responsibility', *Journal of Applied Philosophy*, Vol. 14, No. 3, 1997, pp. 263-275.

Goldstein, R.Z. & Volkow, N.D., 'Dysfunction of the prefrontal cortex in addiction: neuroimaging findings and clinical implications', *Nature Reviews Neuroscience*, Vol. 12, No. 11, 2011, pp. 652-669/

Heyman, G.M., *Addiction: A disorder of choice*, Harvard University Press, Cambridge Massachusetts 2009.

Heyman, G.M., 'Addiction and choice: Theory and new data', *Frontiers in Psychiatry*, Vol. 4, 2013, p. 31.

Hyman, S.E., 'Addiction: a disease of learning and memory', *American Journal of Psychiatry*, Vol. 162, No. 8, 2005, pp. 1414-1422.

Jentsch, J.D. *et al.*, 'Dissecting impulsivity and its relationships to drug addictions', *Annals of the New York Academy of Sciences*, Vol. 1327, No. 1, 2014, pp. 1-26.

Kassel, J.D. *et al.*, 'Negative Affect and Addiction', *in* M. al'Absi (Ed.), *Stress and Addiction*, Academic Press, Burlington 2007, pp. 171-189.

Keiler, J. & Roef, D., *Comparative Concepts of Criminal Law*, 3rd edn, Intersentia, Cambridge 2019.

Kennett, J., *Agency and responsibility: A common-sense moral psychology*. Clarendon Press, Oxford 2001.

Kennett, J., Vincent, N. A. & Snoek, A., 'Drug Addiction and Criminal Responsibility', *in* J. Clausen & N. Levy (Eds.), *Handbook of Neuroethics*, Springer, Dordrecht 2015, pp. 1065-1083.

Leshner, A.I., 'Addiction is a brain disease, and it matters', *Science*, Vol. 278, No. 5335, 1997, pp. 45-47.

Lewis, M., 'Addiction and the Brain: Development, Not Disease', *Neuroethics*, Vol. 10, No. 1, 2017, pp. 7-18.

Lighthart, S.L.T.J., Kooijmans, T. & Meynen, G., 'Een juridisch criterium voor ontoerekeningsvatbaarheid: een uitspraak van het Gerechtshof geanalyseerd', *Delikt & Delinkwent*, Vol. 9, 2018, pp. 101-110.

Maatz, K.R., 'Drogenbedingte Verminderung der Schuldfähigkeit – zum gegenwärtigen Stand der Rechtsprechung des Bundesgerichtshofs', *Tagungsband zum XIII. GTFCh-Symposium, 3.-5.4.2003 in Mosbach*, 2013, pp. 14-27, Retrieved on 25 May 2019 from www.gtfch.org/cms/index.php/en/proceedings/587-gtfch-symposium-2003.

Mackay, R.D., Mitchell, B.J. & Howe, L., 'Yet more facts about the insanity defence', *Criminal Law Review*, 2006, pp. 399-411.

Mackay, R.D., 'Righting the wrong? Some observations on the second limb of the M'Naghten rules', *Criminal Law Review*, Vol. 2, 2009, pp. 80-89.

Maibom, H.L., 'The Mad, the Bad, and the Psychopath', *Neuroethics*, Vol. 1, No. 3, 2008, 167-184.

McSherry, B., 'Defining what is a 'disease of the mind': the untenability of current legal interpretations', *Journal of Law and Medicine*, Vol. 1, No. 2, 1993, pp. 76-90.

Meynen, G., *Legal insanity: Explorations in psychiatry, law, and ethics*. Vol. 71, Springer, Basel 2016.

Moore, M., 'Stephen Morse on the Fundamental Psycho-Legal Error', *Criminal Law and Philosophy*, Vol. 1, 2016, pp. 48-59

Morse, S.J., 'Excusing the crazy: The insanity defense reconsidered', *Southern California Law Review*, Vol. 58, 1985, p. 777.

Morse, S.J., 'Culpability and control', *University of Pennsylvania Law Review*, Vol. 142, 1993, pp. 1587-1660.

Morse, S.J., 'Uncontrollable urges and irrational people', *Virginia Law Review*, Vol. 88, 2002, pp. 1025-1078.

Mumola, C.J. & Karberg, J.C., *Drug use and dependence, state and federal prisoners, 2004*. Retrieved from Washington D.C., 2006.

Penney, S., 'Irresistible impulse and the mental disorder defence: The criminal code, the Charter and the neuroscience of control', *Criminal Law Quarterly*, Vol. 60, 2013, pp. 207-237.

Shea, P., 'M'Naughten revisited – Back to the future? (The mental illness defence – A psychiatric perspective)', *Current Issues in Criminal Justice*, Vol. 12, No. 3, 2000, pp. 347-362.

Smith, J.L. *et al.*, 'Deficits in behavioural inhibition in substance abuse and addiction: a meta-analysis', *Drug and Alcohol Dependence*, Vol. 145, 2014, pp. 1-33.

Verdejo-Garcia, A., Clark, L. & Dunn, B.D., 'The role of interoception in addiction: a critical review', *Neuroscience and Biobehavioral Reviews*, Vol. 36, No. 8, 2012, pp. 1857-1869.

Vincent, N.A., 'On the relevance of neuroscience to criminal responsibility', *Criminal Law and Philosophy*, Vol. 4, No. 1, 2010, pp. 77-98.

Volkow, N.D. & Fowler, J.S., 'Addiction, a disease of compulsion and drive: Involvement of the orbitofrontal cortex', *Cerebral Cortex*, Vol. 10, No. 3, 2000, pp. 318-325.

Zilverstand, A., Huang, A.S., Alia-Klein, N. & Goldstein, R.Z., 'Neuroimaging impaired response inhibition and salience attribution in human drug addiction: A systematic review', *Neuron*, Vol. 98, No. 5, 2018, pp. 886-903.

9 Coercion Changes Sense of Agency?

L. Claydon

1 Introduction

This chapter arises from a paper given in Maastricht in 2018 and from an interdisciplinary project funded by the AHRC.[1] One of the aims of the project was to consider whether interdisciplinary work between cognitive neuroscientists, philosophers and lawyers would assist in understanding issues of importance to the law of England and Wales.[2] An area of particular interest was the subjective experience of agency.

It must be said at the outset that the English criminal law may not accord full weight to the subjective experience of agency in assessing guilt or innocence. The assessment made of guilt will depend upon the definition of the crime and whether there is a defence. In the most serious offences, there is a balance between the subjective and the objective factors that define the criminal offence. However, in determining what may excuse criminal behaviour the criminal law does take account of some of the circumstances of the defendant at the time of the criminal act. The finding of fact in the most serious criminal trials, usually rests with the jury, advised on the law by the judge. The law requires in a limited number of defences that the jury weighs the reaction of the accused against the reaction of a reasonable person in the same circumstances when establishing whether the criminal conduct should be excused.

Cognitive neuroscience in explaining the underpinnings of the subjective experience of agency provides a different perspective for the law. Many of law's normative judgements are based on societal acceptance, or, condemnation of certain types of behaviour. This may be an obvious statement but is worth making. This is because some legal norms have

1 "Project title: Sense of agency and responsibility: integrating legal and neurocognitive accounts. Funded by the Arts and Humanities Research Council (AHRC) as part of its Innovation in Culture Programme. The project aimed to investigate the fact that legal systems generally view individuals as having control over their actions. Yet, expanding scientific knowledge suggests that an individual's actions are the result of brain processes that are independent of consciousness. The study included experiments which assess self-agency and interdisciplinary work between neuroscientists, legal experts, and philosophers. The Principal Investigator on the project was Professor Patrick Haggard of the Institute of Cognitive Neuroscience, University College, London.

2 Hereafter referred to as 'English Law'.

remained in place for many years, and may not have changed to reflect changes in scientific or social viewpoints. Social cognitive neuroscience therefore may provide a critical perspective adding a further dimension to debates within the law.

For those unfamiliar with the development of the law in England, law is derived from two sources. One is the common law: that is the law interpreted and declared by the courts and rooted in legal history and jurisprudence that forms legal precedent to be applied in subsequent cases. The other is legislation passed by Parliament and open to interpretation by the courts. Therefore, an offence or defence defined by the common law has a very different aetiology from that of new offences created by legislation. This will be highlighted as the chapter progresses.

With this in mind, this chapter will examine some recent findings from cognitive neuroscience and consider what those findings might tell us about the criminal culpability of those who are ordered or coerced into committing a criminal act. In particular the agency of those who claim they were ordered to act in a certain manner. Why this may be of relevance to the law is that it will provide a different perspective on the experience of being an individual subject to coercive control. Those who follow orders may not always feel coerced or controlled. The legal interest is in those who claim to be less responsible for a criminal act because they were coerced and controlled into its commission. The claim is not that the description of agent action by neuroscientists is the same as the legal definition of the individual responsible agent. It is rather to look at what evidence there is to assist the structural underpinnings of the legal reasoning when imposing culpability for criminal acts upon those who follow orders.

2 What May Cognitive Neuroscience Tell Us About Our Individual Sense of Agency?

Patrick Haggard, explains how a sense of agency may play a role in our basic actions. Writing about how a sense of agency is experienced in the human brain, he describes agency as follows: "It is the experience of controlling one's own motor acts and through them, the course of external events." Haggard highlights that this is a thinner sense of agency than the sense employed by the social sciences – "in which it typically designates a felt capacity to act (self-efficacy), without reference to any specific motor act."[3] This sense

3 P. Haggard, 'Sense of Agency in the Human Brain', *Nature Reviews Neuroscience*, Vol. 18, No. 4, 2017, p. 197, both quotations.

of controlling the course of future events through motor acts is nowhere near, as complete a sense of foresight of consequences of action, as that required by the criminal law.

Haggard explains very simply how agency generates a basic sense of responsibility. We act to flick a light switch, we know that our motor act in flicking the switch should result in the light coming on and, in that sense, we experience responsibility for turning the light on. Sense of agency 'accompanies' motor acts that are, in a very minimal sense, chosen and directed at bringing about a certain outcome.[4]

Haggard writes that it may be possible to demonstrate empirically that a stronger sense of agency emerges when the selected action brings about the predicted outcome. Thus 'a sense of agency' under certain experimental conditions can be demonstrated "when voluntary actions match outcomes."[5] The relationship between agency attributions and outcomes is however not precisely clear.

Recognising that the legal view of agency requires precision and must take account of the views of society, Haggard poses a question about what sort of evidence might found a defence of self-defence or loss of control. Both contain elements that recognise fear reactions as possibly founding, in the former case, a full defence to certain violent crimes and in the other a partial defence to murder. Cognitive neuroscience has a particular view of fear reactions in terms of fight or flight, this differs somewhat from the legal view.[6] Haggard asks a relevant question about the interrelationship between law and neuroscience:

> Does such 'loss of control' represent involuntary recruitment of a specific neurobiological system subserving 'flight – or – fight' action control or merely a cultural expectation about when extreme behaviour might actually be acceptable? These explanations need not be exclusive: the law can be seen as a normative constraint on basic neurobiological drives to action.[7]

Neuroscience is able to provide a more basic explanation of why we experience self-efficacy in the form of responsibility when we act. What is of interest to this chapter is some recent work carried out by Haggard and collaborators concerning how we experience agency when acting under orders. This work permitted implicit measures of the experience of

---

4 Id., p. 199.

5 Id., p. 201.

6 For the legal viewpoint, *see* J. Horder, *Ashworth's Principles of the Criminal Law*, 9th edn, Oxford University Press, Oxford 2016, pp. 266-267. For a fuller discussion of the thinking behind the neuroscience, *see* A. Damasio, *Self Comes to Mind: Constructing the Conscious Brain*, Heinemann, London 2010, pp. 111-114.

7 Haggard 2017, p. 206.

being ordered to act that could be compared with self-report measures of a reduced sense of agency.

3 An Experimental Paradigm Designed to Test the Experience of Following Orders

Haggard and Casper set up experiments to measure the sense of agency experienced by those who are ordered to act by a third party.[8] The empirical research demonstrated that it is possible to show that the experience of agency was modified for participants when they were ordered to behave in certain ways that caused either a small financial loss or the experience of pain, inflicted by the participant, on another participant in the experiment. This allowed for implicit measurements to be made of the difference in participant responses when they were ordered to inflict financial loss or inflict pain in the form of a mild electric shock; as opposed to when they freely chose to inflict the same amount of financial loss or pain.

The finding of the experiments was that it was possible to establish using accepted scientific methods, that an individual's sense of agency was altered when the subject of the experiment experienced coercion. This correlated with claims made by individuals that they "were only obeying orders". The findings entered the main stream media via *Nature News*.[9] The coverage by BBC Science reported the results of the experiments in lay language, making reference to war crimes committed by those following orders.[10] Patrick Haggard's explanation of the results was more measured:

> When you ask people explicitly about responsibility, they tend to report what they think reflects best on them ... We wanted to know what people actually felt about the action as they made it, and about the outcome. Time perception tells us something about the basic experiences people have when they act, not just about how they think they should have felt. Our results suggest people who obey orders could actually feel less responsible for the outcomes of their action: they may not just be claiming that they feel less responsible. People appear to experience a sort of distance from the outcome of their actions when they are obeying instructions. It's important to distinguish between how our minds

8 E.A. Caspar, J.F. Christensen, A. Cleermans & P. Haggard, 'Coercion Changes the Sense of Agency in the Human Brian', *Current Biology*, Vol. 26, No. 5, 2016, pp. 585-592.

9 A. Abott, 'How the brain reacts to orders', *Nature*, Vol. 530, 2016, pp. 394-395.

10 J. Webb, 'Following orders 'distances us' from our own actions', 2016, www.bbc.co.uk/news/science-environment-35582986, accessed on 1/02/2019.

> generate our subjective feelings of responsibility, and the objective facts of responsibility. Of course, just feeling less responsible does not mean that you aren't responsible, and shouldn't be held responsible by society. In the end, society has to deal with the objective facts of what an individual does.[11]

Caspar felt the findings of the experiment had practical implications for policy makers.

> First, maybe people could be trained to feel more responsible: that might allow them to resist orders that are inappropriate. Second, our results could be particularly important for people who give orders. If people who follow orders feel a reduced sense of responsibility for their actions then perhaps people who give orders should feel increased responsibility.[12]

This research addresses some of the recognised flaws with previous research studies[13] and uses implicit measures to record the experience of agency that yield more objectively verifiable information about the experience of individual participants when ordered to act. In the experiments described above the results from electroencephalogram (EEG), and time perception tests both detected differences in responses when an individual was ordered how to act. The correlated findings of the experiments showed that 'ordered actions' more closely resembled "passive movement than freely chosen voluntary action."[14] There is therefore evidence apart from self-report accounts that when ordered how to act there may be a neuropsychological explanation for why an individual experiences a lower sense of responsibility for the corresponding action.

> Coercive orders thus influenced both explicit judgments of agency and the low-level subjective feeling of agency on which such judgments may be based. The defense of "only obeying orders" is often treated with suspicion by the law because of the clear secondary gain associated with denying responsibility. However, our result suggests that primary feelings and neurophysical processing of agency are indeed reduced by coercion.[15]

11 P. Haggard sets out the results of the experiments on the UCL website: 'Following orders makes us feel less responsible for our actions', 2016, www.ucl.ac.uk/news/2016/feb/following-orders-makes-us-feel-less-responsible-our-actions, accessed 1/02/2019.

12 Id.

13 *See* in particular S. Milgram, 'Behavioral study of obedience', *Journal of Abnormal and Social Psychology*, Vol. 67, No. 4, 1963, pp. 371-378.

14 Caspar *et al.* 2016, p. 589.

15 Id.

It is therefore possible to claim that there is evidence from cognitive neuroscience that an actor's sense of agency is reduced when they are ordered how to act. That is; there is implicit evidence that supports the argument that subjective experience of agency is reduced when people are ordered to perform certain actions. In their conclusions the authors write:

> Our research on the *experience* of agency highlights the fundamental link between law and cognitive neuroscience. The law has to engage with the human capacity to control action if it is to fulfil its function of allowing individuals to live together in societies.[16]

4 PRACTICAL PROBLEMS FOR THE LAW

Providing a legal framework that permits an excuse to be afforded to those who claim that they were ordered, coerced or controlled into committing a crime is problematic. Additionally, there are some structural problems with the criminal law that cannot be ignored. Husak explains this problem well:

> The general problem arises from the lack of a systematic account of relative culpability. An account of relative culpability would identify and defend a set of considerations to assess, whether, why, under what circumstances, and to what extent persons who perform a criminal act with a given culpable state are more or less blameworthy than persons who perform that act with a different culpable state.[17]

English criminal law in the courtroom focusses, in the main, on the criminal act and the immediate circumstances in which the alleged criminal behaviour occurred. The elements that need to be proved in the court room are distinct. Mens rea remains an important measure of culpability but it does not provide an assessment of a defendant's precise mental state at the time of the crime, but only of those elements that are deemed legally relevant.

Traditionally the genesis of mens rea has not been relevant, strictly speaking motive has not been relevant to guilt.[18] An explanation of what is meant by this can be gained by

16 Id., p. 590.
17 D. Husak, *The Philosophy of the Criminal Law*, Oxford University Press, Oxford 2010, p. 177.
18 Certain exculpatory defences most notably insanity may remove issues of mens rea from consideration; but in general, mens rea as a measure of the defendant's culpability remains important in more serious offences as a means of determining guilt. In practice motive is likely to become apparent in the course of a

looking at mens rea states that inculpate people in crime. In inculpatory terms intentional criminal behaviour is the mens rea state likely to attract the most blame.[19] In crimes where the sentence is fixed by law, such as murder, the verdict and sentence will be the same for all those who intentionally kill whether they be mercy killers or assassins. The verdict will be murder and the sentence will be life imprisonment. In crimes where the sentence is not fixed by law what motivated the crime may become a factor to be taken into account in sentencing.

In English criminal law, there is no legal defence of following orders.[20] The nearest criminal law defence would be duress. In duress there are a number of areas that have caused difficulty for the criminal law and required clarification to provide workable precedents on which to base the excuse.

First, and perhaps most notably, the question arose: is the law correct in excluding from the ambit of the defence the offence of murder? Secondly, should the law restrict the defence to a narrow range of defendants, those, who in the view of the courts, most deserve a defence? In order to narrow the defence, the common law courts developed a test of the reasonableness of the accused's action. The reasonableness test generated further difficulties, for example: should that test be an objective or a subjective test? If it is to be an objective test – how is the real experience of the defendant to be heard: what importance should be given to the accused's understanding of and response to the circumstances in which they were forced to commit a criminal act? Is an honest belief in the existence of a threat to be accepted or, should the existence of the threat be objectively verifiable? In answering these questions, the courts developed an approach to claims of threats of death or serious violence that is highly informative in terms of how English courts approach the statement made by Haggard – "Of course, just feeling less responsible does not mean that you aren't responsible, and shouldn't be held responsible by society. In the end, society has to deal with the objective facts of what an individual does."[21]

---

case where a trial is held and is therefore likely to influence the jury decision. It is worth noting in England and Wales that in the year ending January 2018 67% of defendants pleaded guilty, so there was no trial of the facts. A majority of the remaining cases were heard in the Magistrates Court but may be referred to Crown Court for sentencing. Actual trials in the Crown Court before a jury will be very small in number. Source: Ministry of Justice, Criminal Court Statistics, published 28 June 2018.

19 This is dependent on the other elements of the offence that have to be proved. For example, in crimes of violence where the actus reus requires the unlawful application of force self-defence may render the application of force lawful.

20 Though it may be that a member of the police service or armed forces who kills a civilian, whilst on active service, is able to claim that she is acting lawfully via the defence of self-defence. There are limitations on the defence particularly whether the use of force was excessive in the circumstances see *R v. Clegg* [1995] 1 A.C. 482.

21 *See supra* n. 11 and accompanying text.

Duress is very different from less specific claims of coercion and control. Duress is a general defence to crime and that means someone who successfully pleads duress cannot be found guilty. Two forms of duress are recognised: duress by threat and duress of circumstances. In English law duress is a complete defence to any crime with the exception of murder.[22] Duress of circumstances is recognised by the criminal law where the fear that brings the offence about is not from a spoken threat but from threatening circumstances.[23] In order to establish the defence of duress the accused has to demonstrate that there was a threat of death or serious injury, to herself or someone for whom she is responsible. The threat has to be immediate. An assessment of the reasonableness of the belief in the threat will be made, and the crime must be directly linked to the threat. There must be no reasonable opportunity to escape the threat.[24]

5 Difficult Cases that Formed the Law

In the seminal case of *Lynch*, the House of Lords had to grapple with an appeal from Northern Ireland against conviction for aiding and abetting the murder of a policeman. Lynch had assisted in the hijacking of a car and driven an IRA gunman to the site of the crime. He was convicted and his defence of duress, based on his fear for his own life, was withdrawn from the jury by the trial judge. In *Lynch* there is discussion of why the law should recognise duress as a defence. Lord Morris is clear that the law "would be censorious and inhumane if it did not recognise the appalling plight of a person who finds himself in jeopardy unless he submits and obeys."[25]

Lord Morris reviewed the standard of behaviour to be required by the courts of someone experiencing duress. He commented that such a person should not be expected to be 'heroic' but that there is need to establish that a 'real' threat was made.[26] This neatly exposes the paradox at the heart of duress that someone pleading duress may have committed a really serious crime, have fulfilled the actus reus and mens rea requirements of that crime and yet, none the less, be found to have no criminal culpability. Therefore, it is not surprising that the appeal courts have sought to limit the applicability of the defence.

22 *R v. Howe*, 1986 2 WLR 294.
23 *Cole* [1994] Crim LR 582; *Ali* [1995] Crim LR 303.
24 Further restrictions on the defence are that voluntarily opening yourself up to the possibility of such a threat or failing to take evasive action to avoid the crime will remove the accused from the ambit of the defence. *R v. Hasan (Aytach)* [2005] UKHL 22.
25 Lynch v. DPP for Northern Ireland [1975] AC 653, p. 671.
26 Id., p. 670.

But such limitations expose a rift in the development of the law between the expressed intention of judges to recognise the appalling plight of the person who feels she has to submit and obey the threat; and the manner in which the courts have chosen to narrow the defence of duress. As noted earlier the question of the reasonableness of the belief in the threat and the response to the threat has caused some difficulty. In *Graham*[27] the court identified three elements to the test. Firstly, the accused must have reasonably believed in the threat. The belief must be based on a 'good cause' to be fearful. Finally, the response to the fear must be assessed against that of the response of a 'sober person of reasonable firmness'. Then there was the question of whether a defendant should be judged subjectively on whether she foresaw a risk of being exposed to the threat.

In *Hasan* the majority of the House of Lords determined that the test of foresight of the risk should be objective. Lord Bingham stated that: "[t]he policy of the law must be to discourage association with known criminals and should be slow to excuse the criminal conduct of those who do." He continued:

If a person voluntarily becomes or remains associated with others engaged in criminal activity in a situation where he knows or ought reasonably to know that he may be subject to compulsion by them or their associates, he cannot rely on the defence of duress to excuse any act which he is thereafter compelled to do by them.[28]

6 Problems with the Defence

Baroness Hale, in her opinion in *Hasan*, expressed concern at the problems of objectively comparing the accused's assessment of risk to that of a sober person of reasonable firmness. In the context of the legal debate around what the accused should have been able to withstand she said:

> The moral basis of the defence remains a hot topic of debate: ... I accept that even the person with a knife at her back has a choice whether or not to do as the knifeman says. The question is whether she should have resisted the threat. But, perhaps because I am a reasonable but comparatively weak and fearful grandmother, I do not understand why the defendant's beliefs and personal

27 [1982] 1 All ER 801.
28 *Hasan* [2005] UKHL 22 [39], both quotations.

> characteristics are not morally relevant to whether she could reasonably have been expected to resist.[29]

Baroness Hale went on to say that in her view withdrawal of the defence from those who exposed themselves to the "risk of unlawful violence", disadvantaged an abused partner who was subject to domestic violence.

> The battered wife knows that she is exposing herself to the risk of unlawful violence if she stays, but she may have no reason to believe that her husband will eventually use her broken will to force her to commit crimes of some sort.

On that basis she concluded that there was a reason to distinguish those "who had quite a different reason for becoming associated with the duressor and then finds it difficult to escape."[30]

Baroness Hale expressed her support for a more subjective approach to the assessment of the defendant's belief in the reality of the threat. In making this argument she supported the views expressed by the Law Commission, that duress should be measured by the defendant's "reasonable reaction … in the circumstances as he or she believed them to be."[31] She remarked that in the consultation on the Law Commission's proposals there had been no support for the more objective approach to the beliefs of the defendant taken in *Graham*.[32] Moreover, Baroness Hale reiterated the Law Commission's conclusions that duress should not merely mitigate liability but should be a complete defence to all crimes. Her opinion quotes at length from the Law Commission report.

> We believe that it is wrong even in respect of murder to condemn the defendant for not acting heroically rather than reasonably, it would be even more unjust to condemn defendants for lesser acts done under the same conditions. To censure and punish such defendants who found themselves in such circumstances would be to bring the law into disrepute.

Baroness Hale reinforces the idea that duress is not an issue to be left to prosecutorial discretion and that relegating duress, to a plea in mitigation, does not meet the requirements of justice.

29 Id. [73].
30 Id. [78], all quotations.
31 Law Com No. 218, 1993, para. 29.7.
32 *Hasan* [2005] UKHL 22 [68].

> If the reasons for rejecting duress are ones of public policy, it is hard to see that that policy is forwarded by a regime that assumes that convictions are to be purely nominal in nature, or, even in some cases that the law will not be enforced at all.[33]

Norrie commenting on the Supreme Court decision in *Hasan* compares the reasoning of Lord Bingham and Baroness Hale and points out that in framing the requirements of the law: "Different views of the defendant lead to different views of the defence." He comments that Baroness Hale normalises the defendant changing the focus from the 'charter for terrorists' and "back to the defendant's 'miserable and agonising plight."[34] The difference in the tenor of the opinions in *Hasan* is certainly remarkable. It underlines the fact that different views of morality and how that should be reflected in the practice of the criminal law vary quite considerably amongst those who interpret and apply the common law. It also reinforces the point made by Haggard that the law makes a much richer judgement of agency. It must also be accepted that the law does impose its own reductive notions of responsibility on agency that controversially narrows the ambit of excusing conditions. This may be seen from the examination of the development of duress.

Does the fact that it is possible to implicitly measure the fact that the individual experience of acting under orders does make the experience of acting more like that of passive movement make a difference to the legal argument? Is it possible that scientific findings could challenge our existing notions of criminal responsibility?

7 LAW, TRADITIONAL JURISPRUDENCE, AND FOLK PSYCHOLOGY

Traditionally, it is argued that they cannot. The work of Stephen Morse, in particular, points out that the definition of criminal responsibility is both normative and based on folk psychology. Morse argues that "the law is concerned with the mental state itself, rather than the cause of it."[35] Morse's view is that the folk psychological view provides a better explanation of human behaviour. "We are the sort of creatures that can act for and respond

33 Id. [69], both quotations.

34 A. Norrie, *Crime, Reason and History: A Critical Introduction to Criminal Law*, 3rd edn, Cambridge University Press, Cambridge 2014, p. 227.

35 "All affirmative defences of justification and excuse involve an inquiry into the person's mental state, such as belief that self -defensive force was necessary or the lack of knowledge of right from wrong. Of course, the person's mental state is influenced by biological, psychological and knowledge of those variables may help determine was, but the law is concerned with the mental state itself, rather than the cause of it." S. Morse, 'Lost in Translation? An Essay on Law and Neuroscience', *in* M. Freeman, (Ed.), *Law and Neuroscience, Current Legal Issues* Vol. 13, Oxford University Press, Oxford 2011, p. 531.

to reasons, including legal rules and standards that are expressed and understood linguistically." On this view it is our ability to interpret, folk psychologically speaking, how others act that is key to the finders of fact the jury. Morse continues: "[t]he law treats persons generally as intentional creatures and not as mechanical forces of nature." Folk psychological explanations of behaviour see the "person as a conscious (and potentially self-conscious) creature who forms and acts on intentions that are the product of the person's other mental states such as desires, beliefs, willings and plans."[36] Folk psychology may hold true for limited notions of reasons and intention. However, it may be more difficult to rely on such bare understandings and interpretations to attribute culpability when trying to interpret more complex behaviour.

Moreover, the traditional approach of the criminal law to exculpatory defences based on coercion and control is problematic. Horder expresses this as: a failure to recognise that "physical or psychological coercion – especially over a long period – may break D's will to resist. This effectively silences the voice of reason." Horder makes a further argument that when 'reason' is silenced in this manner. The coerced person may only respond to "means end rational guidance in complying with the coercer's demands." He argues that: 'In such cases D's conduct is non-voluntary."[37] Caspar et al make a similar comment: "coercion also reduced the neural processing of the outcomes of one's own action." "Thus, people who obey orders may subjectively experience their actions as closer to passive movements than fully voluntary actions."[38]

In making his argument Horder draws upon the jurisprudential reasoning of Raz. Raz in *Practical Reasons and Norms* considers, at some length, the problem of a conflict of reasons for acting. He concludes that at times acting on the balance of reasons may be defeated by a reason that, because of its nature, prevents the accused person acting in accordance with reason. Raz identifies this type of lack of ability to act for reasons as being distinguished by a dependency "on the circumstances of the agent at the time he decides what to do."[39] Raz offers various alternatives for why a person may not act as might be expected, resulting in a failure to follow what might be viewed as a rational choice. The reason for not acting is described as "a reason for mistrusting one's judgement, rather than not acting for certain reasons."[40] This Raz argues could be alternatively viewed as an incapacity to act in accordance with reason. It is notable that both Raz and Horder give explanations that are

36 Id., p. 531, both quotations.
37 J. Horder, *Excusing Crime*, Oxford University Press, Oxford 2004, p. 94, all quotations.
38 Caspar *et al.* 2016, p. 585.
39 Oxford University Press, Oxford 1990, p. 48.
40 Id., p. 48.

assessing the action after the event, whereas Casper et al are making implicit measurements and these are taken before the action occurs.

It is worth stressing that there is no uniform agreement amongst legal commentators as to the problems underlying the law's approach to coercion and responsibility. The use of reason and rationality to inculpate or exculpate liability itself has a contested history in legal jurisprudence. Kennedy points out that there is another tension here with the reasoning that underpins much of the law: "We are all taught that men are rational and women emotional; the system assigns more worth to reason than to emotion."[41]

8 Does the Law Need Assistance from Experts?

The courts have expressed their concern that those who commit crimes escape liability, but more questionably have rejected expert guidance in helping juries understand the experience of coercion and control. In *R v. EK*[42] the Court of Appeal considered an application from a victim of human trafficking (VOT) who had committed a number of crimes. In the course of the hearing of the appeal, the Court of Appeal questioned the need for any expert evidence on the psychological effect of controlling and coercive behaviour on a victim of trafficking.

The court accepted that EK was a victim of trafficking at the time of committing the crimes. The offences to which she pled guilty included, conspiracy to control prostitution for gain and money laundering. At the time of her conviction and sentencing, there was no trial as she pled guilty, her status as victim of trafficking had been rejected. However, by the time of her appeal that decision had been overturned and her status as a VOT recognised.

This appeal was to hear a claim that EK's prosecution and conviction was an abuse of process. Her status as a victim of human trafficking having been established. She had been granted asylum. The new appeal sought the quashing of her conviction for which she had already served the sentence. The Court of Appeal accepted that if she succeeded in having her criminal conviction quashed her immigration status would be improved as would her employment prospects. The court in its reasoning drew on the common law's approach to risk, money laundering was a serious offence and therefore the judgment also has a deterrence aspect to it. The court stated:

41 H. Kennedy, *Eve Was Shamed: How British Justice is Failing Women*, Chatto and Wyndus, London 2018, p. 7.
42 [2018] EWCA Crim 2961.

> It is, unfortunately, not infrequent that those convicted of criminal offences have been subjected to a malign, sometimes controlling influence. Ordinarily, that does not absolve them from criminal responsibility, ... In the VOT context it is important that the law is not devoid of sympathy or understanding -the evils of human trafficking are well understood; but it is also necessary in the public interest that there neither is, nor ought to be, any blanket immunity. Unfortunately for the appellant, she fell and falls the wrong side of that line.[43]

It seems that the court was wary of quashing the conviction. There is an indication that the court did not feel that the public interest was best served by such action. They might have felt more inclined to quash the conviction if the level of coercion had been "very high".[44] This suggests that some form of folk psychology might be at work here – suggesting to the court that the defendant was rational and her actions were intentional and not to be excused. Is such a conclusion sustainable? This type of pragmatic reasoning is also implicit in the legislation that recognises and criminalises human trafficking in a slightly different form. The Modern Slavery Act 2012 provides a defence in Section 45 for those trafficked and forced to commit crime but not in the case of more serious offences.[45]

Is this reasoning that more serious crime deserves different treatment supportable? It might be – but in order to establish that this was the case it would need to be established that the level of coercion being high or the seriousness of the offence made a difference to the level of culpability of a defendant. The neuroscience suggests that in cases of coercion the experience of acting is changed. This obviously may happen even if the act ordered to be carried out is serious. Indeed, it may be the experience of being ordered to act that is more crucial to an assessment of culpability than the seriousness of the crime. The court in *EK* seems to elide the seriousness of the criminal act with the need to maintain the conviction for policy reasons and thus to deny abuse of process. Thus, taking a pragmatic approach to the fact of coercion: being focussed on deterrence, and holding someone responsible for a serious crime. Problematically the court in *EK* seems to presume that anyone may escape from coercion, as and when, an opportunity to escape is afforded.

---

43 Id. [56].

44 Id. [51].

45 (1) A person is not guilty of an offence if –
(a) the person is aged 18 or over when the person does the act which constitutes the offence,
(b) the person does that act because the person is compelled to do it,
(c) the compulsion is attributable to slavery or to relevant exploitation, and
(d) a reasonable person in the same situation as the person and having the person's relevant characteristics would have no realistic alternative to doing that act.
Schedule 4 of the Act excludes the defence as a plea to a charge for a more serious crime.

Noted in the judgment are comments about the expert evidence before the Court of Appeal – having stated their scepticism about how expert evidence might assist – the court notes that the expert described as a complex trauma specialist cannot identify "the factual cause of the Applicant's complex Post- Traumatic Stress Disorder and or Major Depressive Disorder from the experiences she has suffered."[46] Though, the court appears to accept that EK had been trafficked multiple times and that the tribunal that established her status as a victim of trafficking found, on the balance of probabilities, that she "was at all times under the control of SK and that her experiences have left her in vulnerable psychological state."[47]

Worryingly in *EK* the court seems to be seeking a direct simple linkage between being a victim of trafficking and the crime; and notes a concession by an expert with regard to the evidence she has given: "The freeze response that potentially explains the Applicant's inability to escape from situations of abuse and danger would not of itself fully explain her not removing herself from her association with Sergei Konart."[48] Konart is described in court as her boyfriend. The court does not seem to consider there are a number of other factors that might contribute to her inability to escape – and expert evidence to this effect might be a contributory factor in aiding the court to understand how EK had been controlled by Konart. Victims of trafficking are not alone in this misunderstanding of the issues surrounding the failure to leave a controlling or coercive relationship, there is evidence that women experiencing domestic abuse receive similar treatment.

Writing of her experience as a criminal barrister Helen Kennedy writes:

> Understanding domestic abuse plainly remains a challenge for the courts. To onlookers the response of the battered women seems abnormal, but to her it is a rational response to her abnormal circumstances. Misconceptions litter the court and are reflected in the verdicts of juries: women have ample opportunities to leave; in some perverse way they like the pain; [...] Continuing to live with the tormentor is seen as a testament to the acceptability of his behaviour. A constant refrain in the questioning is "Why did you not leave?" This is something the woman herself can never answer coherently.[49]

46 [2018] EWCA Crim 2961 [28].
47 Id. [29].
48 Id.
49 Kennedy 2018, p. 100.

On the whole the Court of Appeal is sceptical of EK's claims and of the expert evidence to support the claims the judgment notes:

> Scepticism has consistently been expressed as to the value of expert evidence in cases such as this: Lord Judge CJ at *R v N* and *R v Le* [2012] EWCA Crim 189; [2012] 1 Cr App R 35 at [86C]; Lord Thomas CJ in *R v Joseph (Verna)* [2017] EWCA Crim 36; [2017] 1 Cr App R 33, especially at [87] and following; *R v S(G)* at [70] and following. When it comes to the credibility of accounts given by an applicant or appellant, it is for a jury or this court to evaluate them. It is not the function of experts to do so. When it comes to the correctness of a decision to prosecute, expert evidence is ordinarily unlikely to assist.[50]

It seems unlikely that the jury or the court will have a realistic grasp of the experience of coercion or control, or indeed the impact upon behaviour of being a victim of human trafficking. The failure to permit evidence of the effect of coercion and control may in effect open the door to the worst kind of folk psychology interpretation based on prejudice and inexperience.

9 New Approaches to Coercion and Control

In 2015 Parliament legislated, not to create a new defence but, rather to create a new offence of coercive or controlling behaviour in intimate family relationships. The new offence of coercive or controlling behaviour in intimate relationships[51] extends the law by criminalising conduct that is coercive or controlling. The Act is concerned with imposing criminal responsibility for the infliction of harm by such behaviour. The victim has to experience a 'serious effect' defined in 76(4) as causing fear of violence on at least two occasions, or "causing serious alarm and distress which has a substantial adverse effect" on the victim's "day to day activities". The offence carries a maximum sentence of 5 years imprisonment. The inculpatory argument behind the Act seems to be that coercive and controlling

---

50 *R v. EK* [2018] [42].

51 Serious Crime Act 2015 created in Section 76 a new offence of controlling or coercive behaviour in an intimate of family relationships came into force in December 2015.
76 Controlling or coercive behaviour in an intimate or family relationship
(1) A person (A) commits an offence if –
(a) A repeatedly or continuously engages in behaviour towards another person (B) that is controlling or coercive,
(b) at the time of the behaviour, A and B are personally connected,
(c) the behaviour has a serious effect on B, and
(d) A knows or ought to know that the behaviour will have a serious effect on B.

behaviour that compromises an ability to act 'normally' or places someone at fear of violence is harmful to individuals and to society and therefore such behaviour should be criminalised. This is of interest because the new law has been influenced by a kind of expertise not normally recognised by the courts; that of social science.

The Home Office released guidance on the new law.[52] This made it clear that the coercion and control had to be 'repeated' or continuous. The abuser must know or "ought to have known" that the behaviour would have a "serious effect on the victim". The rationale for the offence is explained:

> This offence sends a clear message that this form of domestic abuse can constitute a serious offence particularly in light of the violation of trust it represents and will provide better protection to victims experiencing repeated or continuous abuse. It sets out the importance of recognising the harm caused by coercion or control, the cumulative impact on the victim and that a repeated pattern of abuse can be more injurious and harmful than a single incident of violence.

Beneath this explanation appears a quotation: "Not only is coercive control the most common context in which [women] are abused. It is also the most dangerous."[53]

The quotation is from a monograph written by Evan Stark who cleary was influential in the drafting of the legislation. Therefore, it seems worthwhile to examine his academic arguments in relation to the law, to see how Stark feels that the law should respond to domestic abuse by coercive control.

> The first challenge I pose involves shifting the legal rationales for intervention from 'equal protection' of victim physical integrity to the 'anti-subordination' argument used to preserve individual sovereignty and oppose discrimination. The second challenge is to incorporate the typology into the criminal justice legal response by giving the pattern I describe a name; redefining the abuse as a course of conduct crime ... similar to harassment rather than an incident specific assault; and distinguishing a class of individual behaviours that reinforce inequality and harm liberty [...] The new crime would have much in common

52 Controlling or Coercive Behaviour in an Intimate or Family Relationship: Statutory Guidance Framework, Home Office, 2015.

53 Id., p. 3; the quotation is cited to E. Stark, *Coercive Control. How Men Entrap Women in Personal Life*, Oxford University Press, New York 2007.

> with indentured servitude, terrorism, or hostage taking, but would not merely mimic public law by conflating personal harms with public harms as marital rape statutes have done, unsuccessfully in my view. I hope to stir interest in a class of rights in personal life that could be protected with minimal threat to privacy.[54]

The statutory guidance for the new Act seems to reinforce some of these comments. Particularly those regarding anti-subordination by describing controlling behaviour as "a range of acts designed to make a person subordinate and or dependent." It is notable that this description by Stark does not have its roots in the language of folk psychology in reason or intention. It has its roots in the powerlessness of someone who is the victim of interpersonal coercion and control and the need for society to prevent such harm. It is not weighing the risk of harm but seeking to establish a more equal society.

10 Two Different Approaches to Coercion and Control in English Law

The difference in approach between common law approaches to duress and the approach taken by the new legislation to coercion and control leads to a dissonance in the criminal law. In that behaviour that may inculpate and lead to imprisonment cannot exculpate the person who suffers the abuse. This point may be demonstrated by examining the case of *R v A.*[55]

The defendant was charged with perverting the course of justice by withdrawing her claim that her husband had raped her. The charges laid against her in respect of perverting the course of justice were in the alternative. It was claimed that either that she had made a false allegation of rape or, that she had lied when withdrawing her allegation. A, pled guilty to the second charge. On appeal against conviction[56] there was considerable evidence, that she had experienced abuse at the hands of her husband; and that she had been pressured into withdrawing the allegations of rape by her husband and his sister.

54 E. Stark, 'Rethinking Coercive Control', *Violence against Women*, Vol. 15, No. 12, 2009, pp. 1515-1516.
55 [2012] EWCA Crim 434.
56 Id. [88]. The case states that the situation with regard to her children had deteriorated following her imprisonment meaning that within three weeks of being sentenced she was released her sentence having been commuted to a community sentence.

It is possible to ask why the prosecution took place, why was it in the public interest to prosecute A?[57] Additionally, it might be asked whether it is really humane to inflict the full force of the law on someone who withdraws an allegation of rape in such circumstances. There is something discomforting about reading A's case, particularly when the appeal court shows sympathy for her plight, but does not quash her conviction.[58] But it does reinforce the argument made by Baroness Hale that relying on administrative discretion not to prosecute cannot be relied upon.[59]

In *A* the court gave weight to an argument put forward by an academic commentator Loveless that;

> Leaving aside for the moment the contentious issue of whether an abused woman, even one suffering from BWS, remains a reasonable person or not, the problem of the law is how to translate the medical language of 'learned helplessness, passivity and paralysis' into the legal discourse of duress. It is not simply that there is automatic equivalence between 'learned helplessness' and 'overpowerment of will'; the two are not the same.[60]

In fact, Loveless employed this argument to criticise the pathologizing of women defendants. The court in *A* utilises the same argument to deny the appeal. This seems an odd use of an article that was arguing for a better understanding of the issues surrounding abuse.

In the article in *Nature* Haggard touches upon the problem of domestic abuse and points to the need for scientific research that may provide some understanding of the reactions of those who experience serious domestic violence. He suggests two areas of research that could be of interest. One that might test the idea that profound abuse could affect interactions between the "limbic and motor systems in the brain and thus influence voluntary control of action."[61] He also notes that prolonged abuse "can induce profound changes in cognitive and behavioural capacity, similar to the 'learned helplessness' condition that is

57 Id. [6]. In *A* this is commented upon by the appeal court who note that following newspaper reporting of the case the DPP referred to the need for the "Crown Prosecution Service to organise an improvement in their handling of retraction cases."

58 The court concluded that the appellant had lied when she withdrew her allegations of rape. The appeal court expressed sympathy with the predicament of the appellant who had clearly suffered greatly from the abusive behaviour of her husband. The court did not quash the conviction or concede that a defence of duress may have been arguable at trial. The reason given was that whilst the abusive behaviour was serious and persistent, and there was undoubtedly pressure to withdraw the allegation, there was no evidence of an operative threat of death or serious injury at the time the allegations were withdrawn.

59 *Supra* n. 33.

60 [2012] EWCA Crim 434, [62].

61 Haggard 2017, p. 198.

described in animal behaviour research."[62] The suggestion here is that more evidence and scientific understanding of the effect of prolonged domestic abuse would assist the jury.

The issue of how much moral strength is to be required bedevils the defence of duress. Thus, in *Bowen*,[63] interpreting the *Graham* test the court restricted the characteristics of the accused that could be taken into account by the jury in assessing how a sober person of reasonable firmness might have behaved. In *Bowen* the court excluded any characteristics related to vulnerability and timidity. Thereby excluding the kind of behaviours that might be displayed by someone who had become timid as a result of abuse. But the decision in *Bowen* permitted characteristics to be included within the test that resulted from evidence of psychiatric condition or recognised mental illness. Thus, women who wished to plead the defence and had been abused had to produce psychological or psychiatric evidence to demonstrate that there they possessed a characteristic of relevance to the *Graham* test. It was this focus on the need to show a recognised mental condition that impaired reasoning that Loveless is criticising.

11 THE CIRCUMSTANCES OF R V A

The case report deals with the circumstances of A's unsuccessful appeal on the basis of the defence of duress against conviction for perverting the course of justice. It is possible to review A's husband's behaviour in the light of the new offence of controlling and coercive behaviour under Section 76 of the Serious Crime Act 2015.

A's husband is the subject of a series of allegations that were never tested in court. A's husband denied the allegations. However, the allegations are: that A's husband had raped her on three occasions. There was also evidence of domestic abuse though all the circumstances of this are not given in the report. A's husband pressured her to give up work in a massage parlour. Work that she had undertaken because she was in financial difficulties. He sent her a series of abusive text messages. In the court report it was stated that A's husband was on bail, and under a condition that he should not contact her or have communication with her and he broke those conditions. It was accepted on appeal that she had been pressured to withdraw her allegations by her husband and his sister.

62 Id., p. 198, cited to L.Y. Abraham, M.E. Seligman & J.D. Teasdale, 'Learned Helplessness in Humans: critique and reformulation', *Journal of Abnormal Psychology*, Vol. 87, No. 1, 1978, pp. 49-74.

63 [1996] 4 All ER, 837.

The Home Office Guidance as to when the new offence applies; suggests that the controlling or coercive behaviour must take place 'repeatedly or continuously' and advises the courts to look for a "pattern of behaviour established over a period of time rather than, for example, one or two isolated incidents." The effect on the victim must be evidenced and must show one of two things "either a fear that violence will be used against them on at least two occasions or cause serious alarm or distress which has a substantial adverse effect on the victim's usual day to day activities."

The perpetrator should "know or ought to know" that the behaviour will have "a serious effect on the victim". The offence must take place when the victim and perpetrator are still "personally connected", they must be in an intimate personal relationship.[64]

It is somewhat artificial to examine A to see whether the facts of the abuse might allow a prosecution for coercive and controlling behaviour. However, as a purely academic exercise it seems that a prosecution for coercion and control might have been possible. A seems to have suffered three serious sexual assaults, and her husband's behaviour, in pressurising her to withdraw the allegations against him could be seen to be fulfilling the requirements of the law. The values underpinning the new law, demonstrate signs of concern about subordination and her withdrawal of her allegations seems to fit this category. The CPS legal guidance suggests that pressurising someone to leave their employment is also evidence of coercing or controlling behaviour.[65] It would have to be proved that A's husband knew or ought to have known that the behaviour would have a serious effect on A. The offence carries a maximum sentence of 5 years.

This brief exercise highlights some tensions in the legislative and common law approaches. Duress is looking for a very specific threat. A's appeal fails because she is unable to establish to the court's satisfaction that a threat of death or serious injury was operative at the time she withdrew her statement against her husband.[66] Such a conclusion does not fit happily with the reason for the creation of the offence of coercive or controlling behaviour in intimate relationships. This is to recognise, in the words quoted in the Home Office Statutory Guidance Framework: "Not only is coercive control the most common context in which [women] are abused. It is also the most dangerous."[67]

---

64 Controlling or Coercive Behaviour in an Intimate or Family Relationship: Statutory Guidance Framework, Home Office, 2015, p. 5.

65 www.cps.gov.uk/legal-guidance/controlling-or-coercive-behaviour-intimate-or-family-relationship, accessed on 27/2/2019.

66 [2012] EWCA Crim 434, [70].

67 *Supra* n. 52.

12 CONCLUSION

The law finds it hard to contain within its structures, on the one hand an impulse to fairly recognise, the awful experiences of those who are ordered or coerced into commit crime; and on the other the need to protect society from dangerous individuals. The courts are naturally reluctant to extend the defence of duress to those who voluntarily associate with violent criminals.[68] One way to relieve this pressure would be to avoid the problems related to the older structures of the law by using administrative measures to counteract them. The CPS could conclude there was no public interest in prosecution. But the risk is, that if the CPS do not use that discretion real injustice could result because of the way in which the law is structured. It has been noted in the discussion of *EK*, *A*, and *Hasan* above that the courts have expressed concerns about the use of discretion in this manner. The highest court has also differed as to whether treating, at the sentencing stage, duress as a matter mitigating guilt is an appropriate response. Imposing a criminal conviction but mitigating sentence is not likely to do justice in all cases as Baroness Hale pointed out in *Hasan*.

It has to be accepted that the common law is cautious in extending the ambit of defences. Defences whilst they determine culpability, arguably are not formally part of the normative framework of the law. Offences play a formal role in delineating the accepted norms of the law and defences, where they excuse the actor, ameliorate the harshness of the norms by providing exceptions where the application, or full application, of those norms would not be just. Therefore, one reason why common law defences might lag behind new legislation in recognising harms, is that the common law would need to adjust the rules governing its general defences to meet a wide range of considerations. Whereas, the government when creating new legislation will be aiming to produce a legislative measure to cure a specific harm.

Underlying the issues discussed above in relation to duress is a deeper tension. This seems to be between different approaches to culpability. One approach treats the subject of law as an individual that should be subject to an objective test as to how a person of reasonable firmness in the same position would react. The other approach argues that culpability should take account of a particular defendant's ability to react as a person of reasonable firmness would react. These are radically different approaches and lead to discussions of what should 'count' in terms of excuses. The problem is further compounded when a folk psychological approach is taken to the reaction of people who have suffered long term

68 *See* Lord Simon's opinion in *Lynch* where he warns against the risk of allowing a "countervailing system of sanctions or by terrorism to confer criminal immunity on his gang"; *Lynch v. DPP for Northern Ireland* [1975] AC 653, p. 696.

abuse. There is evidence from neuroscience, social science and from the courtroom that suggests the law does not understand the psychological effects of long-term abuse; or understand that the subjective experience of acting may be changed by the coercive behaviour of others.

Evan Stark in his arguments relating to coercion and control refers to the defendant's capacity to act as a relevant factor, but is also concerned for the defendant's welfare in the broadest sense. He argues that it is the effect of prolonged abuse over a course of conduct that reduces the individual's sense of agency over action, her view of her options for action. The welfare issues are clear in the Home Office Statutory Guidance.[69] The policy is also clearly set out in another Home Office document.[70] The declared strategy – to end violence against women and girls – includes a foreword by the then Home Secretary, Theresa May. The foreword states:

> we need to make tackling violence against women and girls everybody's business. From health providers, to law enforcement, to employers and friends and family we all need to play our part.[71]

As the harm identified by the Home Office is specific to controlling or coercive behaviour, a more robust approach might be to provide a specifically worded defence for those who are coerced or controlled by a partner, or, someone with whom they are in an intimate relationship. If the aims expressed by Stark to create an anti-discrimination, anti-subordination environment are to be realised then the reasonable man test will not meet these aims. A person of reasonable firmness cannot be assumed to have suffered unequal treatment, or, have had her agency impacted by an expectation that carries out the wishes of an abusive or controlling partner. The aims of the law in duress are to restrict access to the defence to anyone who associates with those who are prone to unlawful violence.

Cognitive neuroscience has a part to play in helping the law to establish greater consistency in its reasoning in relation to culpability. Greater understanding of how susceptibility to pressure emerges in intimate, or, coercive relationships would be useful to the courts.

69 *Supra* n. 64, para. 7. Controlling or coercive behaviour is primarily a form of violence against women and girls and is underpinned by wider societal gender inequality. This can contribute to the ability of the offender to retain power and control, and ultimately the ability of the victim to access support and leave safely. It is, therefore, important to consider the role of gender in the context of power and control within a relationship when identifying controlling or coercive behaviour in heterosexual relationships.

70 Ending Violence against Women and Girls Strategy, HM Government, 2016-2020, https://assets.publishing.service.gov.uk/government/uploads/system/uploads/attachment_data/file/522166/VAWG_Strategy_FINAL_PUBLICATION_MASTER_vRBPDF, accessed on 14 June 2019.

71 *Supra* n. 64, para 4.

Expert evidence will arguably be of more use to a jury than a misplaced folk psychological understanding of the effect of prolonged coercion and control. Such an approach requires more interdisciplinary research to gain a clear understanding of the effect of controlling or coercive behaviour. There is a question posed by Casper et al that needs to be addressed: it is – could the law "shift its focus away from those who obey orders towards those who give them, to prevent them from abusing a position that allows them to coerce others"?[72]

What the law at present is not providing is a means of signalling that the highest blame rests with the person who is most responsible. There is need to highlight, recognise and condemn the role coercion and control plays in the commission of some crimes. The principal offender may be caught and punished, or, may escape and therefore leave those who have been forced to commit the crime to face the full force of the law. Pragmatically the law may be content to punish those who are caught rather than highlighting the hierarchy of wrongs committed by various actors in a crime.

However, such an approach seems to be the opposite of the approach espoused by those who created the new legislation; which is to punish the harm done to those who are subject to subordination. One of the aims of the new legislation is to protect those who are abused and reinstate their position in society by recognising the inequality inherent in their position as an abused person. This may contrast with the common law approach which is to punish those who commit serious crimes, even if they are subject to coercion and control.

These two positions are arguably irreconcilable. To answer the question posed at the beginning cognitive neuroscience may tell us much more about our sense of agency. This knowledge together with research from the political social sciences may yield a much stronger knowledge base as to how coercion and control forces individuals to commit crimes. It will be necessary to consider how to apply this knowledge to the law. So far, the courts have avoided that issue. But the nature of the law is such that this fissure in legal reasoning is likely to be exploited by the adversarial system; and soon or later the courts will be faced with choosing the approach they intend to adopt. Both approaches present difficulties; the courts are naturally reluctant to excuse those who have committed crimes but in the words of Baroness Hale regarding the rejection of duress as a defence:

> If the reasons for rejecting duress are ones of public policy, it is hard to see that that policy is forwarded by a regime that assumes that convictions are to be

72 Haggard 2017, p. 590.

> purely nominal in nature, or, even in some cases that the law will not be enforced at all.[73]

In this case perhaps the most just outcome would be the creation of a partial defence to protect those who are subject to demonstrable coercion and control and as a result commit crime. This would permit the fact of coercion to be recognised by a jury or judge, recognising that culpability may be lessened whilst avoiding the outcome that the perpetrator of a crime could go unpunished. Additionally, this solution might encourage courts in severe cases of coercion and control to use their existing sentencing powers to recognise that a defendant deserved an absolute discharge from criminal liability.[74]

73 *Supra* n. 33.
74 www.cps.gov.uk/cps-page/sentencing gives full details of the sentencing options open to English courts.

REFERENCES

Abott, A., 'How the brain reacts to orders', *Nature*, Vol. 530, 2016, pp. 394-395.

Abraham, L.Y., Seligman, M.E. & Teasdale, J.D., 'Learned Helplessness in Humans: critique and reformulation', *Journal of Abnormal Psychology*, Vol. 87, No. 1, 1978, pp. 49-74.

Caspar, E.A., Christensen, J.F., Cleermans, A. & Haggard, P., 'Coercion Changes the Sense of Agency in the Human Brian', *Current Biology*, Vol. 26, No. 5, 2016, pp. 585-592.

Damasio, A., *Self Comes to Mind: Constructing the Conscious Brain*, Heinemann, London 2010.

Haggard, P., 'Sense of Agency in the Human Brain', *Nature Reviews Neuroscience*, Vol. 18, No. 4, 2017, pp. 196-207.

Horder, J., *Excusing Crime*, Oxford University Press, Oxford 2004.

Horder, J., *Ashworth's Principles of the Criminal Law*, 9th edn, Oxford University Press, Oxford 2016.

Husak, D., *The Philosophy of the Criminal Law*, Oxford University Press, Oxford 2010

Kennedy, H., *Eve Was Shamed: How British Justice is Failing Women*, Chatto and Wyndus, London 2018.

Milgram, S., 'Behavioral study of obedience', *Journal of Abnormal and Social Psychology*, Vol. 67, No. 4, F 1963, pp. 371-378.

Morse, S., 'Lost in Translation? An Essay on Law and Neuroscience', *in* M. Freeman, (Ed.), Law and Neuroscience, Current Legal Issues *Vol. 13*, Oxford University Press, Oxford 2011.

Norrie, A., Crime, Reason and History: *A Critical Introduction to Criminal Law*, 3rd edn, Cambridge University Press, Cambridge 2014.

Stark, E., *Coercive Control. How Men Entrap Women in Personal Life*, Oxford University Press, New York 2007.

Stark, E., 'Rethinking Coercive Control', *Violence against Women*, Vol. 15, No. 12, 2009, pp. 1515-1516.

10 Criminal Law for Young Adults in the Netherlands: The Law and the Practice from the Sociology of Childhood Perspective

M. Hopman & D. de Vocht

1 Introduction

Imagine a violent robbery is reported to the police. After investigation, two suspects are arrested: one who is a minor (16 years old) and one who is – legally – an adult (19 years old). Both suspects have priors – a criminal history with violent crimes as well as crimes related to drugs – and their psychological assessment indicates that the 19 year old suffers from a minor developmental disorder. The crime was extremely violent in the sense that weapons (a knife and a gun) were used and two victims were severely injured. How should the criminal justice system deal with the two suspects? Should they be provided with the care and protection offered by juvenile criminal law or does the severity of the crime and/or the difference in age justify taking a more restrictive (adult) approach?

The question whether children should be held responsible for committing criminal offences proves to be difficult to answer, which is also reflected by the fact that there is no global consensus on the minimum age of criminal responsibility (hereafter: MACR). Historically, since the nineteenth century, a distinction is made in criminal law between the adult and the child defendant. The idea is that those categorised as 'children' are considered to have limited, or no, responsibility for their (criminal) acts, and therefore a specific type of punishment (or in a less punitive sense: 'response') is appropriate. This presumption has led states worldwide to introduce specific juvenile criminal law acts, including the introduction of juvenile courts. To which age category of children these specific provisions apply differs per state. In general, the setting of MACR is inextricably linked to the legal doctrine of *doli incapax* which ties the ability to hold someone accountable to rationality, maturity and age.[1] To a certain extent the setting of MACR means that the child is presumed

1 J.J. Titus, 'Juvenile Transfers as Ritual Sacrifice: Legally Constructing the Child Scapegoat', *Youth Violence and Juvenile Justice*, Vol. 3, No. 2, 2005, pp. 116-132, at p. 119.

incapable of criminal intent and therefore cannot be held responsible.[2] Even though the question of finding the appropriate MACR is not new, states these days are continuously struggling with legally determining the line between the child and the adult and the topic is still the subject of political debate. In general, the dividing line seems to move over time and it seems that changes in the determination of the dividing line are subject to cultural, political and normative changes as well as scientific findings.

Several scientific commentators, in particular in the field of sociology of childhood – a critical field of studies that discusses how childhood is perceived in society, and what the consequences are of these sociological views – have criticized these debates, arguing for example that popular discourse categorizes children as 'angelic', 'innocent', unless they commit a serious crime, upon which they are suddenly labelled as 'devils'.[3] As Scott explains, while children are in [American] law generally perceived as "innocent beings, who are dependent, vulnerable, and incapable of making competent decisions":

> When children cross the line to legal adulthood, they are assumed to be autonomous persons who are responsible for their conduct, entitled as citizens to legal rights and privileges, and no longer entitled to support or special protection. This picture is deceptively simple, of course. In fact, the legal regulation of children is extremely complex. Much of the complexity can be traced ultimately to a single source – defining the boundary between childhood and adulthood.[4]

Following this line of reasoning there seems to be "an imposition of the highest rationality and responsibility on children who seriously offend."[5] Others argue that while political arguments related to drawing the line between childhood and adulthood in criminal

2 For example, within the European Union the MACR is usually set at 14 or 15 but sometimes the age limit is lower, which is – for example – the case in England and Wales and Northern Ireland (10) as well as in the Netherlands (12). With both countries setting the age limit as low as 10, before 1963 it was even lower: 8. Interesting to note is that in some countries the MACR will differ per gender (Iran) or type of offence (Ireland, Malaysia). The USA represent a category on its own where the majority of crimes are tried at state level and while most states have no MACR, others set the MACR as low as 6, 7, 9 and 10.

3 *See*, e.g.: S. Hackett *et al.*, 'Community Reactions to Young People Who Have Sexually Abused and Their Families: A Shotgun Blast, Not a Rifle Shot', *Children & Society*, Vol. 29, No. 4, 2005, pp. 243-254, at p. 244; A. Meyer, 'The Moral Rhetoric of Childhood', *Childhood*, Vol. 14, No. 1, 2007, pp. 85-104, at p. 87; Titus 2005, p. 124; E.S. Scott, 'The Legal Construction of Adolescence', *Hofstra Law Review*, Vol. 29, 2000, pp. 547-598, at pp. 557-558.

4 Scott 2000, p. 547.

5 Titus 2005, p. 120.

matters may be presented as scientific, underlying reasons are also of a social-political nature.[6]

In the Netherlands, children can be held criminally liable from the age of 12.[7] In 2014, the new *adolescentenstrafrecht* (criminal law applicable to young adults, hereafter: CLYA) was introduced which stretches the possibility to apply provisions of juvenile criminal law to young adults between the age of 18 and 23. The rationale behind the CLYA, according to its explanatory memorandum (hereafter: EM), are recent findings in neuroscience and developmental psychology. These findings suggest that at the age of 18 young people still have to go through important stages of brain development, which includes emotional, social, moral and intellectual development.[8] According to the memorandum, research shows that young adults do not always have adequate impulse control and are also more sensitive to external influence (such as peer pressure). These characteristics – connected to the incomplete development of certain brain functions – result in particularly risky behaviour. The underdevelopment of young adults in this area partially explains why one third of all criminal offences in the Netherlands take place before the age of 23 and ends after this age.[9] It is also argued that for a small group of young offenders their behaviour is not 'age-bound'. This group can be distinguished by the seriousness of their crimes and the recurring character of their criminal behaviour, which "does not correlate with aforementioned [developmental] factors, but with psychological disorders and/or other criminogenic factors."[10] The goal of the CLYA is to "maximally stimulate the criminal young adult to take on a responsible role in society, whereby s/he will further refrain from criminal behaviour."[11]

In this contribution we focus on how the Dutch judiciary, in practice, decides whether a juvenile defendant should be tried as an adult on the one hand, and whether an adult

6 Scott 2000, p. 564; Titus 2005, pp. 121 and 125; and E. Brown, 'The 'unchildlike child': Making and marking the child/adult divide in the juvenile court', *Children's Geographies*, Vol. 9, No. 3–4, 2011, pp. 361-377, at p. 362.

7 Art. 486 Code of Criminal Procedure. Recently, the Council for the Administration of Criminal Justice and Protection of Juveniles (*Raad voor Strafrechtstoepassing en Jeugdbescherming*) advised the Minister of Justice and Security to raise the age limit from 12 to 14. This proposal was based on the presumption that recent scientific research on the brain development of children indicates that children below the age of 14 are not able to oversee the consequences of their actions: Council for the Administration of Criminal Justice and Protection of Juveniles, '*Verhoging strafrechtelijke minimumleeftijd in context*' ("Raising the age or criminal responsibility – with context"), 20 December 2017.

8 Memorie van Toelichting bij Wijziging van het Wetboek van Strafrecht, het Wetboek van Strafvordering en enige andere wetten in verband met de invoering van een adolescentenstrafrecht, *Kamerstukken II* 2012/13, 33 498, nr. 3, p. 1 (*Explanatory Memorandum*, hereafter: EM).

9 EM, pp. 1 and 12-13.

10 Id., p. 13.

11 Id., p. 1.

defendant should be treated as a juvenile on the other. In addition, we reflect upon this decision-making process from the critical perspective of sociology of the childhood, by wondering how this treatment of the child/adult divide in Dutch criminal law and criminal law courts relates to sociological believes about the child/adult distinction.

In doing so we attempt to answer the following question: *how do Dutch judges make the distinction between child and adult defendants since the introduction of the Criminal Law for Young Adults (CLYA), and how can we understand this practice from the sociology of childhood perspective?*

To answer this question, the following sub questions will be dealt with:
1. What is the relevant legal framework of the CLYA?
2. How is the CLYA applied in practice?
3. How can both the theory and practice of the CLYA be understood from the sociology of childhood perspective?

Each of these sub questions will be discussed in a separate section below followed by some concluding remarks.

2 Methodology

To answer the first sub question, on the framework of the CLYA, we analysed the relevant provisions of the Dutch criminal code, its explanatory memorandum and crosschecked our analysis with secondary literature on the topic.

For the second sub question, we first searched the online database of Dutch case law (www.rechtspraak.nl) for cases that were adjudicated between 1 April 2014 and 15 March 2018, which mentioned the term '*adolescentenstrafrecht*' (criminal law for young adults). This resulted in 211 cases. To have a random sample, we decided to analyse three years, 20 cases per year, since the entering into force of the CLYA. This resulted in the analysis of 60 cases, 20 adjudicated and published online after 1 April 2014, 20 after 1 January 2015 and 20 after 1 January 2016.[12] These cases have been subjected to systematic content analysis[13] according to the following criteria:

1. Number of analysis
2. Case number
3. Date of the (alleged) crime
4. Birth year of the defendant
5. Age of the defendant at the moment of the (alleged) crime[14]
6. Gender of the defendant
7. Crime proven by the court
8. Is the defendant tried according to juvenile or regular criminal law?
9. Expert opinion on the child/adult divide
10. Arguments of the defense lawyer on the child/adult divide
11. Arguments of the prosecutor on the child/adult divide
12. Motivation of the judge to apply juvenile or adult criminal law
13. Sanction(s) applied.

In addition to the case law study, we looked at the instruments developed for experts to advise on the child/adult divide (Probation Service (*Reclassering*) and the Dutch Institute for Forensic Psychiatry and Psychology (NIFP)) and at other published research on the practice of CLYA in the Netherlands.

In the fifth section, we compare our findings under section three with the findings under section four, dealing with whether or not the child/adult divide as it is made in practice by the Dutch judiciary adheres to the intentions of the legislator. We will then proceed to reflect upon these results according to literature on sociology of childhood.

3 CRIMINAL LAW FOR YOUNG ADULTS: THE LEGAL FRAMEWORK

In the Netherlands, a specific juvenile criminal law has been part of Dutch criminal law since 1905. Like in many other countries, the question who can or should be considered to be a child in the context of criminal proceedings has been the subject of continuous debate. As mentioned in the introduction, at present, children in the Netherlands can be

12 One case was excluded, based on the fact that its content did not discuss criminal law for young adults in relation to a decision on the child/adult divide (ECLI:NL:RBGEL:2016:1940).

13 M.A. Hall & R.F. Wright, 'Systematic Content Analysis of Judicial Opinions', *California Law Review*, Vol. 96, 2008, pp. 63-122.

14 Because in the court decisions only the birth year of the defendant is published, the age of the defendant had to be calculated using the year of the crime minus the birth year of the defendant, unless the defendant's age at the time of the crime was indicated elsewhere in the court decision.

held criminally liable from the age of 12.[15] Children below the age of 12 cannot be prosecuted but certain investigative measures can be applied, for example, they can be arrested and interrogated. The age of the juvenile at the moment of the (alleged) committed offence is decisive.[16] Since the introduction of the *adolescentenstrafrecht* (CLYA) in 2014 the judge not only has the possibility to apply adult criminal law to juvenile offenders of age 16 and 17 even though they are below the age of majority (which is set at 18), but also to deal with defendants up until the age of 23 as juveniles (instead of 21 which was the age limit before the law of 2014).[17] The law clearly aims to (further)[18] change the aforementioned divide from a strict binary division into a more flexible grey area. This flexible grey area applies to young adults who committed a crime at the age of 16-23.[19] According to the new law, the standard still is that minors, defined as anyone below the age of 18 at the time of committing the crime, are judged according to juvenile criminal law (*jeugdstrafrecht*) and anyone above the age of 18[20] according to regular criminal law. However, in some cases it may be beneficial to try a 16-17 year old as an adult, and a 18-23 year old as a juvenile. Thus, the fact that a defendant has reached the age of 18 is no longer decisive: the applicability of juvenile criminal law may be indicated by the personality of the suspect or the circumstances of the case up until the age of 23. It is important to note that the introduction of CLYA has only changed the applicability of substantive juvenile criminal law – the age limits of criminal procedural law have remained the same. The decision on which system of sanctions should be applied to the case, is ultimately taken by the judge. This decision is an important one since juvenile criminal law clearly takes a different approach to dealing with criminal behaviour then regular adult criminal law. In a nutshell, juvenile criminal law is more focused on providing second chances by taking an individualistic and more protective (sometimes even paternalistic) approach with a strong focus on re-education and rehabilitation of the child. For this reason, juvenile criminal law provides more options for positive interventions – taking into account the developmental stage of the juvenile

15 Art. 486 Code of Criminal Procedure. Recently, the Council for the Administration of Criminal Justice and Protection of Juveniles advised the Minister of Justice and Security to raise the age limit from 12 to 14. This proposal was based on the presumption that recent scientific research on the brain development of children indicates that children below the age of 14 are not able to oversee the consequences of their actions: Council for the Administration of Criminal Justice and Protection of Juveniles, '*Verhoging strafrechtelijke minimumleeftijd in context*' ("Raising the age or criminal responsibility – with context"), 20 December 2017.

16 Art. 488 Code of Criminal Procedure.

17 Before 2014, application of juvenile criminal law was – as an exception – only possible for young adults aged 18-21.

18 Because this was already the case in the sense that 16 and 17 year olds could be tried as adults depending on the seriousness of their crime, since 1995.

19 Although the government intended to include 15 year olds, this has not been incorporated into the law because it would be contradictory to the UN CRC (EM).

20 From hereon whenever we refer to the age of a defendant, we refer to the age at the time of the crime, unless otherwise indicated.

defendant – compared to adult criminal law. For example, it provides various possibilities for individualised and effective treatment, involvement of family, education *et cetera.*[21]

The judge decides to apply CLYA when this is deemed appropriate given the personality of the defendant or the circumstances surrounding the offence (*omstandigheden waaronder het feit is begaan*). Since the entering into force of the CLYA, juvenile criminal law can be applied to:

1. Defendants age 12-16 (Art. 77a and Art. 77b par. 1 Criminal Code)
2. Defendants age 16-17, unless the judge finds reason to apply regular criminal law, based on (Art. 77b par. 1 Criminal Code):
   a. The seriousness of the alleged crime
   b. The personality of the defendant or
   c. The circumstances under which the alleged crime has been committed
3. Defendants age 18-23, if the judge finds reason to judge them according to juvenile criminal law, based on (Art. 77c par. 1 Criminal Code):
   a. The personality of the defendant or
   b. The circumstances under which the alleged crime has been committed

The characteristics mentioned under 2 and 3 each are sufficient reasons to warrant such a judicial decision.[22] Both situations 2 and 3 need to be read as exceptional. As a general rule, anyone below the age of 18 will be tried according to juvenile criminal law, and anyone above this age will be judged according to regular criminal law.[23]

The wording of this legal framework obviously raises many questions of interpretation. What exactly is meant by "the personality of the defendant", "the circumstances under which the alleged crime has been committed" and "the seriousness of the crime"? Two documents have been issued by the Dutch government which aim to provide answers to these questions: the CLYA's explanatory memorandum (hereafter: EM)[24] and the Guideline and framework for criminal prosecution youth and young adults, including sanction measurements HALT (*Richtlijnen en kader voor strafvordering jeugd en adolescenten, inclusief strafmaten halt*) (hereafter: Guideline (GL)).[25]

21 The wide variety of sanctions available for juveniles can be found in Art. 77g and 77h of the Criminal Code.
22 *See also*: M. van der Laan, M.G.C.J. Beerthuizen, C.S. Barendregt & K.A. Beijersbergen *Adolescentenstrafrecht: Beleidstheorie en eerste empirische bevindingen*, WODC, The Hague 2016, p. 22.
23 EM, p. 25.
24 Id.
25 *Staatscourant* 2014, No. 8284.

In the explanatory memorandum for the CLYA, it is explained that "the seriousness of the alleged crime" (a) refers to "very serious vice- and violent crimes and homicide", crimes that "in society may give rise to the question whether juvenile criminal law, with its orientation towards (re)education of the delinquent and sanctions which are limited in time, enables a fitting reaction [to the crime]."[26] In the Guidelines, in relation to 16 and 17 year olds, it is stated that adult criminal law will only be applied if the alleged crime concerns a "very serious (life)crime" and "the expectation is that the type and duration of treatment in the framework of juvenile criminal law will offer insufficient possibilities to protect the safety of others." Cases of "multiple recidivism, or where young people have been hardened and apply instrumental violence" are supposed to be treated according to juvenile criminal law, so that a change of behaviour can be made possible by taking a personal approach.[27]

"The circumstances under which the alleged crime has been committed" (c) can refer to a situation where a criminal act has been committed in a group setting including both juveniles and adults, in which case a defendant under the age of 18 should be tried similar to his peers above the age of 18 who fulfilled similar roles.[28]

The last criterion, of the "personality of the defendant" (a), is (also) quite complicated. In general, this seems to refer to the developmental phase of the defendant, labelled his/her "developmental age".[29] In the explanatory memorandum, it is argued that young people between the age of 15 and 23 may show risk behaviour partly due to the underdevelopment of certain brain functions. This leads to "yet unfinished emotional, social, moral and intellectual development." Corresponding behavioural characteristics include: inability to inhibit impulses, inability to supress distracting impulses and associations, peers who greatly influence decisions, inability to oversee the consequences of behaviour and adapt one's behaviour accordingly, inability to regulate emotions and unfinished development of empathic ability.[30] The Guidelines reiterate some of these undeveloped qualities (however only in relation to 18-23 year olds), mentioning underdevelopment of "inhibiting impulses, taking long term consequences into account, regulation of emotions and the development of empathetic abilities" It should thereby be considered whether an intervention under juvenile criminal law might offer a more meaningful reaction which still renders justice to the nature and seriousness of the crime and the judicial past of the defendant. Important criteria to take into consideration for applying juvenile criminal law are "whether the suspect: a) still attends school; b) still lives with his/her parents; c) needs support because

26 EM, p. 28.
27 GL, p. 1.
28 EM, p. 25.
29 Id., p. 19; GL, p. 1.
30 EM, p. 19-20.

of a (slight) mental disorder and d) is open for support and a more pedagogical approach." In general, juvenile criminal law should be applied to defendants who cannot yet be considered as completely independent and mature.[31]

The explanatory memorandum states that for 16-17 year olds, the "personality of the defendant" as a reason to try a juvenile defendant as an adult, can include cases where based on personality issues, a behavioural expert may estimate that treatment might take longer than possible according to a juvenile sanction, or if the defendant is 18 years old at the time of the trial.[32] Specifically for 18-23 year olds, a judge may choose to apply juvenile criminal law when it concerns a serious crime, when the young adult is a known repeat offender, or when the young adult belongs to a designated category of clearly vulnerable young adults, which include: a psychological or psychiatric disorder or a developmental disorder such as the group of slightly mentally disabled (*licht verstandelijk beperkten*).[33]

When categorised, the decision of the judge needs to be based on the following considerations (see the table below):

- When considerations are contradictory, the explanatory memorandum has been labelled (EM) and the Guideline has been labelled (GL)
- In some respects, different characteristics apply to either 16-17 year olds on the one hand, and 18-23 year olds on the other. In that case, the 16-17 year old specific characteristics are expressed in *italics*, the 18-23 year old specific characteristics are made **bold**.

Juvenile criminal law	**Regular (adult) criminal law**
Crime: ***is very serious** (EM, p. 30) **where young people have been hardened and apply instrumental violence'* (GL, p. 1) *has been committed in a group setting that includes both minors and adults (EM, p. 25)	Crime: ***is not very serious** (EM, p. 30) **is very serious* (EM, p. 25) **is very serious (vice- and violent crimes and homicide), so that in society it may give rise to the question whether juvenile criminal law enables a fitting reaction;* (EM, p. 28) **is a very serious life crime and it is expected that treatment under juvenile criminal law will not sufficiently protect the safety of others.* (GL, p. 1) * has been committed in a group setting that includes both minors and adults (EM, p. 25)
Criminal history: ***young adult is a known repeat offender** (EM, p. 30) **case of 'multiple recidivism'* (GL, p. 1)	Criminal history: ***crime is first offense** (EM, p. 30)

31 GL, p. 1.
32 EM, p. 25.
33 Id., p. 30.

Juvenile criminal law	Regular (adult) criminal law
Personality: *unfinished emotional, social, moral and intellectual development (EM, p. 20) *developmental phase of defendant (EM, p. 26; GL, p. 1) ***cannot yet be considered completely independent and mature** (GL, p. 1)	Age: **the defendant is 18 years old at the time of the trial* (EM, p. 25)
Personality characteristics: *inability to inhibit impulses (EM, p. 20; **GL, p. 1**) *inability to supress distracting impulses and associations *peers who have a great influence in taking risky decisions *inability to oversee the consequences of behaviour (**GL, p. 1**) and adapt one's behaviour accordingly (EM, p. 20) *inability to regulate emotions (EM, p. 20; GL, p. 1) *unfinished development of empathic ability (EM, p. 20; **GL, p. 1**)	
Personality (disorder) (EM, p. 30): ***has a psychological disorder** ***has a psychiatric disorder disorder** ***has a developmental disorder such as slightly mentally disabled**	
Intervention: ***juvenile criminal law may offer a more meaningful reaction which still renders justice to the nature and seriousness of the crime and the judicial past**	Intervention: **based on personality of the defendant, it is estimated that treatment might take longer than possible according to a juvenile sanction* (EM, p. 25)
Living circumstances suspect (GL, p. 1): ***still attends school** ***still lives with his/her parents** ***needs support because of a (slight) mental disorder** ***is open to support and a more pedagogical approach**	

From this scheme, it seems that some of the considerations are quite contradictory. For example: according to the guidelines, a 16 or 17-year-old who commits a violent crime that does not threaten someone's life should be tried according to juvenile criminal law, whereas according to the explanatory memorandum violent crimes by 16 or 17 year olds should be tried according to adult criminal law. In general, a 16 or 17-year-old can be tried as an adult if (s)he has committed a "very serious crime", whereas for an 18-23 year old the seriousness of the crime is a reason to apply juvenile criminal law. Also, on the one hand the limited responsibility of the defendant is considered when the young adult committed the crime in part due to his/her limited capacity to control impulses and oversee long term consequences of his/her actions. On the other hand, if by the time the case comes to court the defendant has reached the age of 18, this is considered a reason to judge him/her as an adult.

4 CRIMINAL LAW FOR YOUNG ADULTS: THE PRACTICE

In practice, the decision to apply adult or juvenile criminal law is, in first instance, made by the public prosecutor, who decides where to detain the suspect until trial: in a youth detention or in an adult detention centre. The dominant role of the public prosecutor in this respect has been repeatedly criticized in Dutch legal literature highlighting that if the public prosecutor does not decide to ask for the application of juvenile criminal law for young adults in early stages of the proceedings, chances are slim that this will happen at a later stage.[34] During the early stages of proceedings, the defendant will sometimes be evaluated by a psychologist, psychiatrist and/or rehabilitation officers. Their (behavioural) reports will also be used during trial. In some cases, these experts use a checklist to help them evaluate the defendant. There are two different lists; one developed by the Dutch Institute for Forensic Psychiatry and Psychology (DIFP)[35] and the other by the rehabilitation office/Ministry of Justice (RO/MoJ).[36] Both lists consist of indications and counter-indications for applying criminal law for young adults to 18-23 year olds. Unfortunately, there is no list for 16 and 17 year olds. When combined with the legal criteria described above, this results in the following scheme (see below). Again, in some respects, different characteristics apply to either 16-17 year olds on the one hand, and 18-23 year olds on the other. For that reason, the 16-17 year old specific characteristics are expressed in *italics* and the 18-23 year old specific characteristics are made **bold**.

34 *See*, for a critical perspective on the Dutch practice (among others), E.M. Mijnarends & E.R. Rensen, 'De officier van justitie en het adolescentenstrafrecht: Twee geloven op één kussen?', *Tijdschrift voor Familie- en Jeugdrecht*, No. 3, 2017, pp. 58-63; E.M. Mijnarends & E.R. Rensen, 'De toepassing van het adolescentenstrafrecht in de praktijk: is het genoeg of kan er nog wat meer bij?', *Tijdschrift voor Familie- en Jeugdrecht*, No. 11, 2017, pp. 280-285; A.H. Tiemens, 'Adolescentenstrafrecht: herbezinning op een onevenwichtige praktijk', *Tijdschrift Praktijkwijzer Strafrecht*, No. 24, 2018, pp. 64-71; A.M. van der Laan, M.G.C.J. Beerthuizen, C.S. Barendrecht & K.A. Beijersbergen 2016; L.J.C. Prop, A.M. van der Laan, C.S. Barendregt, M.G.C.J. Beerthuizen & Ch. van Nieuwenhuizen, *Adolescentenstrafrecht – Kenmerken van de doelgroep, de strafzaken en de tenuitvoerlegging*, Cahier 9, WODC, The Hague 2018; and T. Liefaard & S. Rap, 'Het adolescentenstrafrecht in Nederland: de stand van zaken vier jaar na invoering van de Wet Adolescentenstrafrecht', *Tijdschrift voor Criminologie*, No. 3, 2018, pp. 365-376.

35 DIFP (2014) Wegingslijst adolescentenstrafrecht.

36 Van Montfoort (2014) Instructies en toelichting Wegingskader Adolescentenstrafrecht 2014-02-17.

Gvmt: juvenile criminal law	**Gvmt: adult criminal law**	**NIFP: juvenile criminal law** ***(18-23 year olds)***	**NIFP: adult criminal law** ***(18-23 year olds)***	**RO/MoJ: juvenile criminal law** ***(18-23 year olds)***	**RO/MoJ: adult criminal law** ***(18-23 year olds)***
Crime: ***is very serious** (EM, p. 30) **where young people have been hardened and apply instrumental violence'* (GL p. 1) *has been committed in a group setting that includes both minors and adults (EM, p. 25)	Crime: ***is not very serious** (EM, p. 30) **is very serious* (EM, p. 25) **is very serious (vice- and violent crimes and homicide), so that it may give rise in society to question whether juvenile criminal law enables a fitting reaction;* (EM, p. 28) **is very serious life crime and there's expectation that treatment under juvenile criminal law will not sufficiently protect the safety of others.* (GL, p. 1) *has been committed in a group setting that includes both minors and adults (EM, p. 25)				
Criminal history: ***young adult is a known repeat offender (EM, p. 30)** **case of 'multiple recidivism'* (GL, p. 1)	Criminal history: ***crime is first offense** (EM, p. 30)		Criminal history: *has a criminal history of years *has let previous legal sanctions fail *is not impressed by legal authorities *there is an increase in seriousness of crimes *has had PIJ measurement before		Criminal history: *has a long criminal history *has let previous legal sanctions fail *is not impressed by legal authorities *current crime shows an increase in seriousness of crimes

Gvmt: juvenile criminal law	**Gvmt: adult criminal law**	**NIFP: juvenile criminal law *(18-23 year olds)***	**NIFP: adult criminal law *(18-23 year olds)***	**RO/MoJ: juvenile criminal law *(18-23 year olds)***	**RO/MoJ: adult criminal law *(18-23 year olds)***
					*has had PIJ measurement before *has been previously convicted as a leader and current fact concerns leadership of a group crime
Personality: *unfinished emotional, social, moral and intellectual development (EM, p. 20) *developmental phase of defendant (EM, p. 26; GL, p. 1) ***cannot yet be considered completely independent and mature** (GL, p. 1)	Age: **the defendant is 18 years old at the time of the trial* (EM, 25)			Physical appearance: *appears younger than calendar age	
Personality characteristics: *inability to inhibit impulses (EM, p. 20; GL, p. 1) *inability to supress distracting impulses and associations *peers who have a great influence in taking risky decisions *inability to oversee the consequences of behaviour (**GL, p. 1**) and adapt one's behaviour accordingly (EM, 20) *inability to regulate emotions		Personality characteristics: *cannot estimate risks of own acts *can hardly organize own behaviour *acts without thinking *in contact, seems younger than calendar age		Personality characteristics: *can hardly estimate risks of own acts *can hardly organize own behaviour *acts impulsively *shows more childish behaviour than one would expect based on calendar age *shows copycat behaviour with friends / acquaintances	Personality characteristics: *does not take victim(s) into consideration (shows no empathy)

Gvmt: juvenile criminal law	**Gvmt: adult criminal law**	**NIFP: juvenile criminal law** ***(18-23 year olds)***	**NIFP: adult criminal law** ***(18-23 year olds)***	**RO/MoJ: juvenile criminal law** ***(18-23 year olds)***	**RO/MoJ: adult criminal law** ***(18-23 year olds)***
(EM, p. 20; **GL, p. 1**) *unfinished development of empathic ability (EM, p. 20; GL, p. 1)					
Personality (disorder): (EM, p. 30) ***has a psychological disorder** ***has a psychiatric disorder disorder** ***has a developmental disorder such as slightly mentally disabled**		Personality (disorder): *functions at cognitively limited level	Personality (disorder): *displays psychopathic characteristics *has antisocial personality issues *uses others for personal goals	Personality (disorder): *functions at cognitively limited level	Personality (disorder): *displays psychopathic characteristics *has antisocial personality issues *uses others for personal goals
Living circumstances suspect (GL, 1): ***still attends school** ***still lives with his/her parents** ***needs support because of a (slight) mental disorder**				Living circumstances: *there is a current threat of neglect, mistreatment or abuse (for the defendant)	
			Criminal lifestyle: *chooses to commit crimes *is embedded in criminal environment *shows off with criminal activities		Criminal lifestyle: *chooses a criminal lifestyle: consciously plans criminal activities *is embedded in criminal environment *Is proud of (profit from) criminal activities

Gvmt: juvenile criminal law	**Gvmt: adult criminal law**	**NIFP: juvenile criminal law** ***(18-23 year olds)***	**NIFP: adult criminal law** ***(18-23 year olds)***	**RO/MoJ: juvenile criminal law** ***(18-23 year olds)***	**RO/MoJ: adult criminal law** ***(18-23 year olds)***
Sanction: *intervention under juvenile criminal law may offer a more meaningful reaction which still renders justice to the nature and seriousness of the crime and the judicial past	Sanction: *intervention: based on personality of the defendant, it is estimated that treatment might take longer than possible according to a juvenile sanction (EM, p. 25)	Sanction: *treatment through behavioural intervention under juvenile criminal law fits best	Sanction: *long protection of society is necessary *treatment through behavioural intervention under adult criminal law fits best *treatment expected to last until after age 22 *disorder demands possible transfer to psychiatric centre	Sanction: *possible threat to person of defendant by other detainees *detention in youth detention centre is best fitting (because schooling can be continued, fellow detainees are less threatening, different treatment security)	Sanction: *detention in adult detention centre is best fitting (because would otherwise feel 'between kids', or treated 'like a child') *long protection of society is necessary
Potential pedagogical effect: ***is open to support and a more pedagogical approach** (GL, p. 1)		Potential pedagogical effect: *can be (re-)educated *needs to continue schooling, *actively participates in family, *has a dependent relationship with caretakers, *needs community-oriented environment.	Potential pedagogical effect: *pedagogical treatment is not possible *will negatively influence other young detainees *is unfit for group oriented living environment	Potential pedagogical effect: *pedagogical treatment is feasible * pedagogical treatment is necessary *continuing school is necessary *actively participates in the family *family-oriented treatment is necessary *has a dependent relationship with parents/caretakers *it is possible to have influence through parents/caretakers *needs a group oriented living environment	Potential pedagogical effect: *pedagogical treatment is not feasible *will negatively influence other fellow detainees of the same age group *cannot stand his/her ground in group oriented living environment

Again, we see potential contradicting elements in the different indication criteria. According to the law (and its explanatory memorandum), if the suspect is a repeat offender, this is a reason to apply juvenile criminal law, whereas according to the DIFP and RO/MoJ this is a reason to apply adult criminal law. According to the legislator, if the defendant has a psychiatric or psychological disorder this is an indication for the application of juvenile criminal law, whereas according to DIFP and RO/MoJ a person displaying psychopathic and/or antisocial personality characteristics is a reason to apply adult criminal law. In the same sense, the lack of empathy on the part of the defendant is – according to the law – an indication to apply juvenile criminal law, whereas – according to the RO/MoJ list – it is an indication for applying adult criminal law.

It is also clear from this scheme that both the NIFP and the RO/MoJ indicate certain characteristics for the child/adult distinction, which cannot be derived from the law, such as the criminal lifestyle of the defendant and his/her physical appearance. On the other hand, other indications mentioned by the law are ignored, such as the seriousness of the crime and the unfinished social, moral and intellectual development of the defendant. Lastly, there are some differences between the list of the DIFP on the one hand and the list of the RO/MoJ on the other: for example, the type of treatment that is most suitable for the defendant is not taken into consideration by the DIFP whereas it is mentioned as relevant both by the RO/MoJ and the law.

Results from the Analysis of Court Cases

Taking into account these different and at times contradicting reasons for applying adult or juvenile criminal law, the next question that automatically comes to mind is: what does this mean in court?. Without a doubt, the decision of a judge to apply adult or juvenile criminal law in a specific case is based on a weighing of many reasons. The law and the weighing lists give certain criteria, reasons for one or the other, but they do not indicate how they should be weighed in a particular case and thus they do not provide for a calculation with one fixed, 'correct' answer. Taking this into account, we have focused our analysis on which reasons (pro/contra application of juvenile criminal law) were expressed in court. A difficulty in this respect is the fact that participants to the proceedings – at least as can be derived from the published decisions – do not clearly state whether a certain observation (say, a psychiatric disorder) is considered to be a pro- or contra indication. Neither do judges always indicate the specific reason(s) for their decision on what criminal law system to apply. This lack of motivation can be explained by the fact that the application of juvenile law to young adults is the exception and – consequently – application of adult criminal law is the rule.[37] The practice illustrates that judges often use limited and standardized explanations for (not) applying juvenile criminal law to young adults. In many cases judges state that they choose one or the other 'based on the personality of the defendant and the seriousness of the crime', which does not give the reader much information other than the – rather general – criteria provided by law. As a result, of all cases analyzed, we were only able to select a small number in which reasons were clearly stated and indicated as reasons pro or contra the application of juvenile criminal law.

In the scheme below, you will find an overview of the reasons used in at least two of the 60 court cases analyzed, categorized according to its different sources (government law and regulation, DIFP/RO&MoJ guidelines, newly introduced in court[38]). The total number of times a certain reason was used by any of the actors involved in the court case is indicated. The number in between brackets is how often a certain indicator was mentioned by the judge. Whenever new indicators were added in court, these are listed in the right column, on the condition that they were mentioned in more than one case.

Gvmt: reasons for applying juvenile criminal law	**Gvmt: reasons for applying adult criminal law**	**NIFP & RO/MoJ: reasons for applying juvenile criminal law (insofar not mentioned by government)**	**NIFP & RO/MoJ: reasons for applying adult criminal law (insofar not mentioned by government)**	**Other court reasons: reasons for applying juvenile criminal law**	**Other court reasons: reasons for applying adult criminal law**
	Crime: *is very serious (16-18 yo) | 12		Criminal history: *has failed previous legal sanctions | 5(5)	Criminal lifestyle: *defendant takes responsi-	Criminal history: *case of 'multiple

37 Already in 2016 the Dutch Supreme Court stated that the judge is not obliged to motivate the decision not to apply juvenile criminal law: HR 29 november 2016, ECLI:NL:HR:2016:2716.

38 Meaning: reasons introduced in court as a motivation for applying one or the other (Juvenile or Adult Criminal Law), which are not mentioned in the different core documents.

Gvmt: reasons for applying juvenile criminal law	Gvmt: reasons for applying adult criminal law	NIFP & RO/MoJ: reasons for applying juvenile criminal law (insofar not mentioned by government)	NIFP & RO/MoJ: reasons for applying adult criminal law (insofar not mentioned by government)	Other court reasons: reasons for applying juvenile criminal law	Other court reasons: reasons for applying adult criminal law
	(11) (only mentioned in relation to > 18 yo)			bility for actions | 7(6)	recidivism' | 6(5)
Personality: *unfinished emotional development | 4(0) *unfinished social development | 4(0) *unfinished intellectual development | 9(0) *cannot yet be considered completely independent and mature | 2(0) *general behind in development | 9(4) *personality/identity insufficiently developed | 3(0)		Personality (disorder): *functions at cognitively limited level | 8(4)	Personality (disorder): *has antisocial personality issues | 5(2)	Personality (disorder): *limited learning capacity | 2(1) *general: disorder | 2(1) *vulnerable personality | 3(1)	
Personality characteristics: *inability to inhibit impulses | 3(0) *peers who have a great influence in taking risky decisions | 4(1) *inability to oversee the consequences of behaviour and adapt one's behaviour accordingly | 2(1) *inability to regulate emotions | 2(0)		Personality characteristics: *can hardly organize own behaviour | 4(0) *shows more childish behaviour than one would expect based on calendar age | 7(0)	Personality characteristics: *does not take victim(s) into consideration (shows no empathy) | 3(3)	Personality characteristics: *weak verbal conceptual understanding | 3(1)	Personality characteristics: *lack of empathetic ability | 3(1) *manipulative/calculating | 3(3)
Living circumstances suspect: *still attends school | 4(2)				Living circumstances: *actively participates in	Living circumstances: *works/has a job | 2(2)

Gvmt: reasons for applying juvenile criminal law	Gvmt: reasons for applying adult criminal law	NIFP & RO/MoJ: reasons for applying juvenile criminal law (insofar not mentioned by government)	NIFP & RO/MoJ: reasons for applying adult criminal law (insofar not mentioned by government)	Other court reasons: reasons for applying juvenile criminal law	Other court reasons: reasons for applying adult criminal law
*still lives with his/her parents | 5(4)				(parental) family | 3(2) *dependant relationship with parents | 4(0) *has young children, wants to take care of them | 2(0)	
		Sanction: *detention in youth detention centre is best fitting (because schooling can be continued, fellow detainees are less threatening, different treatment security) | 4(2)	Sanction: *long protection of society is necessary | 2(2) * detention in adult detention centre is best fitting (because would otherwise feel 'between kids', or treated 'like a child') | 3(0)	Sanction: *expert advises JCL | 6(6)	Sanction: *expert advises CLYA | 2(2) *CLYAmore appropriate | 2(2)
Potential pedagogical effect: *expect (more) value/effect from pedagogical approach | 11 (7)		Potential pedagogical effect: *pedagogical treatment is feasible | 4(1) *pedagogical treatment is necessary | 7(3) *it is possible to have influence through parents/caretakers | 3(3)			

Other lessons learned from practice are what judges consider to be a "serious crime", and the role of age as a reason for determining whether a young person should be tried as a juvenile or an adult:

What is considered to be a serious crime (according to judges)?

*burglary, extortion	1
*extortion (together with others), threatening with violence	1
*theft combined with violence and threats	1
*violent robbery	2
*several counts of dealing harddrugs	1
*several counts of theft (+attempt), entrance house	3
*committing extortion (together with others)	1
*causing explosion of illegal fireworks, causing serious physical harm	1
*public violent act, in group, against person or thing	1

Not serious enough:	
*larceny	1

Age is regularly mentioned in court in the context of deciding between the application of Juvenile Criminal Law (JCL) or Adult Criminal Law (AdCL):

Age	Pro JCL	PRO AdCL
Defendant is young	1(0)	
Defendant was 18 at the time of the crime	3(2)	
Defendant was only just 18 at the time of the crime	2(2)	
Defendant was almost 19 at the time of the crime	3(0)	1(1)
Defendant was 19 at the time of the crime		1(1)
Defendant was 20 at the time of the crime		1(1)
Defendant was 21 at the time of the crime	1(0)	
Defendant was 22 at the time of the crime	1(0)	
Defendant was almost 23 at the time of the crime		1(1)

Summing up, the following reasons are given by judges for applying juvenile criminal law on the one hand or adult criminal law on the other:

Juvenile Criminal Law (JCL)	Adult Criminal Law (ACL)
Defendant takes responsibility for his actions | (6)	Crime is very serious | (11)
Defendant is behind in development | (4)	Defendant has let previous legal sanctions fail | (5)
Defendant functions at cognitively limited level | (4)	Case of 'multiple recidivism' | (5)

Juvenile Criminal Law (JCL)	Adult Criminal Law (ACL)
Defendant still attends school | (2)	Defendant is manipulative/calculating | (3)
Defendant still lives with his/her parents | (4)	defendant does not take victim(s) into consideration (shows no empathy) | (3)
Defendant actively participates in (parental) family | (2)	Defendant has antisocial personality issues | (2)
Detention in youth detention centre is best fitting (because schooling can be continued, fellow detainees are less threatening, different treatment security) | 4(2)	Defendant works/has a job | (2)
Expert advises JCL | (6)	Long protection of society is necessary (2)
Expect (more) value/effect from pedagogical approach | (7)	Expert advises CLYA | (2)
Pedagogical treatment is necessary | (3)	CLYA more appropriate | (2)
Influence through parents/caretakers is considered possible| (3)	

5 Comparing the Law, Guidelines and Court Practice

As illustrated above, the law and official guidelines for applying the criteria to decide whether a young defendant has to be tried as an adult or a juvenile are in many respects contradictory. Looking at the arguments expressed in court (by the different participants of the proceedings) and the arguments given by judges to explain their choices, it is perhaps hardly surprising that judges do not clearly follow the law and/or the official guidelines.

A first element considered important by judges for making this decision seems to be the personality of the defendant. A more "social" defendant who takes responsibility for his/her actions is more likely to be tried as a child, while an anti-social defendant who is manipulative/calculating, who shows no empathy and/or has antisocial personality issues, will therefore be tried as an adult. This contradicts the law and its official interpretations (EM, GL). According to the law, certain anti-social personality characteristics may be attributed to the unfinished development of the juvenile, such as an "unfinished development of empathic ability" or psychological/psychiatric disorders (*e.g.* anti-social personality disorder), which should be reasons to try the defendant as a juvenile. Arguably, personality characteristics that lead judges to try defendants as juveniles, such as 'taking responsibility for one's actions', could in fact under the legal framework be considered a sign of maturity. In general, the types of pro-social behaviour that judges cite as reasons to try defendants as juveniles are quite opposite to certain legal indications for childhood in terms of personality characteristics of the defendant, such as "inability to inhibit impulses", "inability to oversee consequences of behaviour" and "inability to regulate emotions."

In terms of "showing empathy" as well as categorizing the "anti-social personality disorder", judges seem to follow the view of the DIFP and RO/MoJ guidelines. These guidelines, however, also indicate that impulsive, unorganized behaviour of someone who can hardly estimate the risks of his/her own acts are indications for treating the defendant as a juvenile, behaviour which may not automatically be connected to "taking responsibility for one's actions." According to the law, "showing empathy" is explicitly considered a sign of maturity and lack of empathy, as well as "vulnerability of the young adult", expressed for example in a psychological or psychiatric disorder, are reasons to try a defendant as a juvenile. A second reason for the court to try someone as an adult is when the crime is considered "serious", when the defendant is a repeat offender and/or when previous sanctions have not had the intended effect. In all cases where this was mentioned as a reason for the decision, the defendant was below 18 years at the time of the crime. This therefore also goes directly against the law and its official interpretations, according to which both committing a very serious crime and being a repeat offender are in fact indications to apply juvenile criminal law to 18-23 year olds. In this respect, too, the judges are more aligned with the DIFP and RO/MoJ guidelines, which indeed indicate these as reasons for applying adult criminal law. The fact that the seriousness of the crime is considered a reason to try the young adult according to common ('adult') criminal law is most likely also related to the 'sanctioning gap' between juvenile criminal law on the one hand and adult criminal law on the other. According to juvenile criminal law, the maximum sentence is 24 months of detention, which in case of a severe criminal offence might be considered too lenient.

In three respects the judges do seem to follow the law:

- when considering the development of the defendant (a limited development is a reason for applying JCL),
- when considering the potential (pedagogical) effect of intervention (whenever positive effects are expected, this is a reason for applying JCL), and
- in considering the living circumstances of the defendant ('childhood typical' living circumstances such as living with parents and going to school are reasons for applying JCL).

In this respect, the law and the DIFP and RO/MoJ guidelines are aligned, or at least not contradicting and the case law illustrates that judges regularly follow the advice of experts. It seems that these experts base their advice not on the law, but on the NIFP and RO/MoJ guidelines, therefore the advice may contradict the law (see above).

Lastly, it has to be noted that judges often did not take arguments expressed by parties based on the law into account in their ruling, such as arguments about the limited development of the defendant, personality characteristics, living circumstances and the necessity of pedagogical treatment. However, on the basis of the published decisions it is impossible to tell whether that happens because the judge considered the arguments invalid or irrelevant.

6 Taking a Different View: The Critical Perspective of Sociology of Childhood

Of course, one may wonder how it is possible that the law, the subsequent formal interpretation and official guidelines and what is actually practiced in courts, can be so very different when it comes to creating a dividing line between children and adult defendants. It is our hypothesis that (at least part of) this practice can be explained by looking at the matter from the perspective of sociology of childhood.

Research in sociology of childhood on the topic of this child/adult division in criminal law and proceedings in the Western world, has shown on several occasions how this division is made not based on scientific findings and facts. Rather, arguments for categorizing defendants as either 'child' or 'adult' have most often been based on popular sentiment, politics and other non-scientific considerations.[39] Who would or would not be considered a child has been based mostly on popular 'feelings' related to the crime committed, and accompanying classification of children as either 'good and innocent' or 'evil'. Those who committed relatively minor crimes could be considered innocent, and in that sense childlike. A pedagogical approach to punishment would benefit them, and thereby, society. Children on the other hand who committed very serious crimes that shocked society, would be considered 'evil' and therefore would be beyond help and in some sense, beyond 'childlike', and therefore should be judged as adults.

To some extent, the Dutch government seems to have wanted to transcend this line of reasoning by founding the child/adult divide in criminal law on (neuro)scientific findings on the development of children. The goal of this policy was to 'optimally stimulate the criminal young adult to take on a responsible role in society, whereby he/she will further refrain from criminal behaviour'.[40] However, it seems that large parts of this law are not applied in practice.

39 *See*, among others: C. Jenks, *Childhood*, Routledge, London 1996; Scott 2000, p. 564; Titus 2005, pp. 121 and 125; Brown 2011, p. 362.

40 EM, p. 1.

So how can both the law and its practical application be explained? We have seen that the law allows for 16 and 17 year olds ('children' in the sense that they are below the age of majority) to be tried as adults if they commit a serious offence. This type of regulation is quite common in Western countries. According to several authors, if the dominant discourse of society is that of the child as pure, innocent, and in need of protection, the child who commits a violent crime disrupts this romantic image.[41] According to Titus, "a deep social anxiety is provoked when a child's act violate normative regularities to such an extent that our incompatible frames for understanding childhood conformity and aberrance collide."[42] Meyer adds: "if children and childhood are *defined* by innocence then children who do not conform to this image are excluded."[43] In other words: because children who commit serious crimes, challenge society's image of childhood, they need to be considered as not-children. As Titus explains: "the crisis is resolved when the offender is expelled from the juvenile justice system for being insufficiently child-like…declared not to be a child and denied the social protections associated with the juvenile court".[44] According to Titus, the child in this instance is a sacrificial victim, and by sacrificing this child, the state protects morality in society at large "to assure people that society is not out of control. Juvenile transfers serve the symbolic function of reaffirming the community's belief that there are cases of violence and absolute evil that demand a violent collective response."[45]

However, while the Dutch legislator meant for only 16 and 17 year old defendants to be 'sacrificed', and only those who committed one serious crime and not those who "have been hardened and apply instrumental violence", the judge seems to apply this type of reasoning to all 16-23 year olds. In all these cases, the seriousness of the crime and recidivism are reasons to try the young adult as an adult, while – originally – the Dutch legislator meant for 18-23 year olds who commit serious crimes to be tried under juvenile criminal law.

We have also shown that the Dutch judge considers certain anti-social personality characteristics of the young defendant as a reason to try the child as an adult, whereas according to the law this should be a reason to try the defendant as a juvenile. At the same time, judges do apply the law when they consider the development of the defendant, the potential pedagogical effect of intervention and the (childlike/adult) living circumstances of the defendant.

41 Jenks 1996; Hackett *et al.* 2005, p. 244; Meyer 2007, p. 87; and Titus 2005, p. 116.
42 Meyer 2007, p. 87.
43 Id., p. 94.
44 Titus 2005, p. 119.
45 Id., pp. 122-125.

All these factors combined align with the image presented in research on sociology of childhood, namely that the basic consideration for the judge who finds a young delinquent in his/her courtroom, is whether it concerns a vulnerable, innocent, inherently virtuous child who is in need of protection, or whether it concerns an 'unchildlike-child' who cannot be considered a child at all, a young adult who is inherently evil and against whom society needs to be protected. The question of the child/adult divide thereby becomes a question of good versus evil, whereby the good will be tried under juvenile criminal law, and the evil will be tried according to adult criminal law.

7 Conclusion

With the Criminal Law for Young Adults, the legislator envisaged to facilitate a more flexible and individualistic approach in cases concerning young adults. The underlying presumption of the law is that certain young adults are better 'served' with sanctions of the juvenile criminal law allowing for a more pedagogical approach, taking into account the personality of the defendant and his developmental 'deficits'. Recent findings from neuroscience and developmental psychology – including the view that the human brain continues to develop until the age of 25 – confirm the view of the legislator that considering the age of 18 as a magic number automatically transforming the juvenile into an adult is not realistic and in some cases even untrue.

Despite the intentions of the legislator, applying the Criminal Law for Young Adults in daily practice has turned out to be difficult. Turning back to the main question of this contribution: *how do Dutch judges make the distinction between child and adult defendants since the introduction of the Criminal Law for Young Adults (CLYA), and how can we understand this practice from a sociology of childhood perspective?* We can first of all conclude that practice shows an inconsistent picture which is most likely partly caused by contradicting criteria provided by the law on the hand and official guidelines on the other. The case law shows that often there is still a strong focus on the severity of the crime leading away from the personal characteristics of the child defendant from a neuroscientific or developmental perspective. In some cases, the law itself and the criteria it sets forth are completely disregarded.

Trying to understand this practice from a sociology of childhood perspective, it seems that the judicial reluctance to apply juvenile criminal law to young adults – especially in case of severe crimes – is inextricably linked to the fact that we tend to base our decision on 'who is a child?' mostly on 'popular feelings' instead of scientific findings and facts. In a way, the severity of the crime shifts the focus away from the 'child friendly' approach and legitimizes the judge to deal with the defendant as an adult. The popular saying 'If you can do the crime, you can do the time' seems to be a guiding principle in this respect.

Although the current state of case law indicates that – for now – the Criminal Law for Young Adults has not (fully) succeeded to transcend the superficial line of reasoning expressed in the sociology of childhood, we need not be too pessimistic. After all, it has only been five full years after the entering into force of the law which – of course – is a relatively short period. In a way, (juvenile) criminal justice is only at the beginning of incorporating new insights from other disciplines such as neuroscience. This takes time. In order to fully realize the goal of the Criminal Law for Young Adults – taking a more substantive and individualistic approach and taking full account of the 'unfinished development' of the young adult – it will be necessary to shift the focus from the crime to the person. Only then will we be able to slowly move away from the unrealistic and maybe even damaging view considering young adults who commit severe crimes or who illustrate certain anti-social personality characteristics as 'unchildlike'. It forces us to see the – maybe ugly and hard – truth that also children are capable of committing severe crimes. But this does not necessarily mean that they can no longer be treated as children in the courtroom.

References

Brown, E., 'The 'unchildlike child': Making and marking the child/adult divide in the juvenile court', *Children's Geographies*, Vol. 9, No. 3–4, 2011, pp. 361–377.

Green, D.A., 'Suitable vehicles: Framing blame and justice when children kill a child', *Crime Media Culture*, Vol. 4, No. 2, 2008, pp. 197-220.

Hackett, S. *et al.*, 'Community Reactions to Young People Who Have Sexually Abused and Their Families: A Shotgun Blast, Not a Rifle Shot', *Children & Society*, Vol. 29, No. 4, 2005, pp. 243-254.

Jenks, C., *Childhood*, Routledge, London 1996.

Liefaard, T. & Rap, S., 'Het adolescentenstrafrecht in Nederland: de stand van zaken vier jaar na invoering van de Wet Adolescentenstrafrecht', Kroniek van het jeugdrecht, *Tijdschrift voor Criminologie*, No. 3, 2018, p. 365-376.

Meyer A., 'The Moral Rhetoric of Childhood', *Childhood*, Vol. 14, No. 1, 2007, pp. 85-104.

Mijnarends, E.M. & Rensen, E.R., 'De officier van justitie en het adolescentenstrafrecht: Twee geloven op één kussen?', *Tijdschrift voor Familie- en Jeudgrecht*, No. 3, 2017, pp. 58-63.

Mijnarends, E.M. & Rensen, E.R., 'De toepassing van het adolescentenstrafrecht in de praktijk: is het genoeg of kan er nog wat meer bij?', *Tijdschrift voor Familie- en Jeugdrecht*, No. 11, 2017, pp. 280-285.

Prop, L.J.C., Van der Laan, A.M., Barendregt, C.S., Beerthuizen, M.G.C.J. & Van Nieuwenhuizen, Ch., *Adolescentenstrafrecht – Kenmerken van de doelgroep, de strafzaken en de tenuitvoerlegging*, Cahier 9, WODC, The Hague 2018.

Scott, E.S. 'The Legal Construction of Adolescence', *Hofstra Law Review*, Vol. 29, 2000, pp. 547-598.

Tiemens, A.H., 'Adolescentenstrafrecht: herbezinning op een onevenwichtige praktijk', *Tijdschrift Praktijkwijzer Strafrecht*, No. 24, 2018, pp. 64-71.

Titus, J.J., 'Juvenile Transfers as Ritual Sacrifice: Legally Constructing the Child Scapegoat', *Youth Violence and Juvenile Justice*, Vol. 3, No. 2, 2005, pp. 116-132.

Van der Laan, A.M., Beerthuizen, M.G.C.J., Barendrecht, C.S. & Beijersbergen, K.A., *Adolescentenstrafrecht: Beleidstheorie en eerste empirische bevindingen*, WODC, The Hague 2016.

Affiliation of Contributors

Christoph Bublitz is a post-doc at the Faculty of Law, University of Hamburg and fellow of the Center for Interdisciplinary Research (ZiF) in Bielefeld.

Paul Catley is Head of the Law School at the Open University.

Lisa Claydon is a Senior Lecturer in Law at the Open University.

Federica Coppola is a Presidential Scholar in Society and Neuroscience at the Center for Science and Society at Columbia University in the City of New York.

Anna E. Goldberg is a PhD researcher (department of criminal law and criminology) at the Faculty of Law of Maastricht University.

Jaap Hage is professor of legal theory at the Faculty of Law of Maastricht University.

Marieke Hopman is assistant professor at the Faculty of Law (department of international and European law) of Maastricht University.

Marko Jelicic is professor of neuropsychology and law, Faculty of Psychology & Neuroscience, and Faculty of Law, Maastricht

Sjors L.T.J. Ligthart is PhD candidate at the Department of Criminal Law of Tilburg University.

Gerben Meynen is professor of forensic psychiatry, Willem Pompe Institute for Criminal Law and Criminology and Utrecht Centre for Accountability and Liability Law (UCALL), Utrecht University, and endowed professor of ethics and psychiatry, Faculty of Humanities, Vrije Universiteit Amsterdam.

David Roef is associate professor criminal law and extraordinary professor criminal law and neuroscience at the Faculty of Law of Maastricht University.

Dorris de Vocht is assistant professor at the Faculty of Law (department of criminal law and crimology) of Maastricht University and honorary judge with the District Court of Limburg.

Antonia M. Waltermann is assistant professor of legal theory at the Faculty of Law of Maastricht University.

Maastricht Law Series

The Maastricht Law Series is created in 2018 by Boom juridisch and Eleven International Publishing in association with the Maastricht University Faculty of Law. The Maastricht Law Series publishes books on comparative, European and International law. The series builds upon the tradition of excellence in research at the Maastricht Faculty of Law, its research centers and the Ius Commune Research School. The Maastricht Law Series is a peer reviewed book series that allows researchers an excellent opportunity to showcase their work.

Series editors

Dr. Bram Akkermans (editor-in-chief)
Prof. dr. Monica Claes
Prof. dr. Fons Coomans
Prof. dr. Mariolina Eliantonio
Prof. dr. Michael Faure
Dr. Bram van Hofstraeten
Prof. dr. Saskia Klosse
Dr. Denise Prevost
Prof. dr. David Roef
Dr. Marcel Schaper
Prof. dr. Jan M. Smits

Published in this series:

Volume 1: Reinhard Zimmermann, Does the Law of Succession Reflect Cultural Differences?, ISBN 978-94-6236-856-9
Volume 2: Anna Berlee, Access to personal data in public land registers, ISBN 978-94-6236-841-5
Volume 3: Marcus Meyer, The Position of Dutch Works Councils in Multinational Corporations, ISBN 978-94-6236-848-4
Volume 4: Jaap Hage, Foundations and Building Blocks of Law, ISBN 978-94-6236-860-6
Volume 5: Bastiaan van Zelst, The End of Justice(s)?, ISBN 978-94-6236-881-1
Volume 6: Lars van Vliet & Agustin Parise (eds.), Re- De- Co-dification? New Insights on the Codification of Private Law, ISBN 978-94-6236-900-9
Volume 7: Caroline Rupp, Rafael Ibarra Garza & Bram Akkermans, Property Law Perspectives VI, ISBN 978-94-6236-904-7
Volume 8: Aalt Willem Heringa, Europees Nederlands Staatsrecht, ISBN 978-94-6290-604-4
Volume 9: Symeon C. Symeonides, The "Private" in Private International Law, ISBN 978-94-6236-949-8
Volume 10: Jaap Hage, European Integration: A Theme, ISBN 978-94-6236-981-8

Volume 11: Jan M. Smits, Five Uneasy Pieces. Essays on Law and Evolution, ISBN 978-94-6236-982-5
Volume 12: Hannah Brodersen, Vincent Glerum, & André Klip, The European Arrest Warrant and In Absentia Judgements, ISBN 978-94-6236-985-6
Volume 13: Bram Akkermans & Gijs van Dijck, Sustainability and Private Law, ISBN 978-94-6236-986-3
Volume 14: Antonia Waltermann, David Roef, Jaap Hage & Marko Jelicic, Law, Science, Rationality, ISBN 978-94-6236-989-4

9 789462 369894

Printed by Libri Plureos GmbH in Hamburg,
Germany